Thirsty for Love

恋の渇き

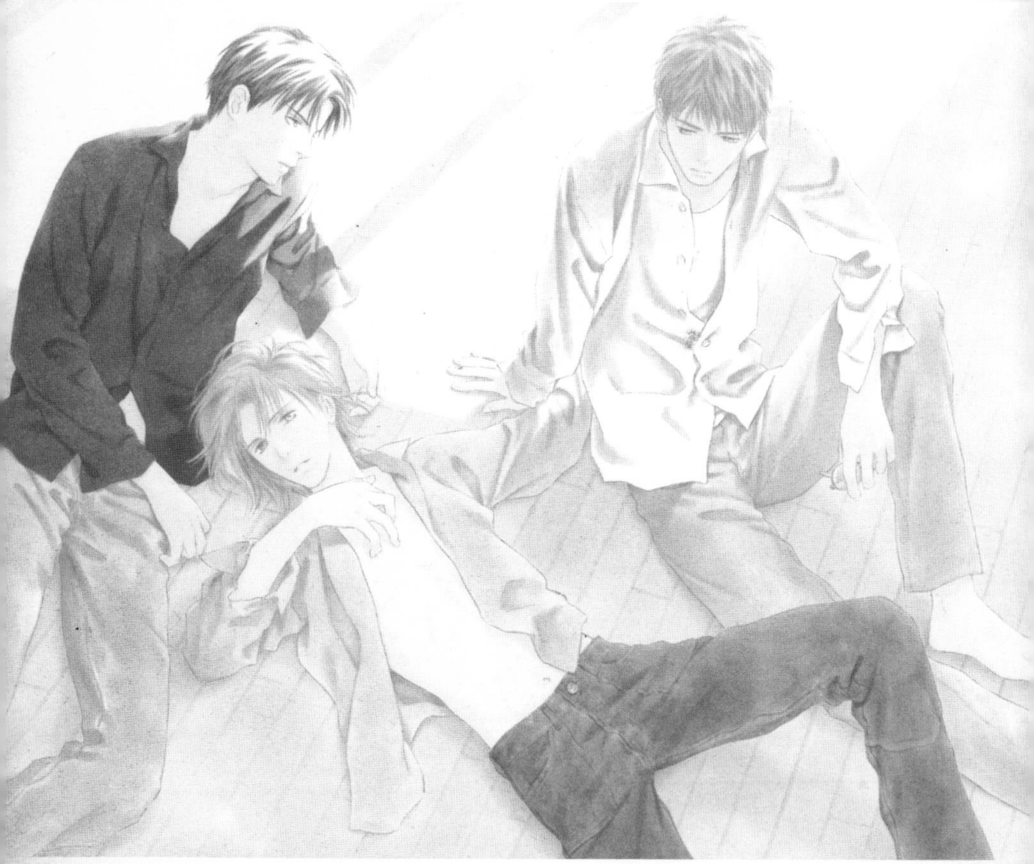

Yukine Honami X Satosumi Takaguchi

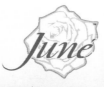

June

Thirsty for Love

恋の渇き

Translation	Melanie Schoen
Lettering	Replibooks
Graphic Design	Fred Lui / Wendy Lee / Matt Akuginow
Editing	Bambi Eloriaga
Editor in Chief	Fred Lui
Publisher	Hikaru Sasahara

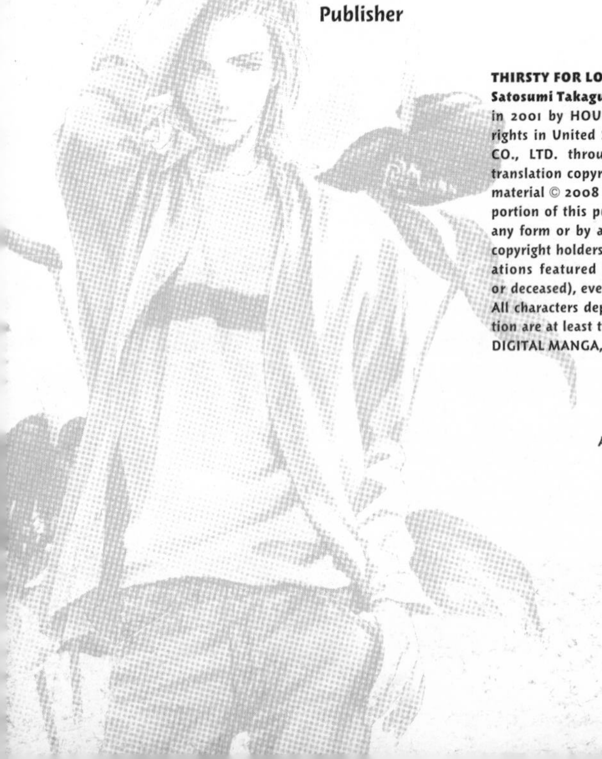

English Edition Published by
DIGITAL MANGA PUBLISHING
A division of DIGITAL MANGA, Inc.
1487 W 178th Street, Suite 300
Gardena, CA 90248

www.dmpbooks.com

First Edition: April 2008
ISBN-10: 1-56970-743-X
ISBN-13: 978-1-56970-743-2

1 3 5 7 9 10 8 6 4 2

Printed in China

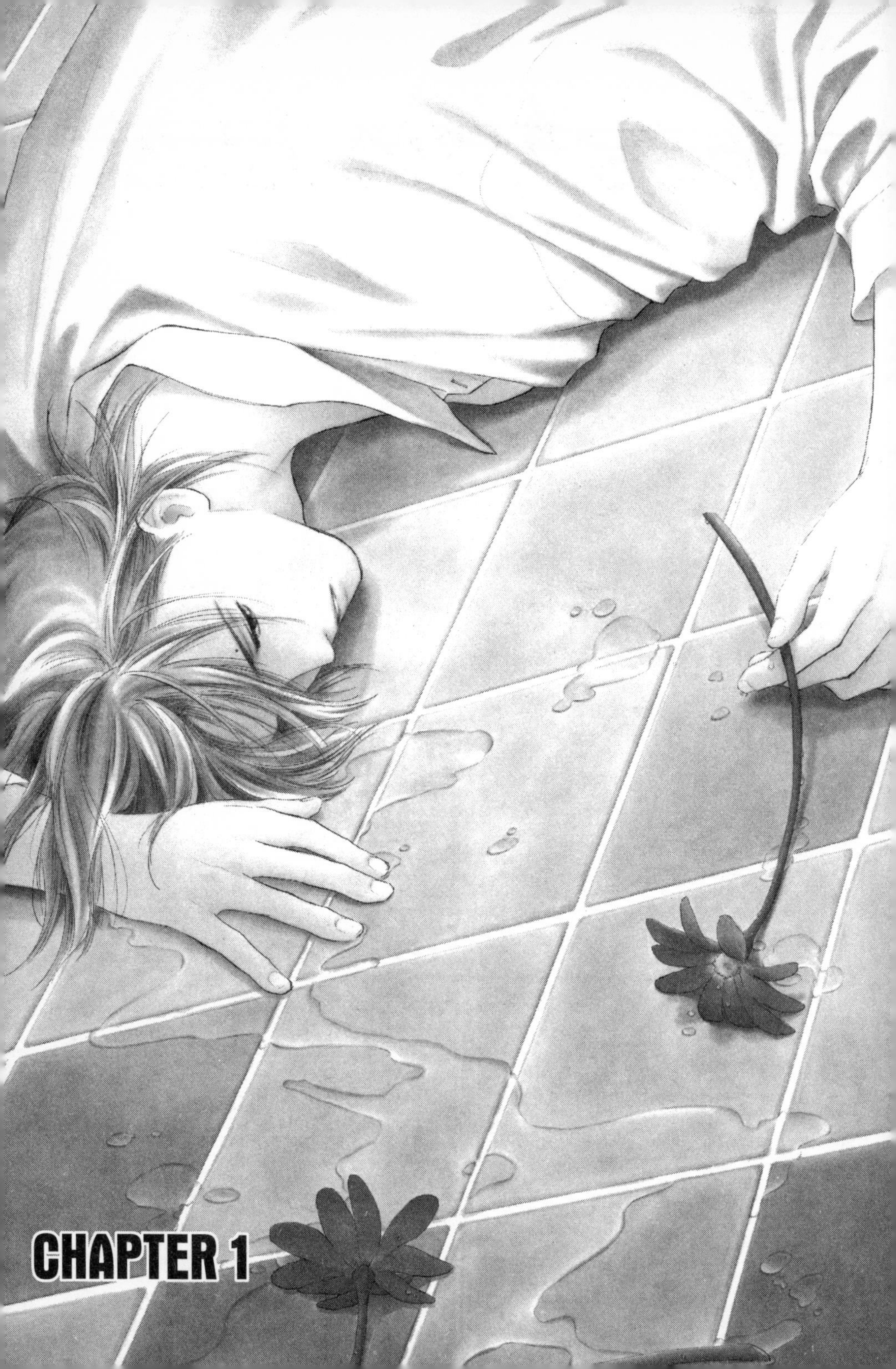
CHAPTER 1

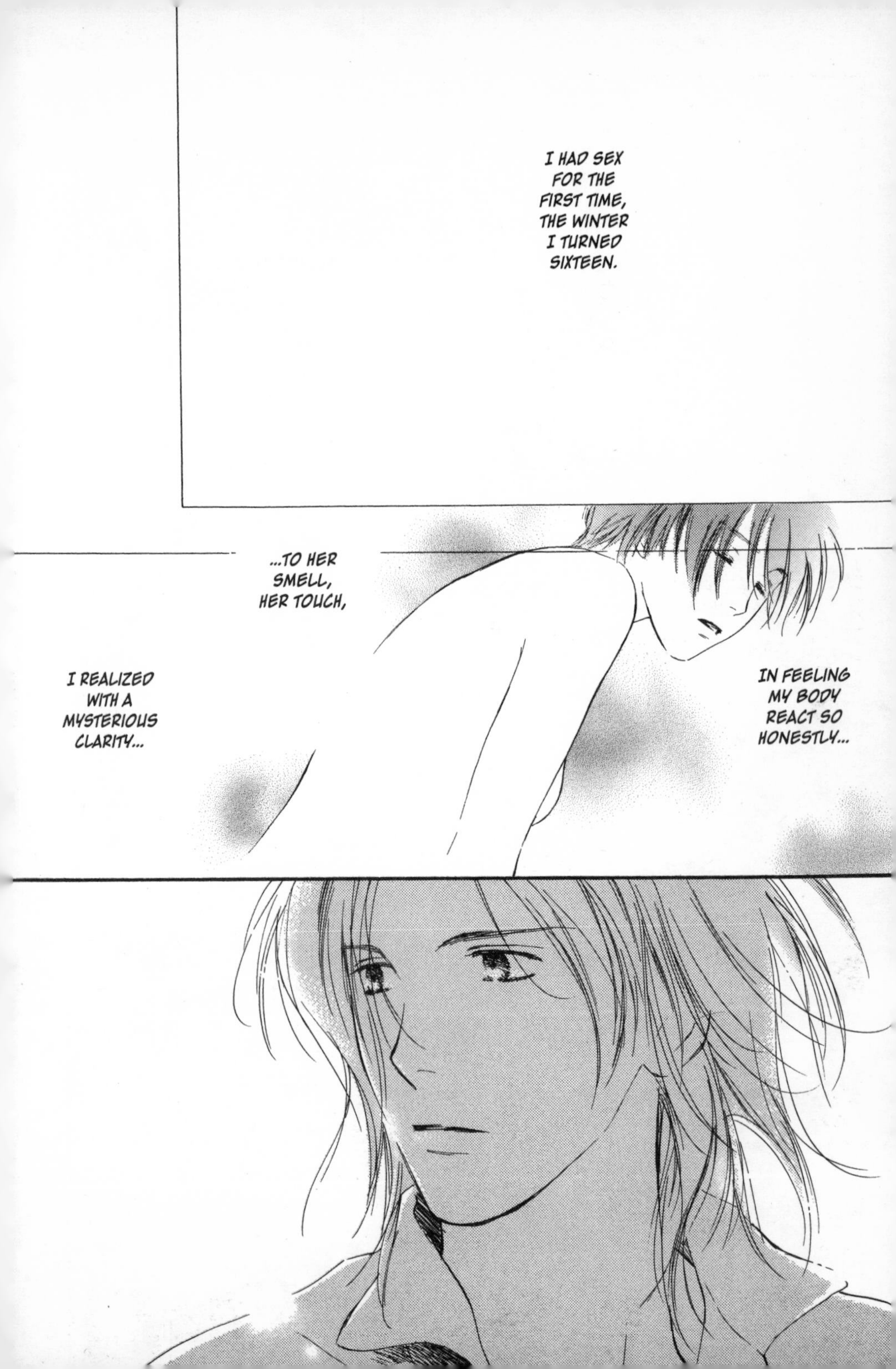
I HAD SEX FOR THE FIRST TIME, THE WINTER I TURNED SIXTEEN.
IN FEELING MY BODY REACT SO HONESTLY...
...TO HER SMELL, HER TOUCH,
I REALIZED WITH A MYSTERIOUS CLARITY...

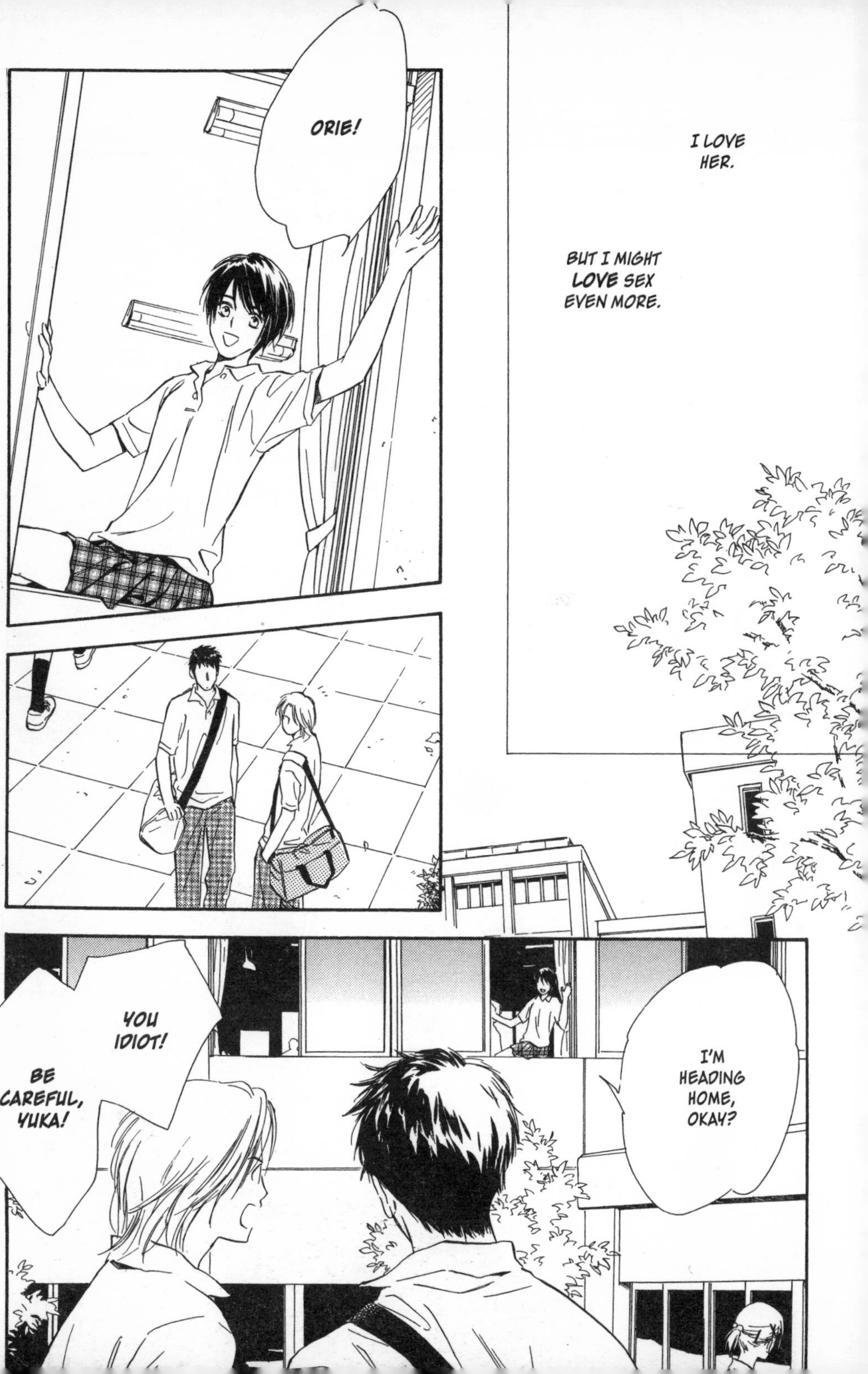
I LOVE HER.
BUT I MIGHT LOVE SEX EVEN MORE.
ORIE!
I'M HEADING HOME, OKAY?
YOU IDIOT!
BE CAREFUL, YUKA!

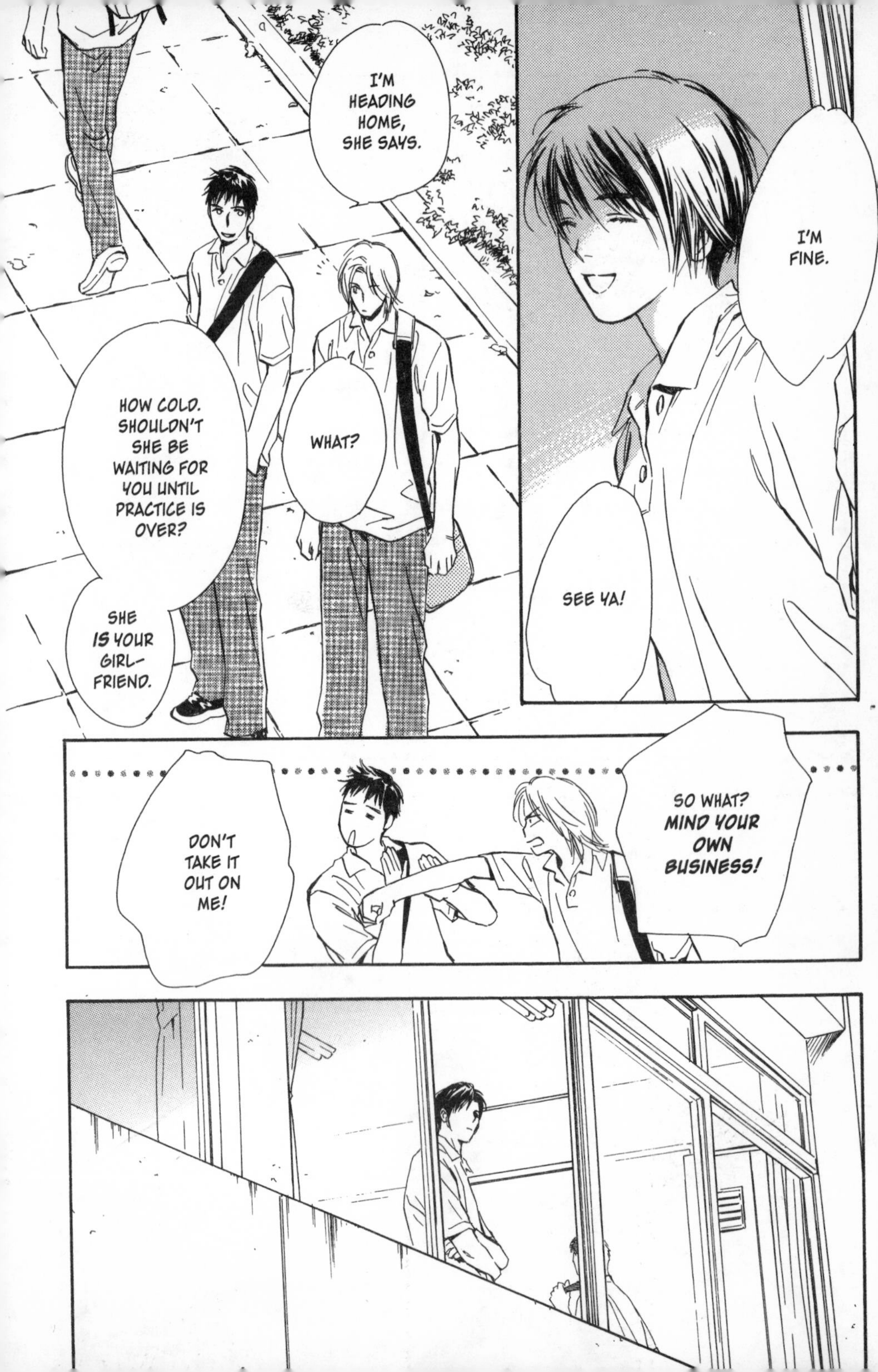
I'M FINE.
SEE YA!
I'M HEADING HOME, SHE SAYS.
WHAT?
HOW COLD. SHOULDN'T SHE BE WAITING FOR YOU UNTIL PRACTICE IS OVER?
SHE IS YOUR GIRLFRIEND.
SO WHAT? MIND YOUR OWN BUSINESS!
DON'T TAKE IT OUT ON ME!

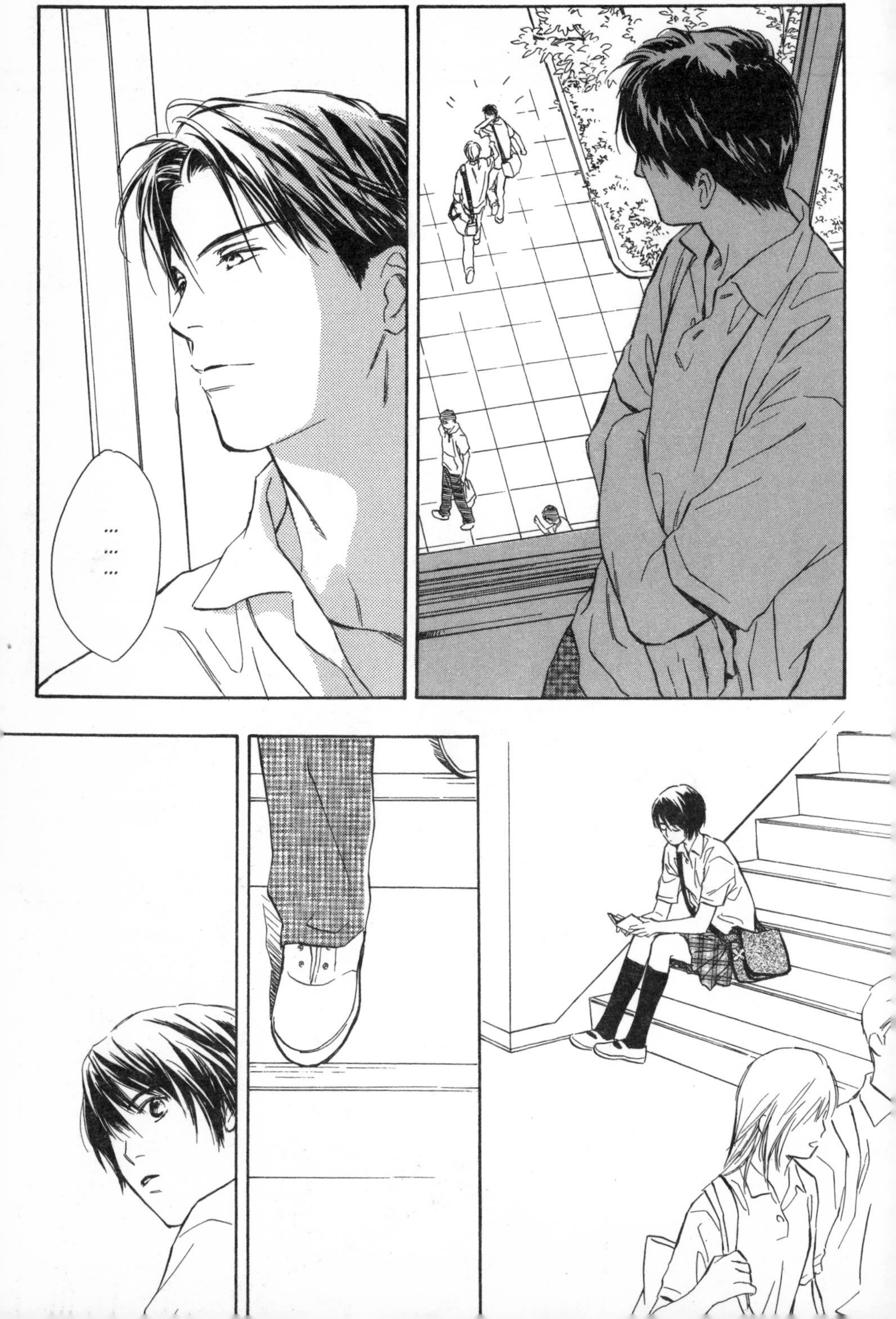
…
…
…

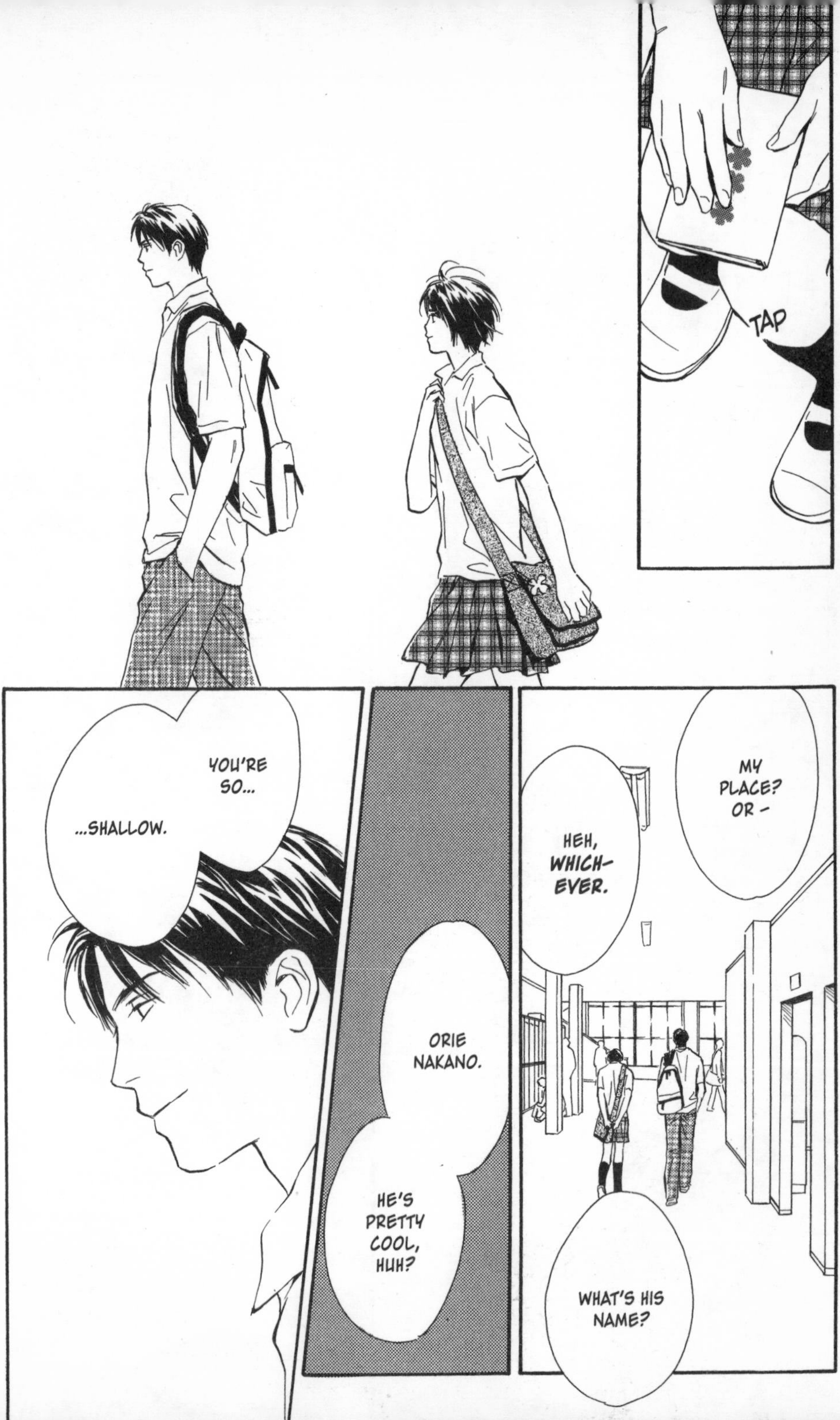
TAP
MY PLACE? OR -
HEH, WHICH-EVER.
WHAT'S HIS NAME?
ORIE NAKANO.
HE'S PRETTY COOL, HUH?
YOU'RE SO...
...SHALLOW.

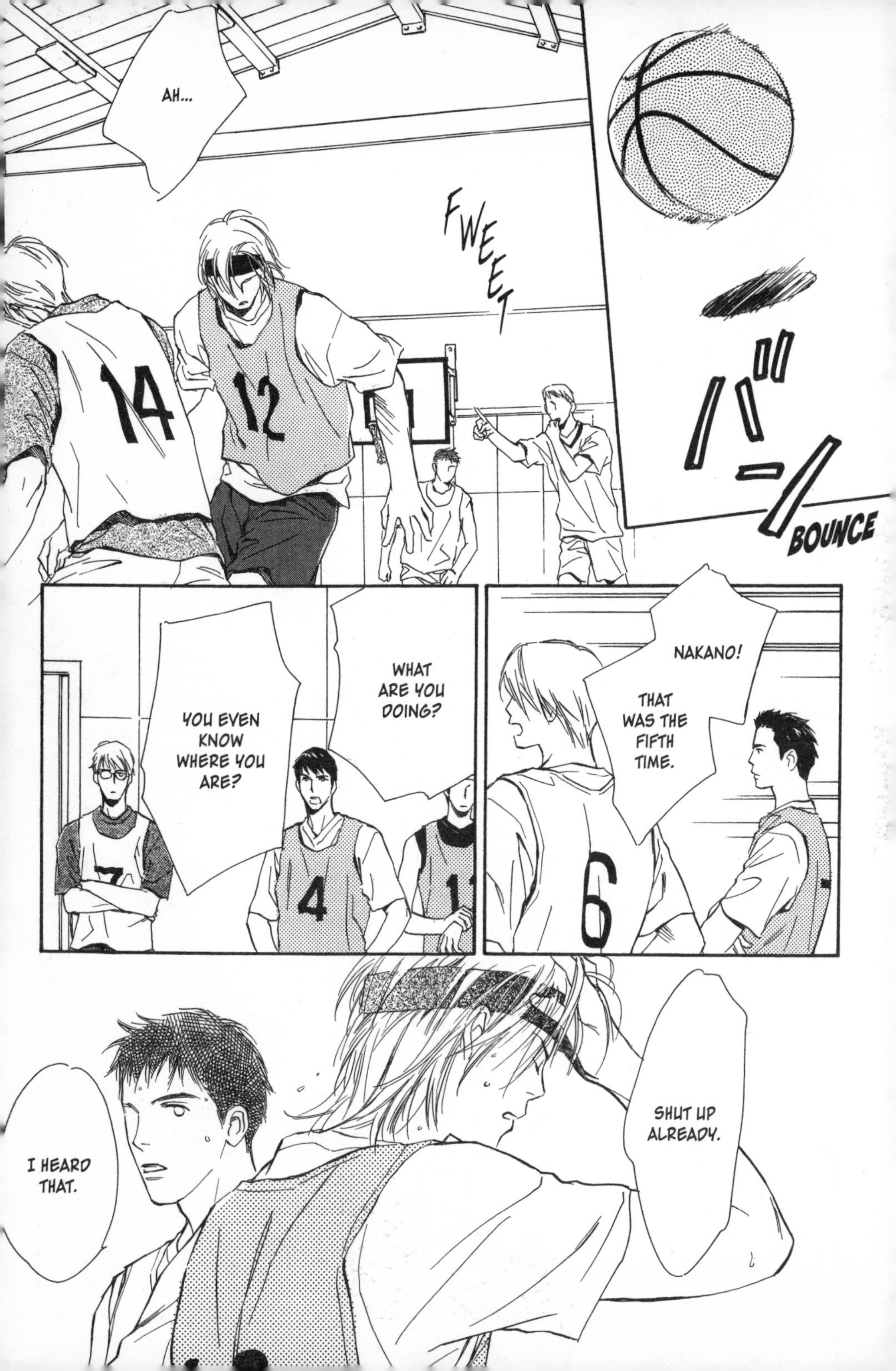
BOUNCE
AH...
FWEET
NAKANO!
THAT WAS THE FIFTH TIME.
WHAT ARE YOU DOING?
YOU EVEN KNOW WHERE YOU ARE?
SHUT UP ALREADY.
I HEARD THAT.

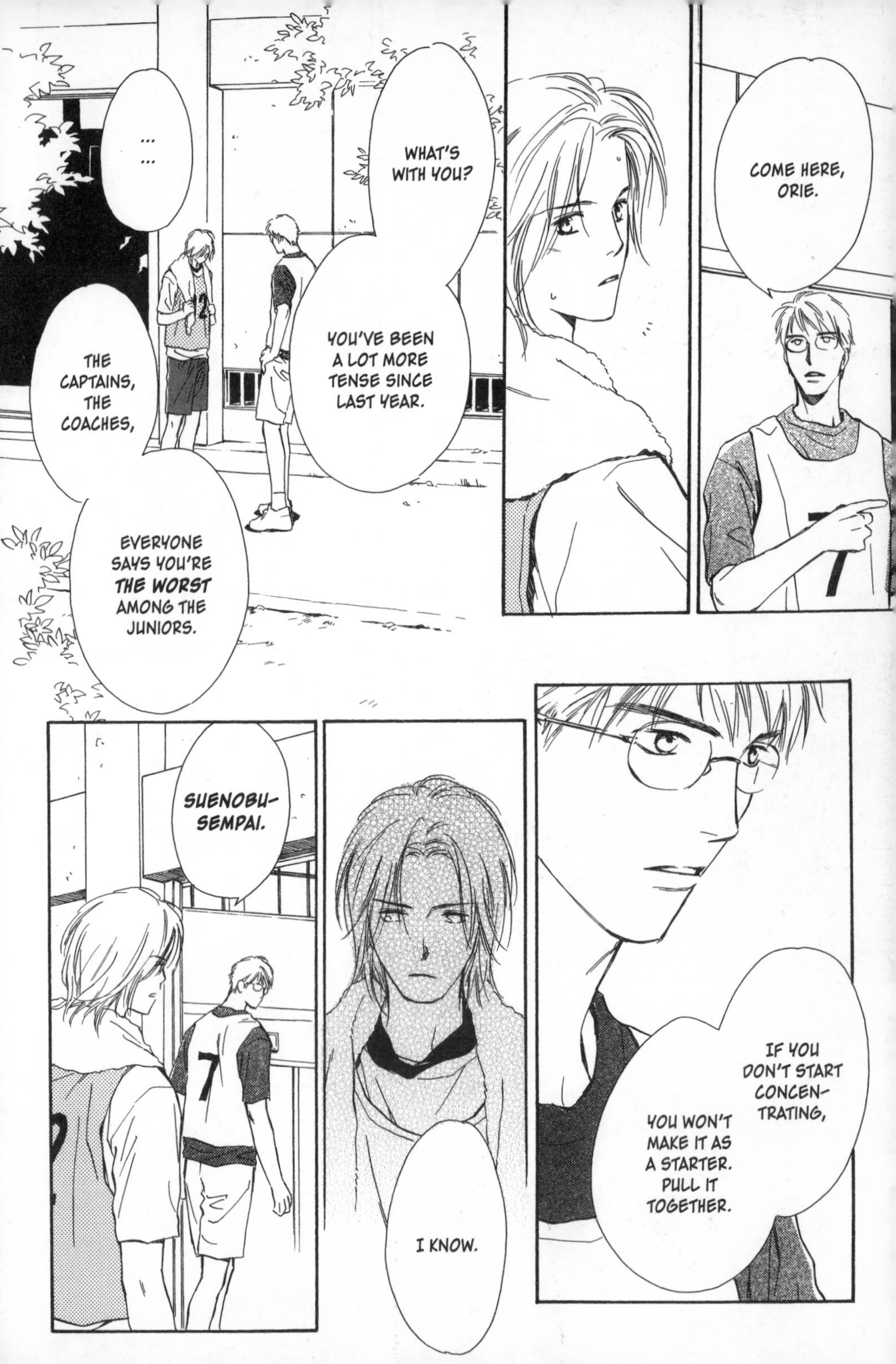
COME HERE, ORIE.
WHAT'S WITH YOU?
YOU'VE BEEN A LOT MORE TENSE SINCE LAST YEAR.
... ...
THE CAPTAINS, THE COACHES,
EVERYONE SAYS YOU'RE **THE WORST** AMONG THE JUNIORS.
IF YOU DON'T START CONCEN-TRATING,
YOU WON'T MAKE IT AS A STARTER. PULL IT TOGETHER.
I KNOW.
SUENOBU-SEMPAI.

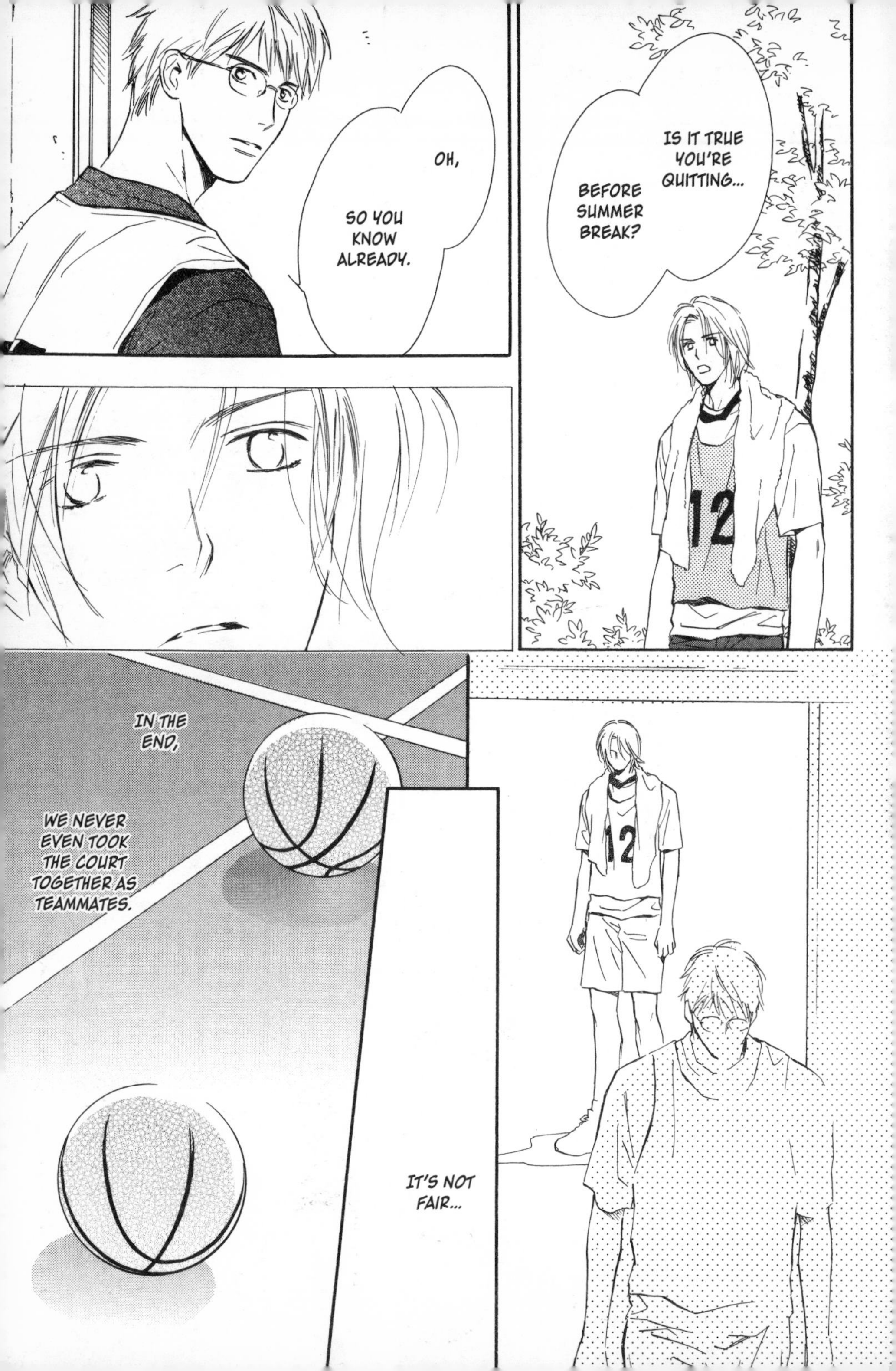
IS IT TRUE YOU'RE QUITTING...
BEFORE SUMMER BREAK?
OH,
SO YOU KNOW ALREADY.
IN THE END,
WE NEVER EVEN TOOK THE COURT TOGETHER AS TEAMMATES.
IT'S NOT FAIR...

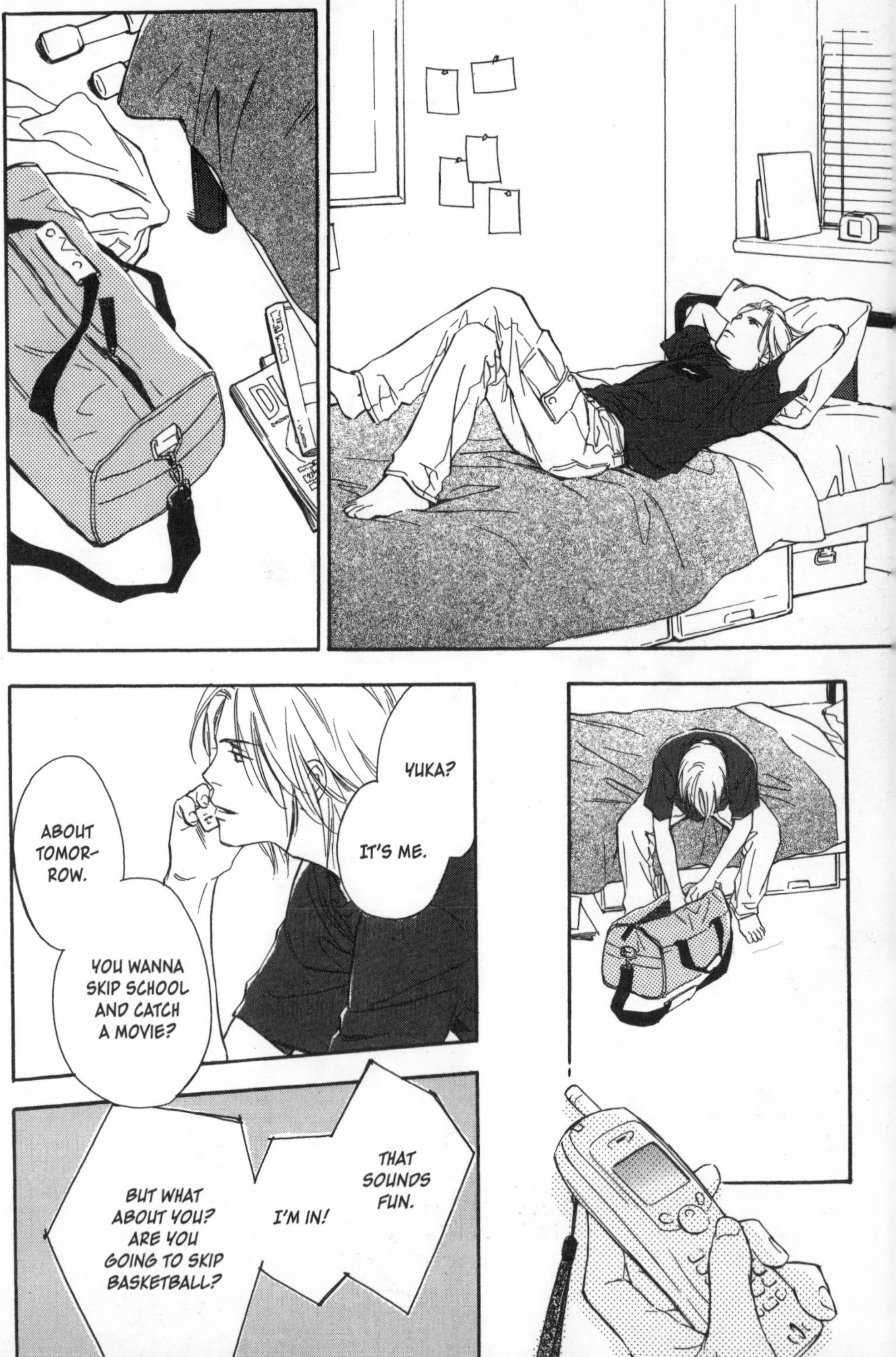
YUKA?
IT'S ME.
ABOUT TOMOR-ROW.
YOU WANNA SKIP SCHOOL AND CATCH A MOVIE?
THAT SOUNDS FUN.
I'M IN!
BUT WHAT ABOUT YOU? ARE YOU GOING TO SKIP BASKETBALL?

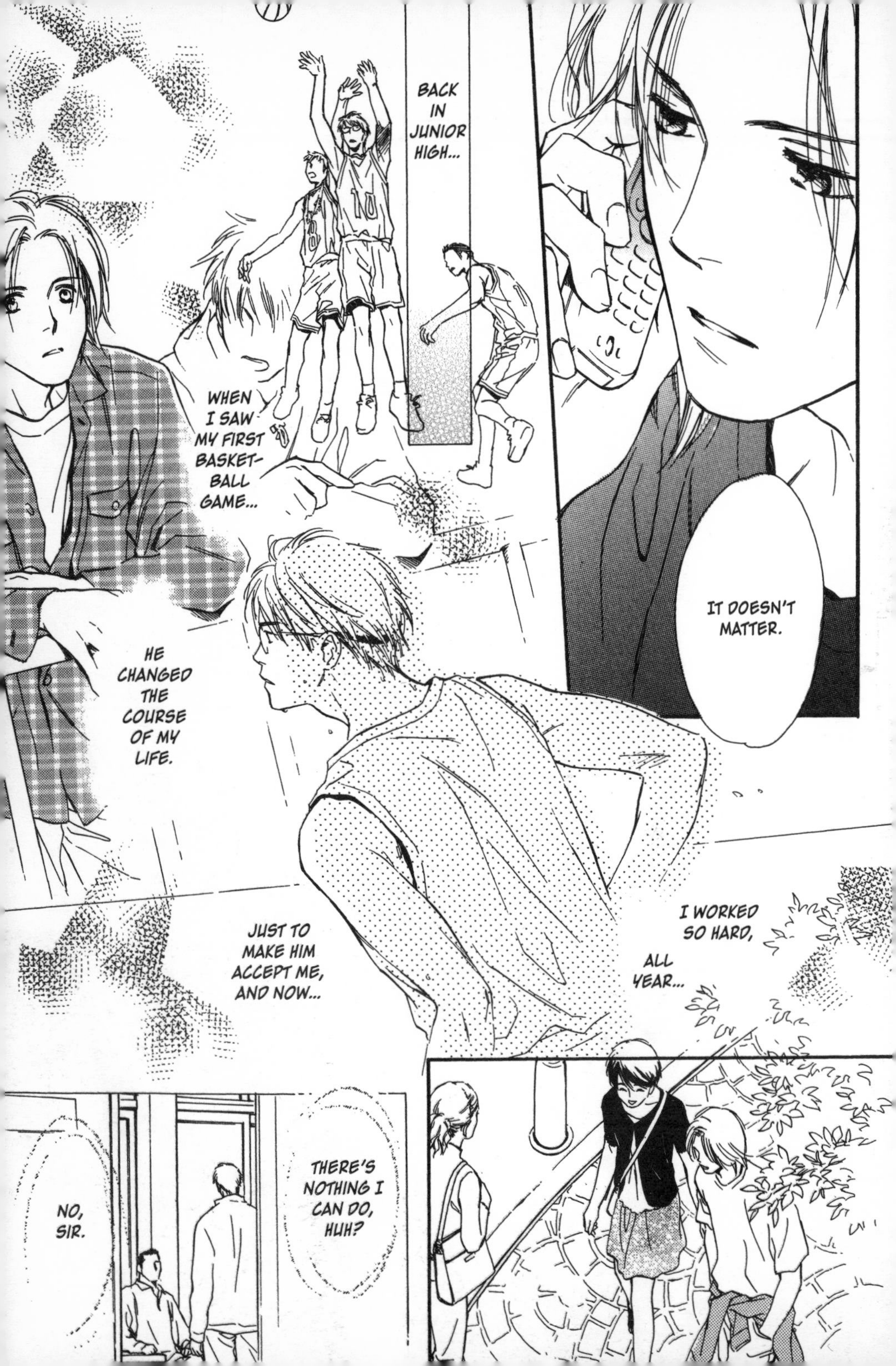

IT DOESN'T MATTER.
BACK IN JUNIOR HIGH...
WHEN I SAW MY FIRST BASKET-BALL GAME...
HE CHANGED THE COURSE OF MY LIFE.
I WORKED SO HARD,
ALL YEAR...
JUST TO MAKE HIM ACCEPT ME, AND NOW...
THERE'S NOTHING I CAN DO, HUH?
NO, SIR.

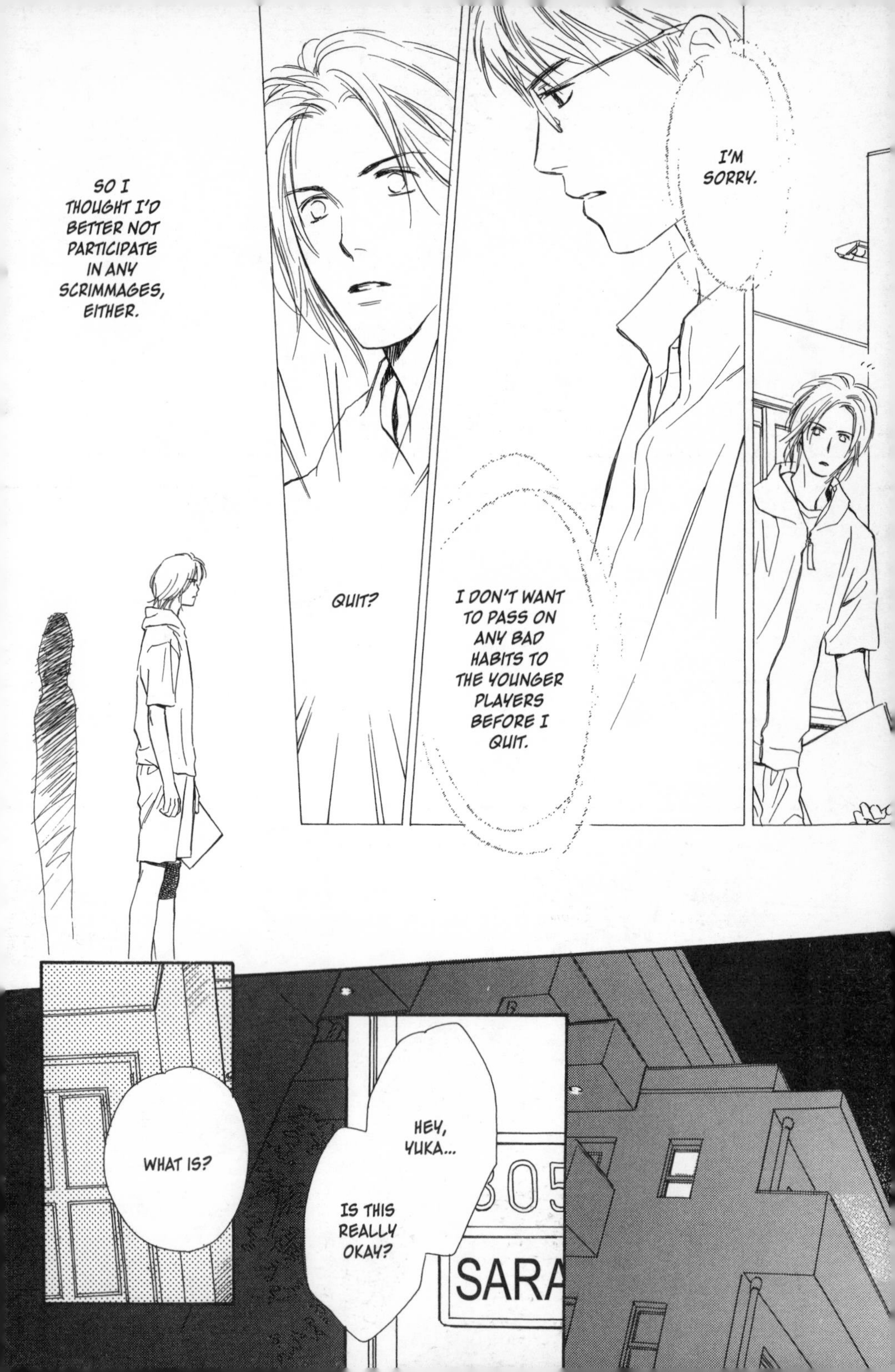
I'M SORRY.
I DON'T WANT TO PASS ON ANY BAD HABITS TO THE YOUNGER PLAYERS BEFORE I QUIT.
QUIT?
SO I THOUGHT I'D BETTER NOT PARTICIPATE IN ANY SCRIMMAGES, EITHER.
305
SARA
HEY, YUKA...
IS THIS REALLY OKAY?
WHAT IS?

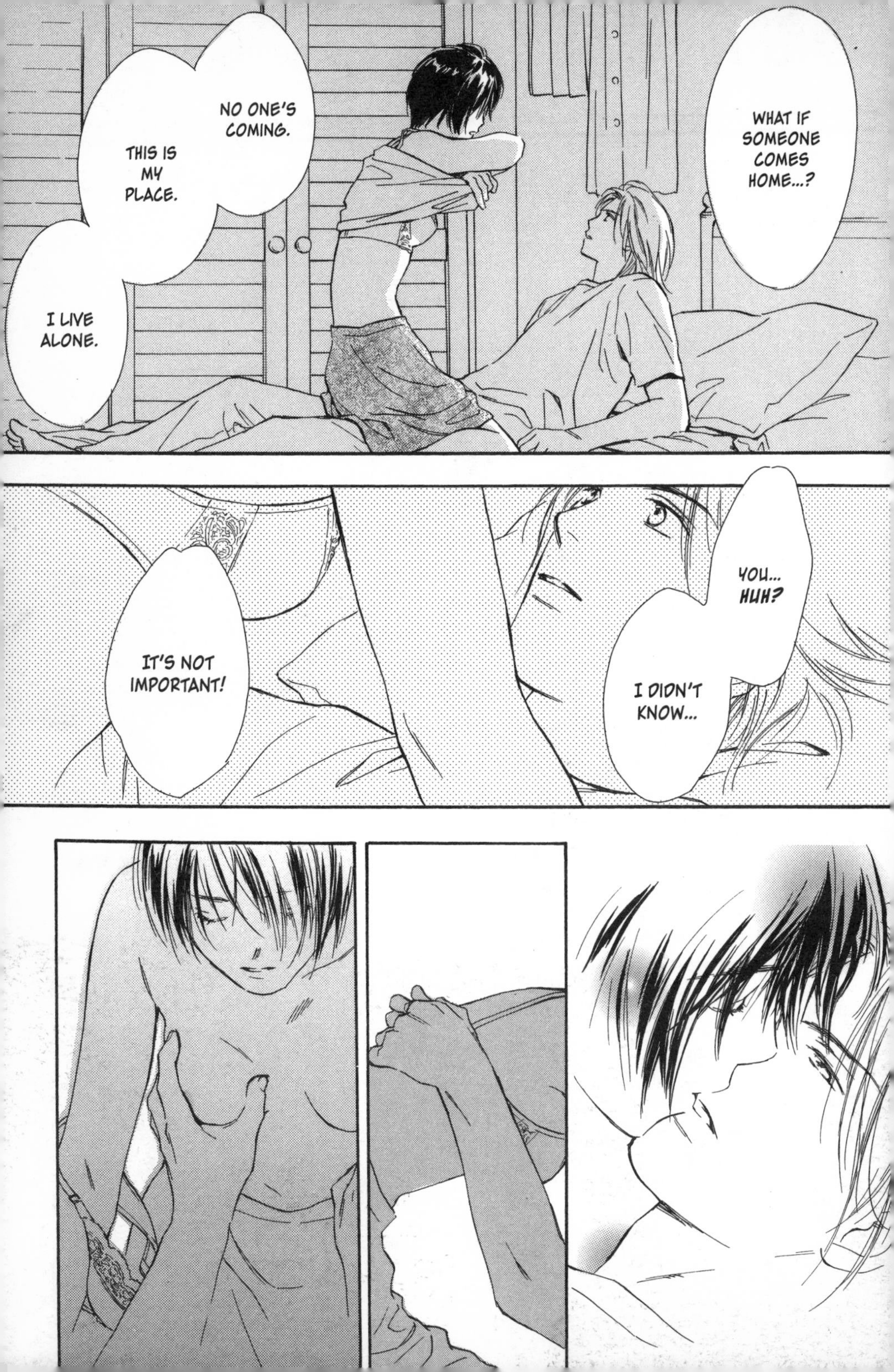
WHAT IF SOMEONE COMES HOME...?
NO ONE'S COMING.
THIS IS MY PLACE.
I LIVE ALONE.
YOU... HUH?
I DIDN'T KNOW...
IT'S NOT IMPORTANT!

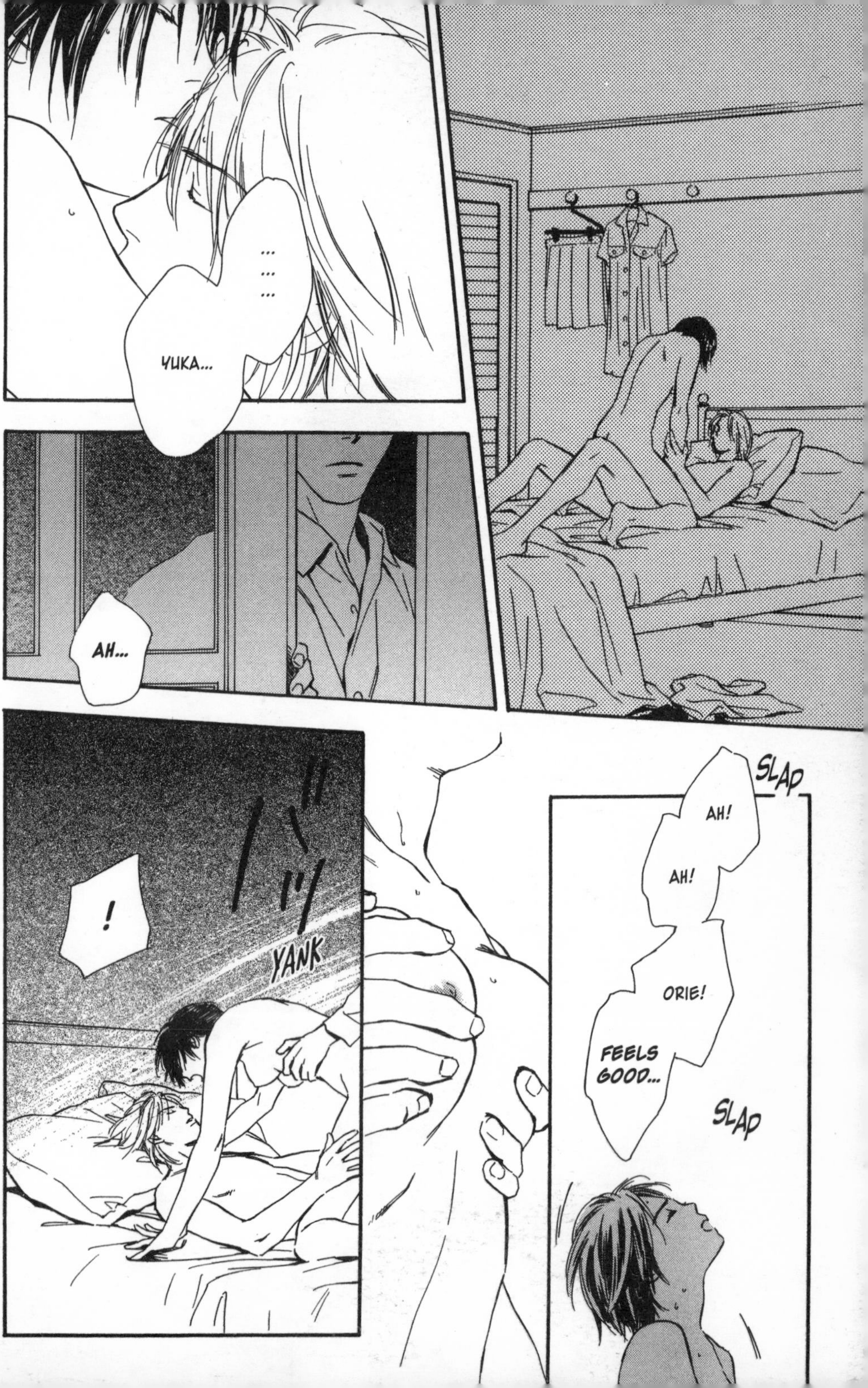

...
...
...
YUKA...
AH...
SLAP
AH!
AH!
ORIE!
FEELS GOOD...
SLAP
!
YANK

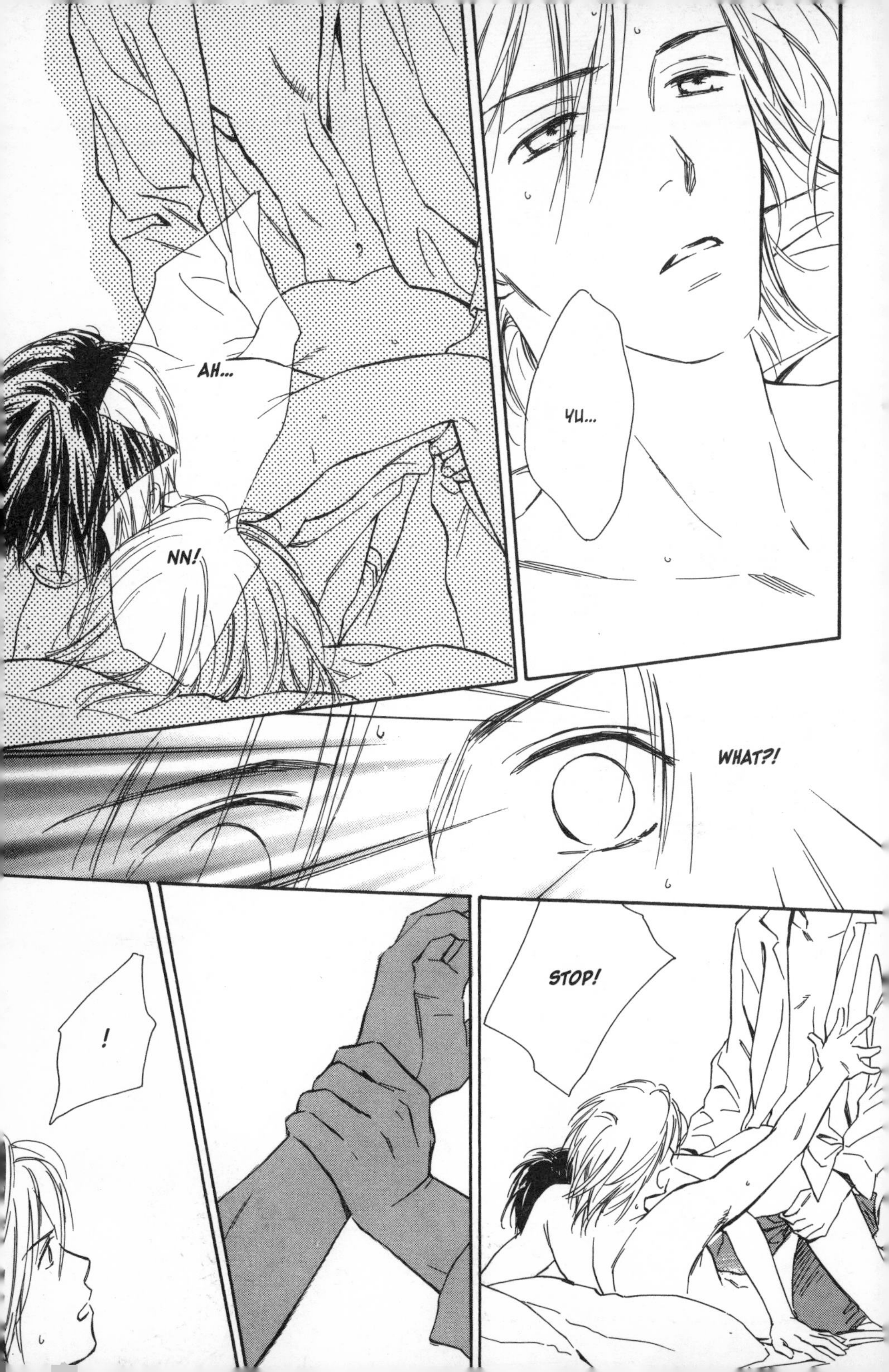
YU...
AH...
NN!
WHAT?!
STOP!
!

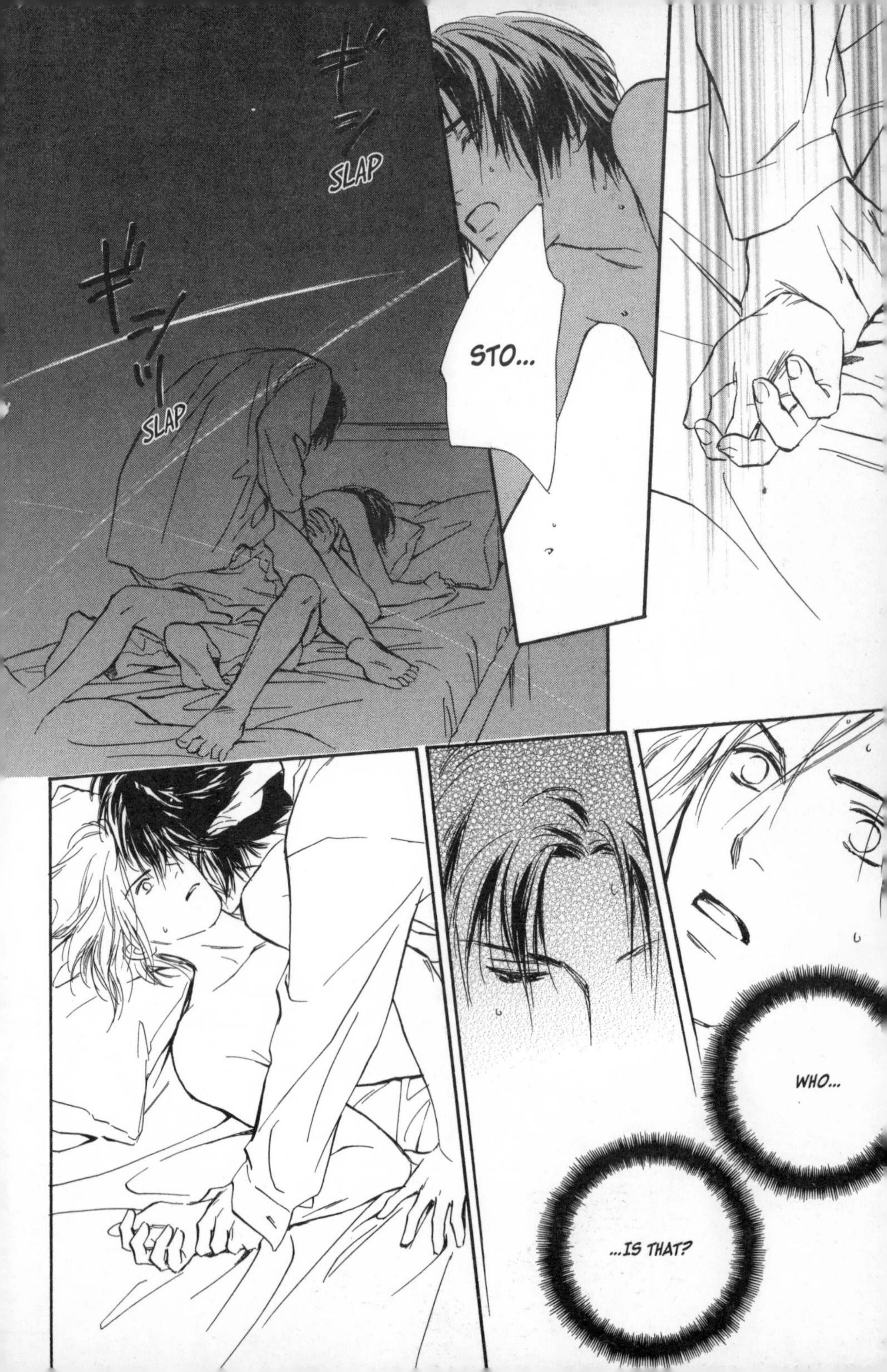
STO...
SLAP
SLAP
WHO...
...IS THAT?

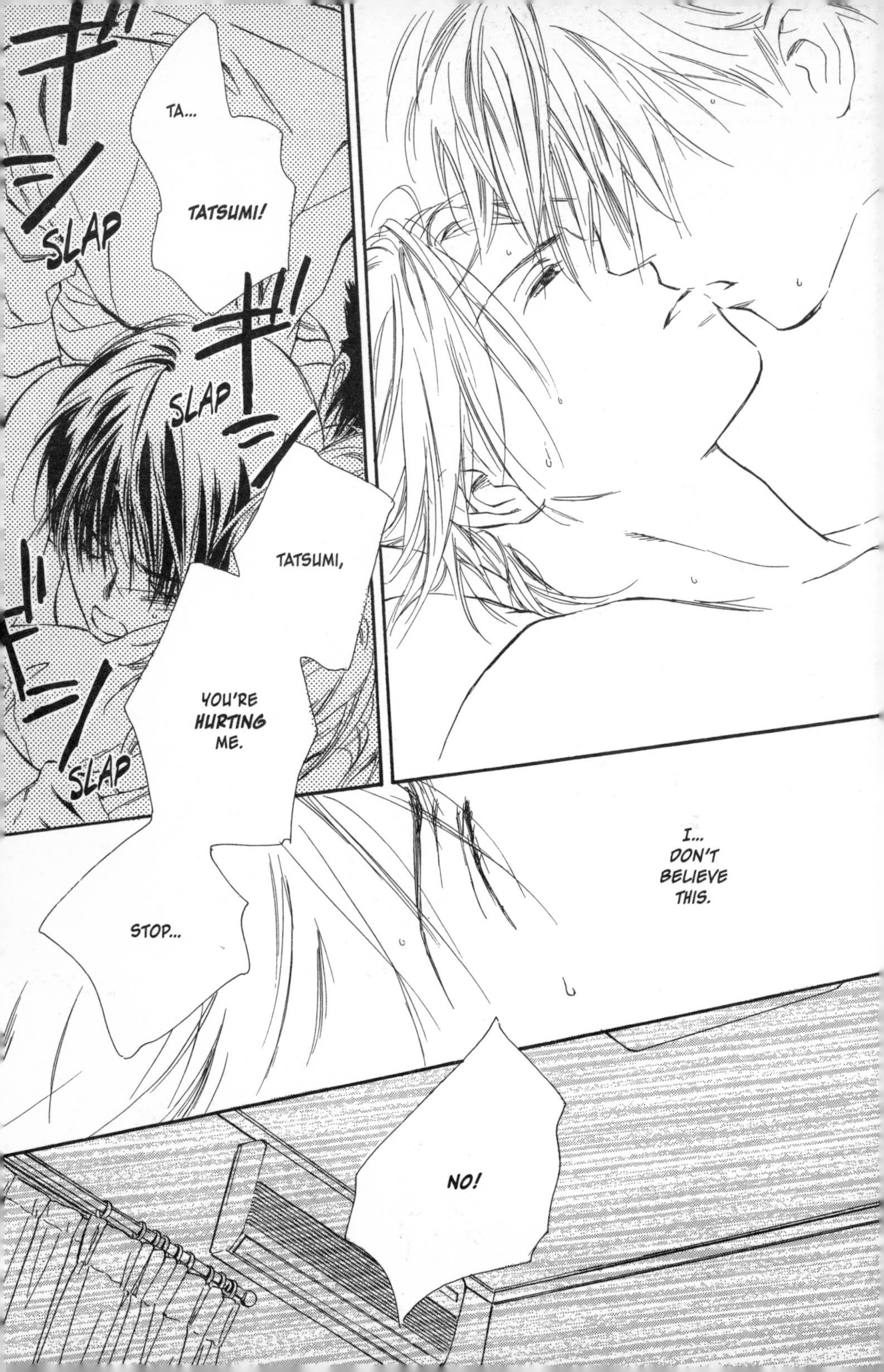
TA...
TATSUMI!
SLAP
SLAP
TATSUMI,
YOU'RE HURTING ME.
SLAP
I... DON'T BELIEVE THIS.
STOP...
NO!

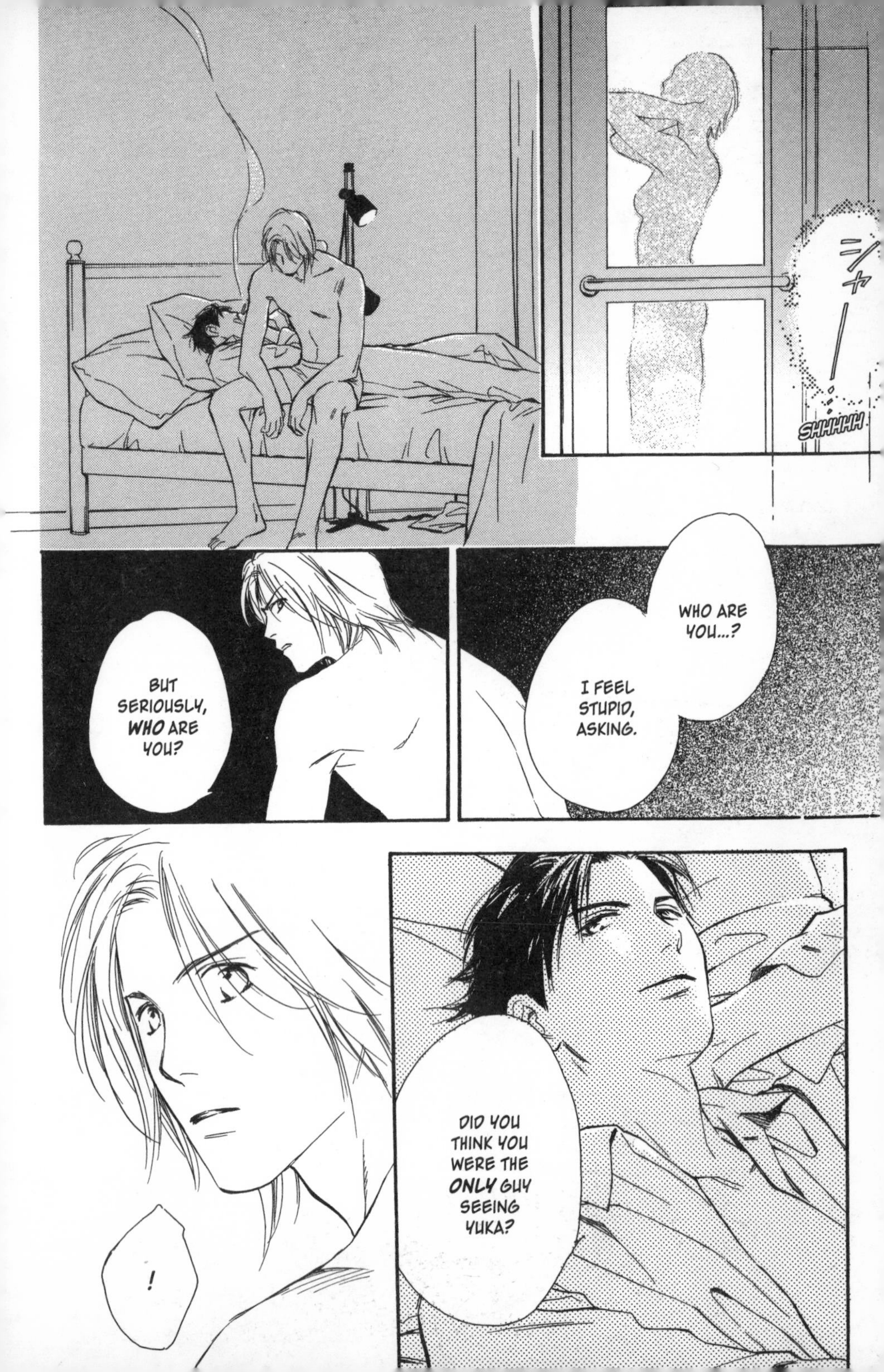
シャー
SHHHHH
WHO ARE YOU...?
I FEEL STUPID, ASKING.
BUT SERIOUSLY, WHO ARE YOU?
DID YOU THINK YOU WERE THE ONLY GUY SEEING YUKA?
!

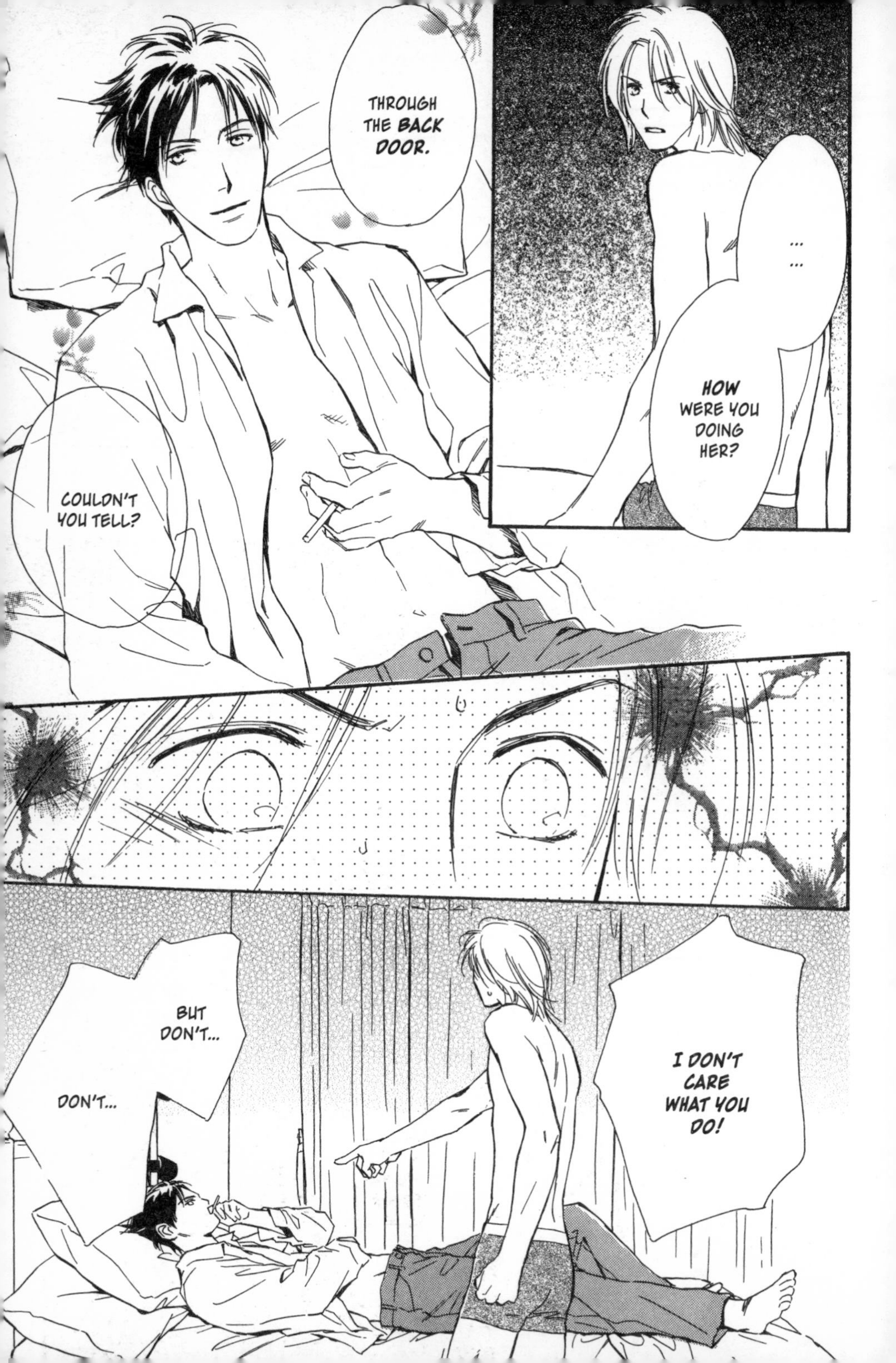

... ...
HOW WERE YOU DOING HER?
THROUGH THE BACK DOOR.
COULDN'T YOU TELL?
I DON'T CARE WHAT YOU DO!
BUT DON'T...
DON'T...

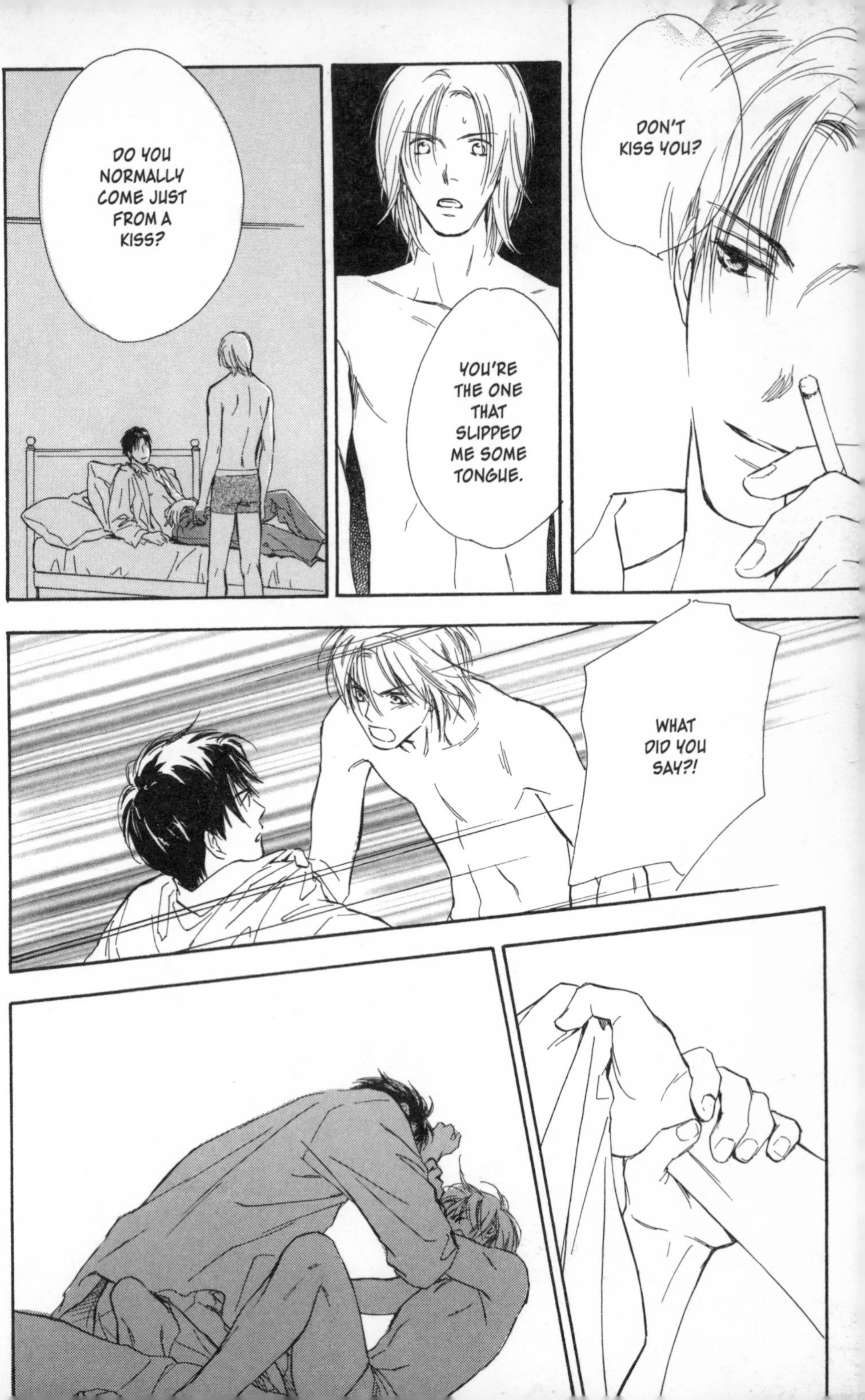
DON'T KISS YOU?
YOU'RE THE ONE THAT SLIPPED ME SOME TONGUE.
DO YOU NORMALLY COME JUST FROM A KISS?
WHAT DID YOU SAY?!

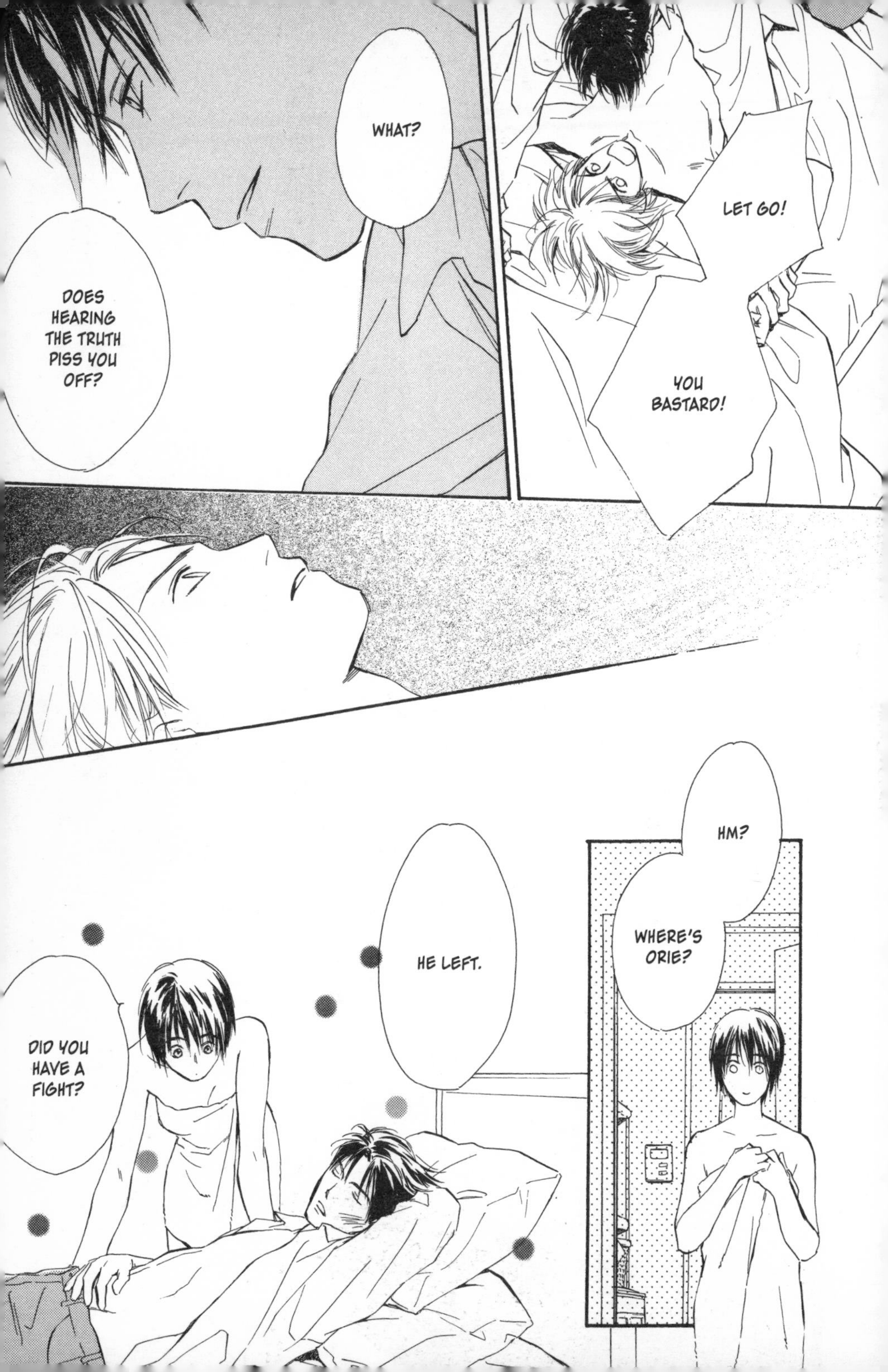

LET GO!
YOU BASTARD!
WHAT?
DOES HEARING THE TRUTH PISS YOU OFF?
HM?
WHERE'S ORIE?
HE LEFT.
DID YOU HAVE A FIGHT?

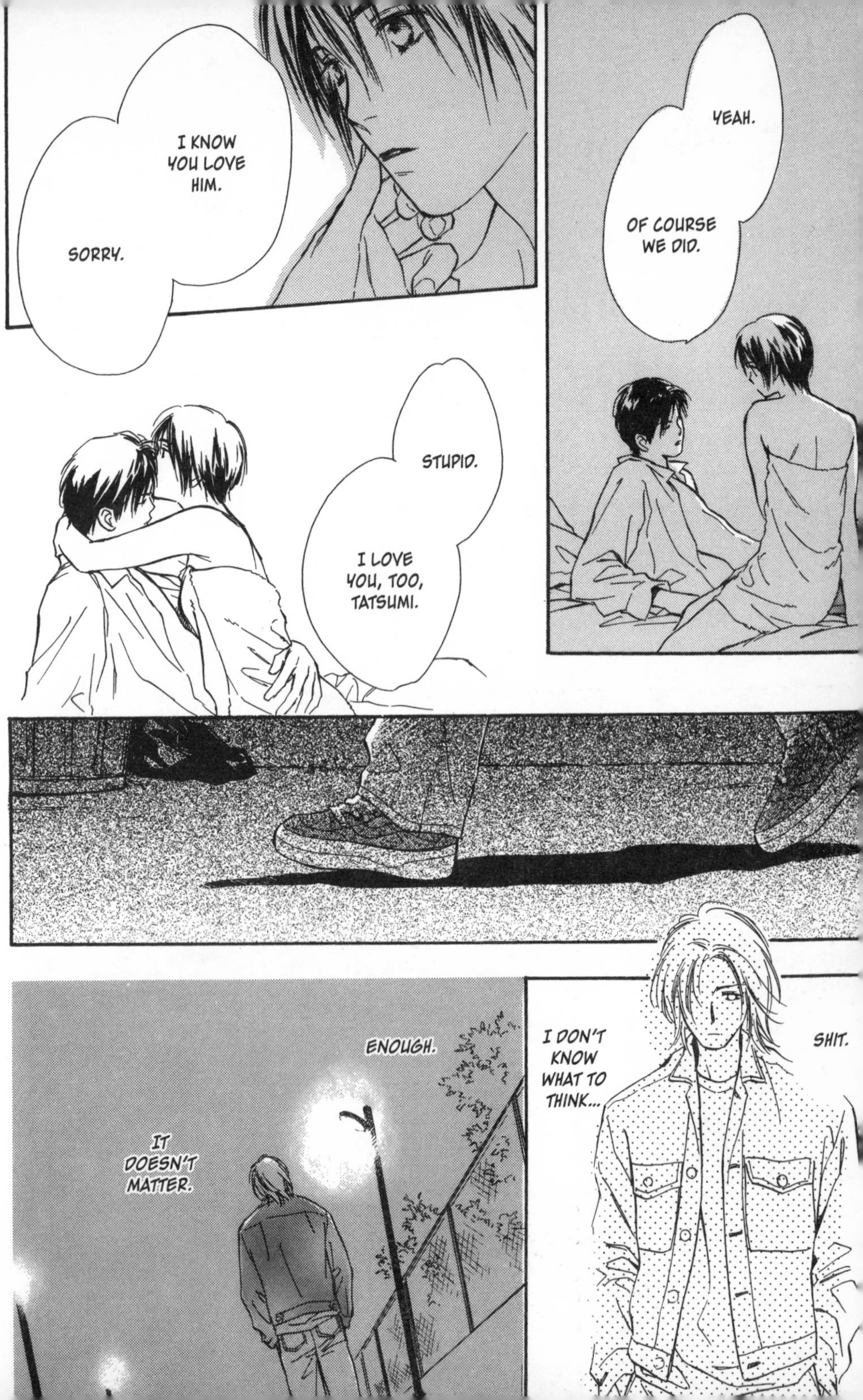
YEAH.
OF COURSE WE DID.
I KNOW YOU LOVE HIM.
SORRY.
STUPID.
I LOVE YOU, TOO, TATSUMI.
SHIT.
I DON'T KNOW WHAT TO THINK...
ENOUGH.
IT DOESN'T MATTER.

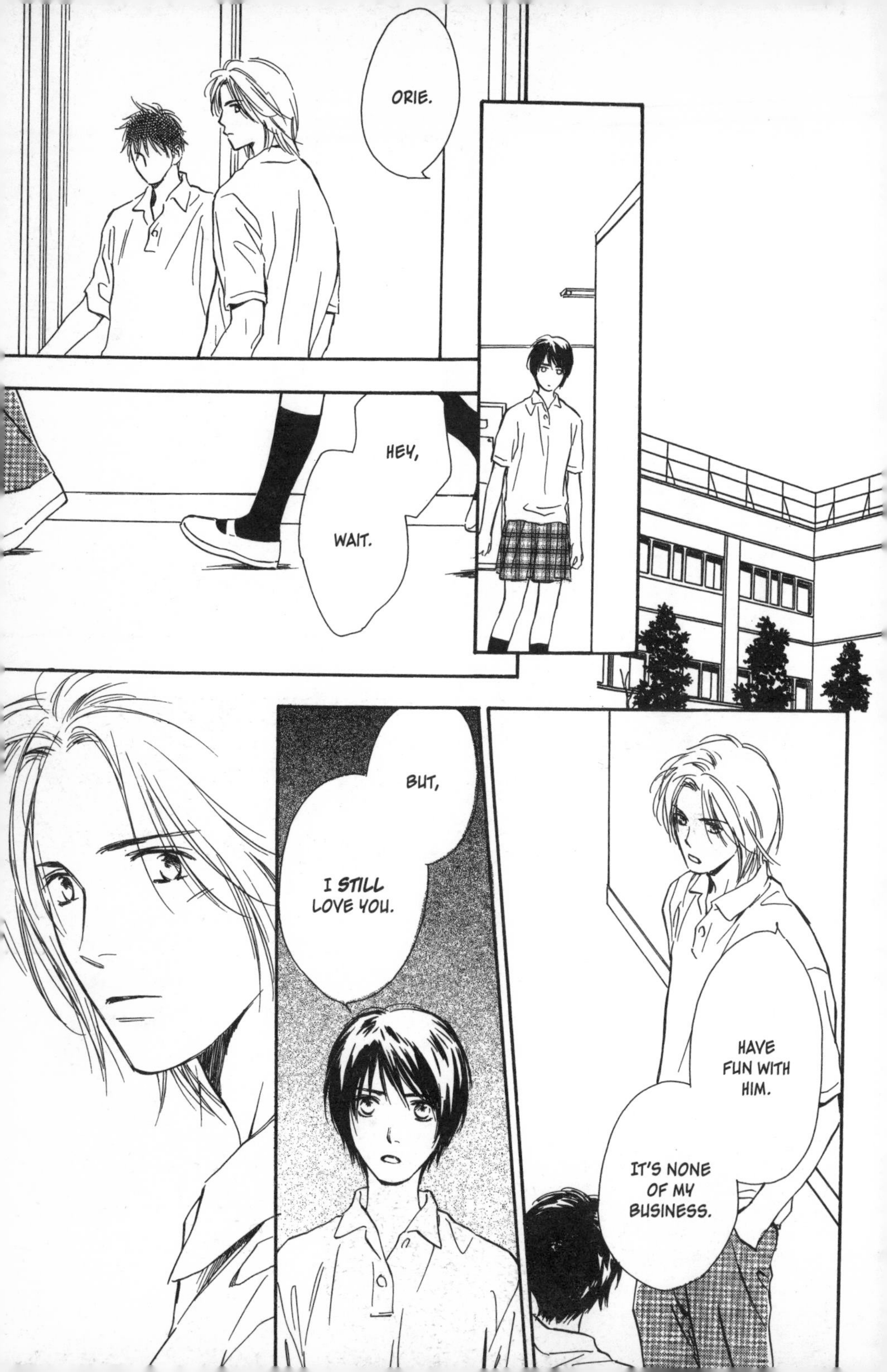
ORIE.
HEY,
WAIT.
HAVE FUN WITH HIM.
IT'S NONE OF MY BUSINESS.
BUT,
I STILL LOVE YOU.

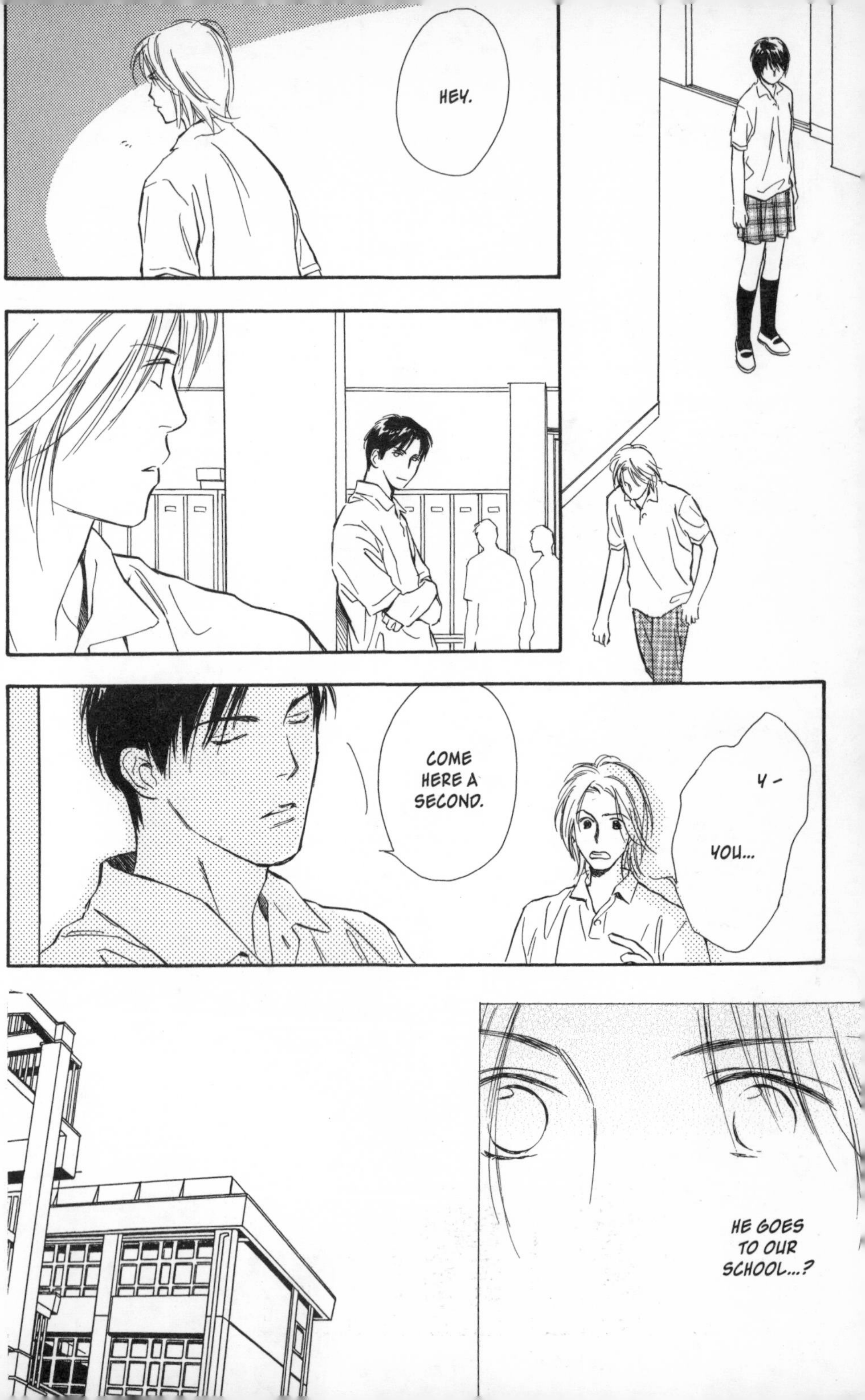
HEY.
Y -
YOU...
COME HERE A SECOND.
HE GOES TO OUR SCHOOL...?

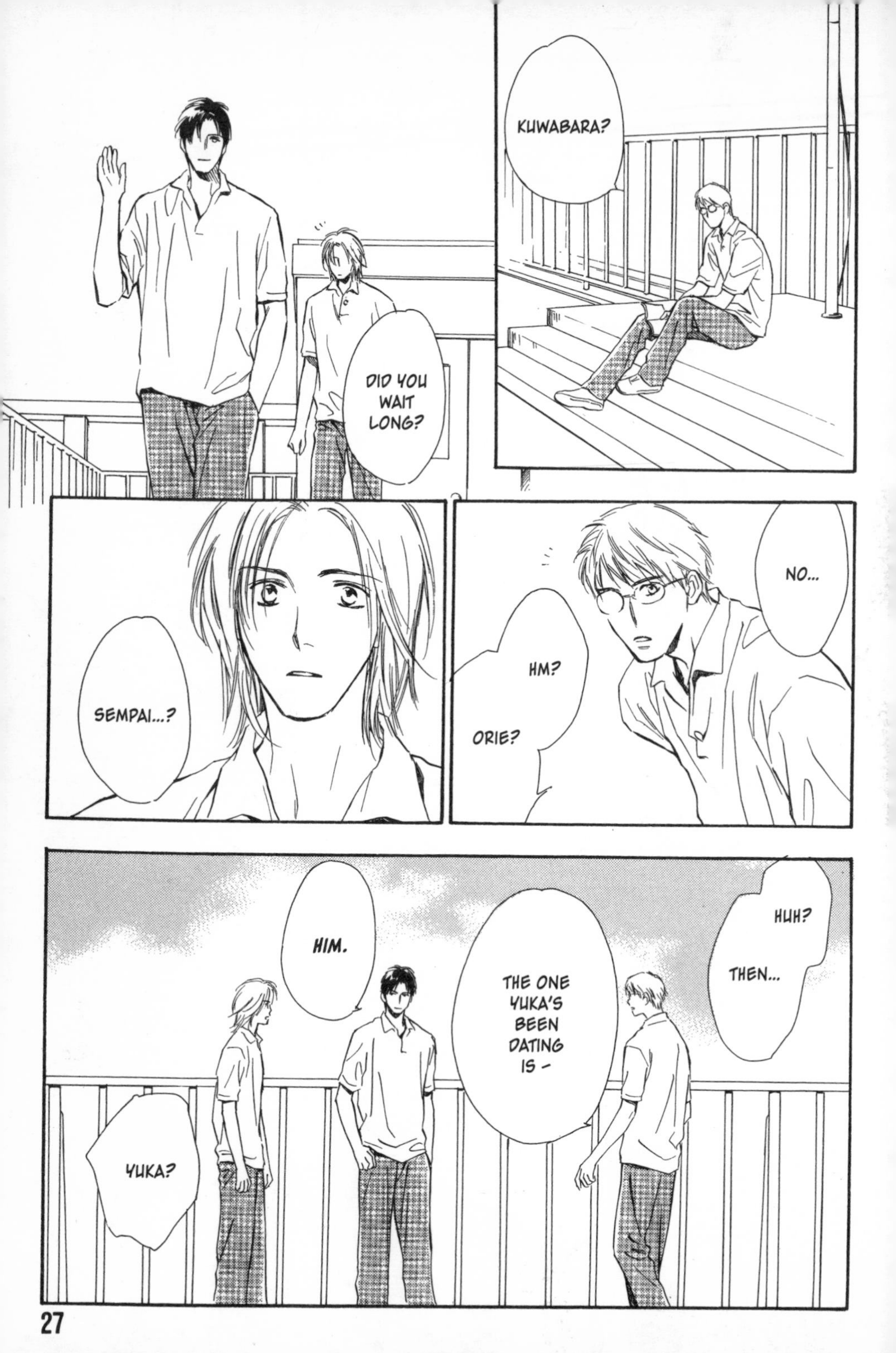
KUWABARA?
DID YOU WAIT LONG?
NO...
HM?
ORIE?
SEMPAI...?
HUH? THEN...
THE ONE YUKA'S BEEN DATING IS –
HIM.
YUKA?

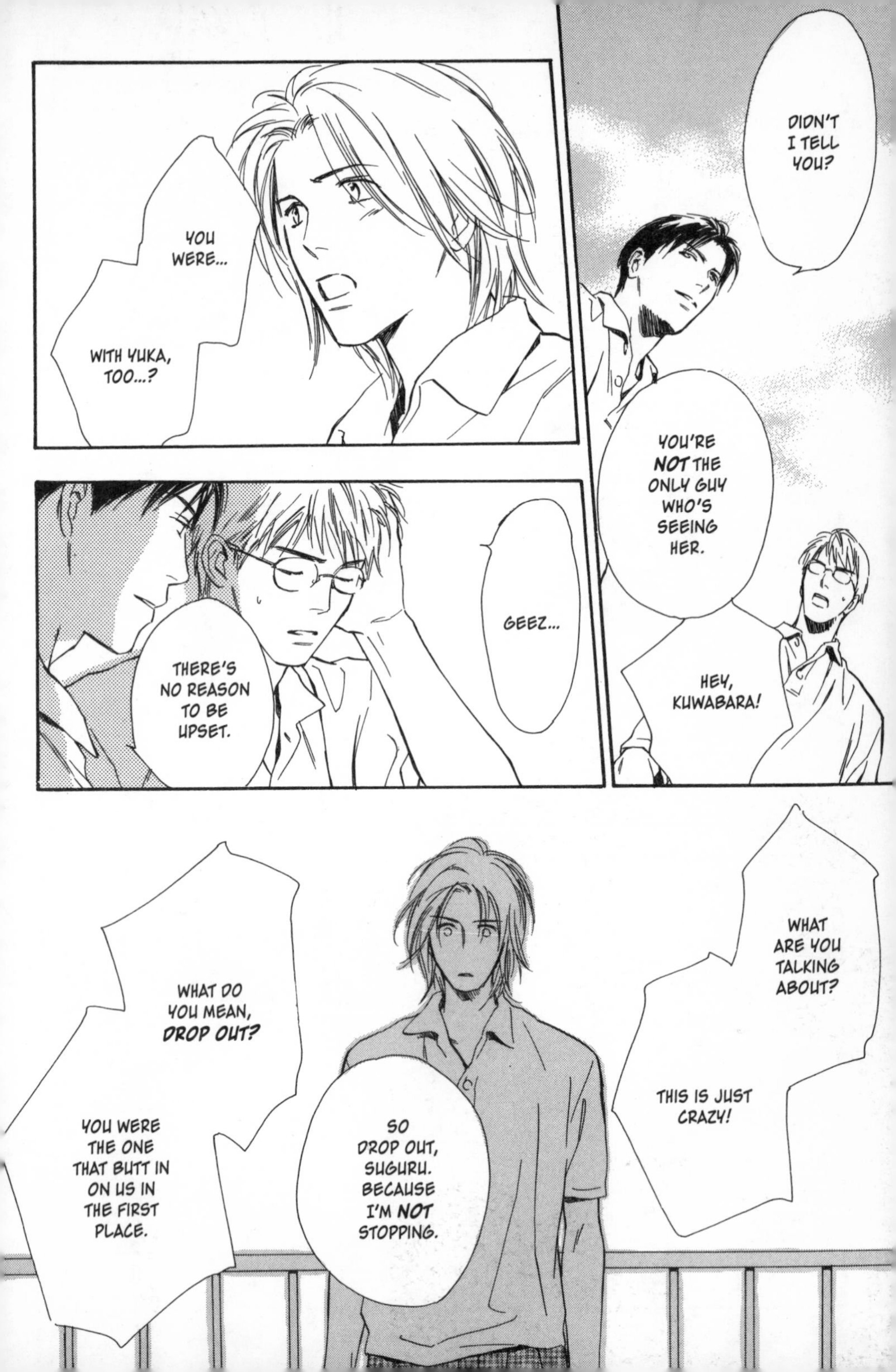
DIDN'T I TELL YOU?
YOU'RE **NOT** THE ONLY GUY WHO'S SEEING HER.
HEY, KUWABARA!
YOU WERE...
WITH YUKA, TOO...?
GEEZ...
THERE'S NO REASON TO BE UPSET.
WHAT ARE YOU TALKING ABOUT?
THIS IS JUST CRAZY!
SO DROP OUT, SUGURU. BECAUSE I'M **NOT** STOPPING.
WHAT DO YOU MEAN, ***DROP OUT?***
YOU WERE THE ONE THAT BUTT IN ON US IN THE FIRST PLACE.

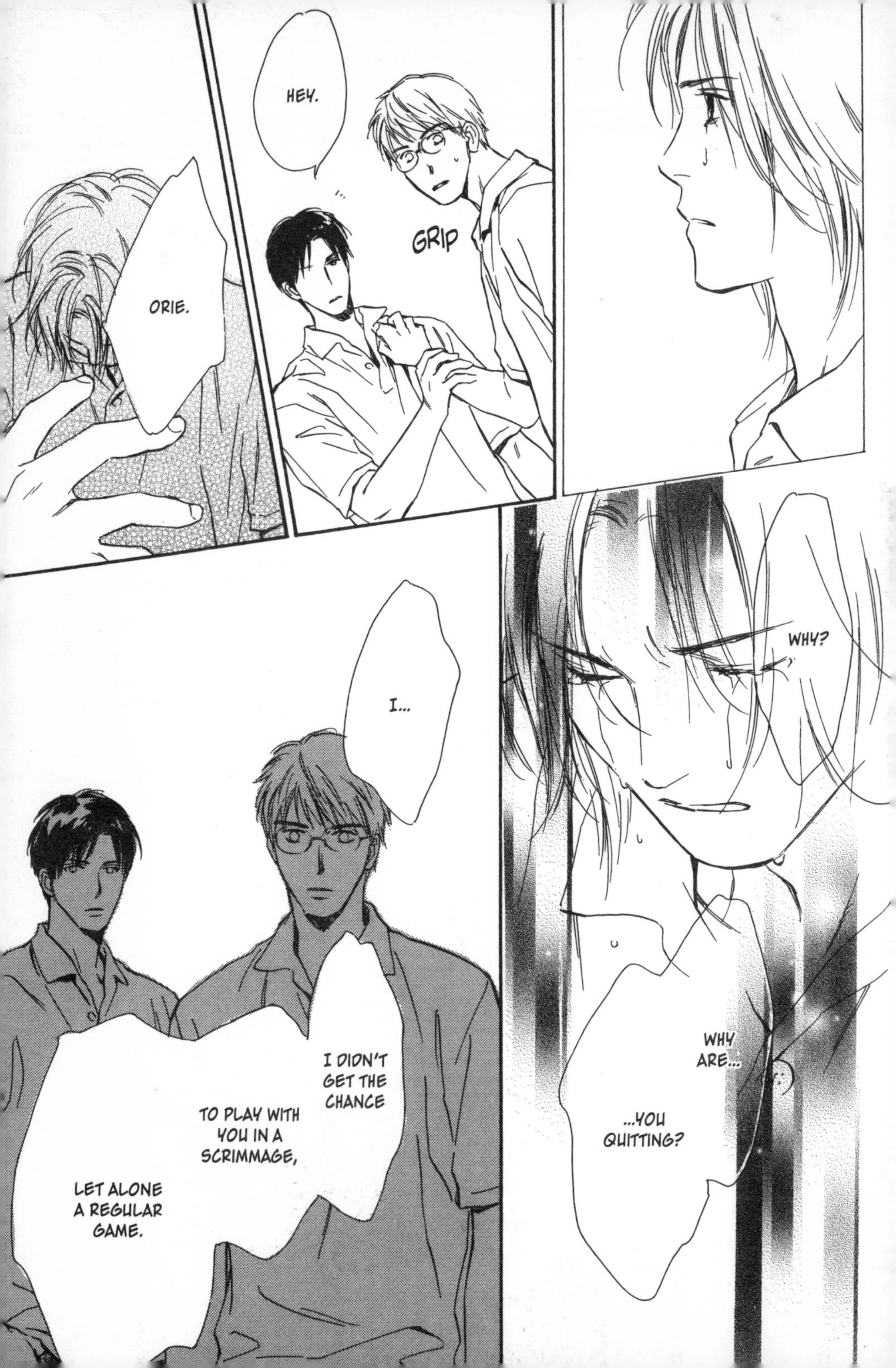
HEY.
GRIP
ORIE.
WHY?
WHY ARE...
...YOU QUITTING?
I...
I DIDN'T GET THE CHANCE
TO PLAY WITH YOU IN A SCRIMMAGE,
LET ALONE A REGULAR GAME.

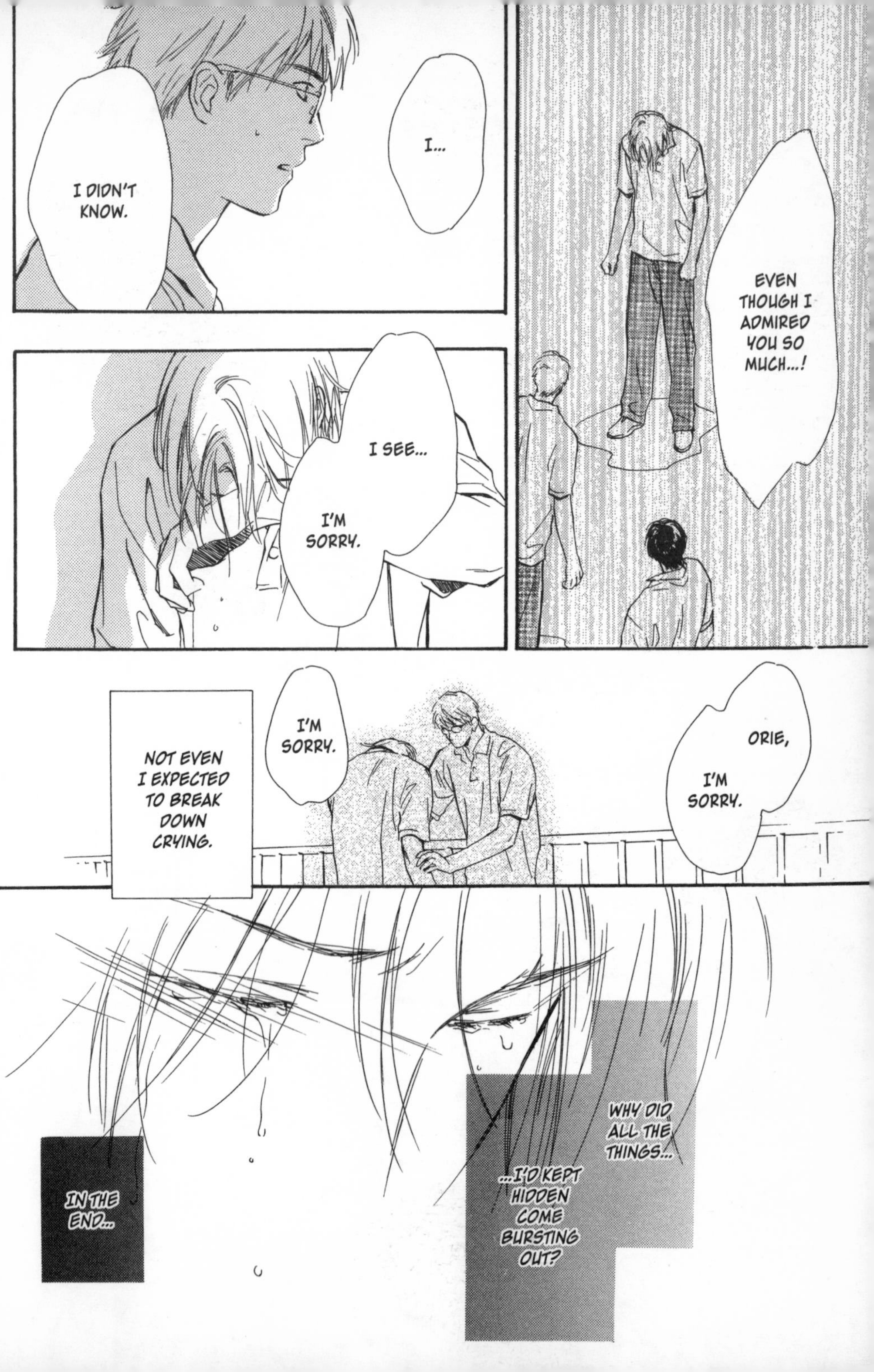
EVEN THOUGH I ADMIRED YOU SO MUCH...!
I...
I DIDN'T KNOW.
I SEE...
I'M SORRY.
ORIE,
I'M SORRY.
I'M SORRY.
NOT EVEN I EXPECTED TO BREAK DOWN CRYING.
WHY DID ALL THE THINGS...
...I'D KEPT HIDDEN COME BURSTING OUT?
IN THE END...

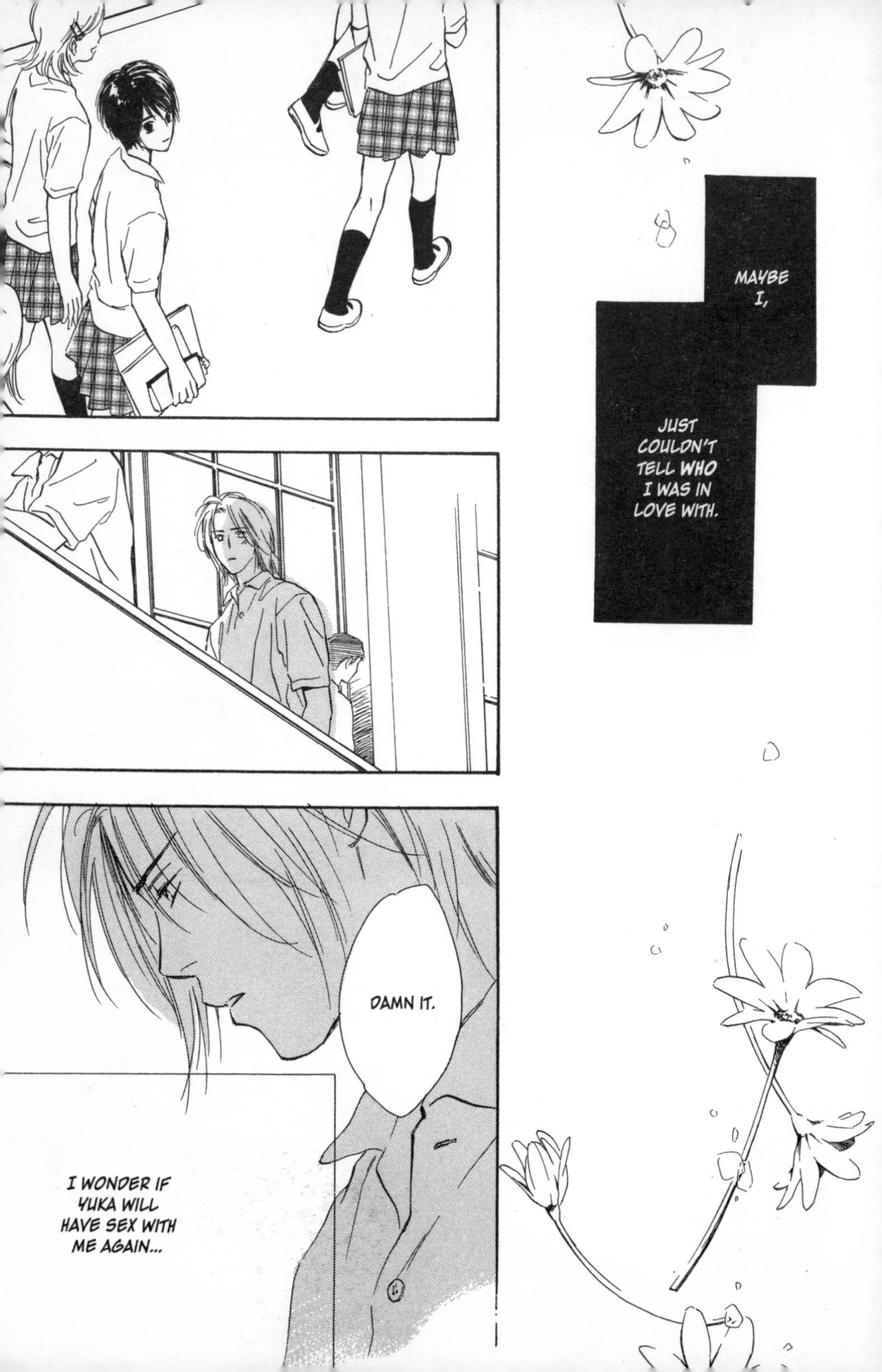
MAYBE I,
JUST COULDN'T TELL WHO I WAS IN LOVE WITH.
DAMN IT.
I WONDER IF YUKA WILL HAVE SEX WITH ME AGAIN...

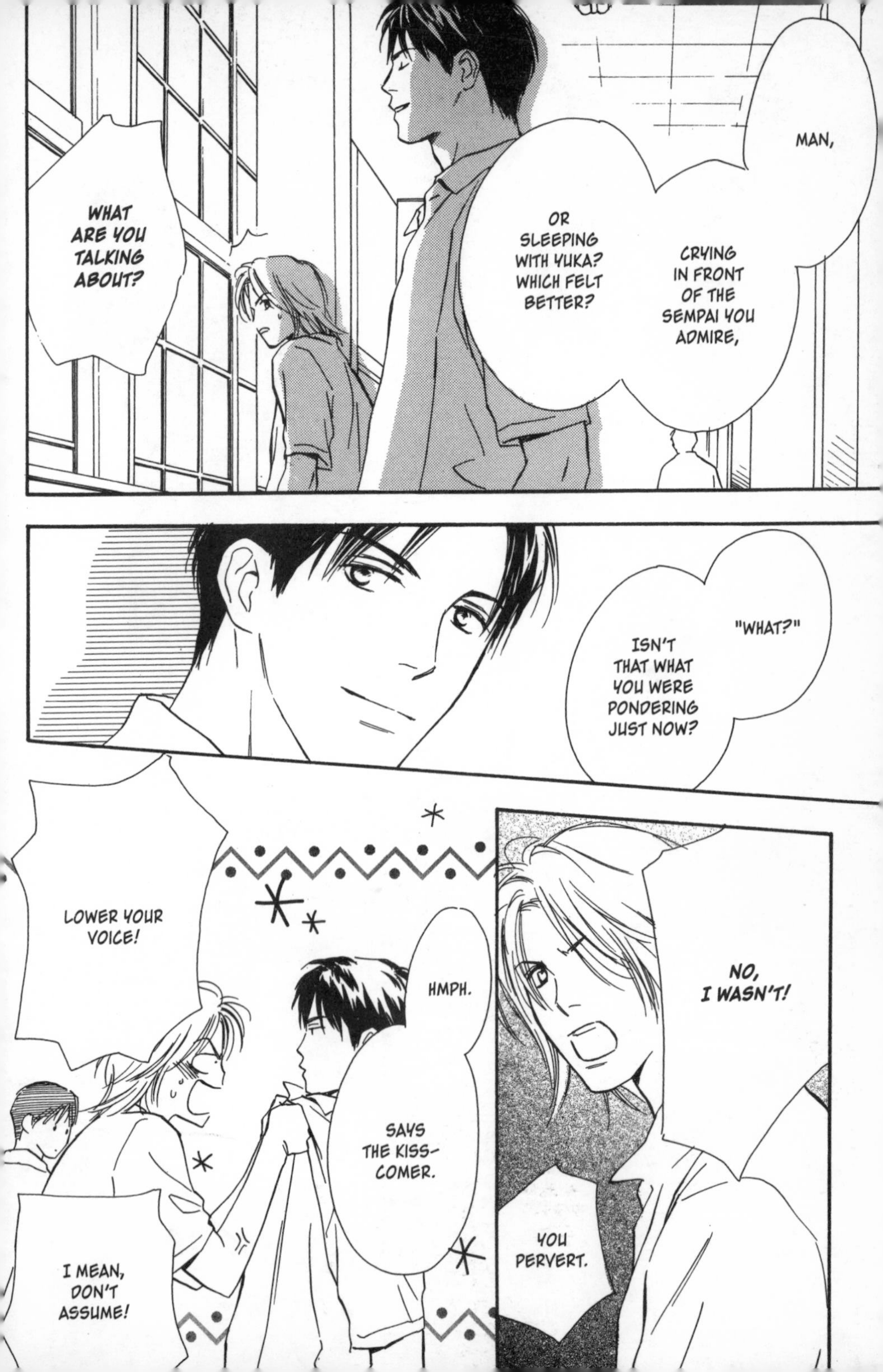
MAN,
CRYING IN FRONT OF THE SEMPAI YOU ADMIRE,
OR SLEEPING WITH YUKA? WHICH FELT BETTER?
WHAT ARE YOU TALKING ABOUT?
"WHAT?"
ISN'T THAT WHAT YOU WERE PONDERING JUST NOW?
NO, I WASN'T!
YOU PERVERT.
LOWER YOUR VOICE!
HMPH.
SAYS THE KISS-COMER.
I MEAN, DON'T ASSUME!

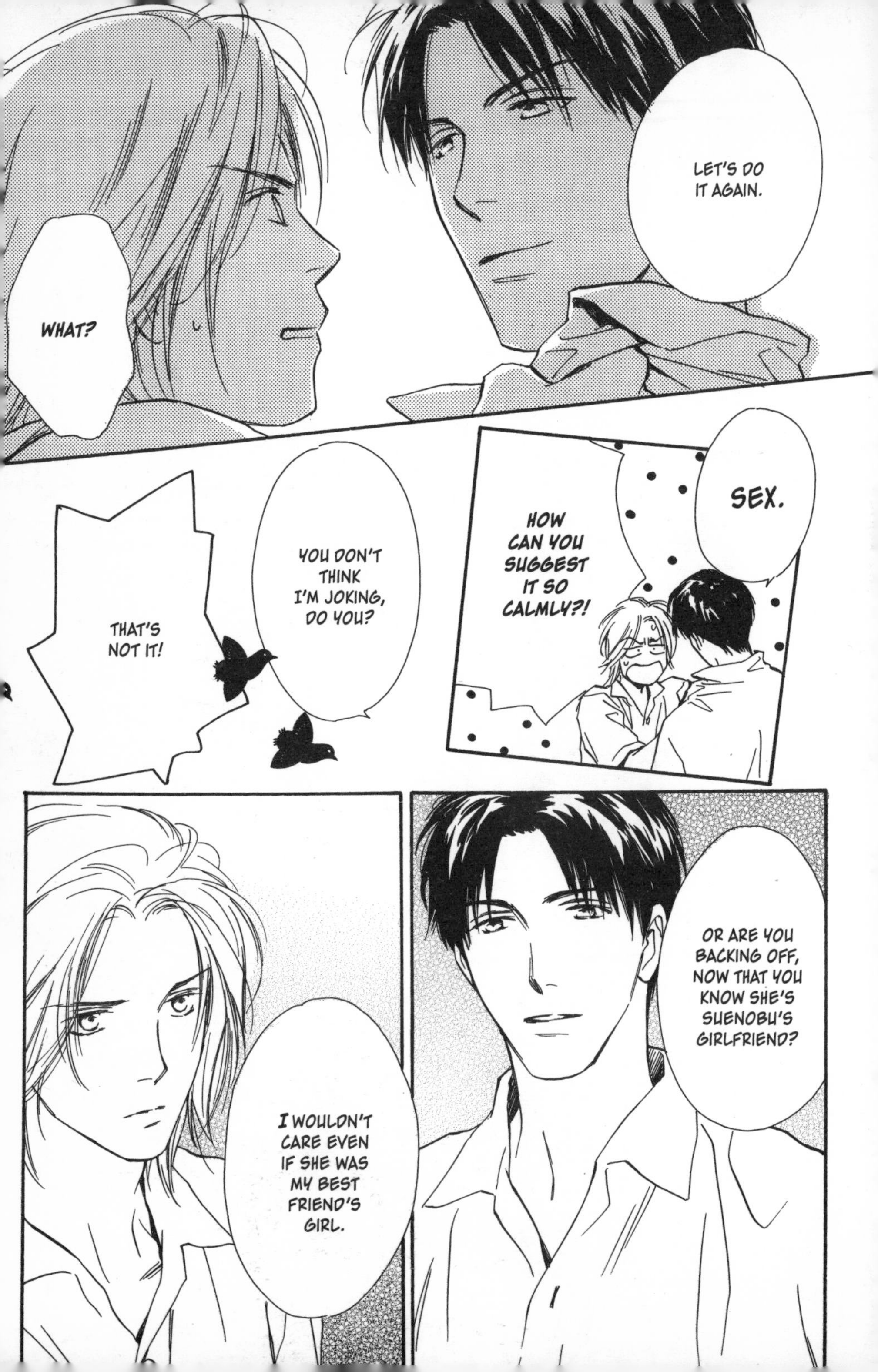
LET'S DO IT AGAIN.
WHAT?
SEX.
HOW CAN YOU SUGGEST IT SO CALMLY?!
YOU DON'T THINK I'M JOKING, DO YOU?
THAT'S NOT IT!
OR ARE YOU BACKING OFF, NOW THAT YOU KNOW SHE'S SUENOBU'S GIRLFRIEND?
I WOULDN'T CARE EVEN IF SHE WAS MY BEST FRIEND'S GIRL.

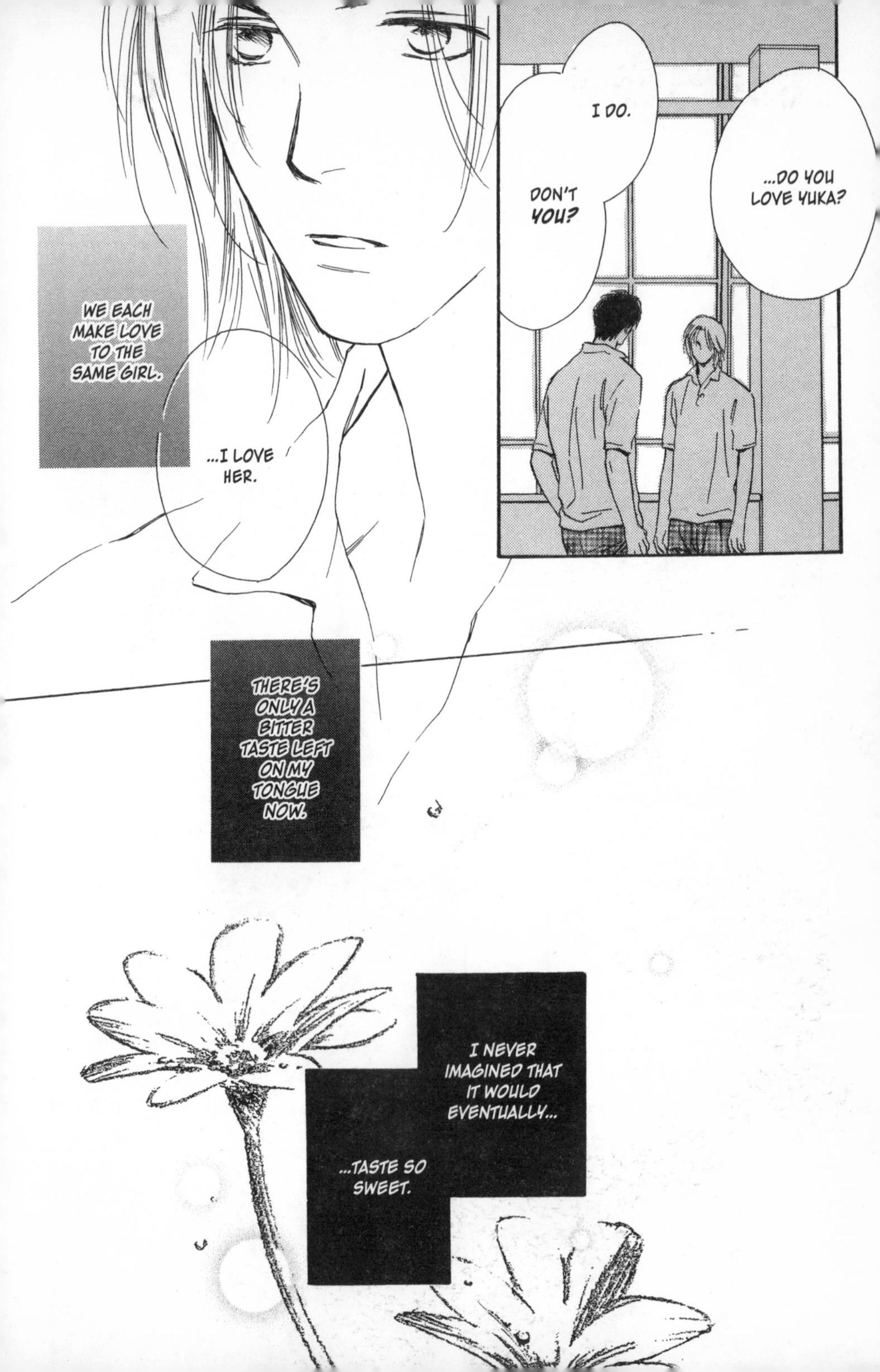
...DO YOU LOVE YUKA?
I DO.
DON'T YOU?
...I LOVE HER.
WE EACH MAKE LOVE TO THE SAME GIRL.
THERE'S ONLY A BITTER TASTE LEFT ON MY TONGUE NOW.
I NEVER IMAGINED THAT IT WOULD EVENTUALLY...
...TASTE SO SWEET.

CHAPTER 2

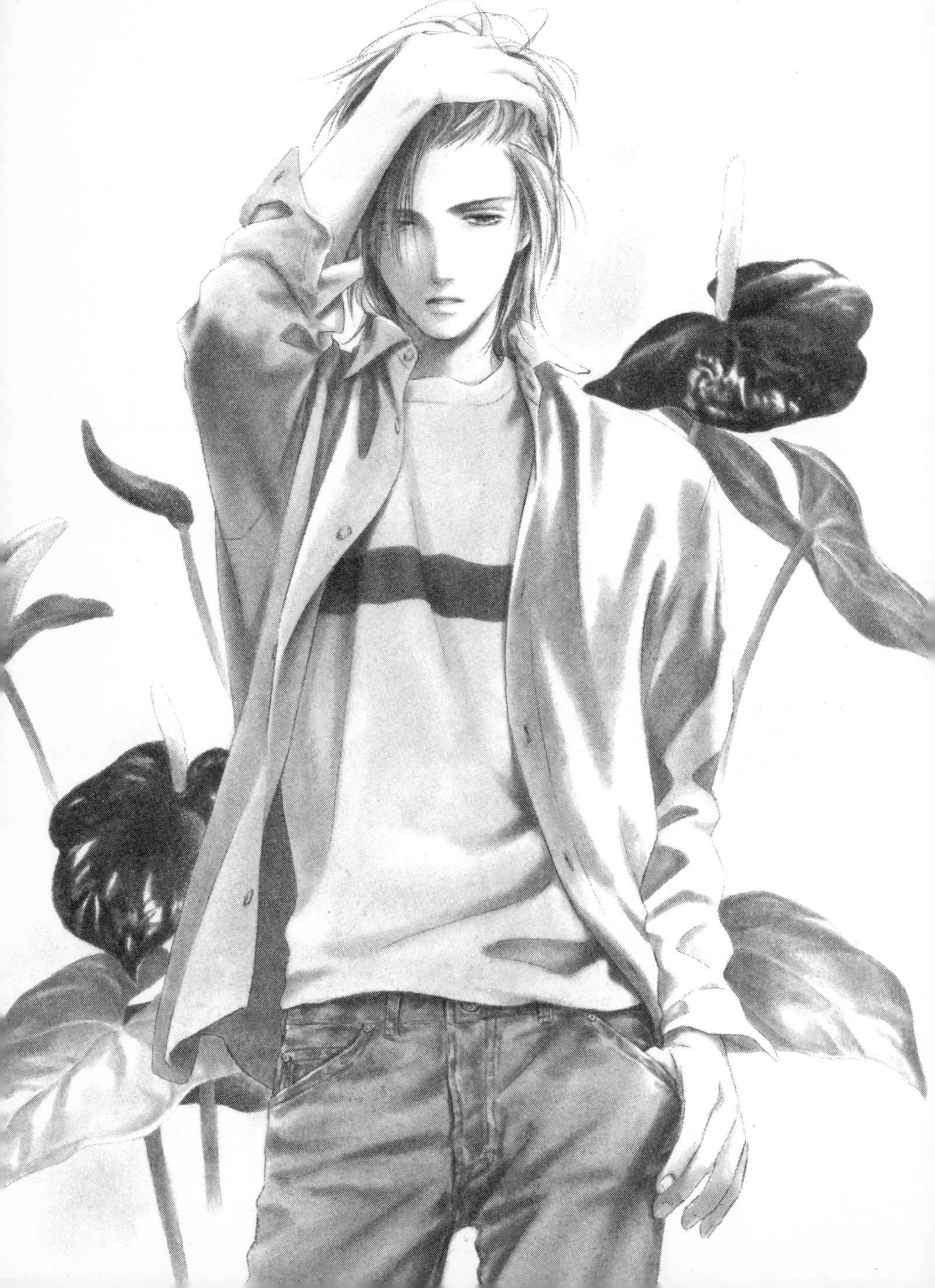

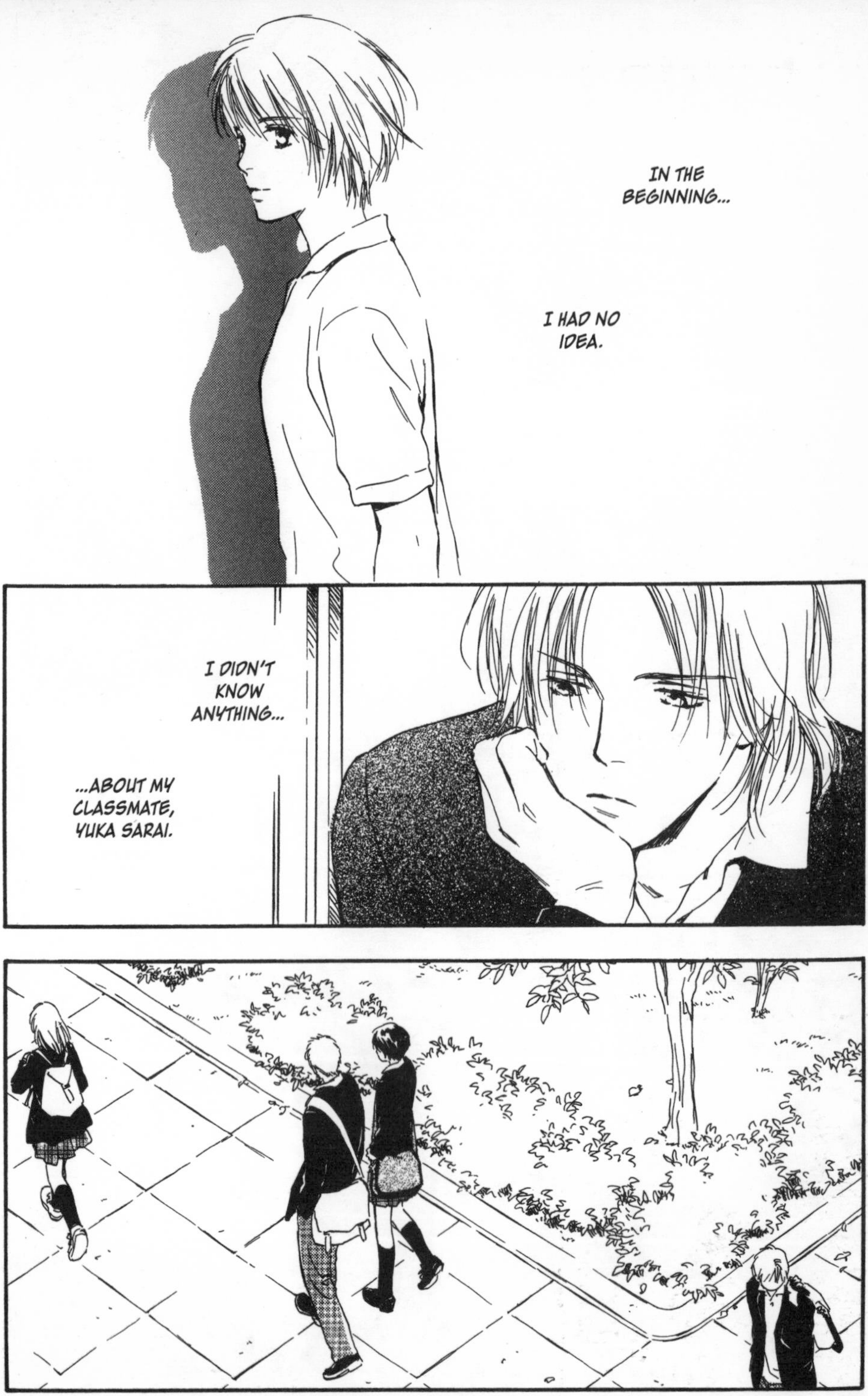
IN THE BEGINNING...
I HAD NO IDEA.
I DIDN'T KNOW ANYTHING...
...ABOUT MY CLASSMATE, YUKA SARAI.

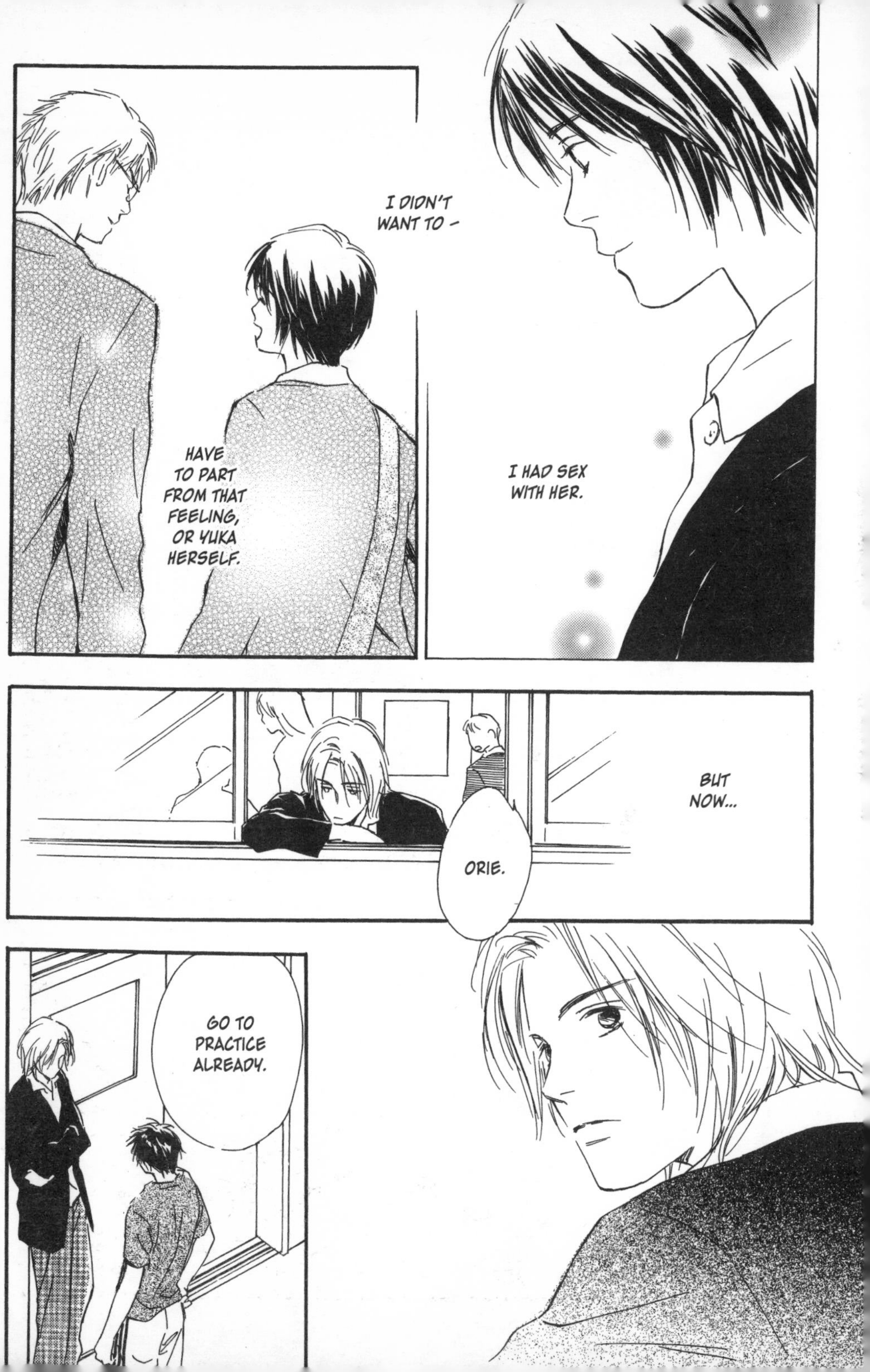
I HAD SEX WITH HER.
I DIDN'T WANT TO -
HAVE TO PART FROM THAT FEELING, OR YUKA HERSELF.
BUT NOW...
ORIE.
GO TO PRACTICE ALREADY.

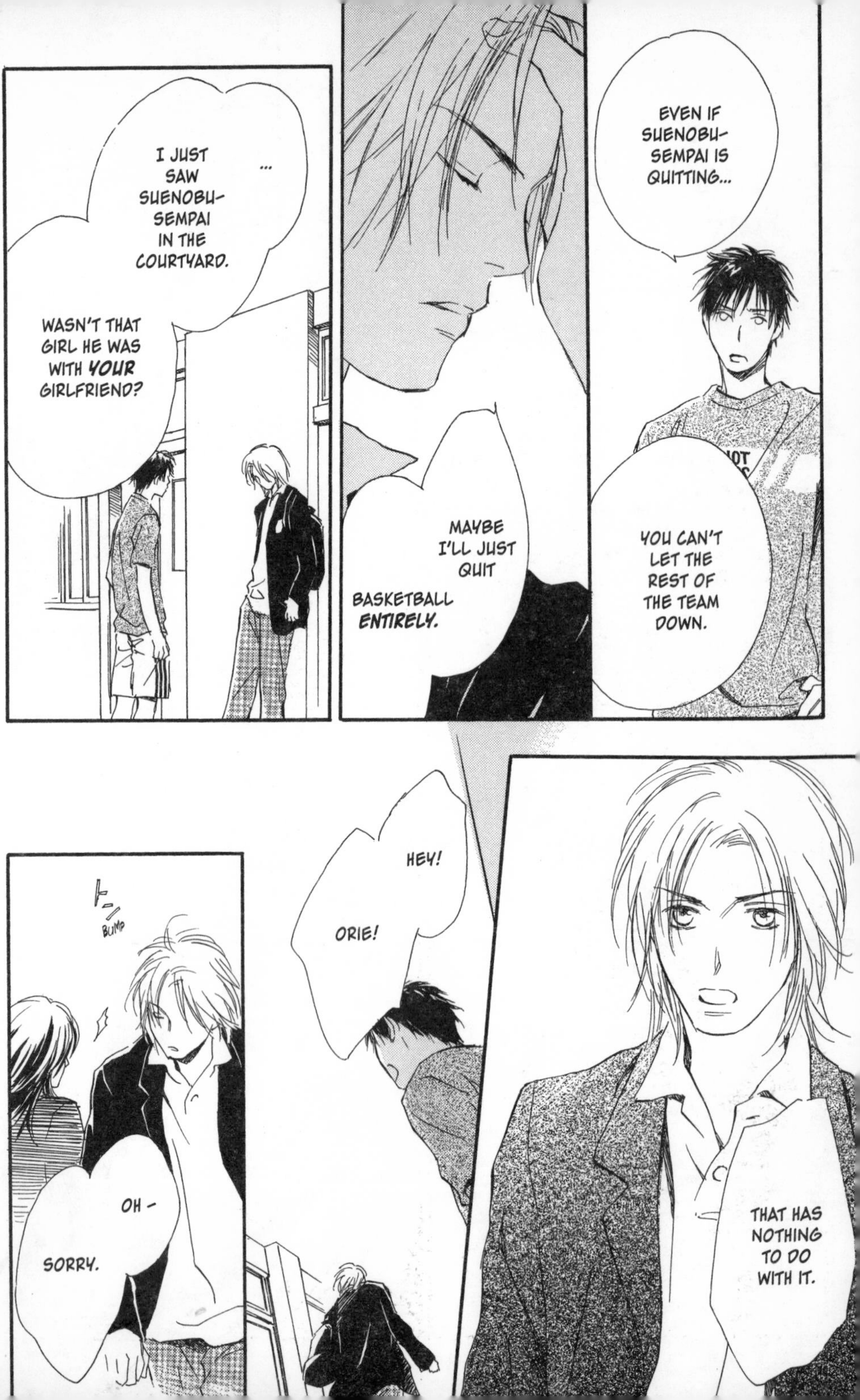
EVEN IF SUENOBU-SEMPAI IS QUITTING...
YOU CAN'T LET THE REST OF THE TEAM DOWN.
MAYBE I'LL JUST QUIT BASKETBALL ENTIRELY.
...
I JUST SAW SUENOBU-SEMPAI IN THE COURTYARD.
WASN'T THAT GIRL HE WAS WITH YOUR GIRLFRIEND?
THAT HAS NOTHING TO DO WITH IT.
HEY!
ORIE!
BUMP
OH -
SORRY.

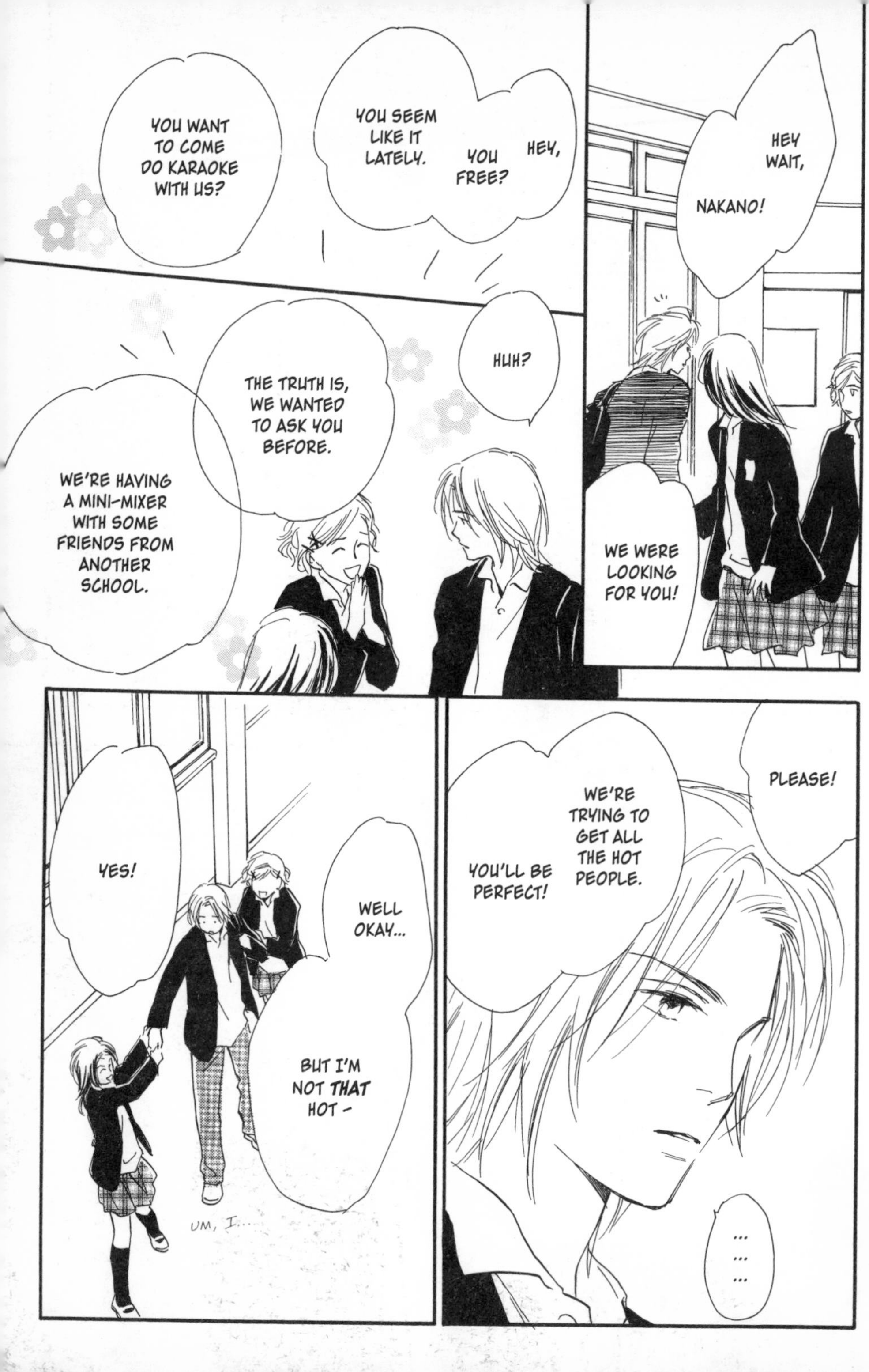
HEY WAIT, NAKANO!
WE WERE LOOKING FOR YOU!
HEY, YOU FREE?
YOU SEEM LIKE IT LATELY.
YOU WANT TO COME DO KARAOKE WITH US?
HUH?
THE TRUTH IS, WE WANTED TO ASK YOU BEFORE.
WE'RE HAVING A MINI-MIXER WITH SOME FRIENDS FROM ANOTHER SCHOOL.
PLEASE!
WE'RE TRYING TO GET ALL THE HOT PEOPLE.
YOU'LL BE PERFECT!
… … …
WELL OKAY...
BUT I'M NOT **THAT** HOT -
YES!
UM, I...

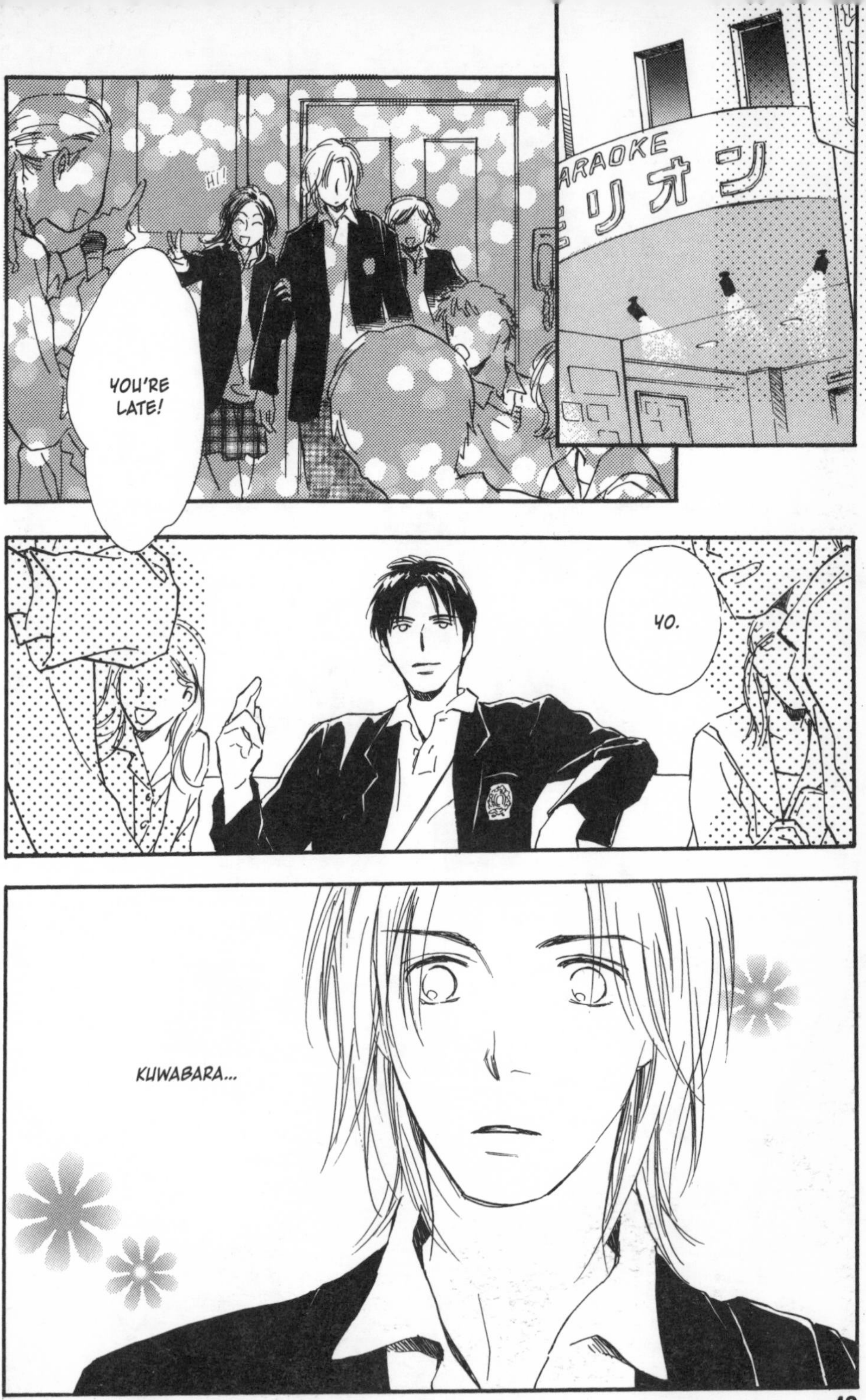
ARAOKE
リオン
HI!
YOU'RE LATE!
YO.
KUWABARA...

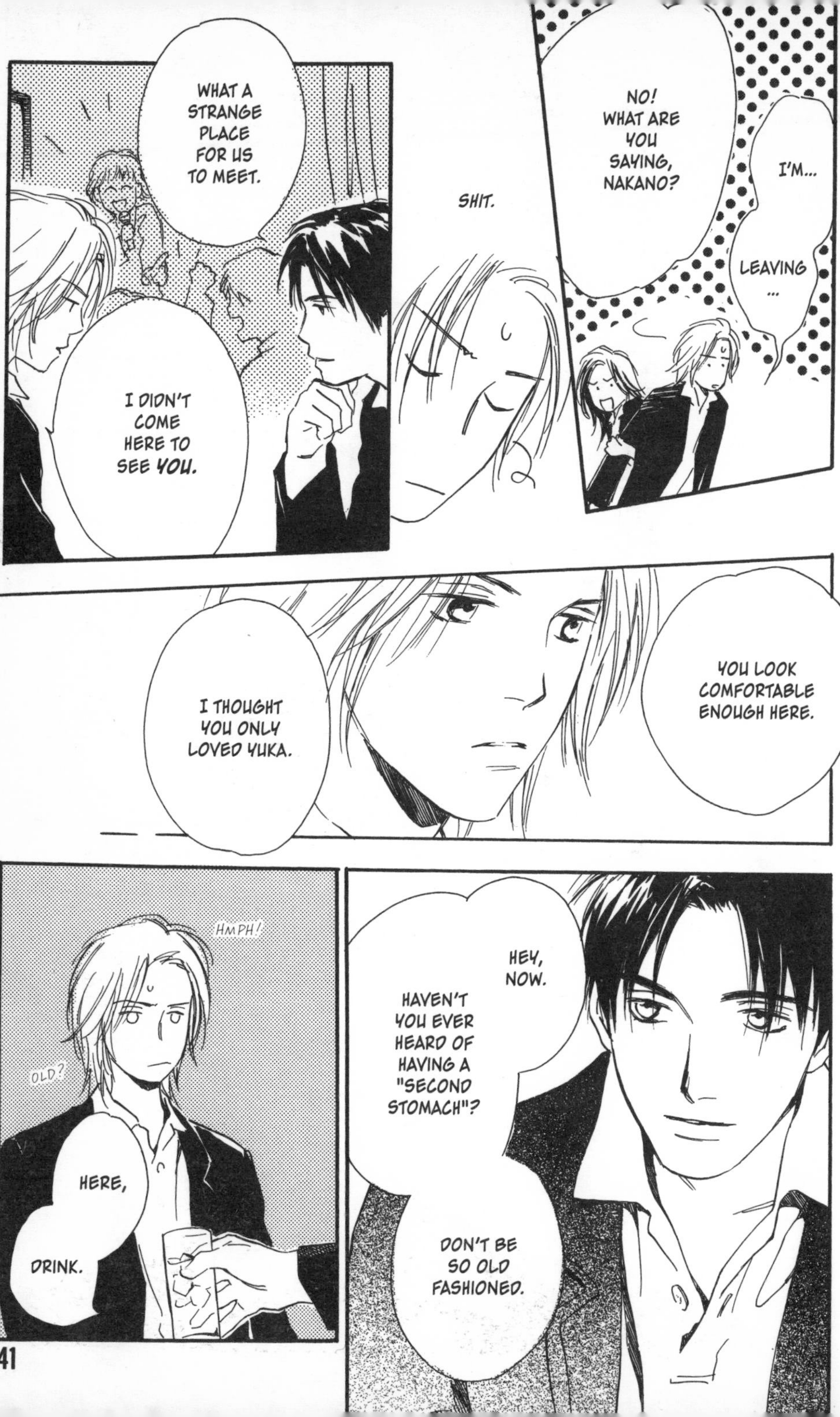
I'M... LEAVING...
NO! WHAT ARE YOU SAYING, NAKANO?
SHIT.
WHAT A STRANGE PLACE FOR US TO MEET.
I DIDN'T COME HERE TO SEE YOU.
YOU LOOK COMFORTABLE ENOUGH HERE.
I THOUGHT YOU ONLY LOVED YUKA.
HEY, NOW.
HAVEN'T YOU EVER HEARD OF HAVING A "SECOND STOMACH"?
DON'T BE SO OLD FASHIONED.
HMPH!
OLD?
HERE, DRINK.

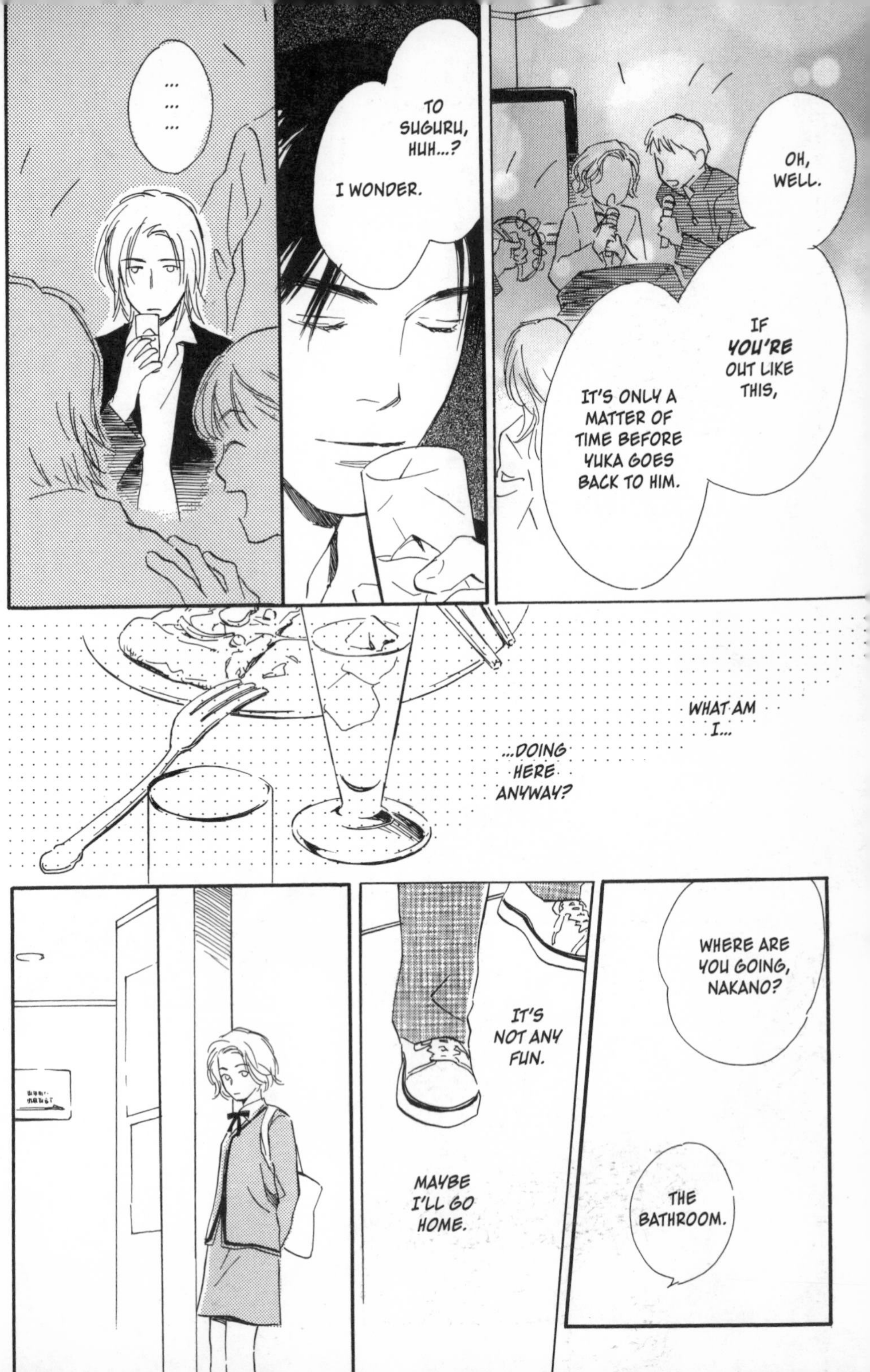
OH, WELL.
IF *YOU'RE* OUT LIKE THIS,
IT'S ONLY A MATTER OF TIME BEFORE YUKA GOES BACK TO HIM.
TO SUGURU, HUH...?
I WONDER.
...
...
...
WHAT AM I...
...DOING HERE ANYWAY?
WHERE ARE YOU GOING, NAKANO?
THE BATHROOM.
IT'S NOT ANY FUN.
MAYBE I'LL GO HOME.

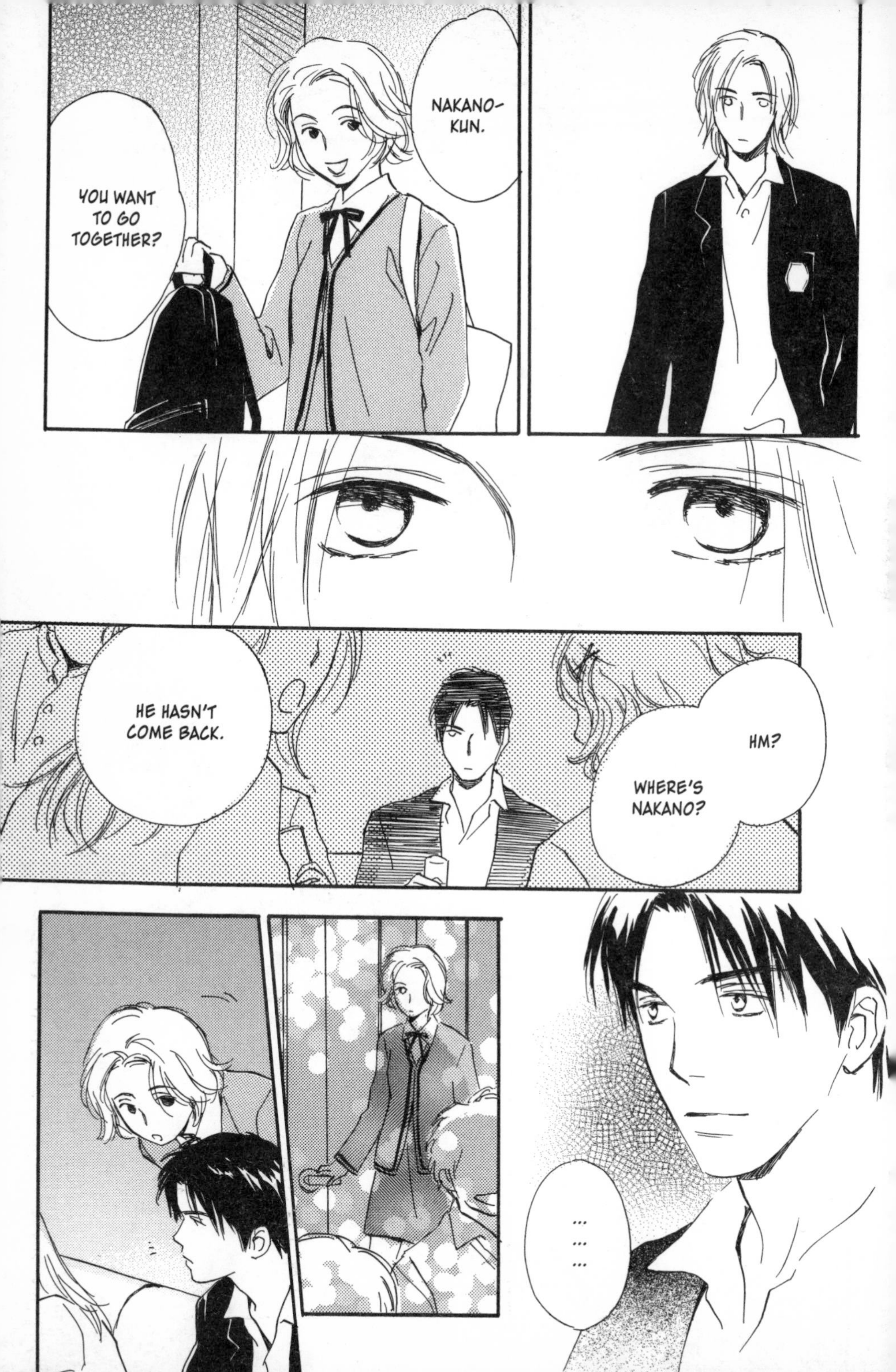
NAKANO-KUN.
YOU WANT TO GO TOGETHER?
HM?
WHERE'S NAKANO?
HE HASN'T COME BACK.
...
...
...

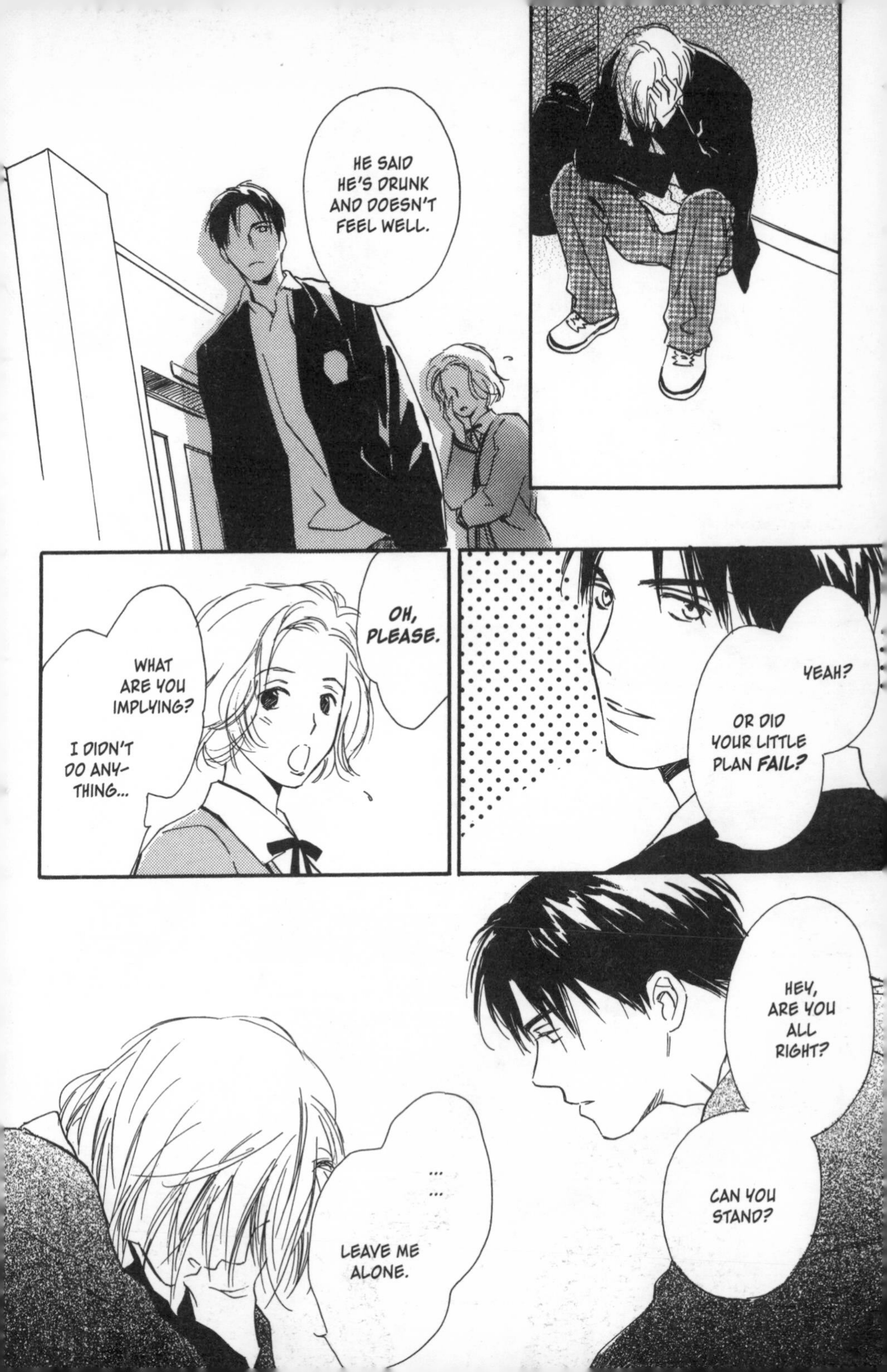
HE SAID HE'S DRUNK AND DOESN'T FEEL WELL.
YEAH?
OR DID YOUR LITTLE PLAN **FAIL?**
OH, PLEASE.
WHAT ARE YOU IMPLYING?
I DIDN'T DO ANY-THING...
HEY, ARE YOU ALL RIGHT?
CAN YOU STAND?
... ...
LEAVE ME ALONE.

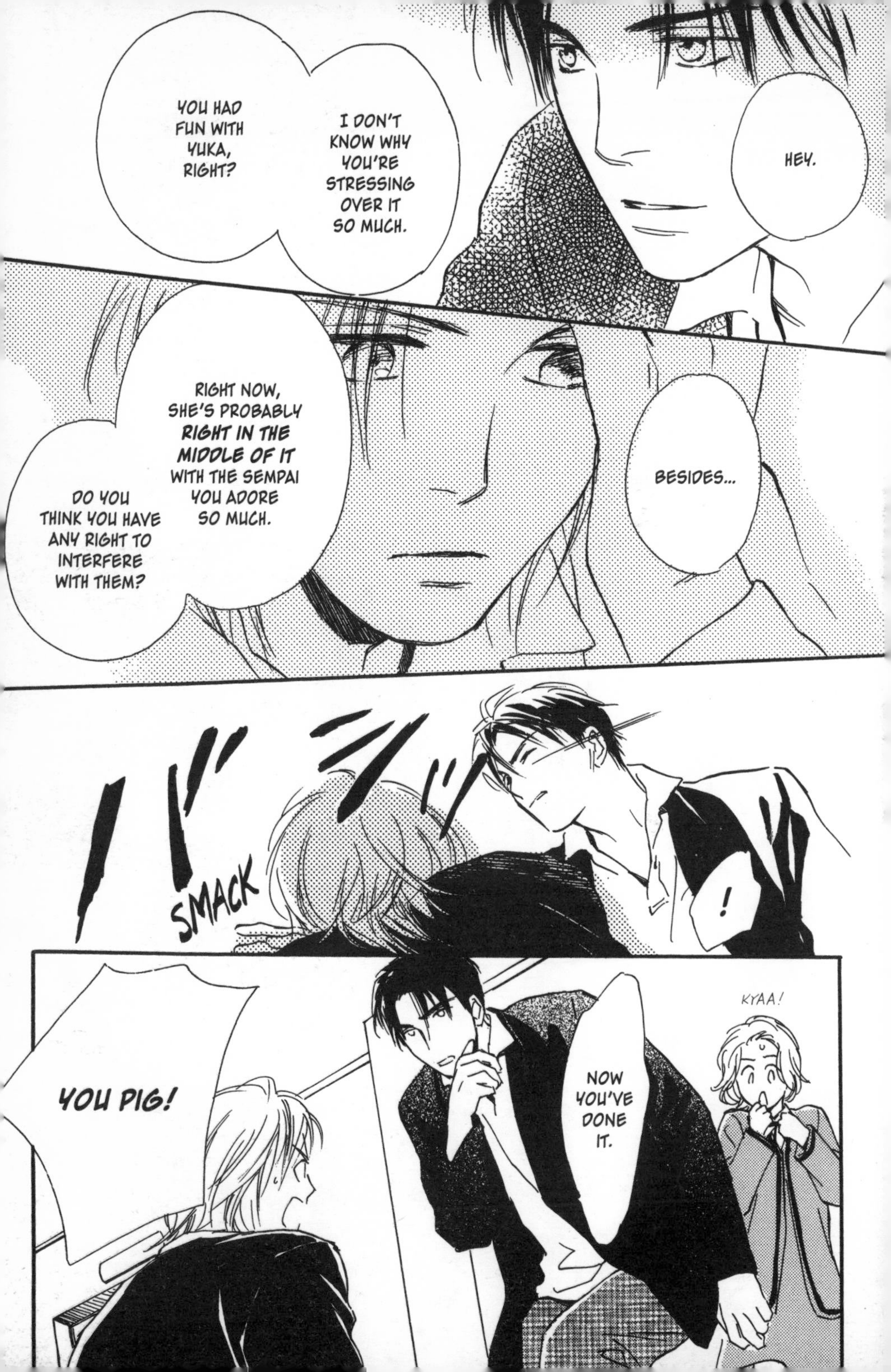
HEY.
I DON'T KNOW WHY YOU'RE STRESSING OVER IT SO MUCH.
YOU HAD FUN WITH YUKA, RIGHT?
BESIDES...
RIGHT NOW, SHE'S PROBABLY **RIGHT IN THE MIDDLE OF IT** WITH THE SEMPAI YOU ADORE SO MUCH.
DO YOU THINK YOU HAVE ANY RIGHT TO INTERFERE WITH THEM?
!
SMACK
KYAA!
NOW YOU'VE DONE IT.
YOU PIG!

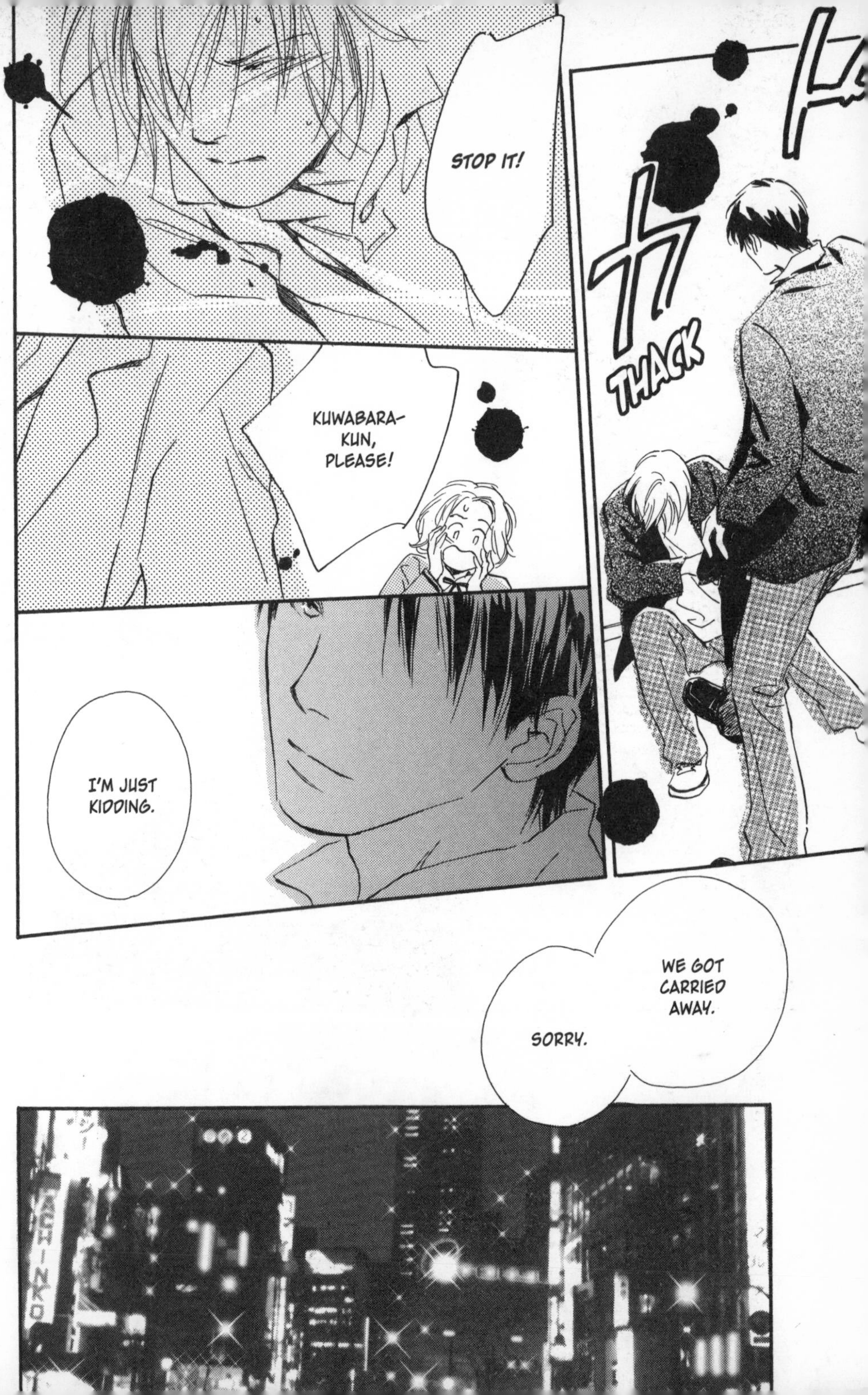
THACK
STOP IT!
KUWABARA-KUN, PLEASE!
I'M JUST KIDDING.
WE GOT CARRIED AWAY.
SORRY.

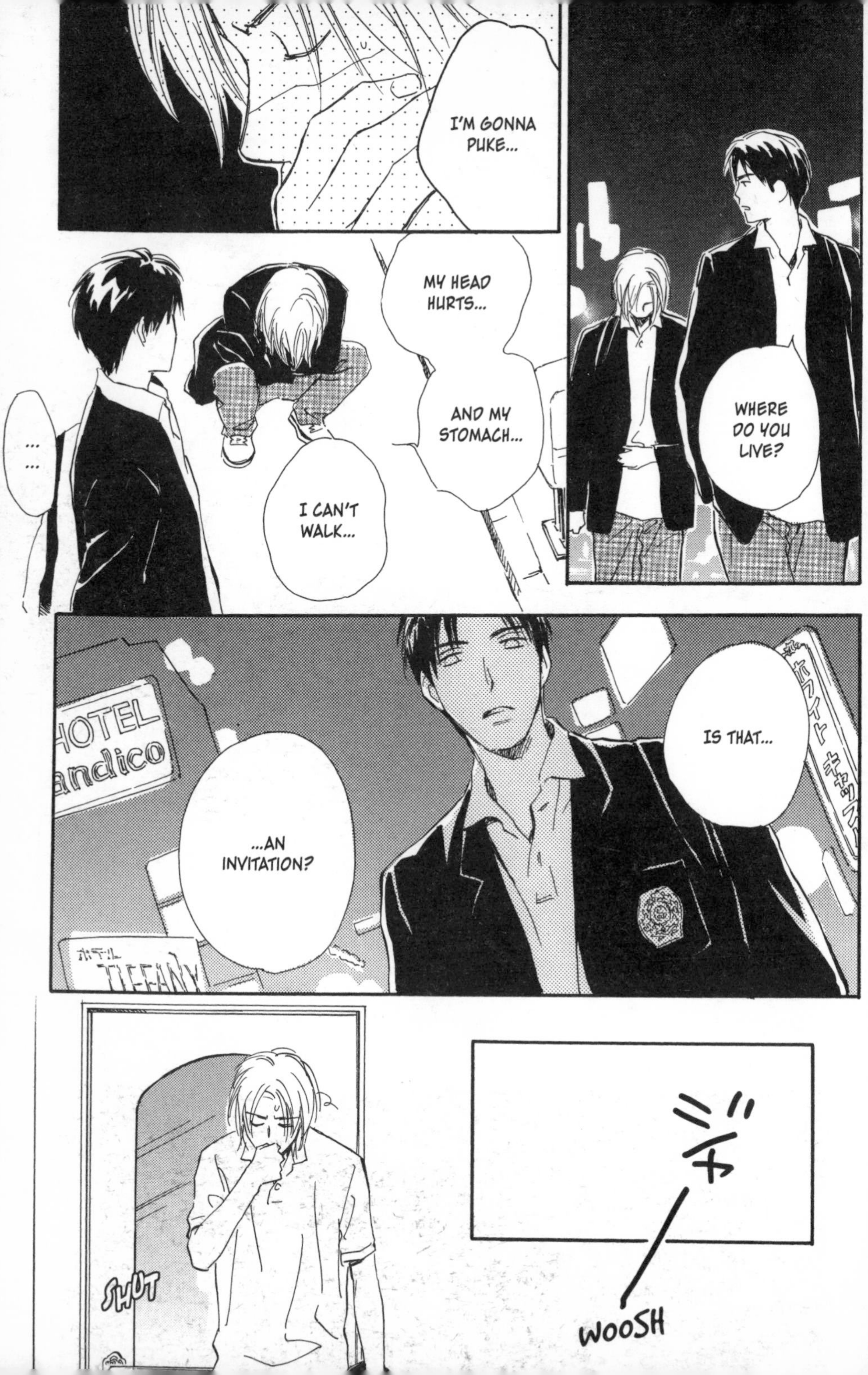
WHERE DO YOU LIVE?
I'M GONNA PUKE...
MY HEAD HURTS...
AND MY STOMACH...
I CAN'T WALK...
... ...
IS THAT...
...AN INVITATION?
HOTEL
andico
ジャー
WOOSH
SHUT

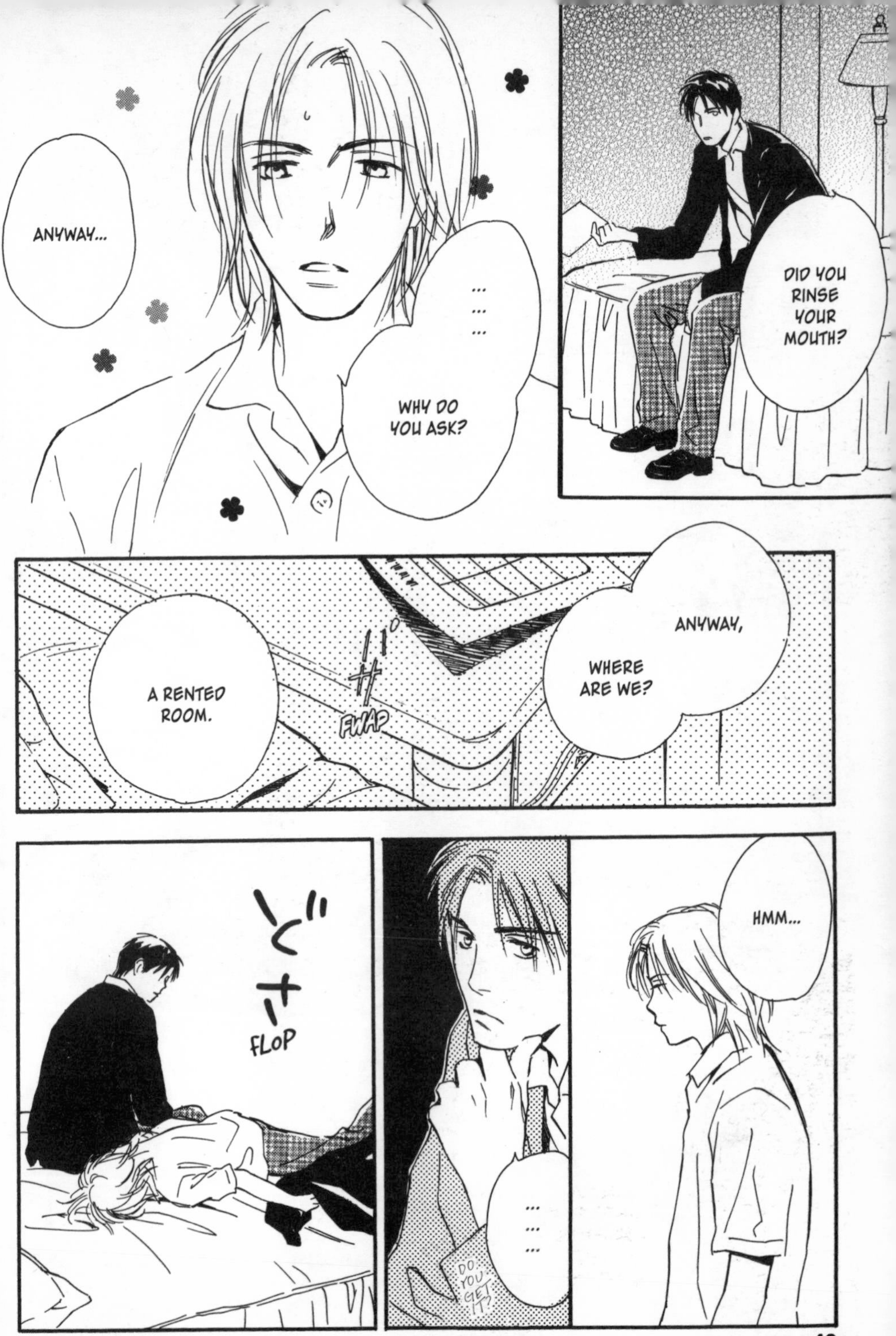
DID YOU RINSE YOUR MOUTH?
... ...
WHY DO YOU ASK?
ANYWAY...
ANYWAY,
WHERE ARE WE?
FWAP
A RENTED ROOM.
HMM...
... ...
DO YOU GET IT?
FLOP

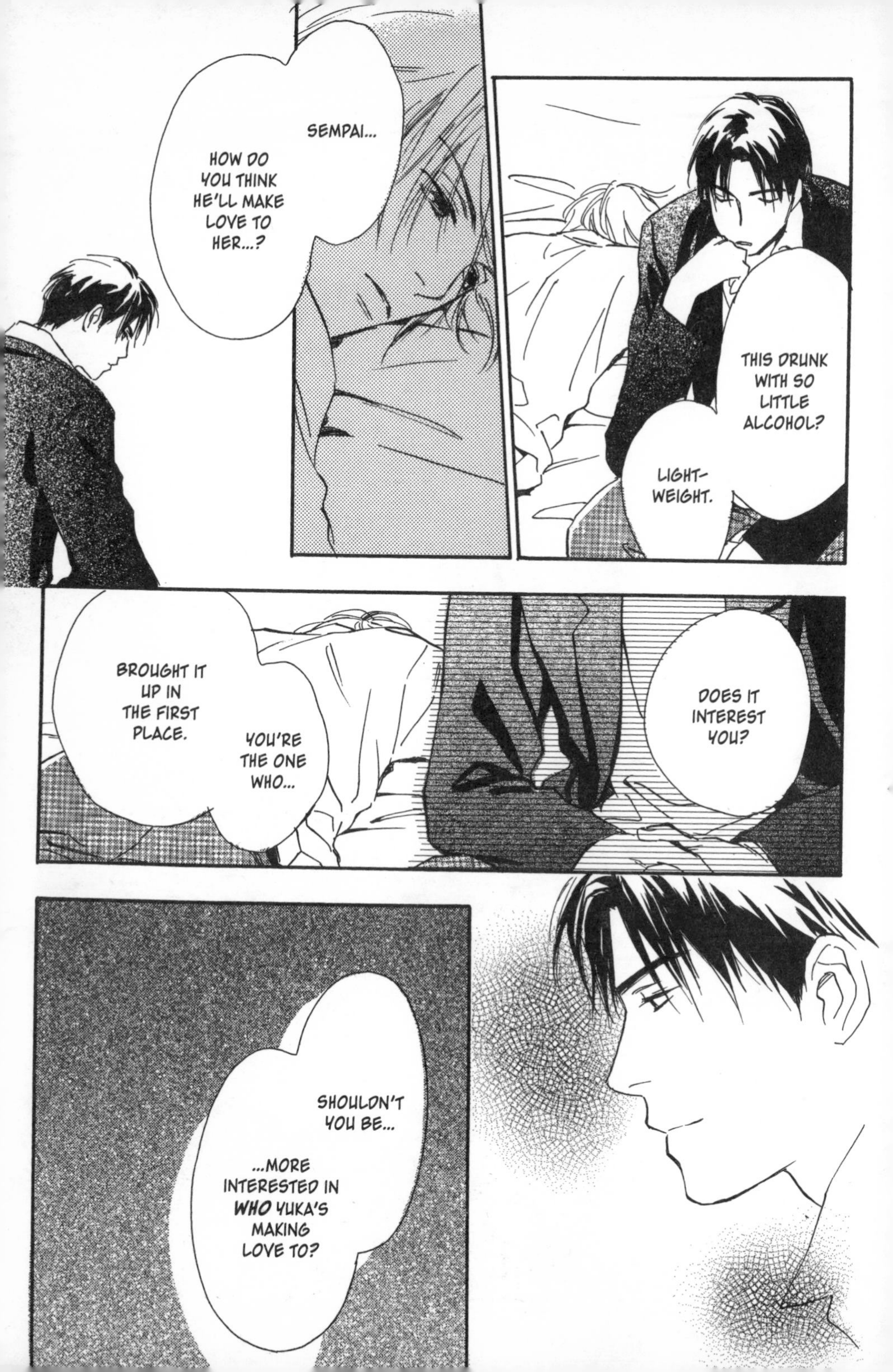
THIS DRUNK WITH SO LITTLE ALCOHOL?
LIGHT-WEIGHT.
SEMPAI...
HOW DO YOU THINK HE'LL MAKE LOVE TO HER...?
DOES IT INTEREST YOU?
YOU'RE THE ONE WHO...
BROUGHT IT UP IN THE FIRST PLACE.
SHOULDN'T YOU BE...
...MORE INTERESTED IN **WHO** YUKA'S MAKING LOVE TO?

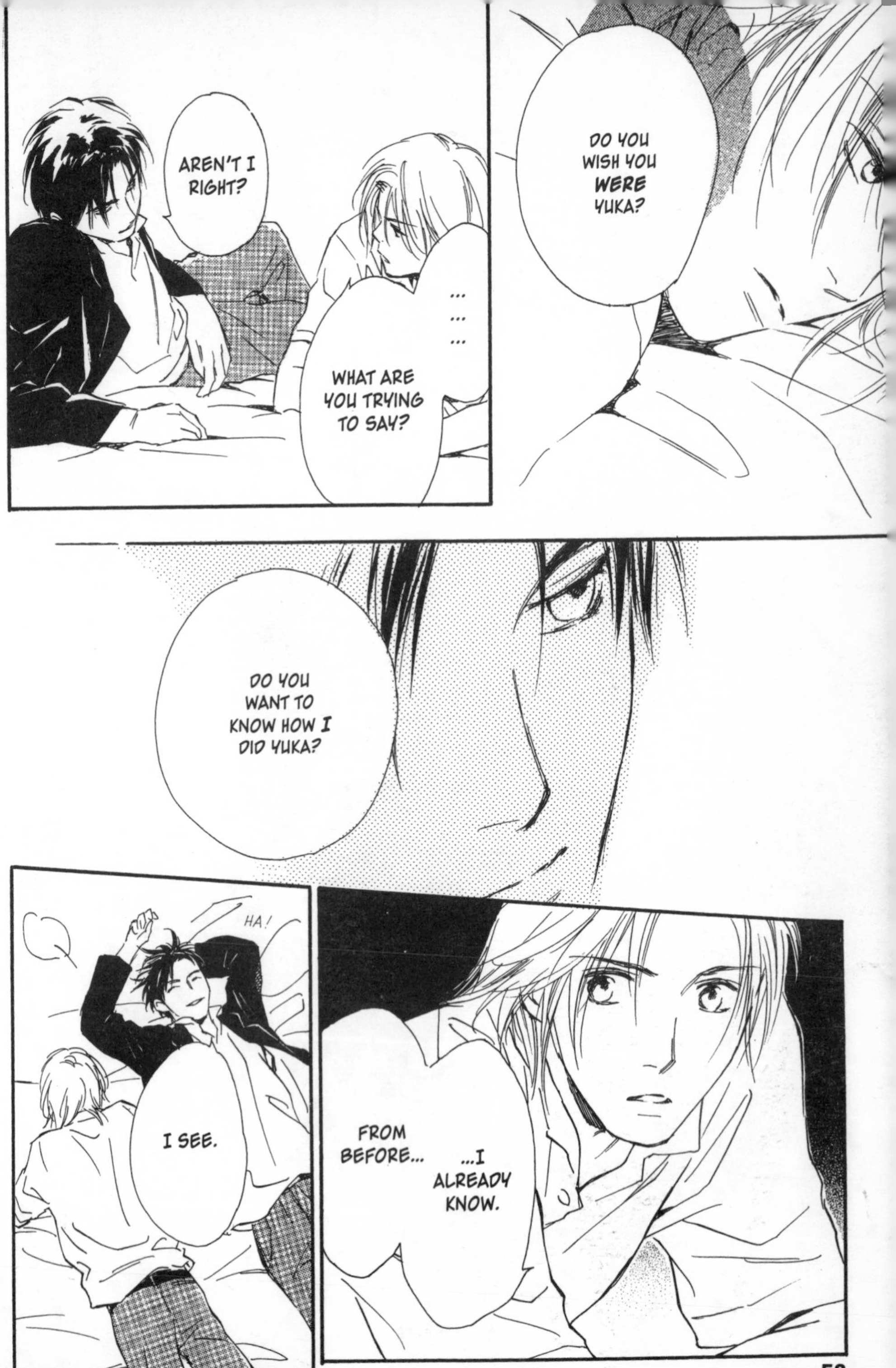
DO YOU WISH YOU WERE YUKA?
AREN'T I RIGHT?
... ... WHAT ARE YOU TRYING TO SAY?
DO YOU WANT TO KNOW HOW I DID YUKA?
FROM BEFORE...
...I ALREADY KNOW.
HA!
I SEE.

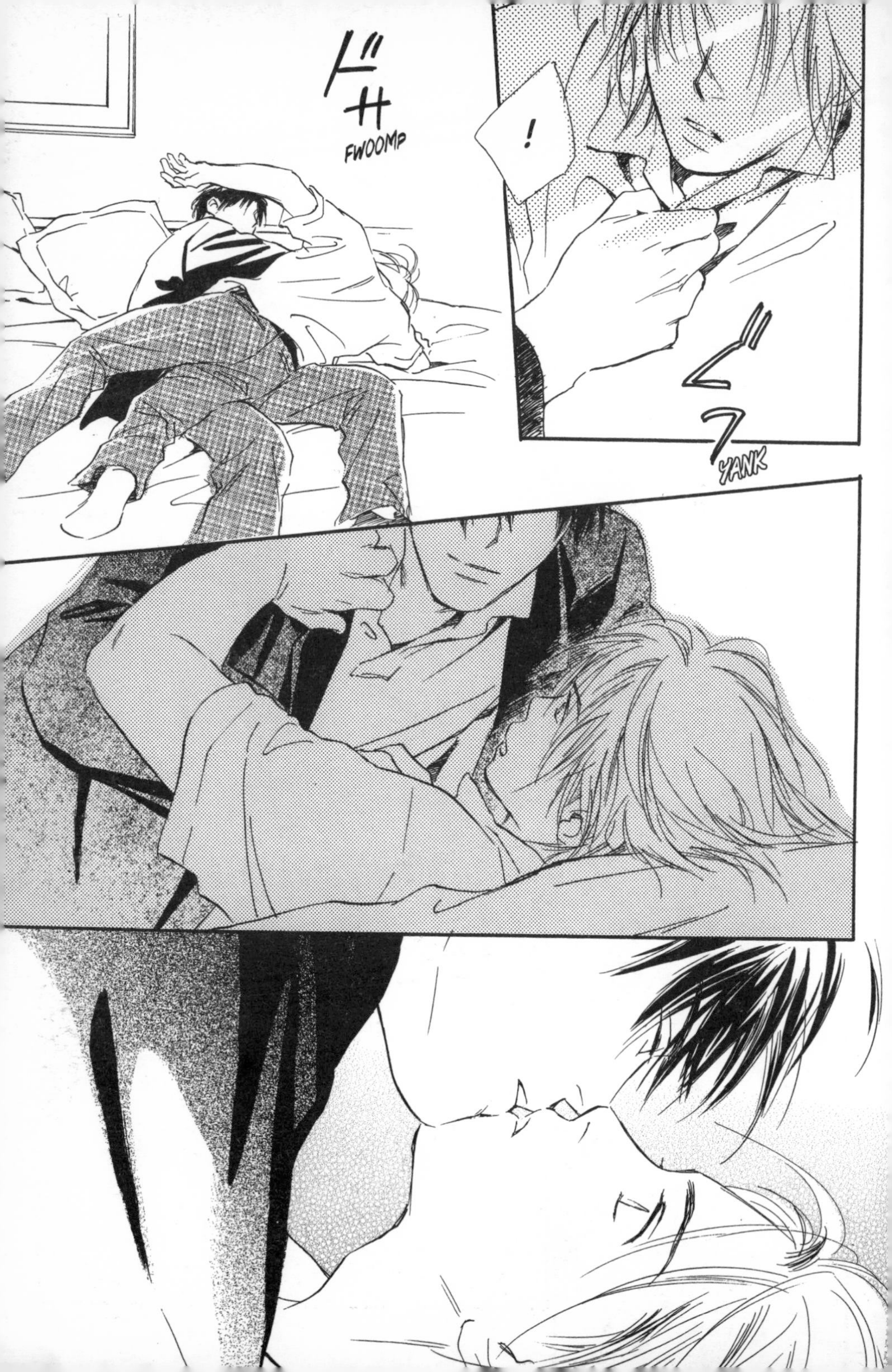
!
YANK
ドサ
FWOOMP

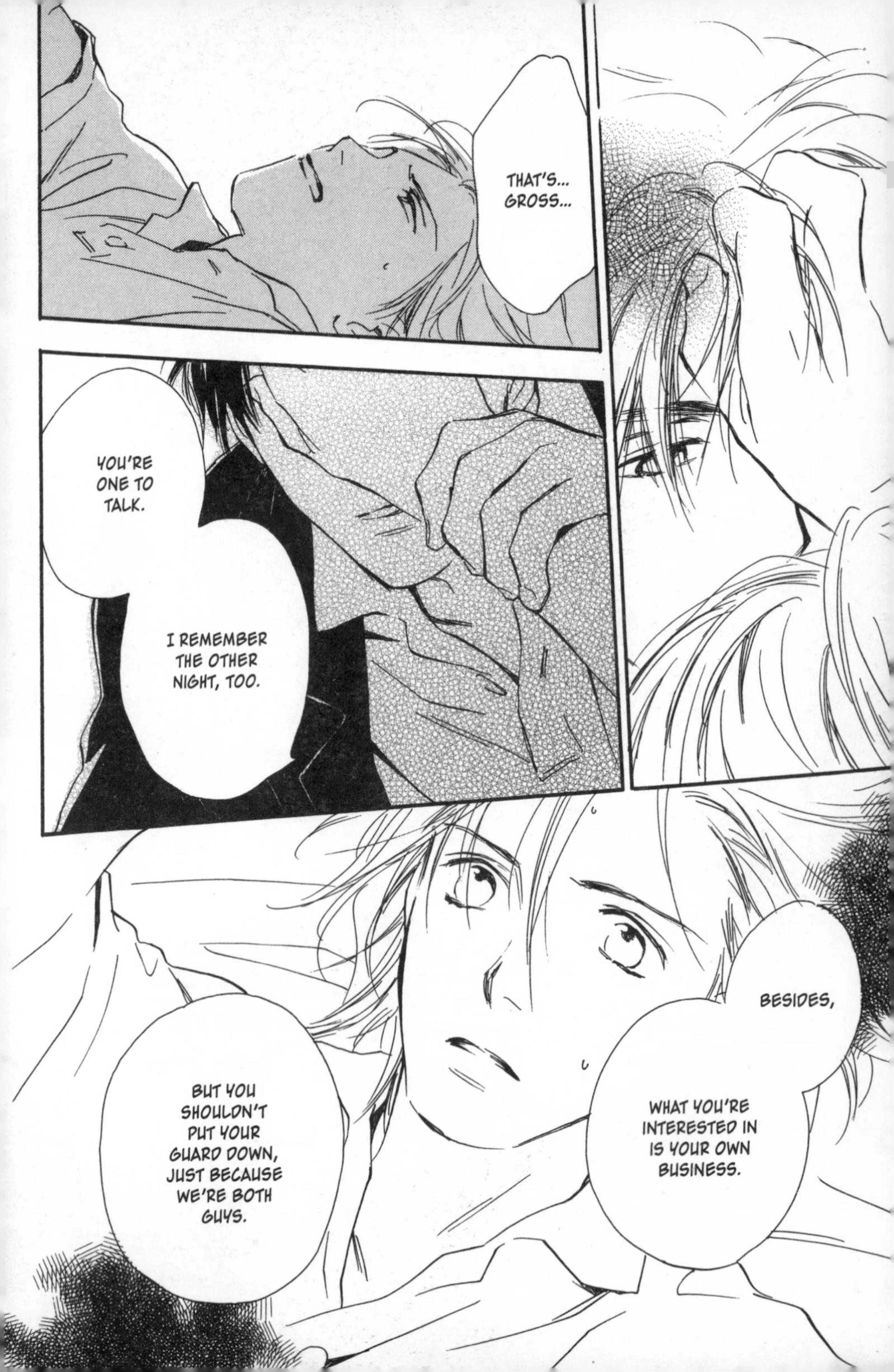
THAT'S... GROSS...
YOU'RE ONE TO TALK.
I REMEMBER THE OTHER NIGHT, TOO.
BESIDES,
WHAT YOU'RE INTERESTED IN IS YOUR OWN BUSINESS.
BUT YOU SHOULDN'T PUT YOUR GUARD DOWN, JUST BECAUSE WE'RE BOTH GUYS.

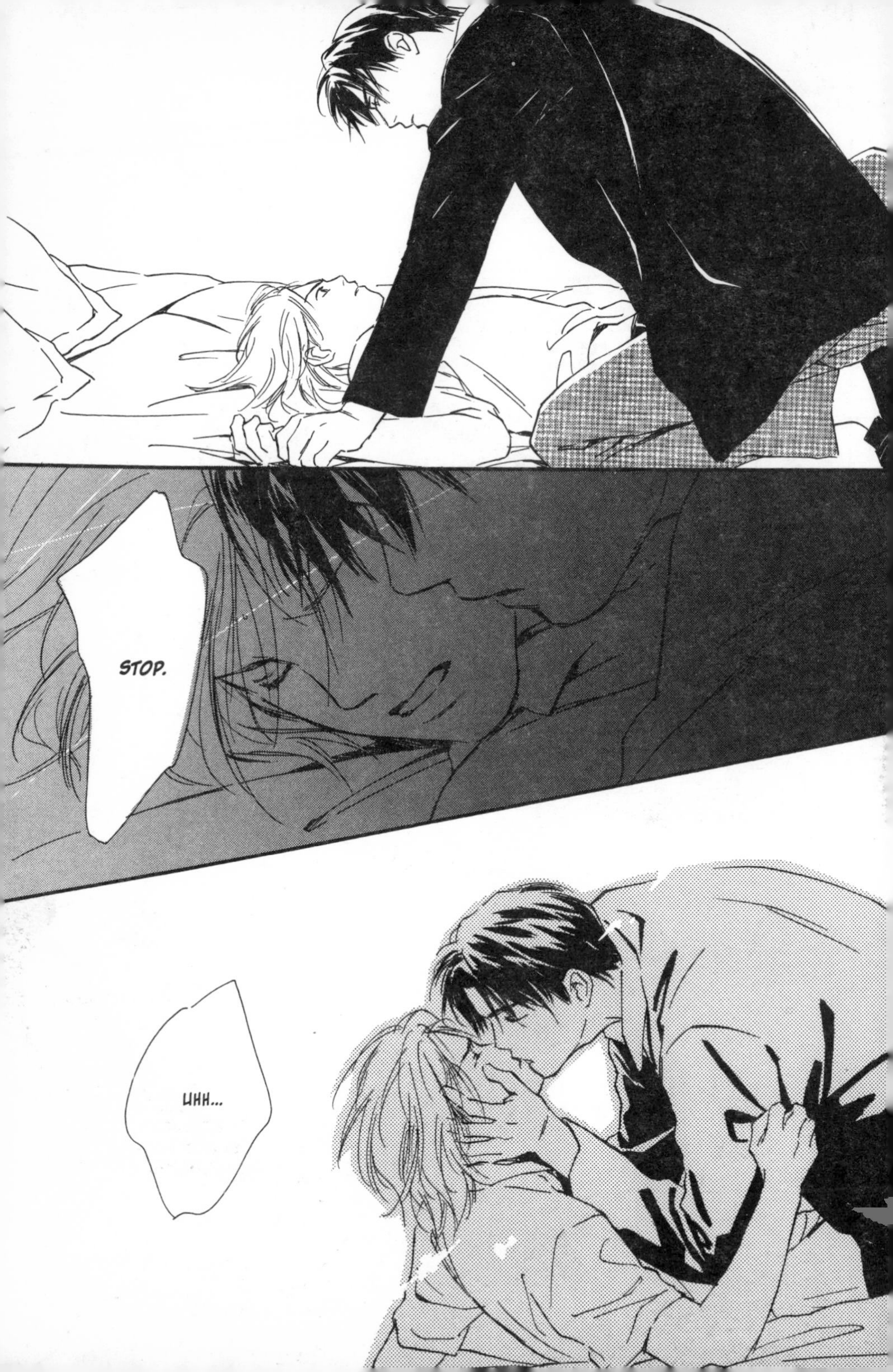
STOP.
UHH...

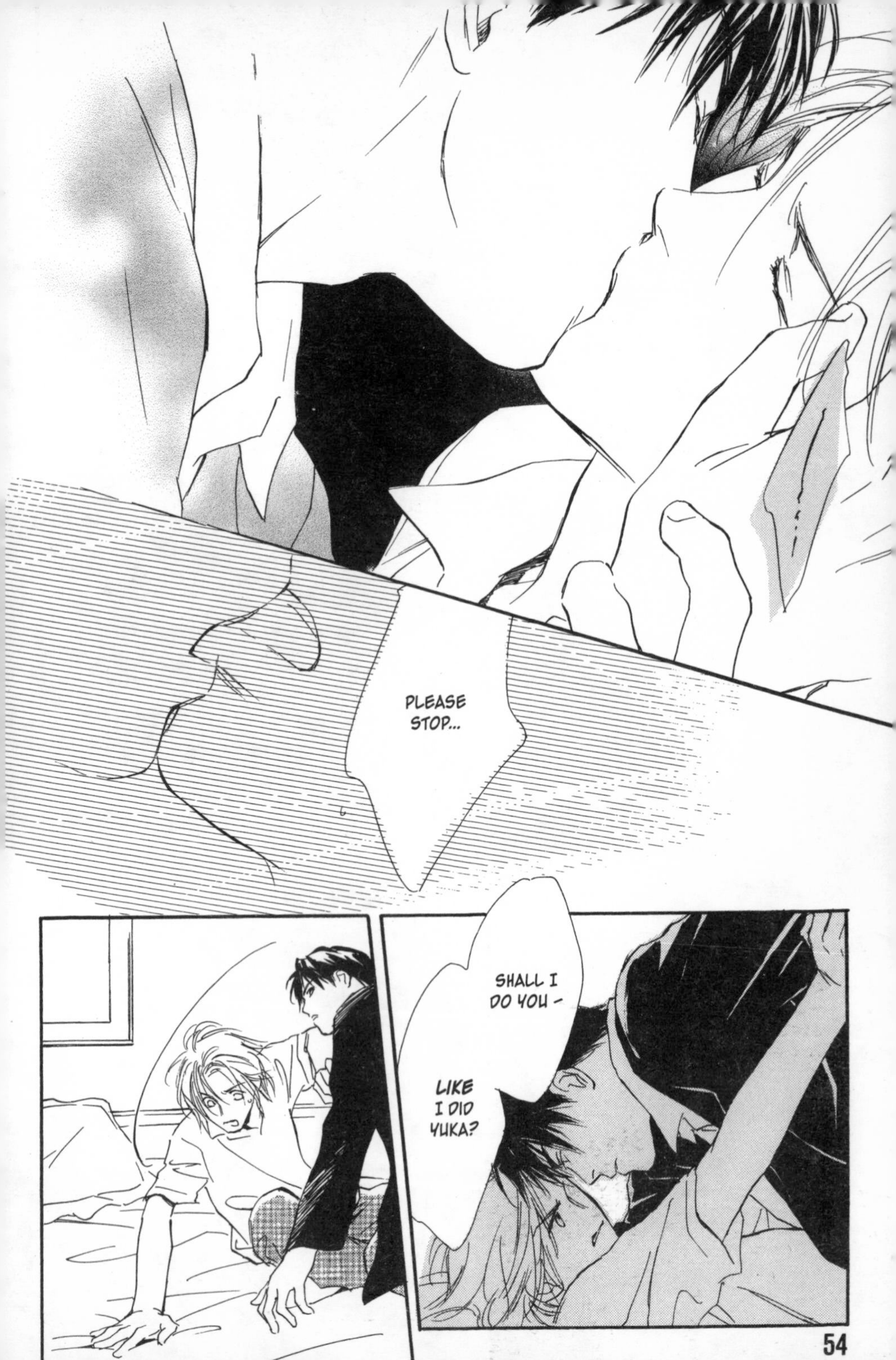
PLEASE STOP...
SHALL I DO YOU -
LIKE I DID YUKA?

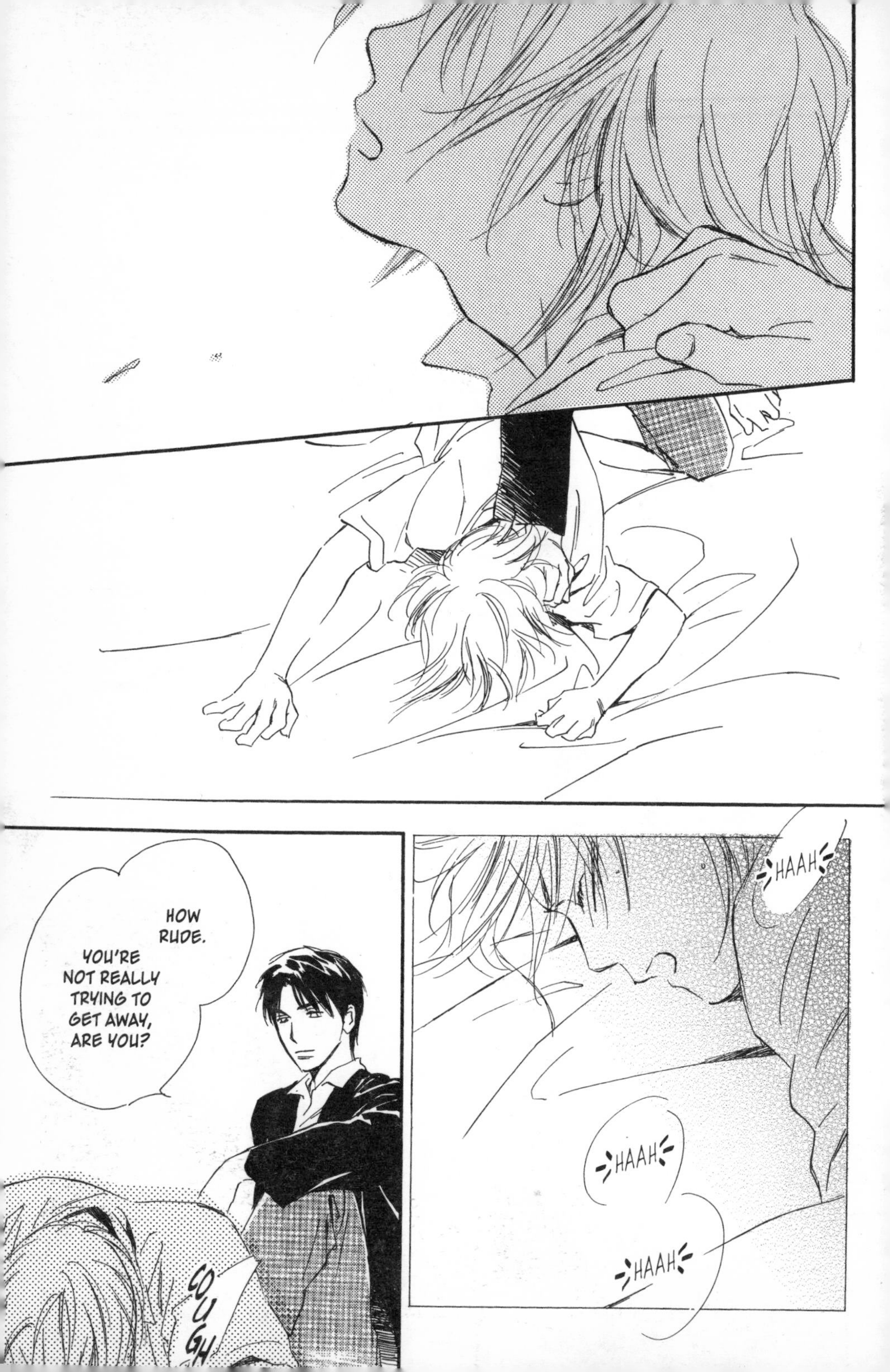
HAAH
HAAH
HAAH
HOW RUDE. YOU'RE NOT REALLY TRYING TO GET AWAY, ARE YOU?
COUGH

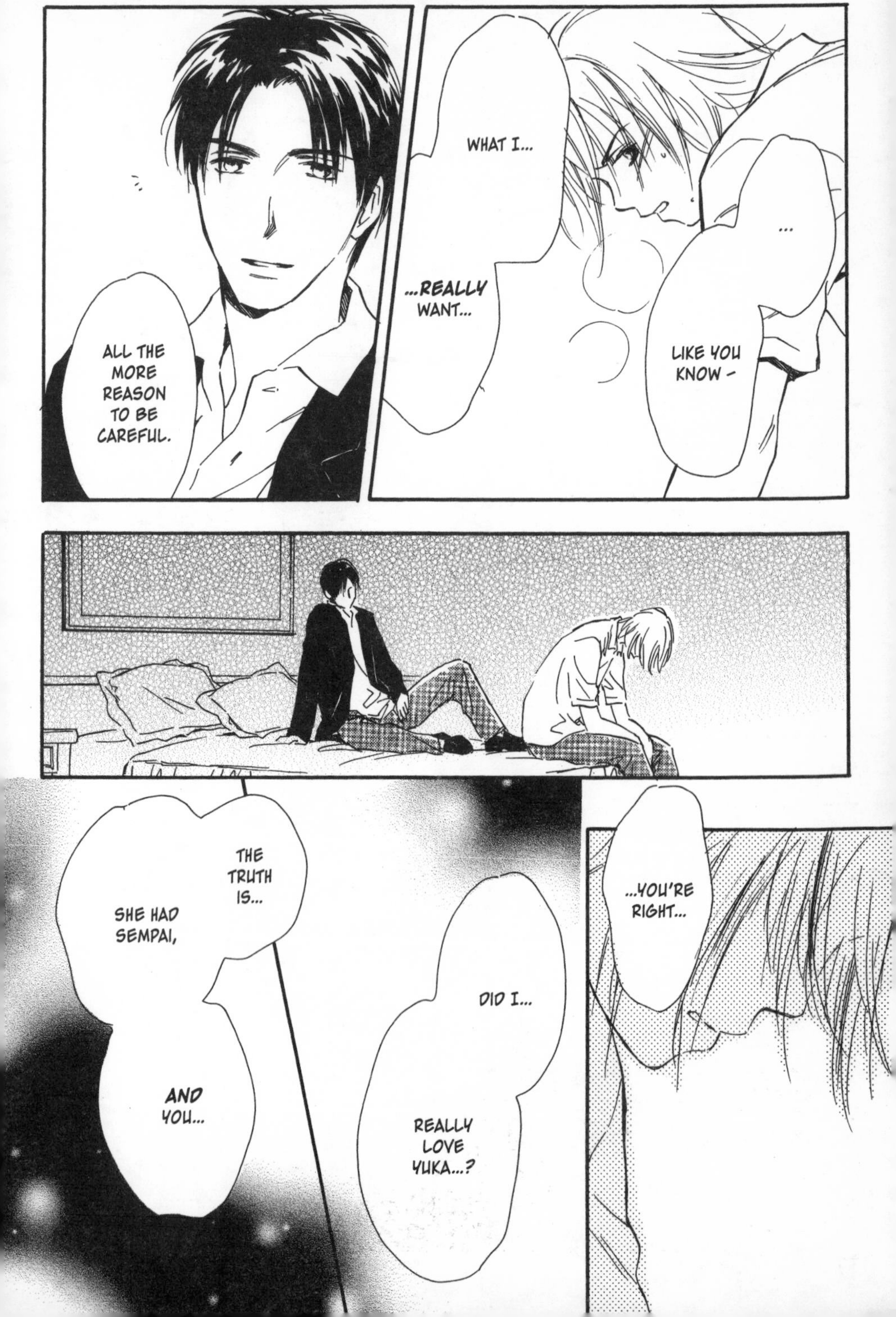

... LIKE YOU KNOW -
WHAT I... ...REALLY WANT...
ALL THE MORE REASON TO BE CAREFUL.
...YOU'RE RIGHT...
DID I... REALLY LOVE YUKA...?
THE TRUTH IS... SHE HAD SEMPAI,
AND YOU...

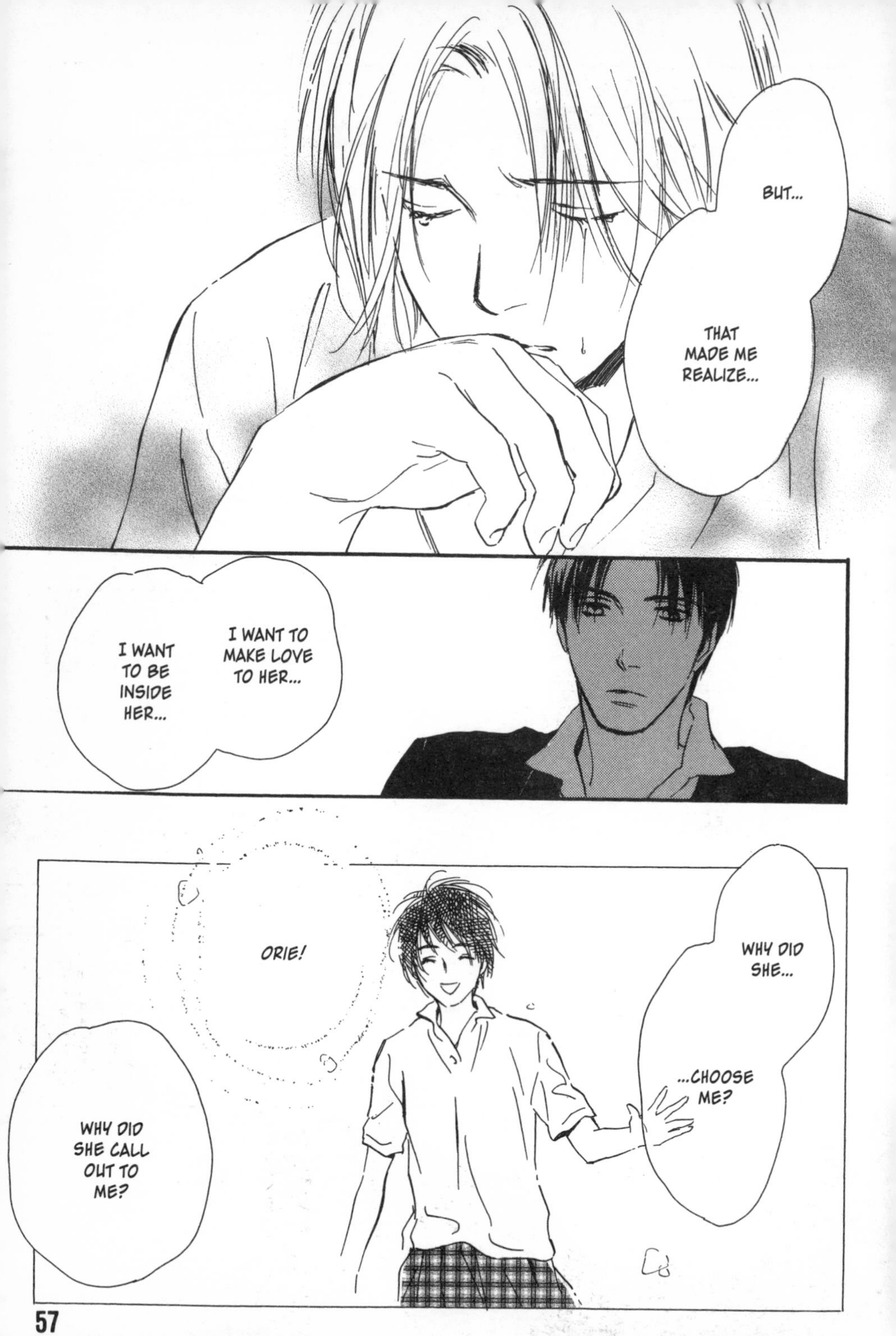
BUT...
THAT MADE ME REALIZE...
I WANT TO MAKE LOVE TO HER...
I WANT TO BE INSIDE HER...
WHY DID SHE...
...CHOOSE ME?
ORIE!
WHY DID SHE CALL OUT TO ME?

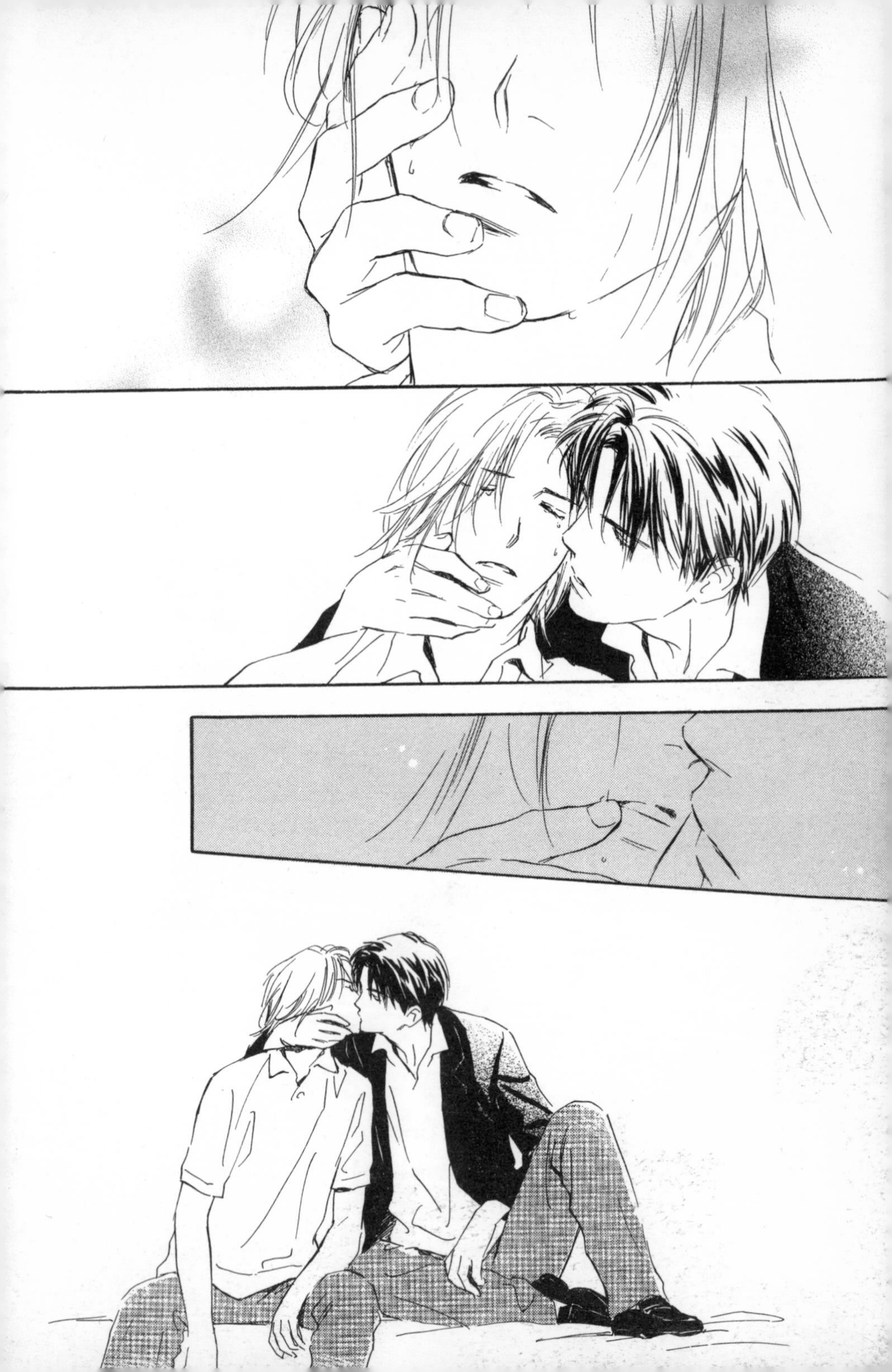

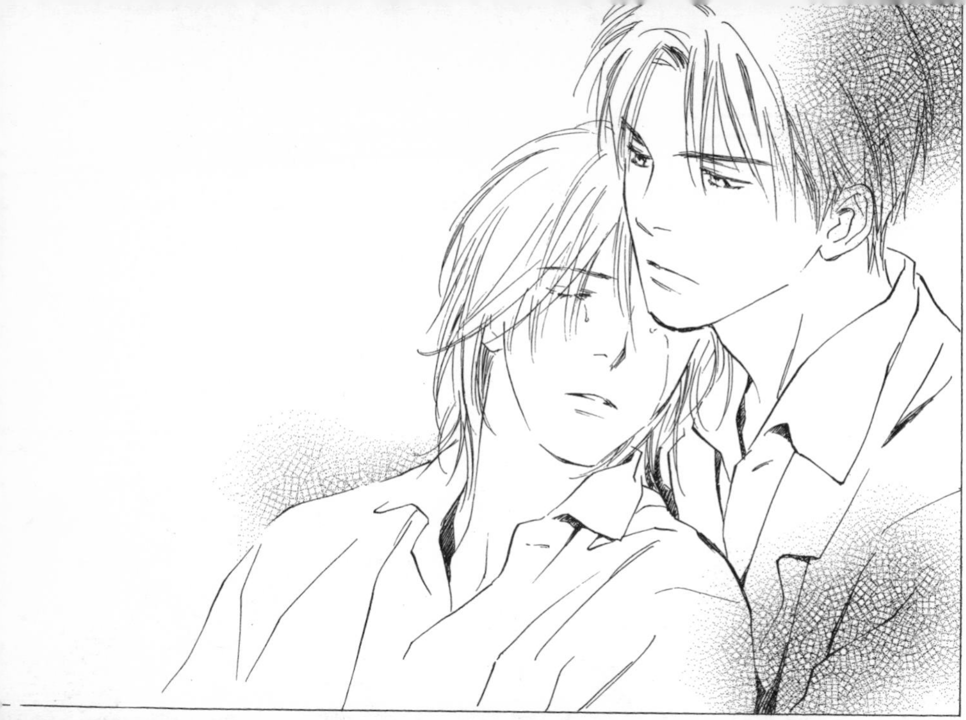

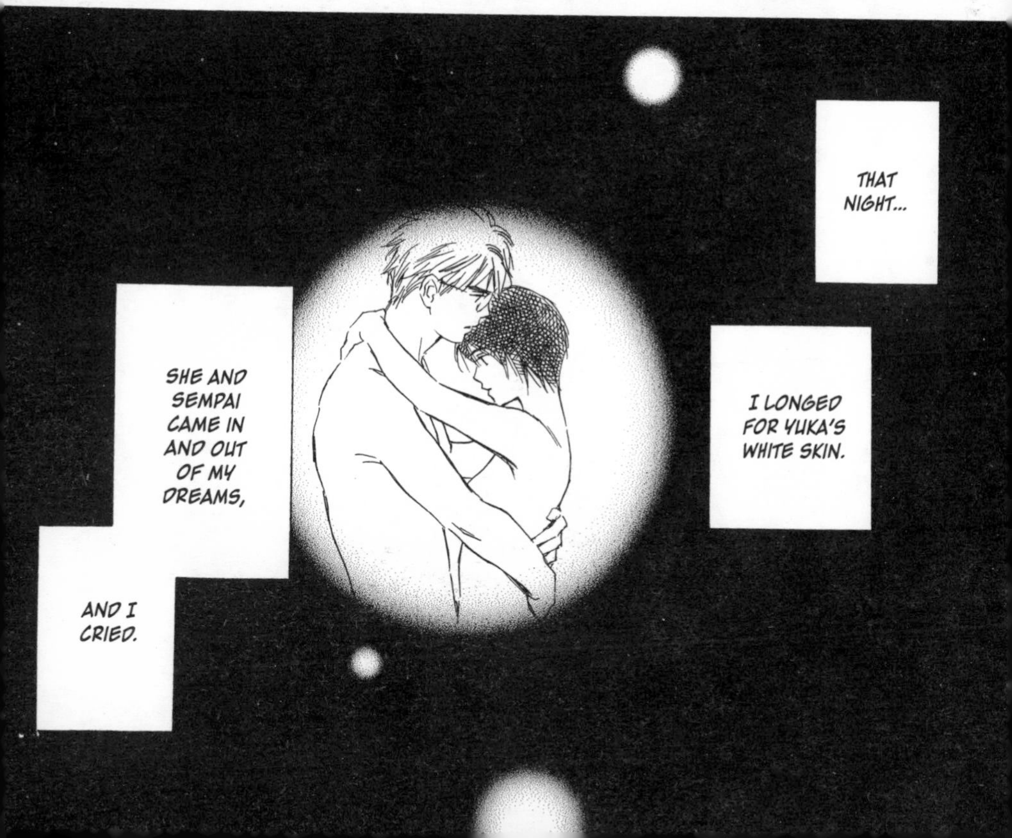
THAT NIGHT...
I LONGED FOR YUKA'S WHITE SKIN.
SHE AND SEMPAI CAME IN AND OUT OF MY DREAMS,
AND I CRIED.

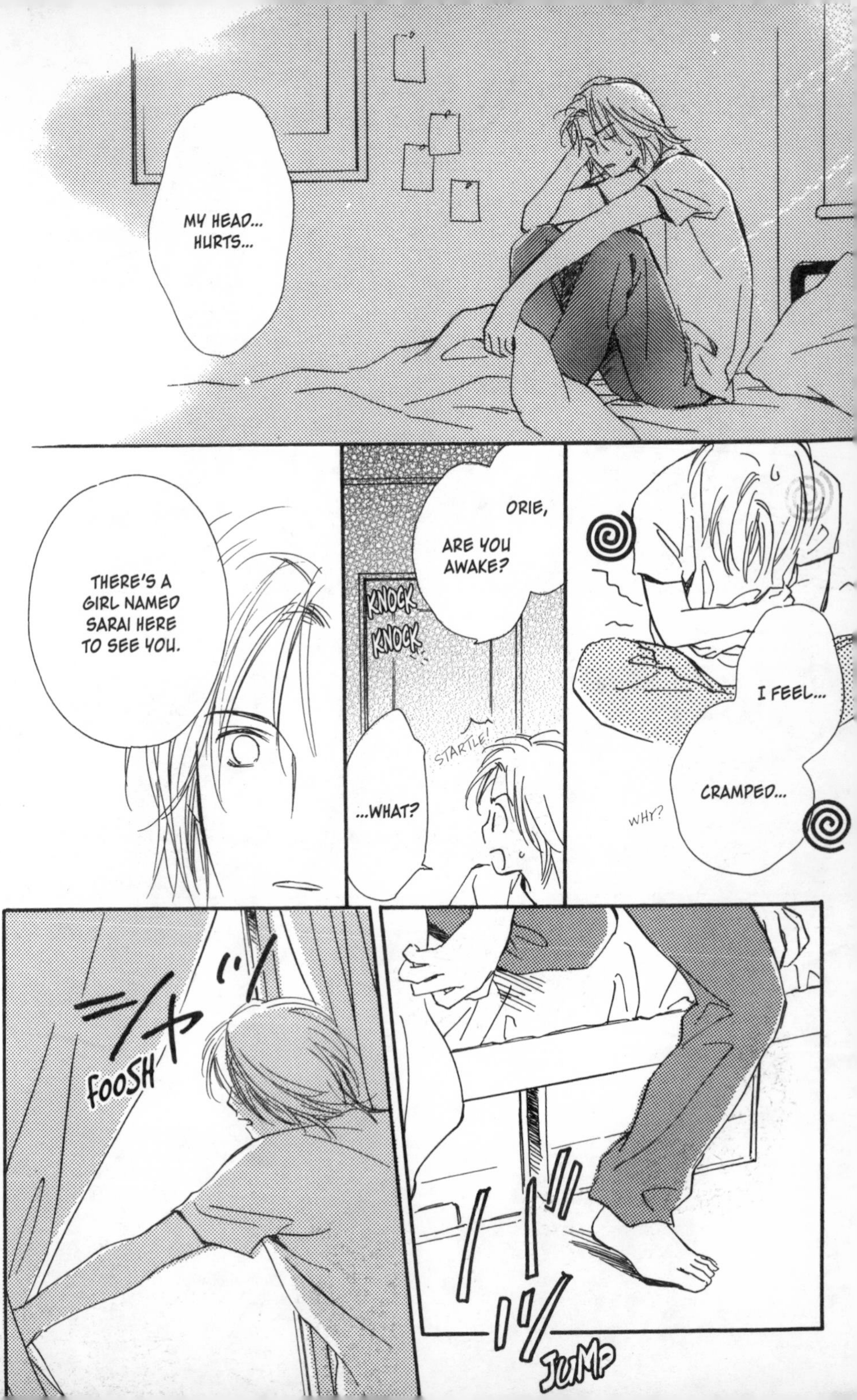
MY HEAD... HURTS...
I FEEL...
CRAMPED...
WHY?
ORIE,
ARE YOU AWAKE?
KNOCK KNOCK
STARTLE!
...WHAT?
THERE'S A GIRL NAMED SARAI HERE TO SEE YOU.
JUMP
FOOSH

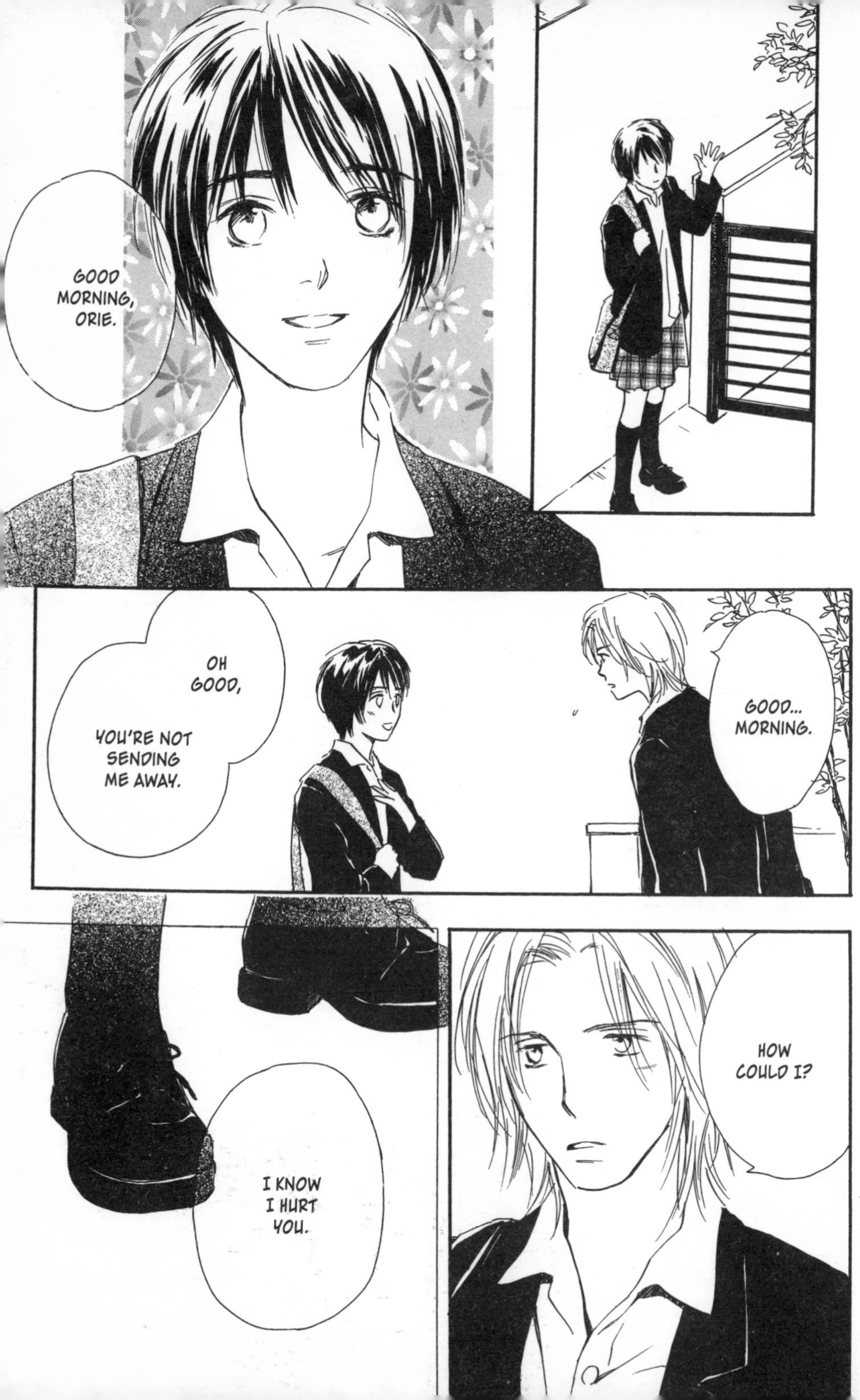
GOOD MORNING, ORIE.
GOOD... MORNING.
OH GOOD,
YOU'RE NOT SENDING ME AWAY.
HOW COULD I?
I KNOW I HURT YOU.

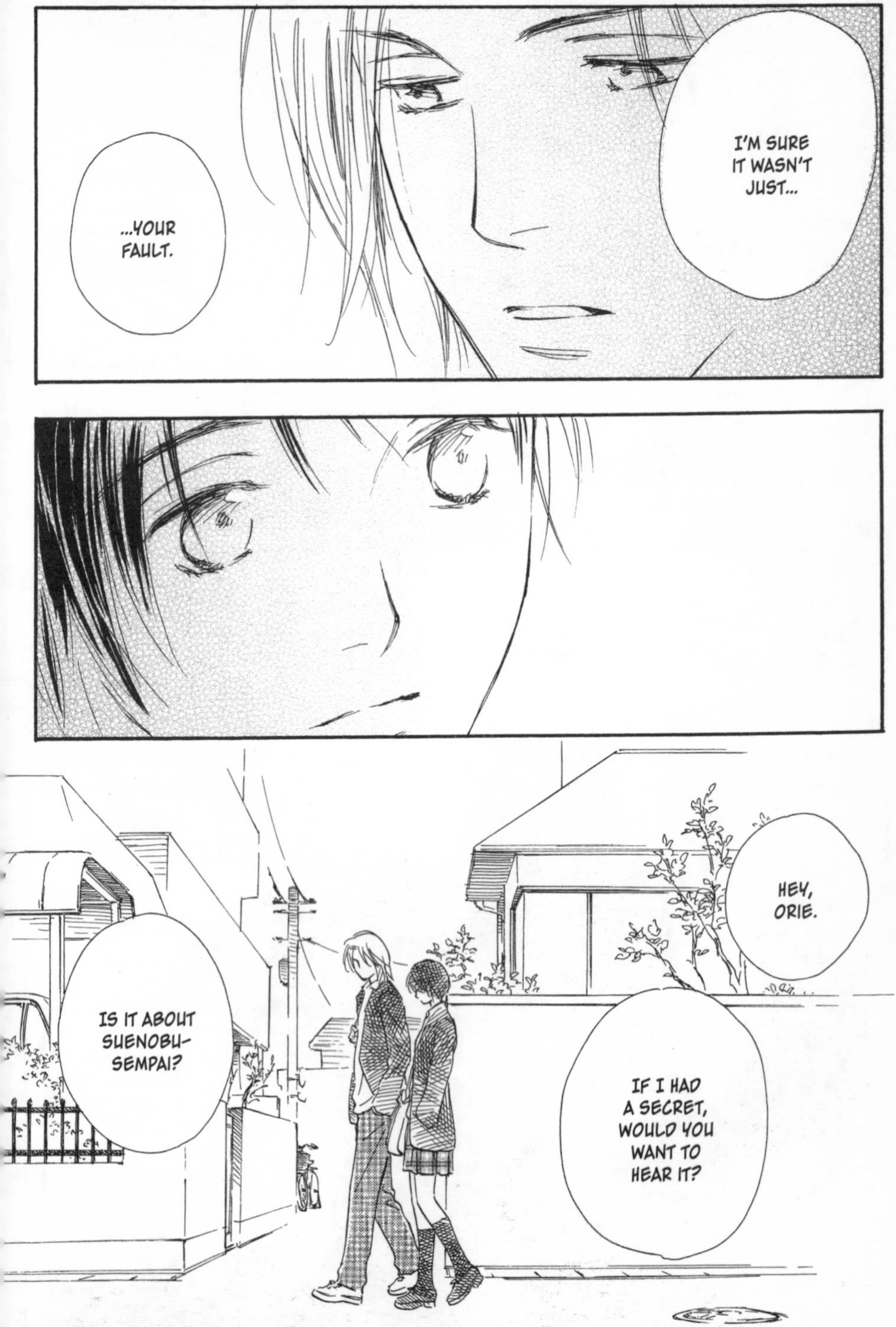
I'M SURE IT WASN'T JUST...
...YOUR FAULT.
HEY, ORIE.
IF I HAD A SECRET, WOULD YOU WANT TO HEAR IT?
IS IT ABOUT SUENOBU-SEMPAI?

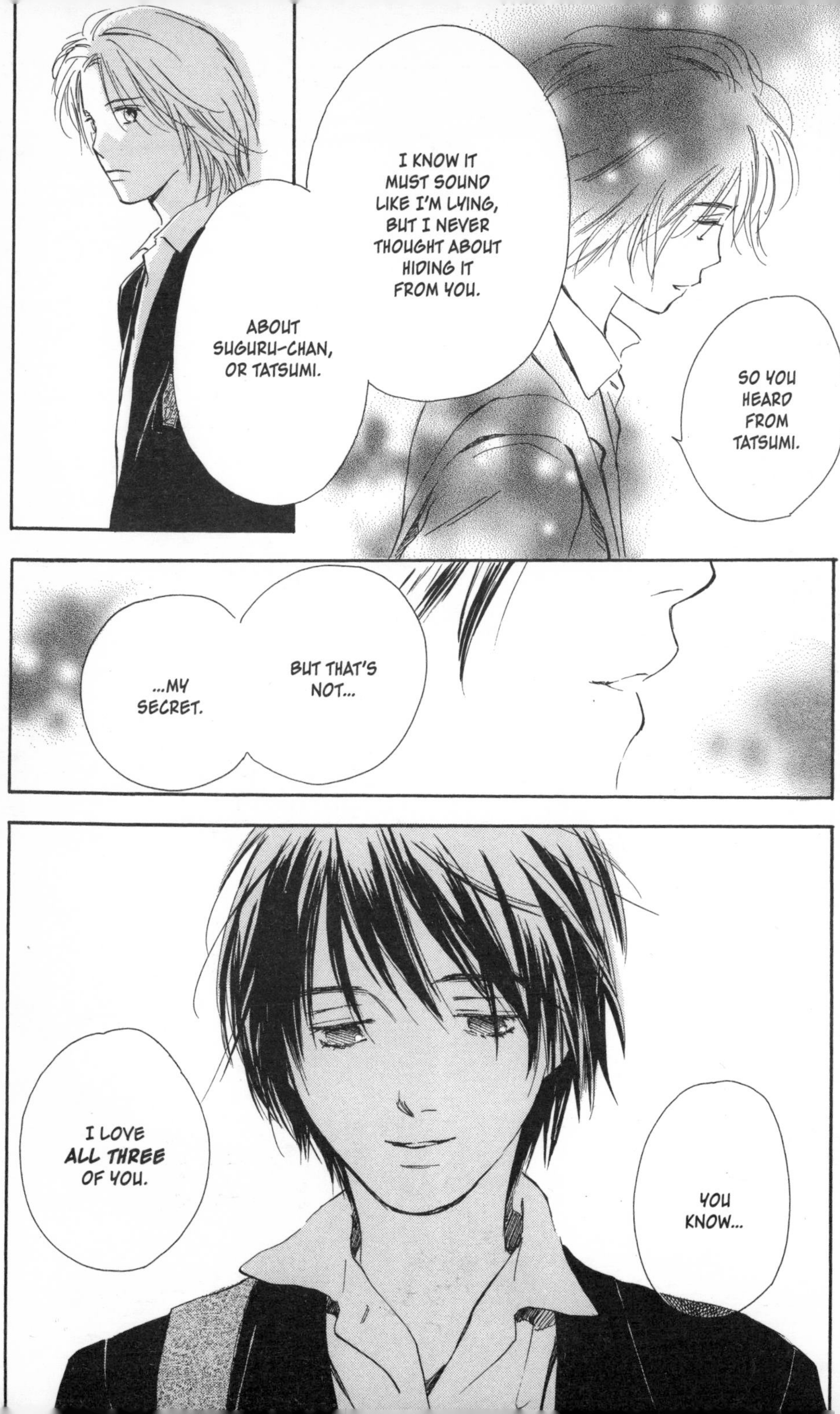
SO YOU HEARD FROM TATSUMI.
I KNOW IT MUST SOUND LIKE I'M LYING, BUT I NEVER THOUGHT ABOUT HIDING IT FROM YOU.
ABOUT SUGURU-CHAN, OR TATSUMI.
BUT THAT'S NOT...
...MY SECRET.
YOU KNOW...
I LOVE **ALL THREE** OF YOU.

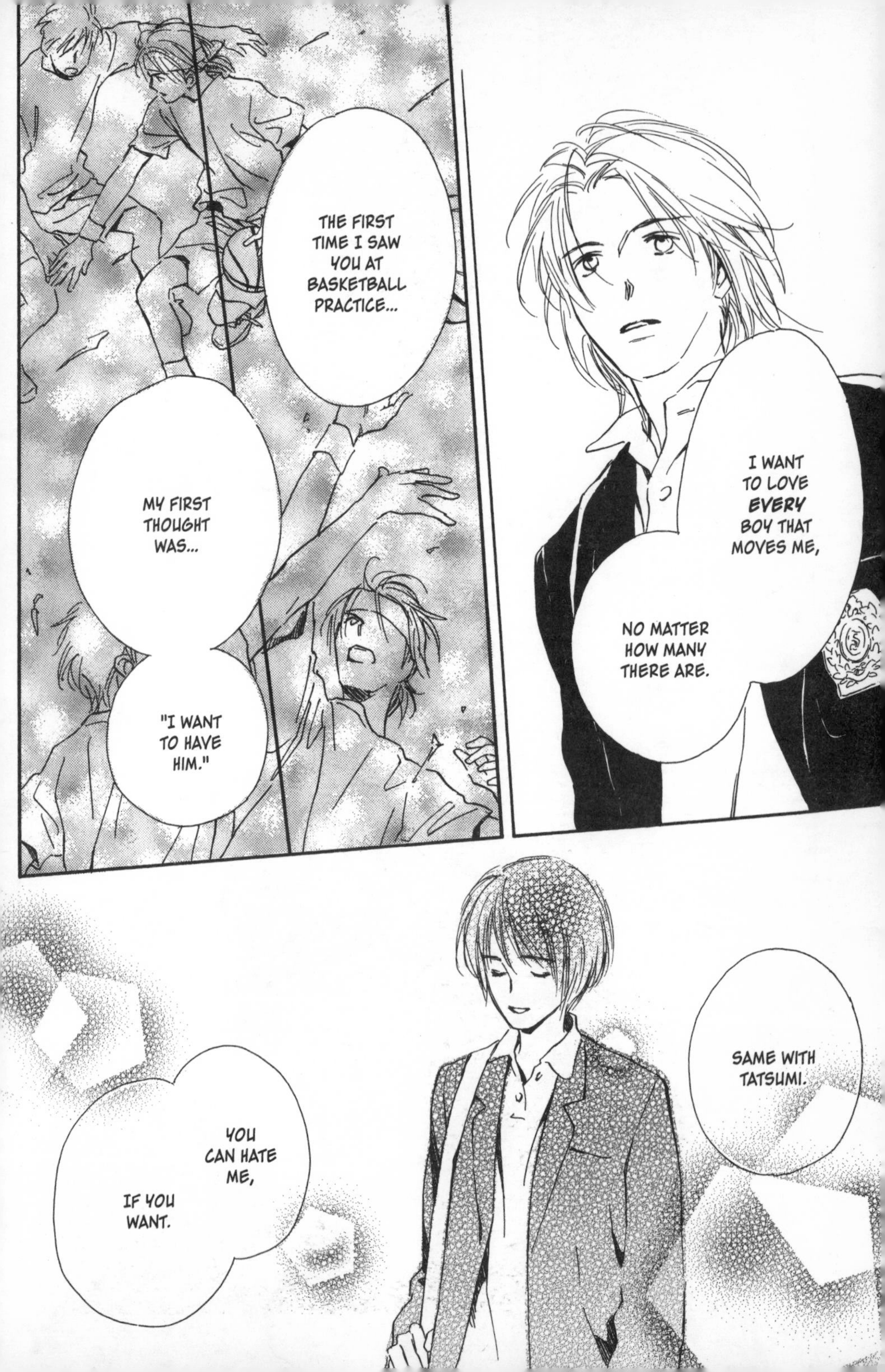
I WANT TO LOVE **EVERY** BOY THAT MOVES ME,
NO MATTER HOW MANY THERE ARE.
THE FIRST TIME I SAW YOU AT BASKETBALL PRACTICE...
MY FIRST THOUGHT WAS...
"I WANT TO HAVE HIM."
SAME WITH TATSUMI.
YOU CAN HATE ME,
IF YOU WANT.

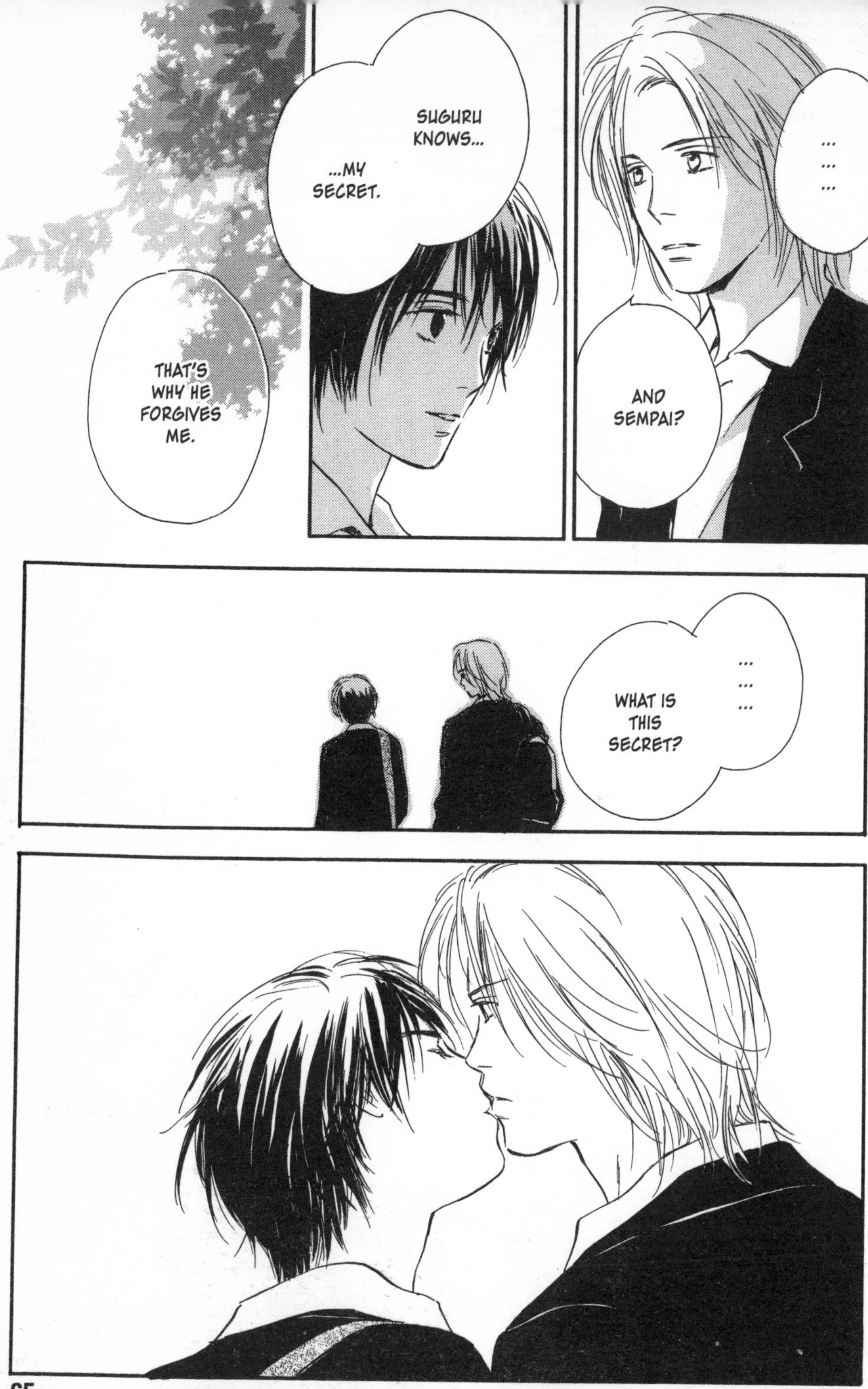
... ...
AND SEMPAI?
SUGURU KNOWS...
...MY SECRET.
THAT'S WHY HE FORGIVES ME.
... ...
WHAT IS THIS SECRET?

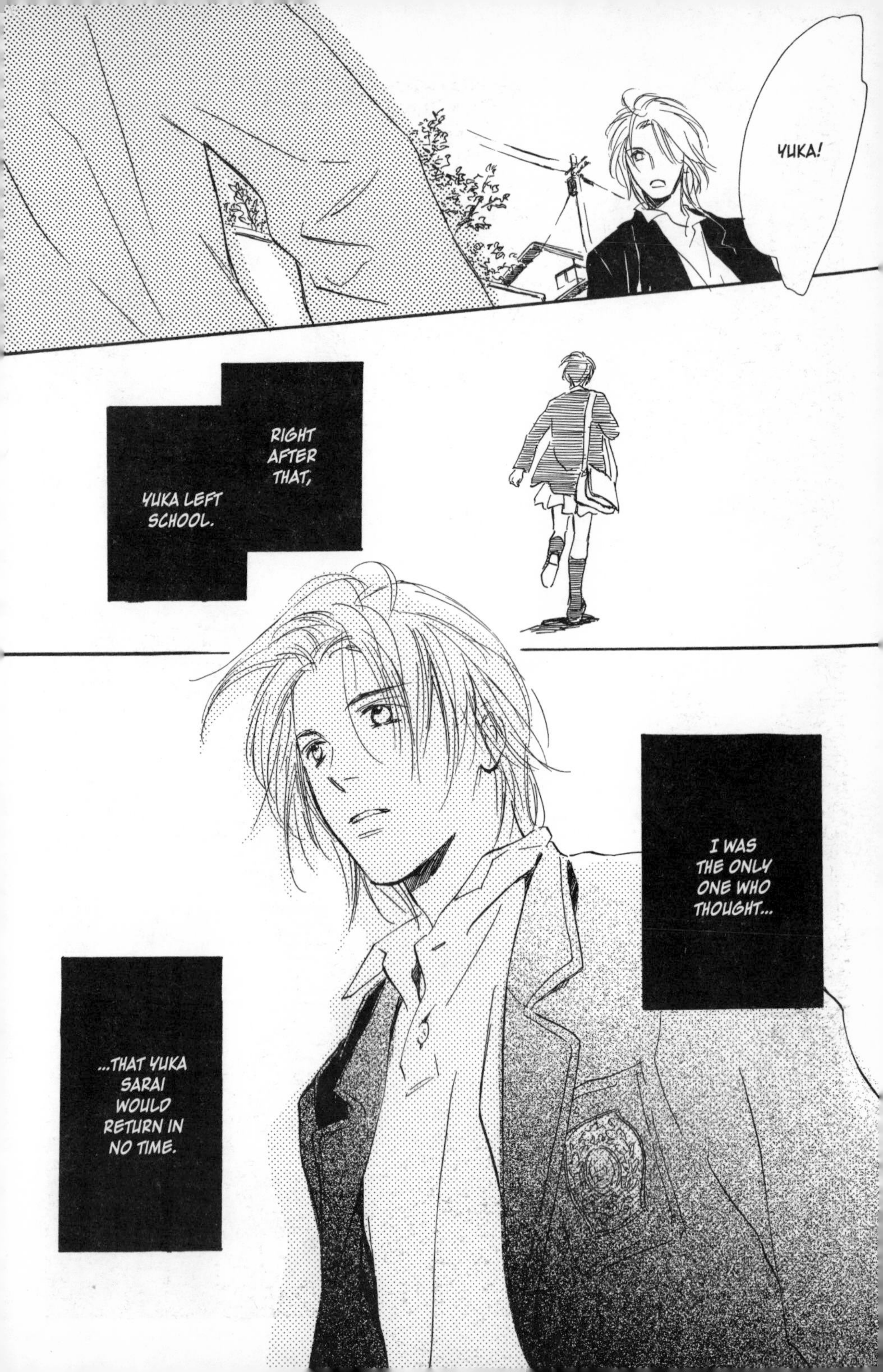
YUKA!
RIGHT AFTER THAT,
YUKA LEFT SCHOOL.
I WAS THE ONLY ONE WHO THOUGHT...
...THAT YUKA SARAI WOULD RETURN IN NO TIME.

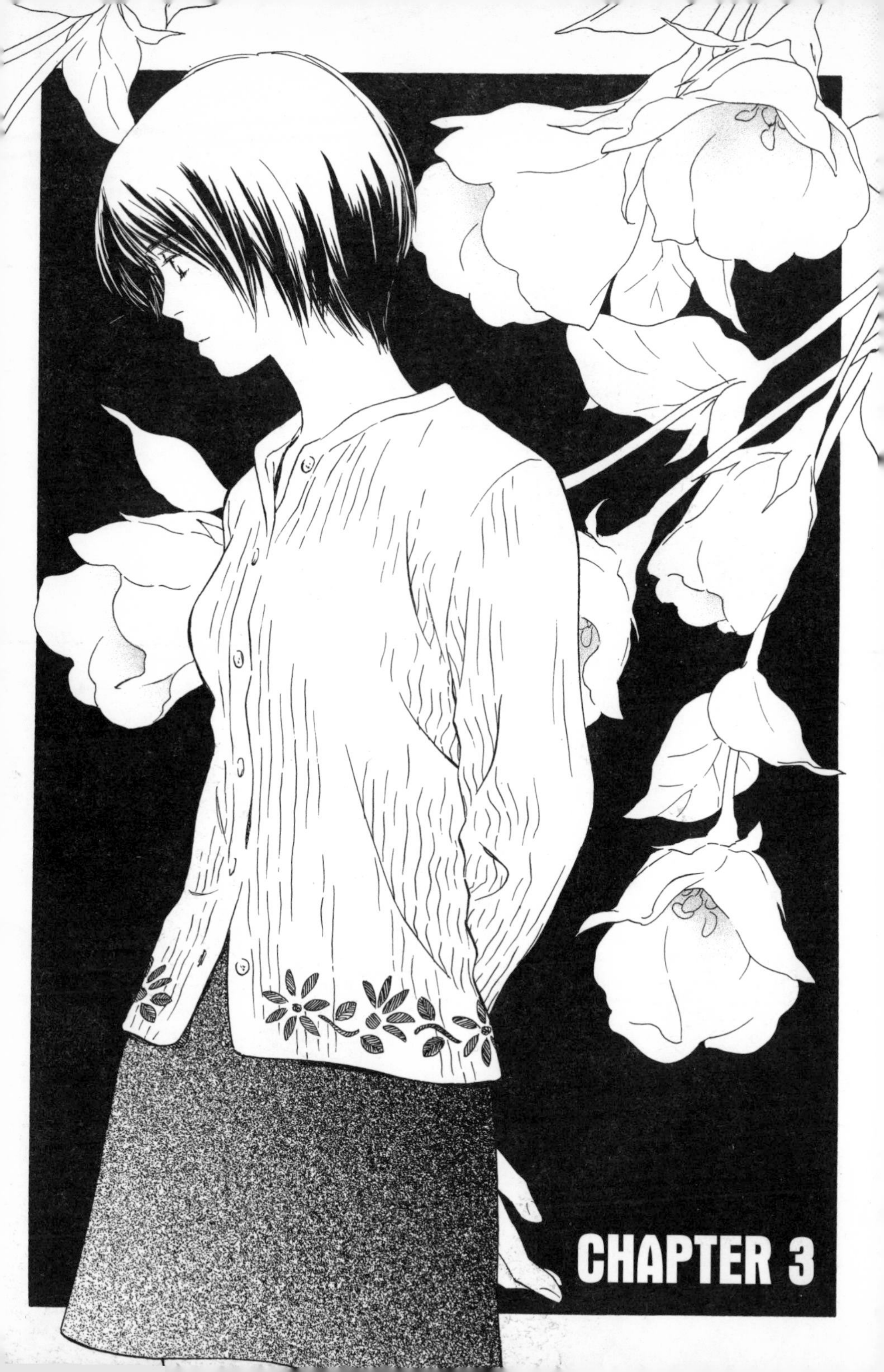
CHAPTER 3

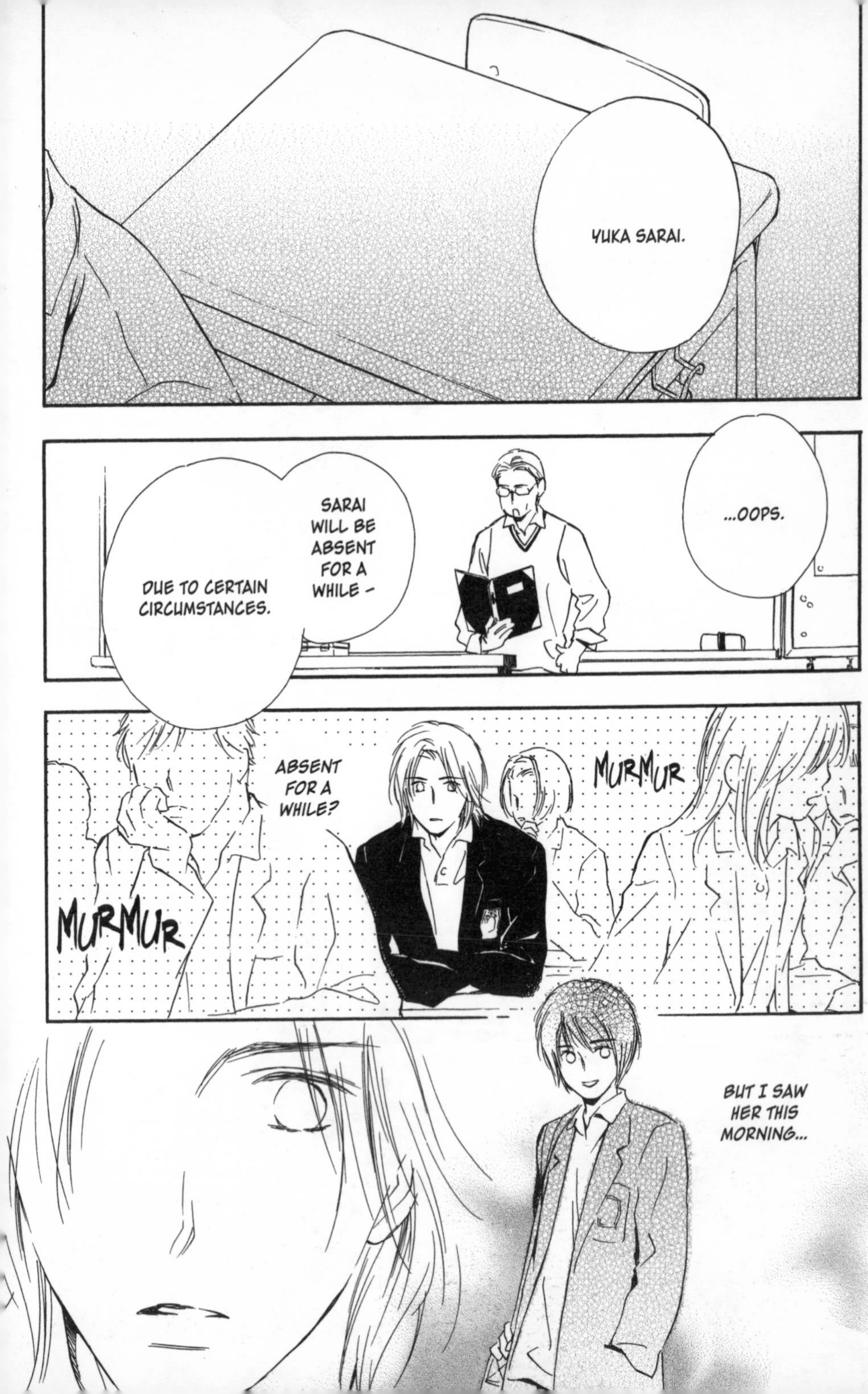
YUKA SARAI.
...OOPS.
SARAI WILL BE ABSENT FOR A WHILE -
DUE TO CERTAIN CIRCUMSTANCES.
MURMUR
ABSENT FOR A WHILE?
MURMUR
BUT I SAW HER THIS MORNING...

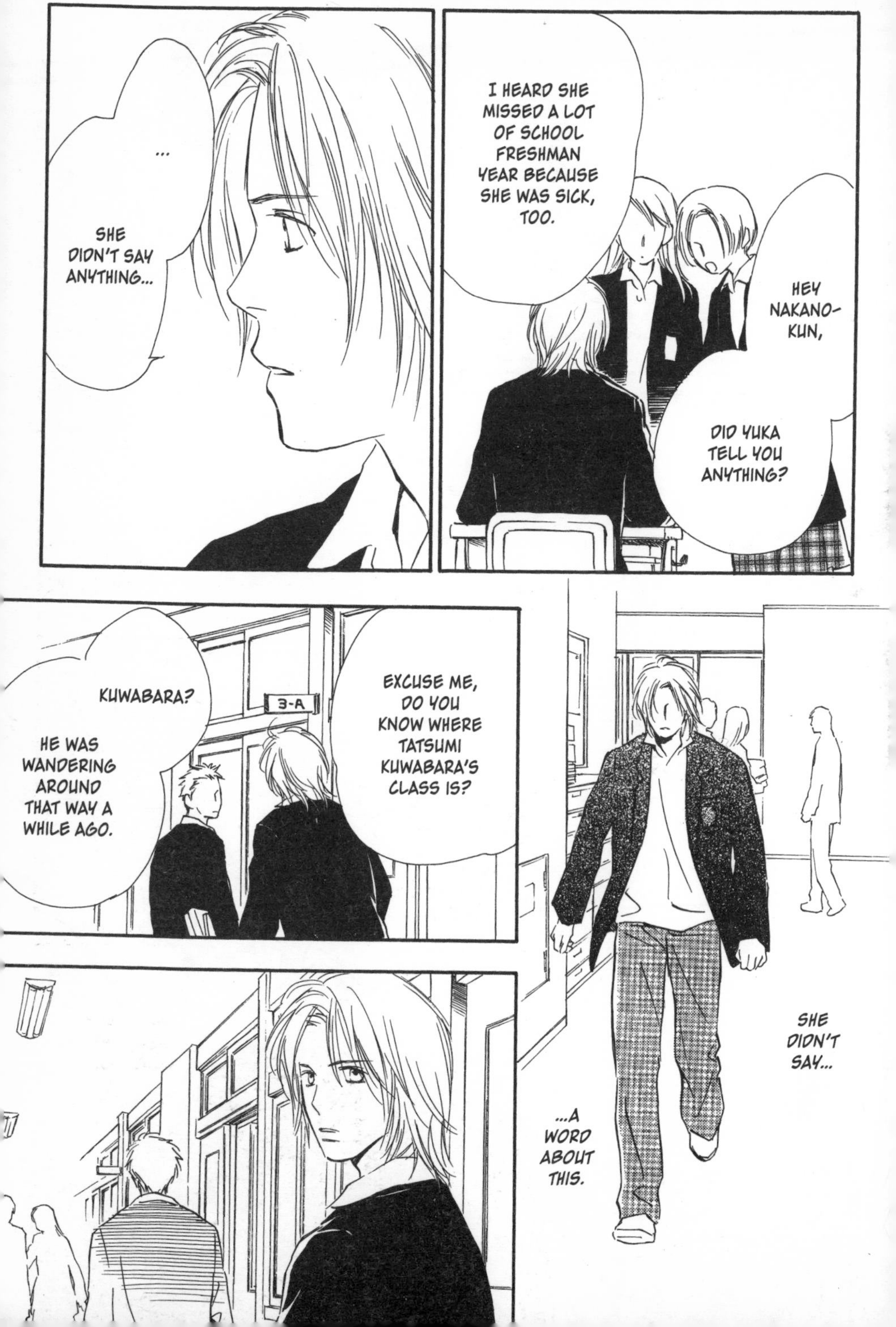
HEY NAKANO-KUN,
DID YUKA TELL YOU ANYTHING?
I HEARD SHE MISSED A LOT OF SCHOOL FRESHMAN YEAR BECAUSE SHE WAS SICK, TOO.
...
SHE DIDN'T SAY ANYTHING...
SHE DIDN'T SAY...
...A WORD ABOUT THIS.
EXCUSE ME, DO YOU KNOW WHERE TATSUMI KUWABARA'S CLASS IS?
3-A
KUWABARA?
HE WAS WANDERING AROUND THAT WAY A WHILE AGO.

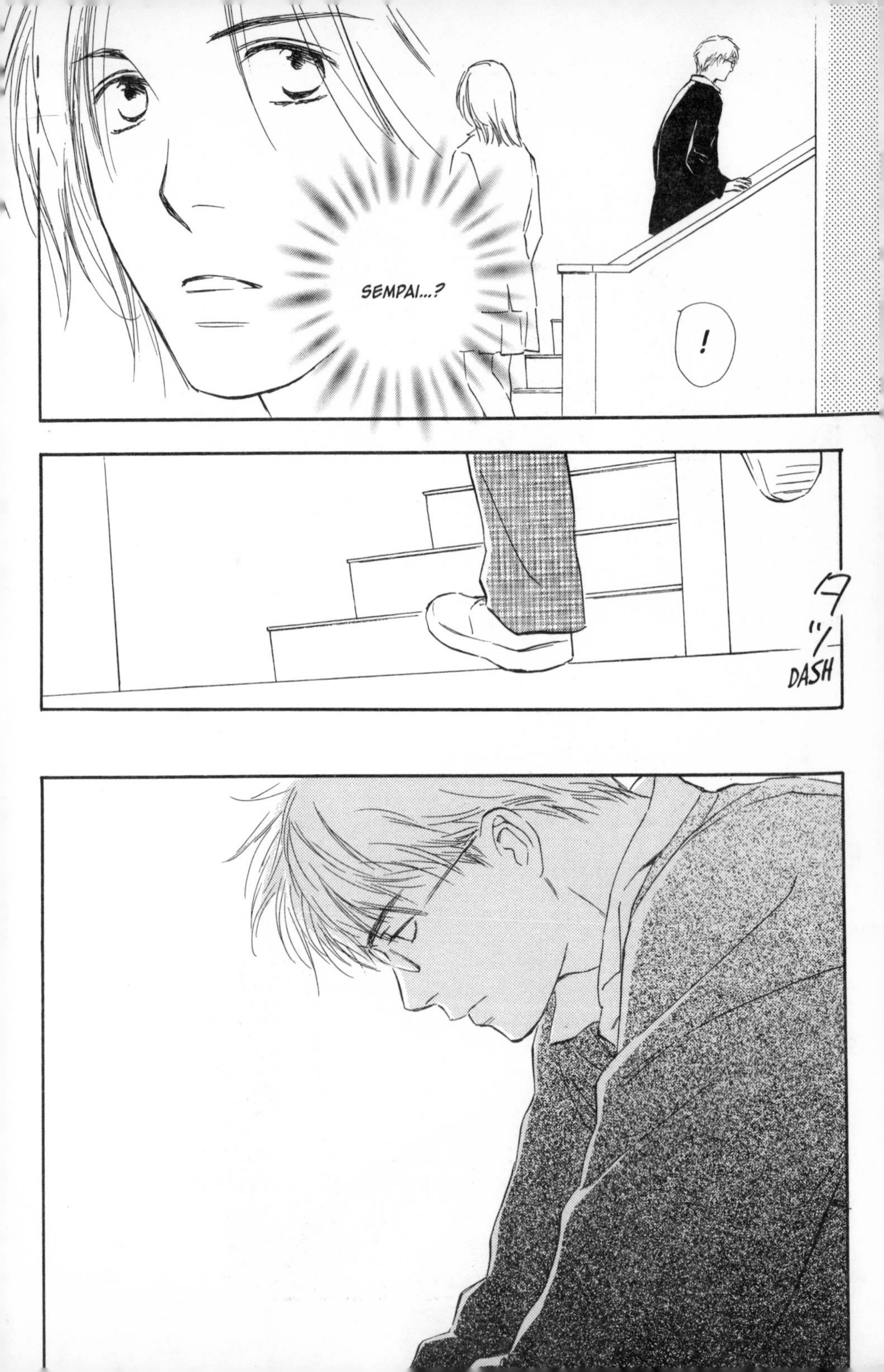
!
SEMPAI...?
タッ
DASH

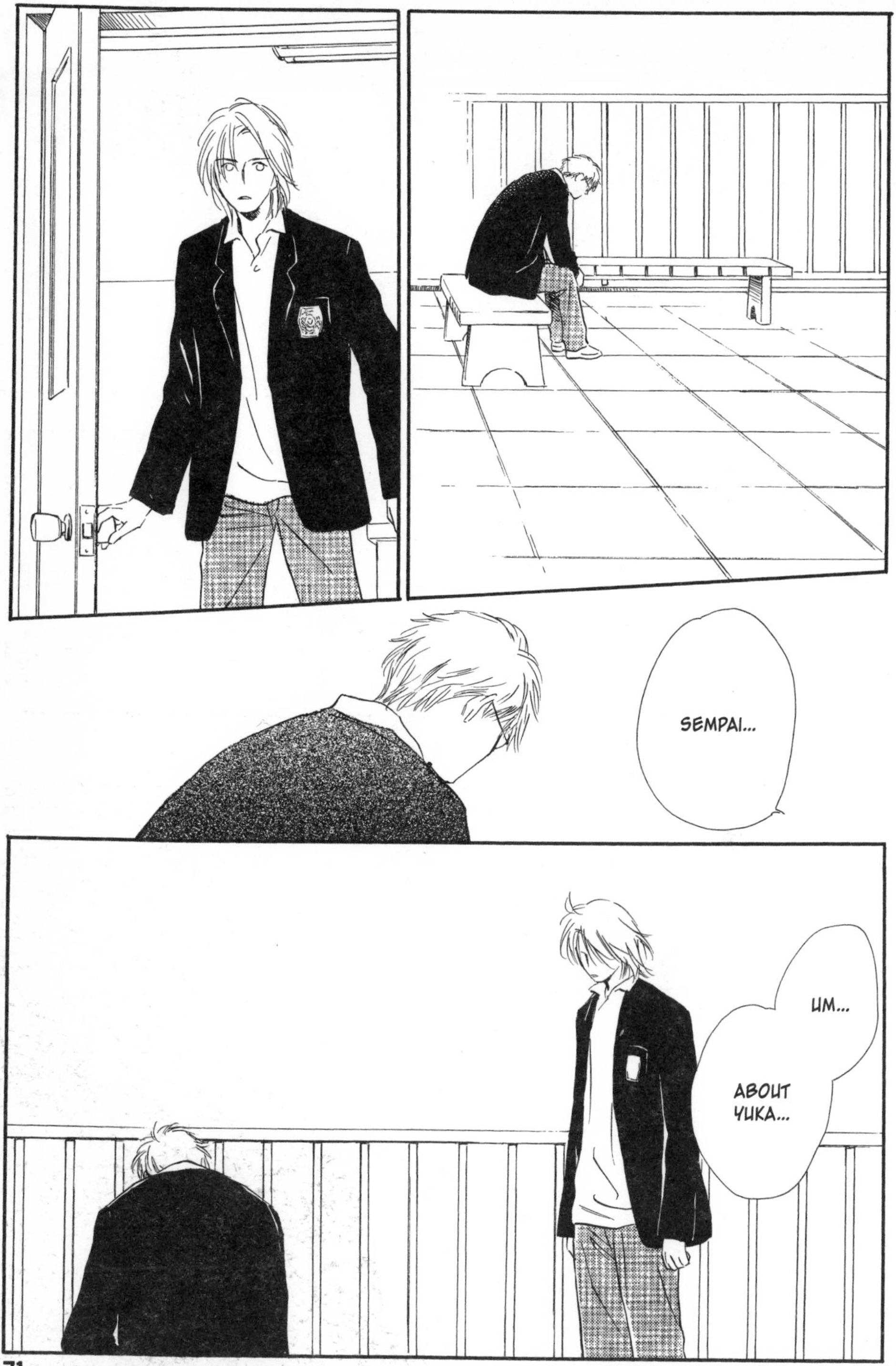
SEMPAI...
UM...
ABOUT YUKA...

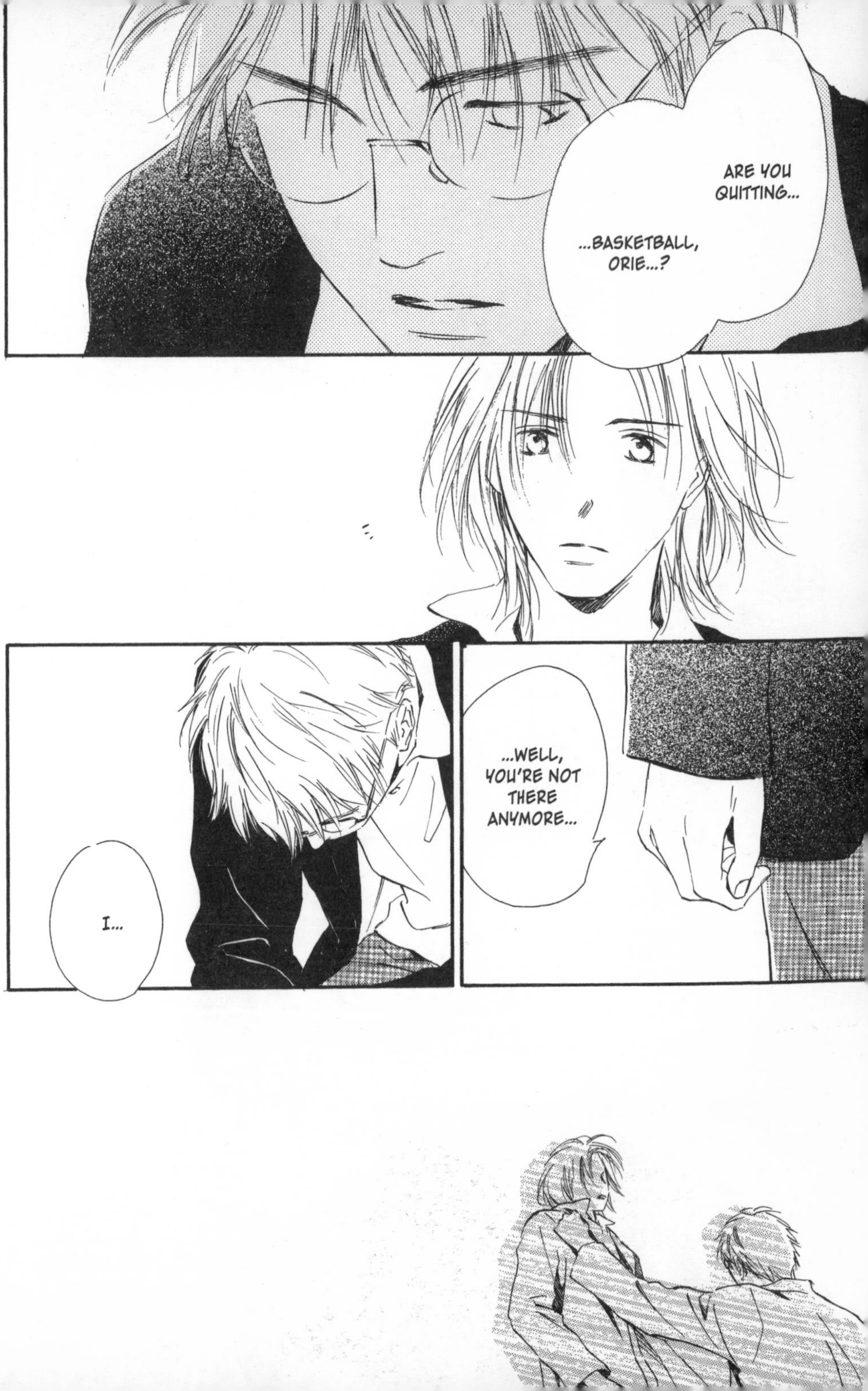
ARE YOU QUITTING...
...BASKETBALL, ORIE...?
...WELL, YOU'RE NOT THERE ANYMORE...
I...

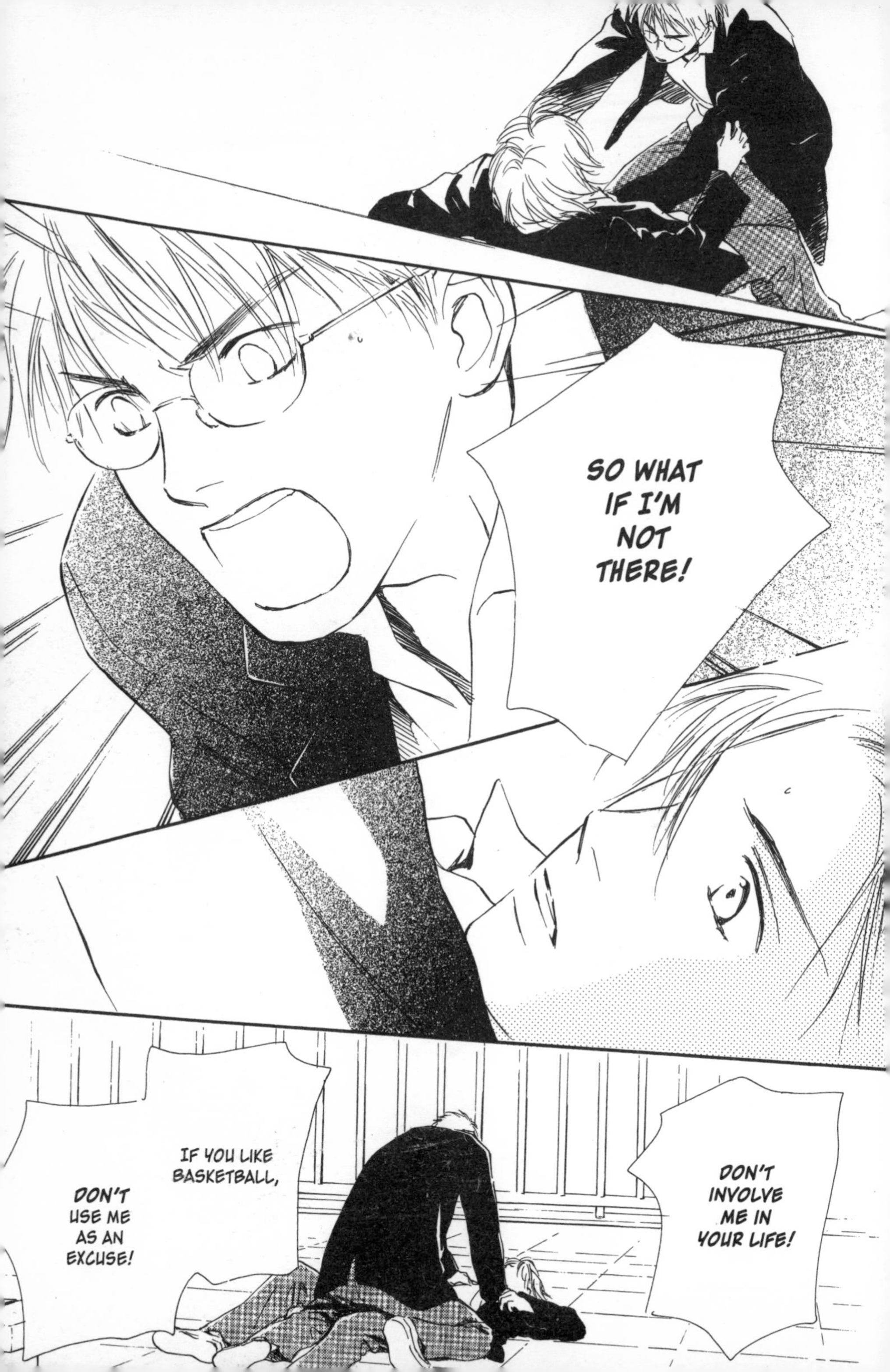
SO WHAT IF I'M NOT THERE!
IF YOU LIKE BASKETBALL,
DON'T USE ME AS AN EXCUSE!
DON'T INVOLVE ME IN YOUR LIFE!

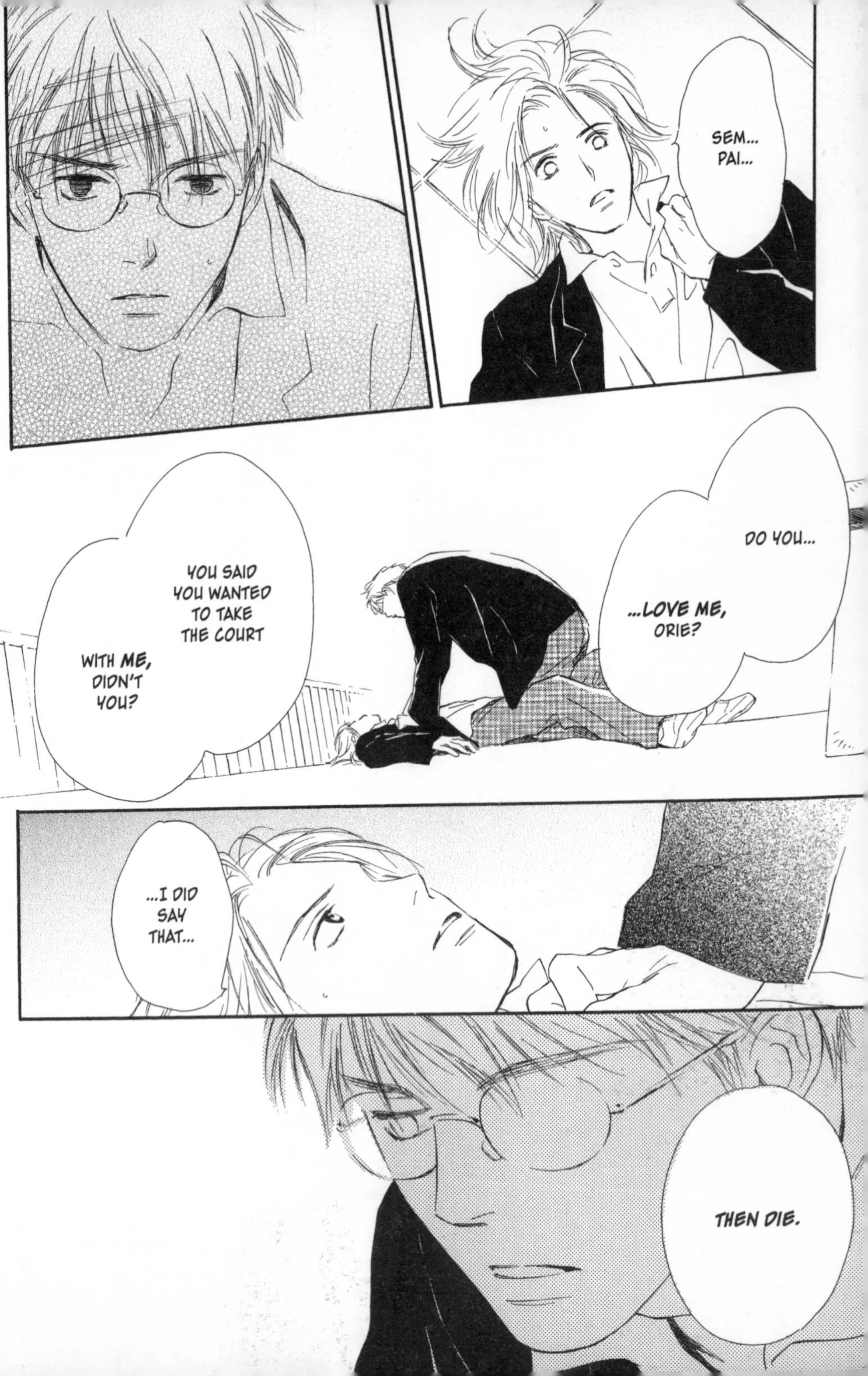
SEM... PAI...
DO YOU...
...LOVE ME, ORIE?
YOU SAID YOU WANTED TO TAKE THE COURT
WITH ME, DIDN'T YOU?
...I DID SAY THAT...
THEN DIE.

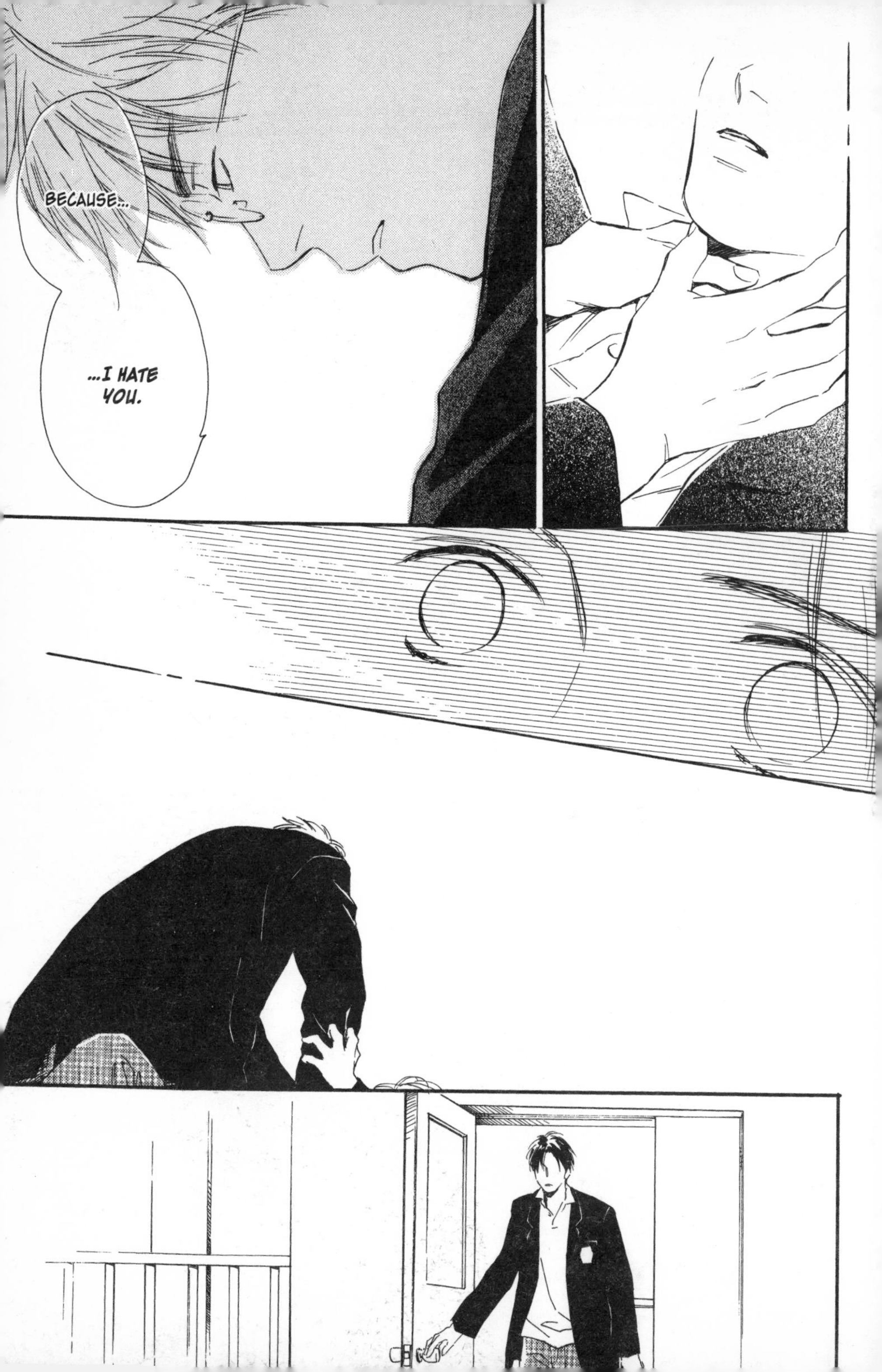
BECAUSE...
...I HATE YOU.

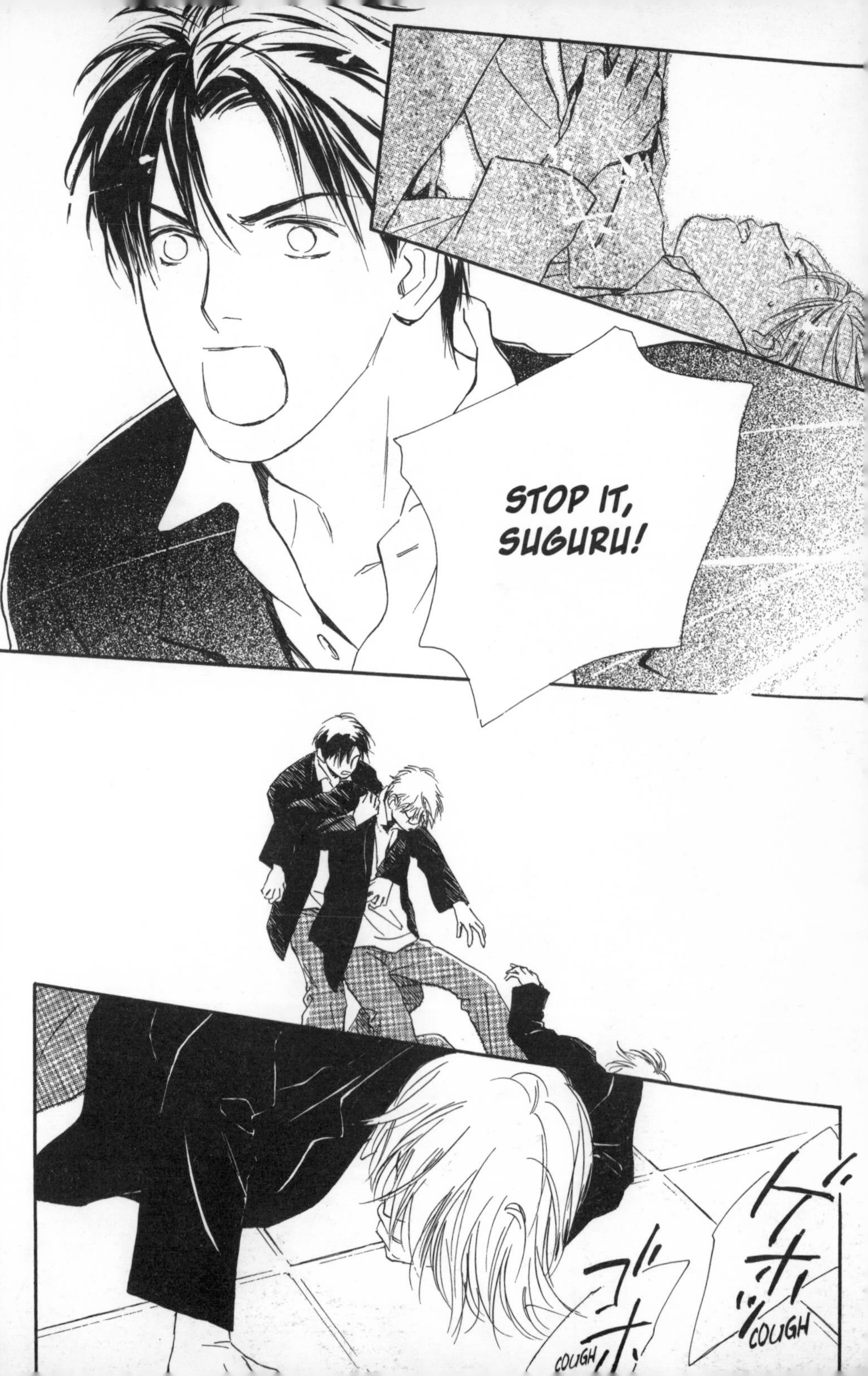
STOP IT, SUGURU!
COUGH
COUGH

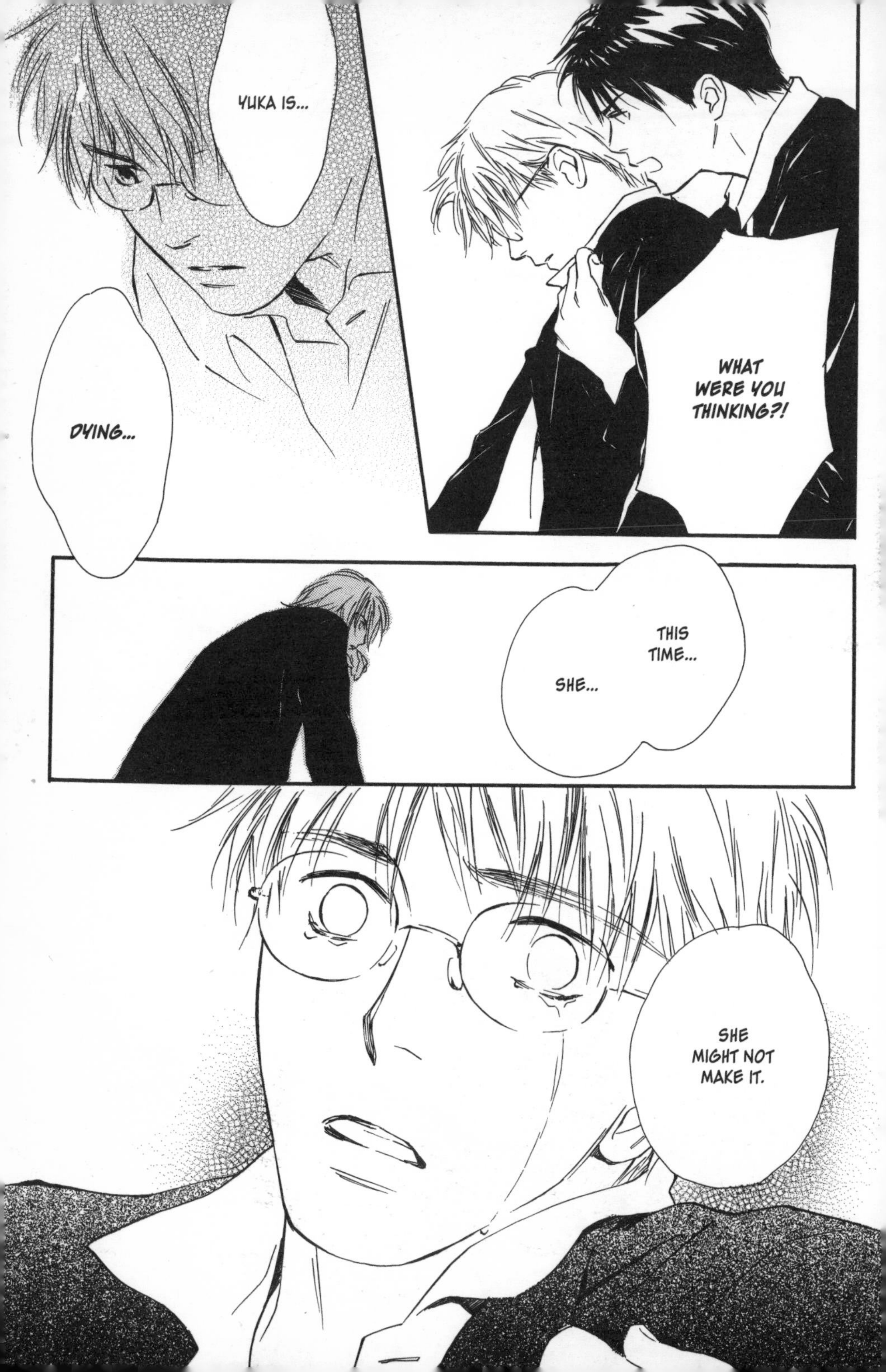
WHAT WERE YOU THINKING?!
YUKA IS...
DYING...
THIS TIME...
SHE...
SHE MIGHT NOT MAKE IT.

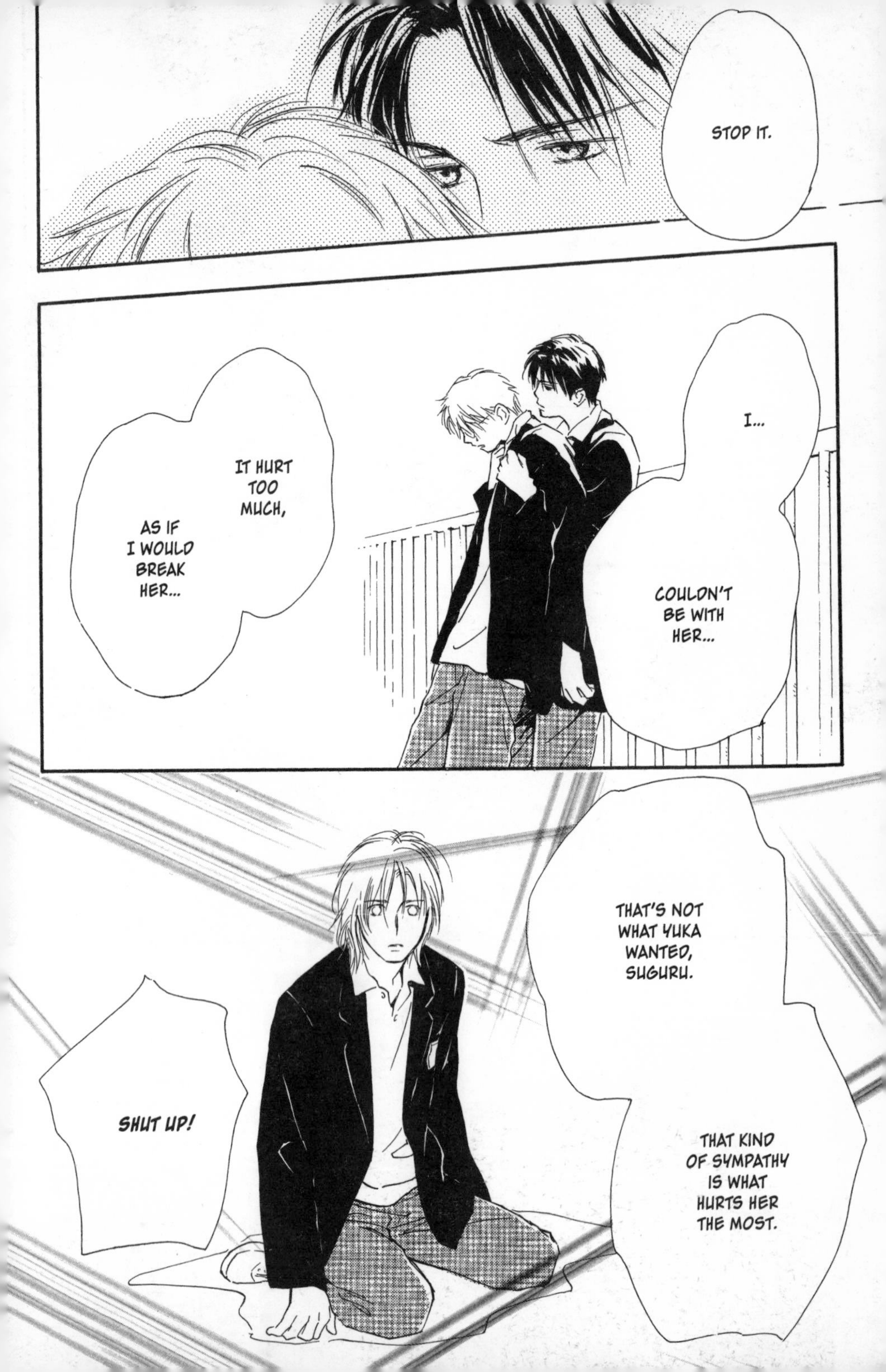
STOP IT.
I...
COULDN'T BE WITH HER...
IT HURT TOO MUCH,
AS IF I WOULD BREAK HER...
THAT'S NOT WHAT YUKA WANTED, SUGURU.
THAT KIND OF SYMPATHY IS WHAT HURTS HER THE MOST.
SHUT UP!

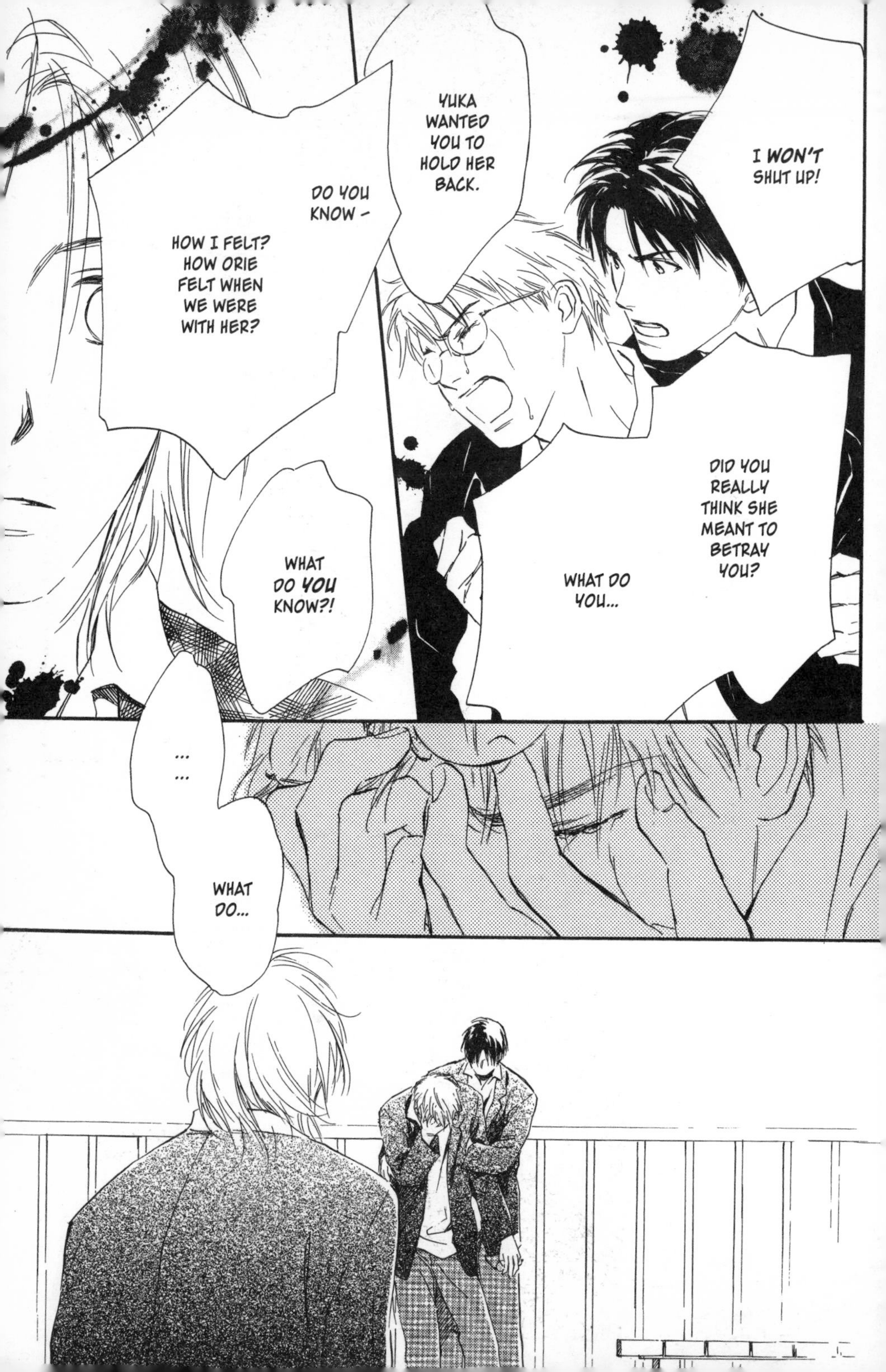
I WON'T SHUT UP!
YUKA WANTED YOU TO HOLD HER BACK.
DID YOU REALLY THINK SHE MEANT TO BETRAY YOU?
WHAT DO YOU...
DO YOU KNOW –
HOW I FELT? HOW ORIE FELT WHEN WE WERE WITH HER?
WHAT DO YOU KNOW?!
... ...
WHAT DO...

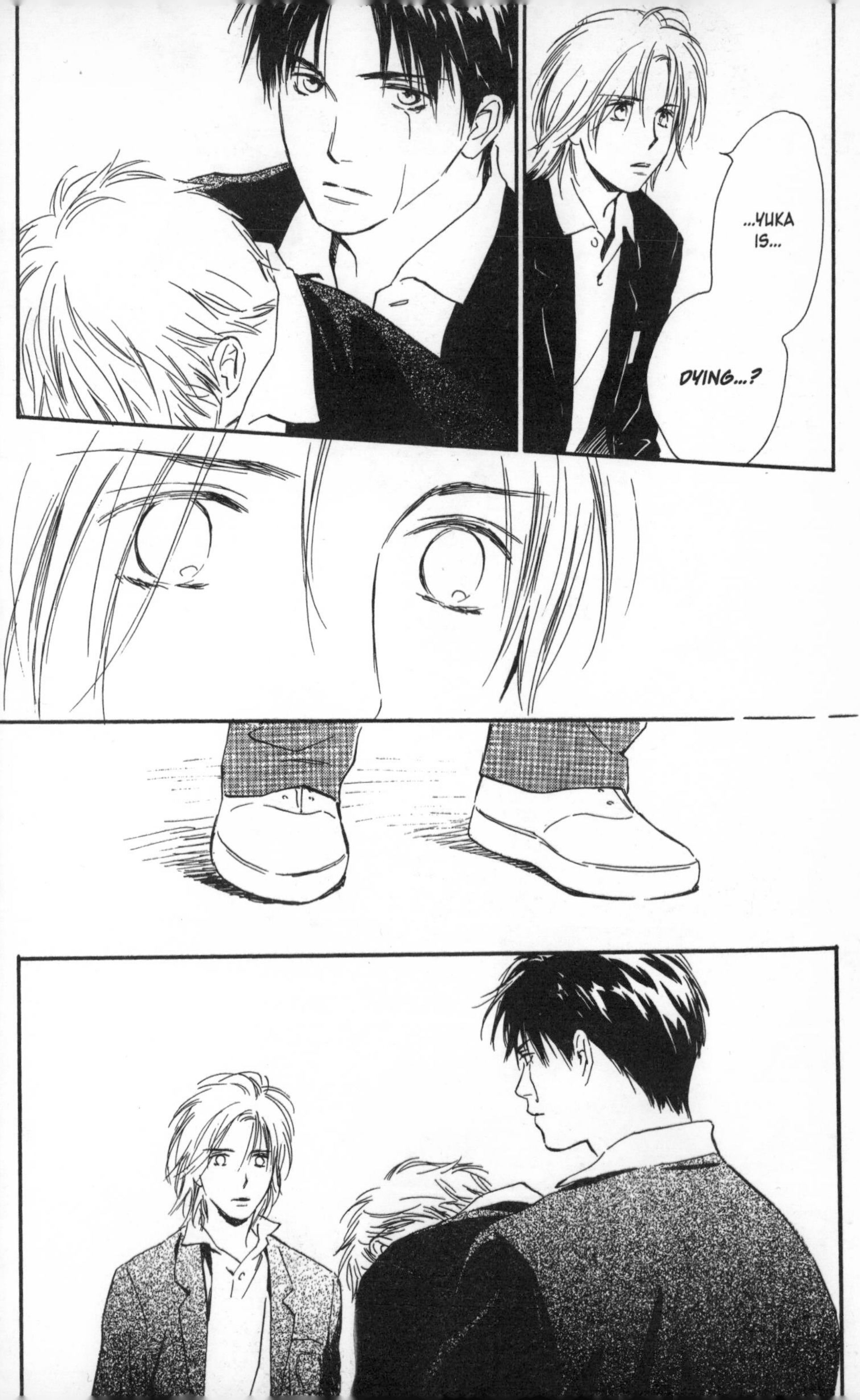
...YUKA IS... DYING...?

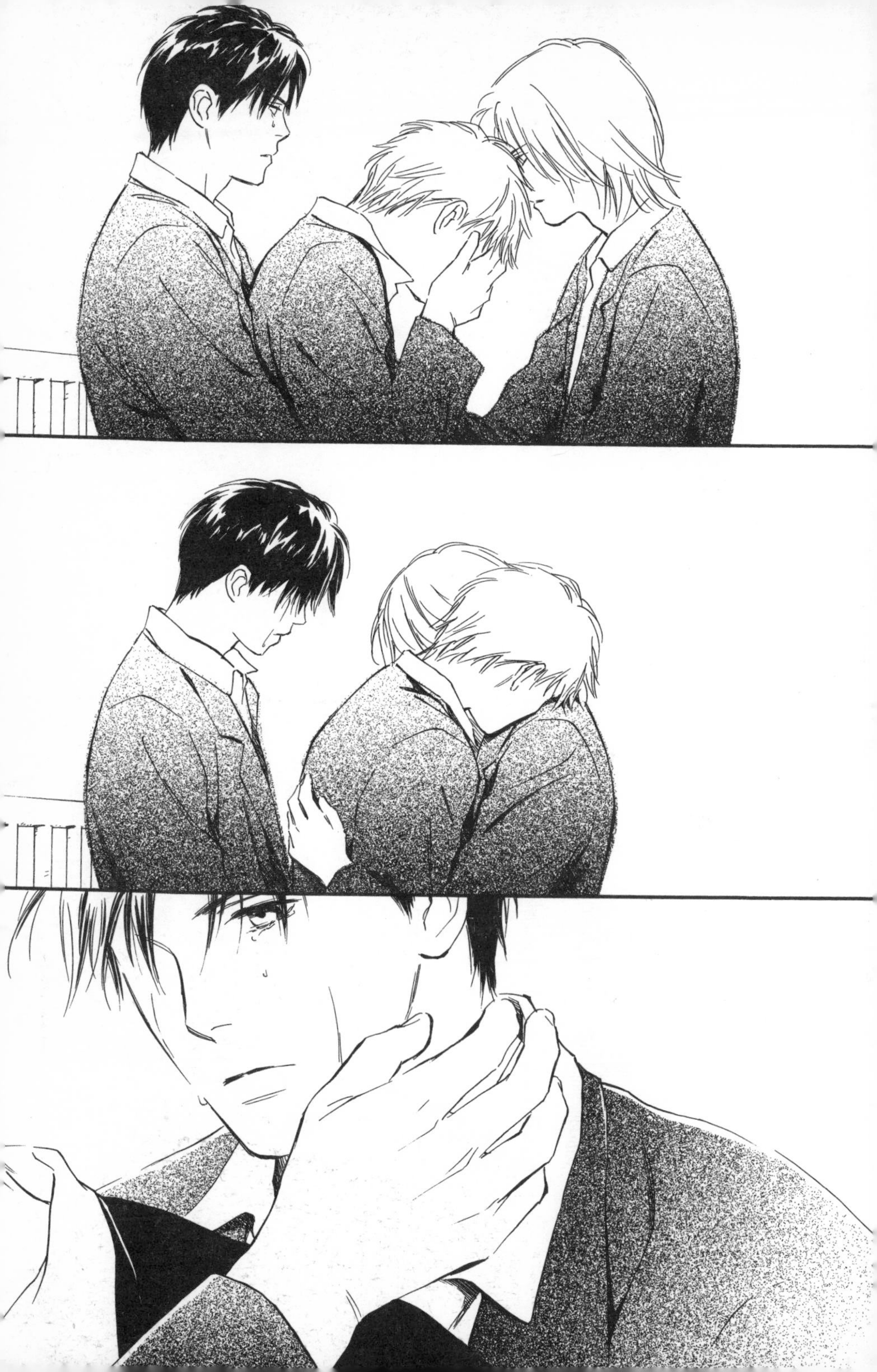

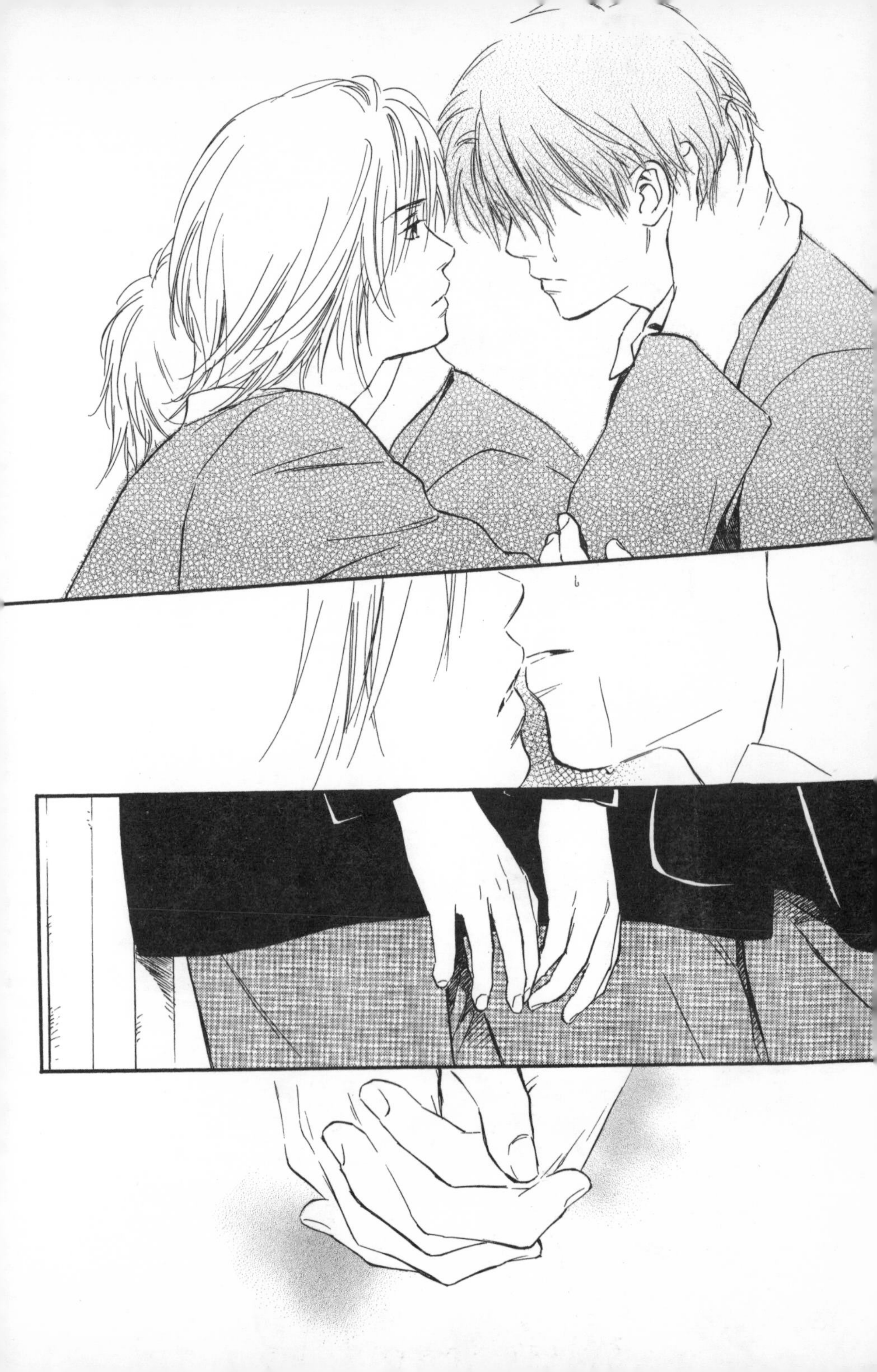

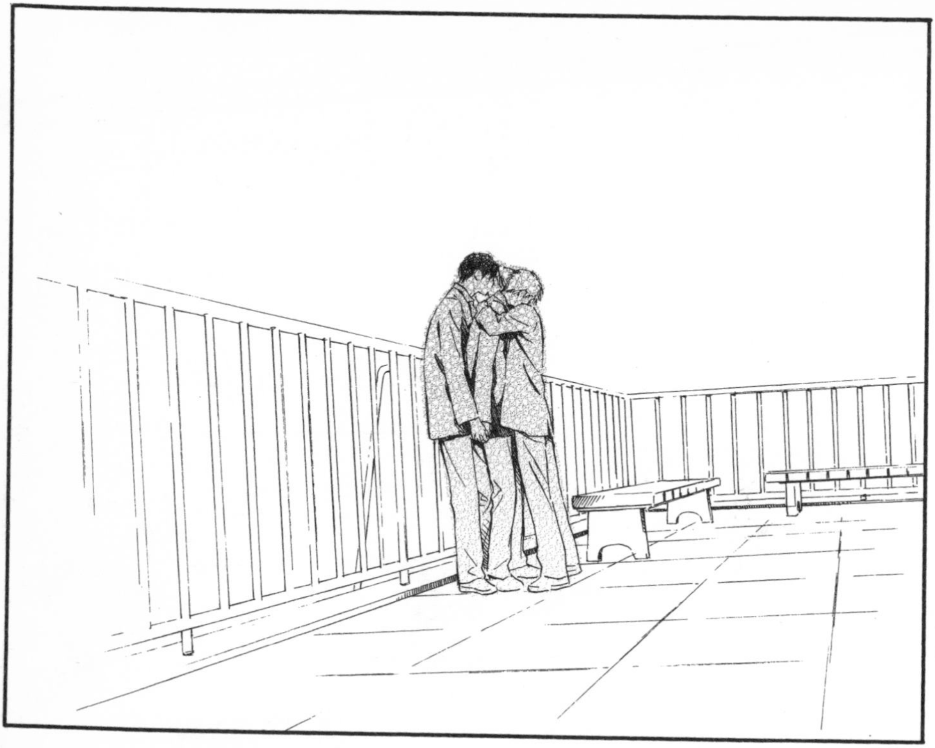

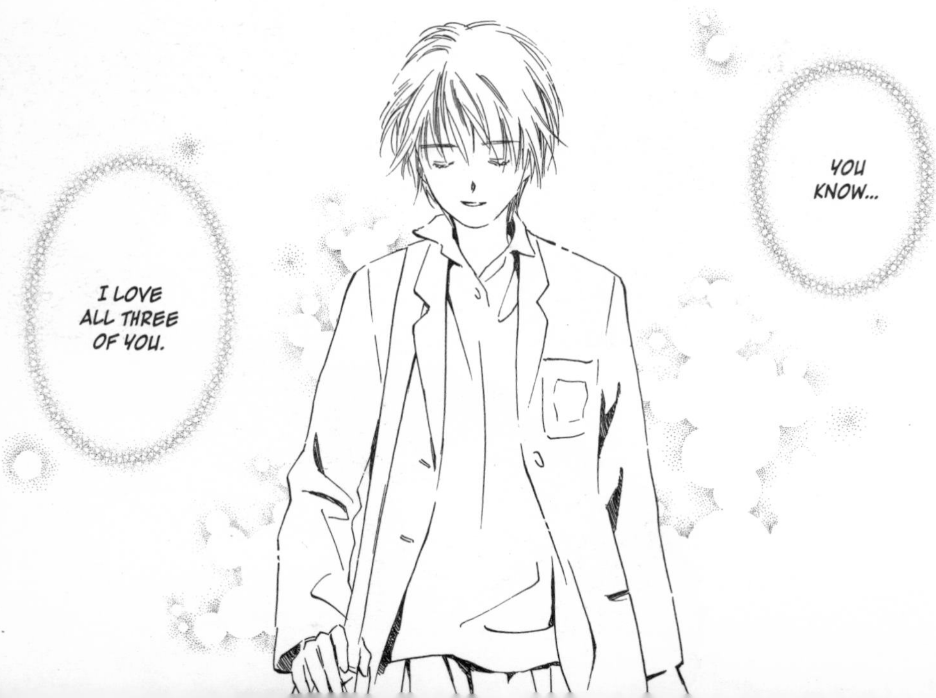
YOU KNOW...
I LOVE ALL THREE OF YOU.

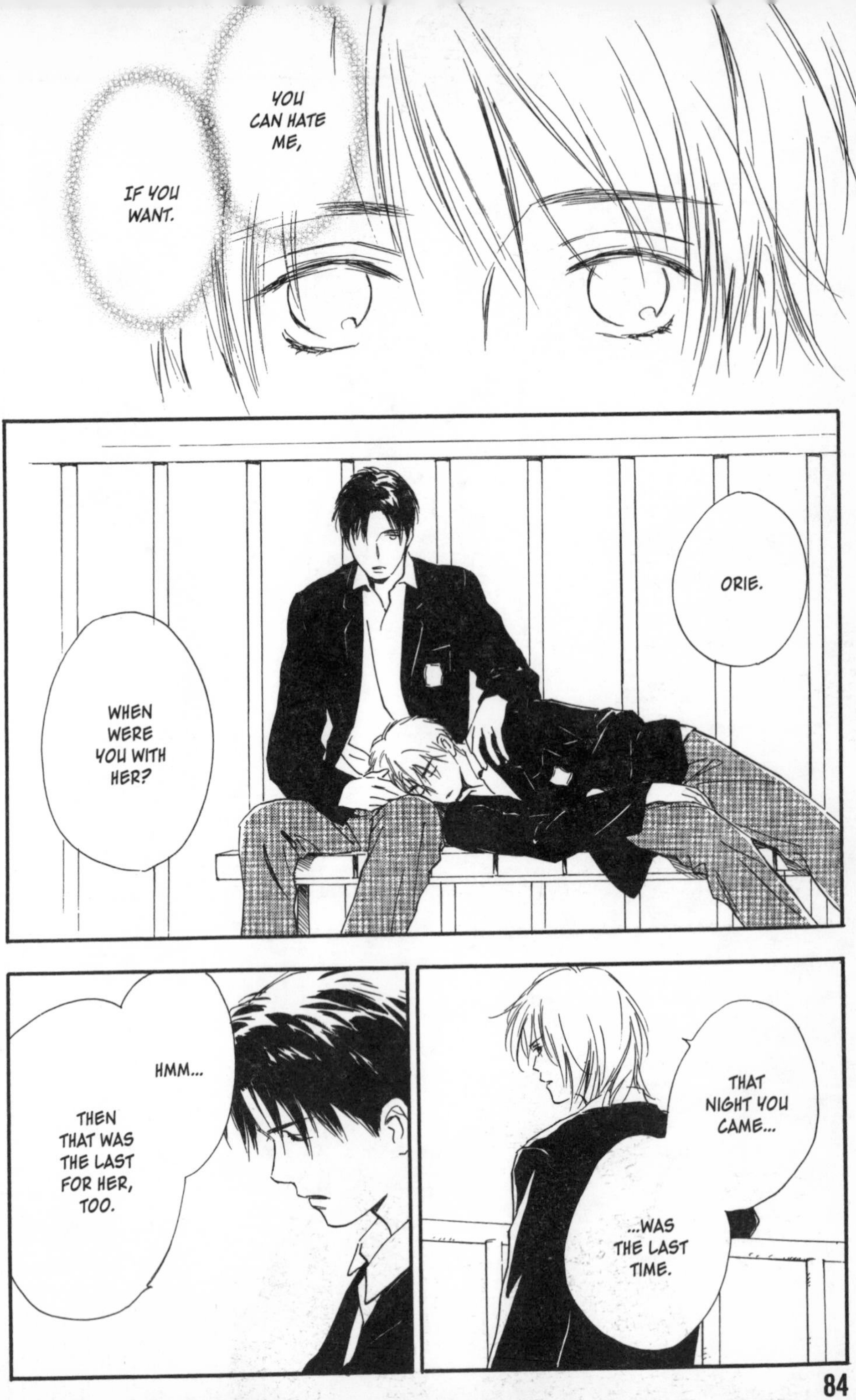
YOU CAN HATE ME,
IF YOU WANT.
ORIE.
WHEN WERE YOU WITH HER?
THAT NIGHT YOU CAME...
...WAS THE LAST TIME.
HMM...
THEN THAT WAS THE LAST FOR HER, TOO.

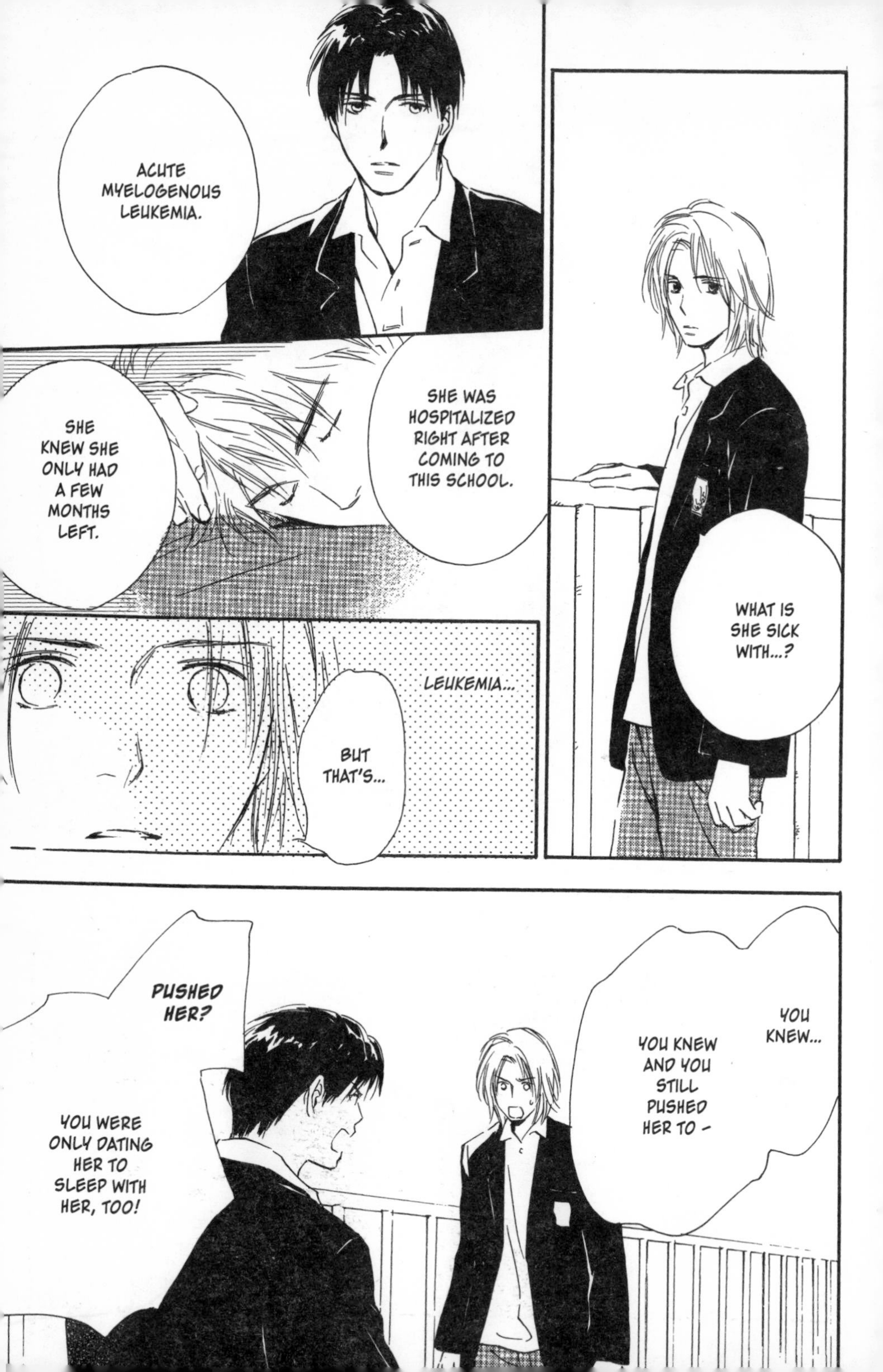
WHAT IS SHE SICK WITH...?
ACUTE MYELOGENOUS LEUKEMIA.
SHE WAS HOSPITALIZED RIGHT AFTER COMING TO THIS SCHOOL.
SHE KNEW SHE ONLY HAD A FEW MONTHS LEFT.
LEUKEMIA...
BUT THAT'S...
YOU KNEW...
YOU KNEW AND YOU STILL PUSHED HER TO -
PUSHED HER?
YOU WERE ONLY DATING HER TO SLEEP WITH HER, TOO!

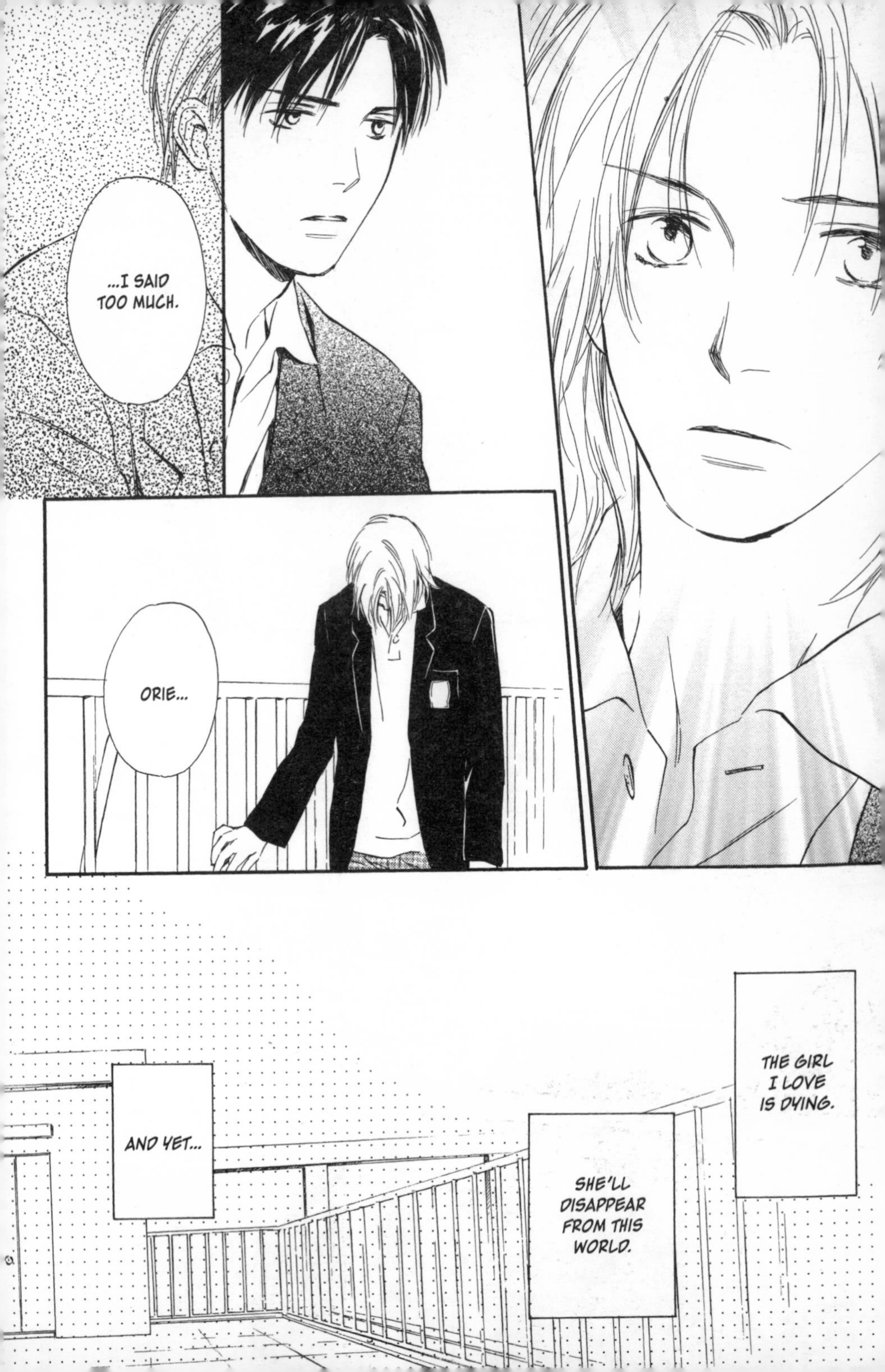
...I SAID TOO MUCH.
ORIE...
THE GIRL I LOVE IS DYING.
SHE'LL DISAPPEAR FROM THIS WORLD.
AND YET...

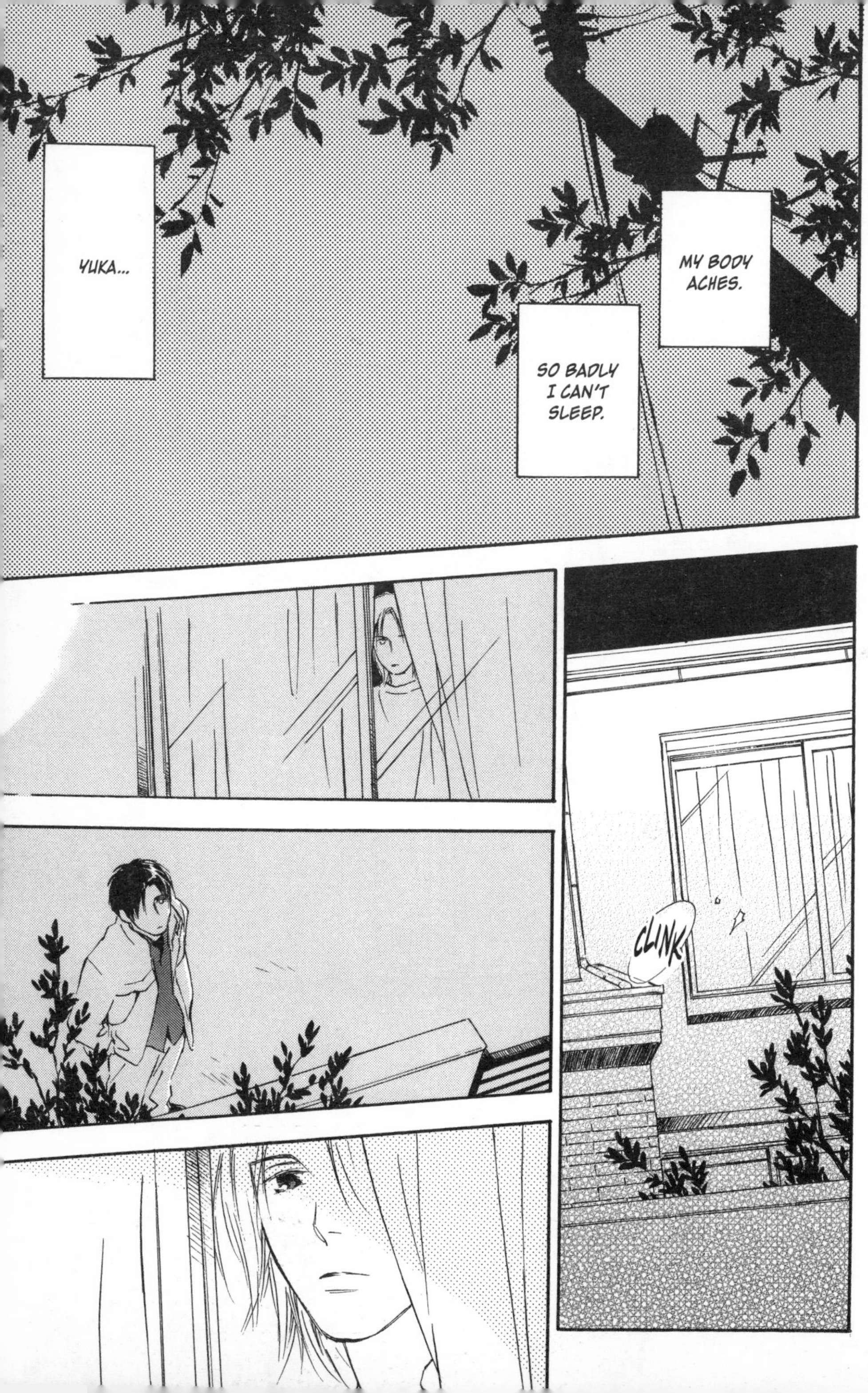
MY BODY ACHES.
SO BADLY I CAN'T SLEEP.
YUKA...
CLINK

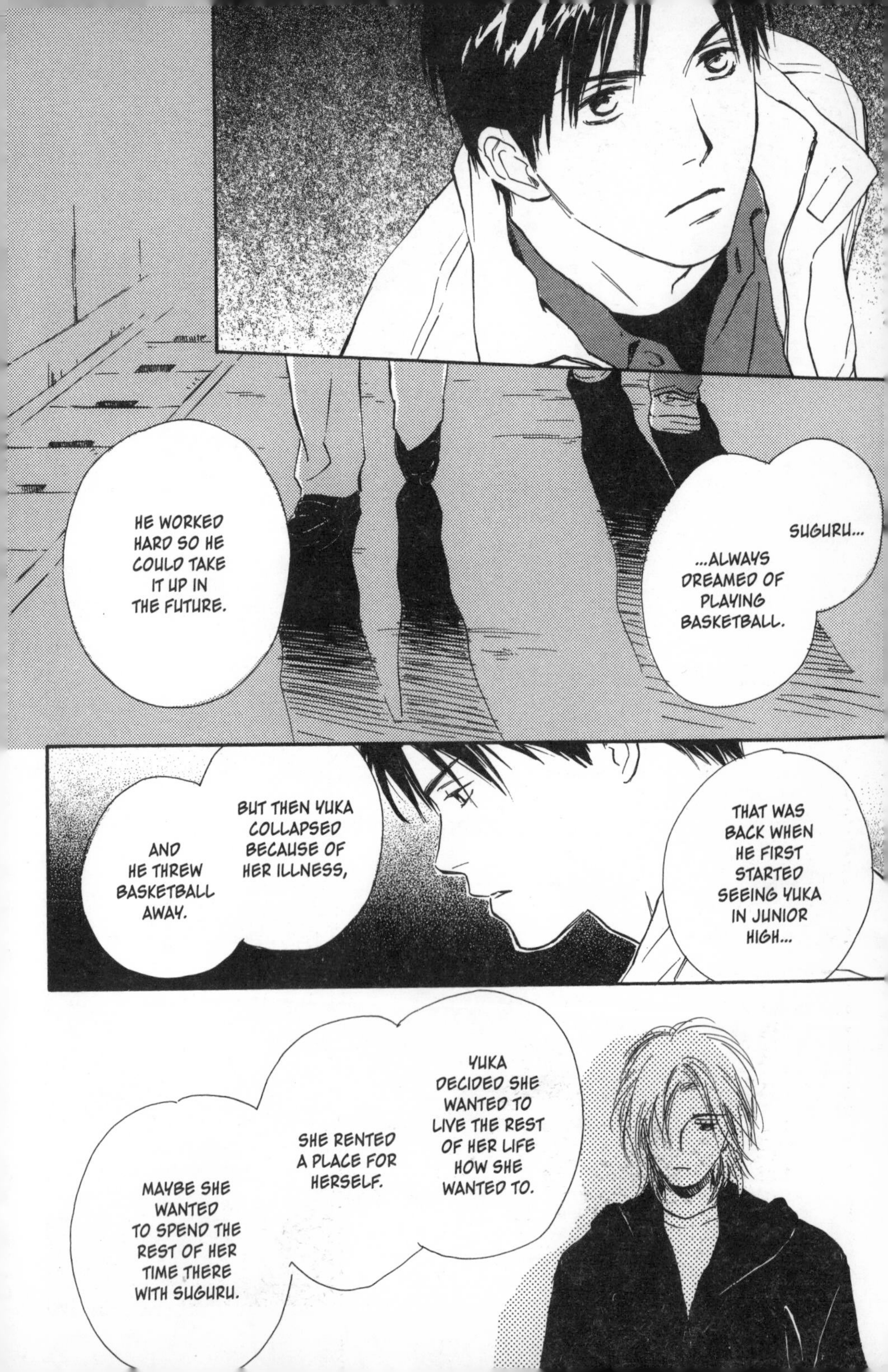
SUGURU... ...ALWAYS DREAMED OF PLAYING BASKETBALL.
HE WORKED HARD SO HE COULD TAKE IT UP IN THE FUTURE.
THAT WAS BACK WHEN HE FIRST STARTED SEEING YUKA IN JUNIOR HIGH...
BUT THEN YUKA COLLAPSED BECAUSE OF HER ILLNESS,
AND HE THREW BASKETBALL AWAY.
YUKA DECIDED SHE WANTED TO LIVE THE REST OF HER LIFE HOW SHE WANTED TO.
SHE RENTED A PLACE FOR HERSELF.
MAYBE SHE WANTED TO SPEND THE REST OF HER TIME THERE WITH SUGURU.

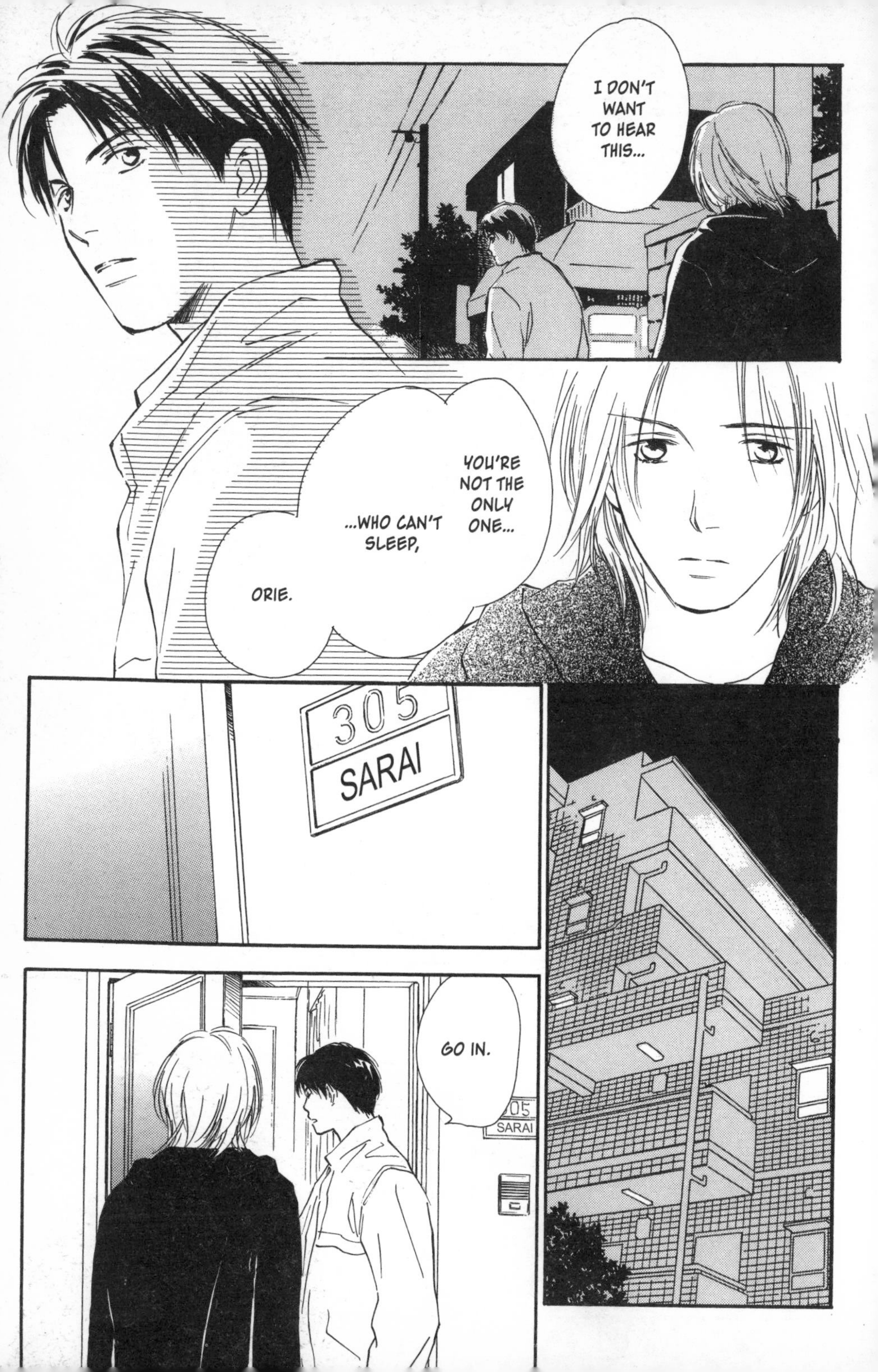
I DON'T WANT TO HEAR THIS...
YOU'RE NOT THE ONLY ONE...
...WHO CAN'T SLEEP,
ORIE.
305
SARAI
GO IN.

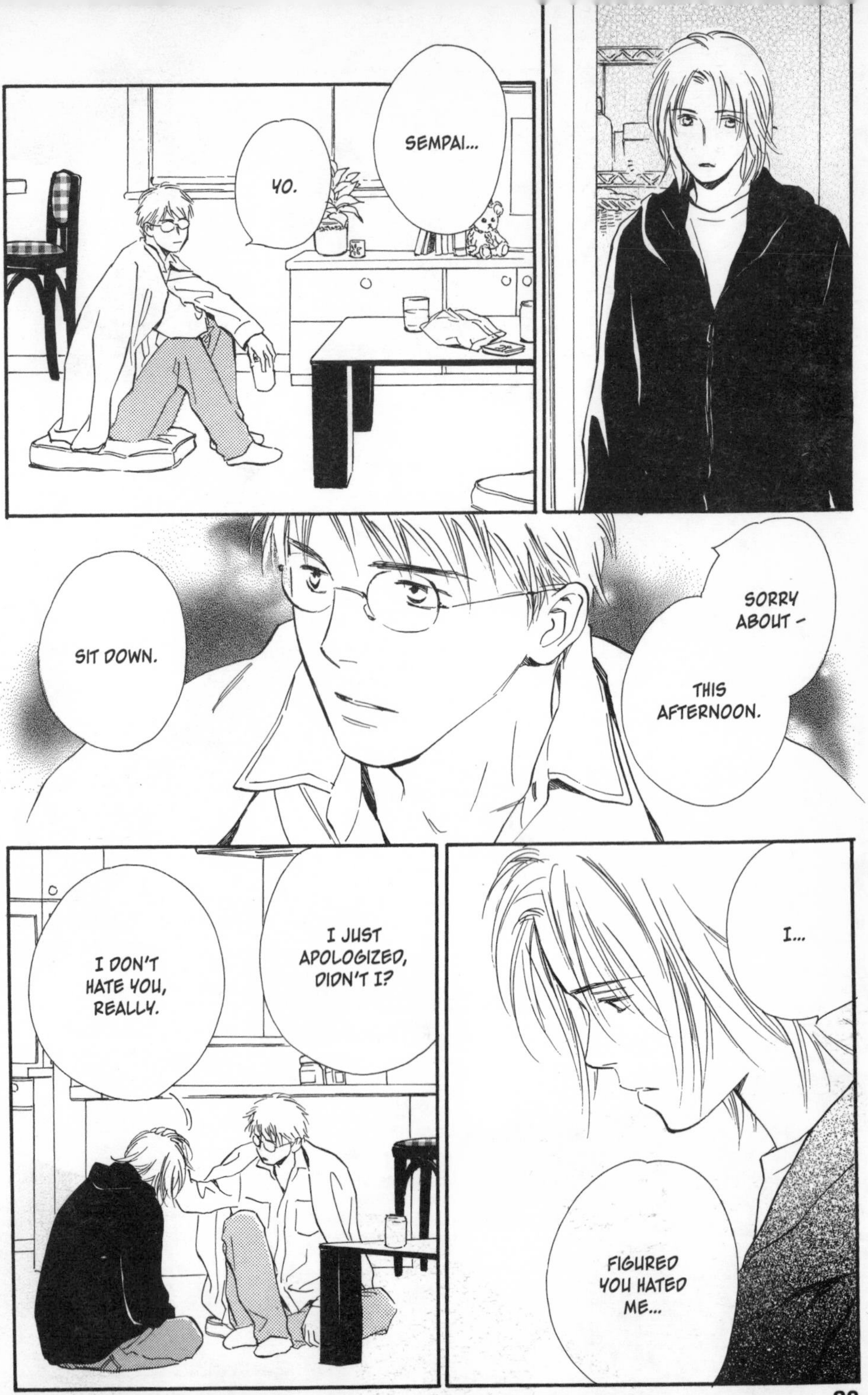
SEMPAI...
YO.
SORRY ABOUT – THIS AFTERNOON.
SIT DOWN.
I...
FIGURED YOU HATED ME...
I JUST APOLOGIZED, DIDN'T I?
I DON'T HATE YOU, REALLY.

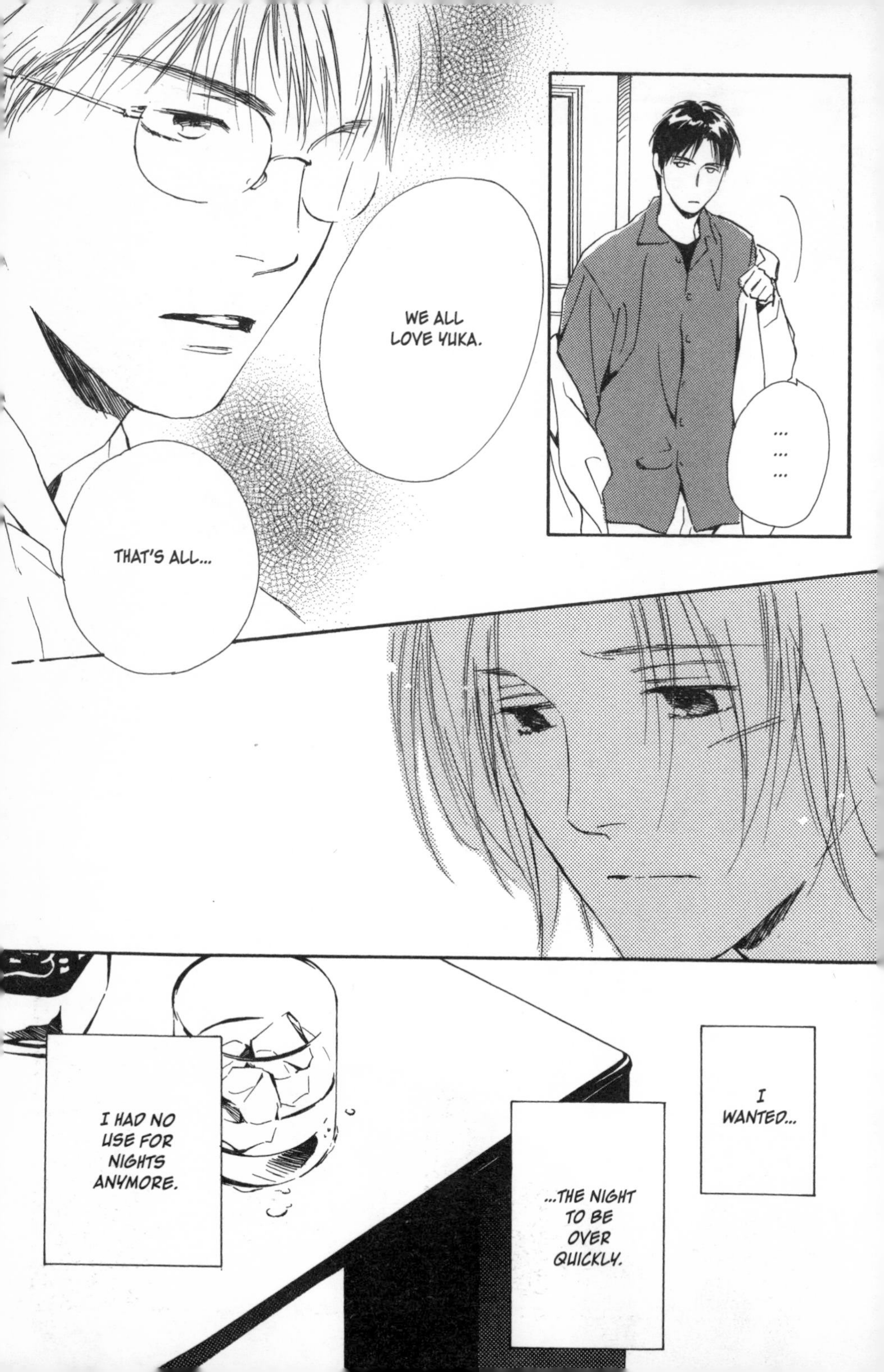
... ...
WE ALL LOVE YUKA.
THAT'S ALL...
I WANTED...
...THE NIGHT TO BE OVER QUICKLY.
I HAD NO USE FOR NIGHTS ANYMORE.

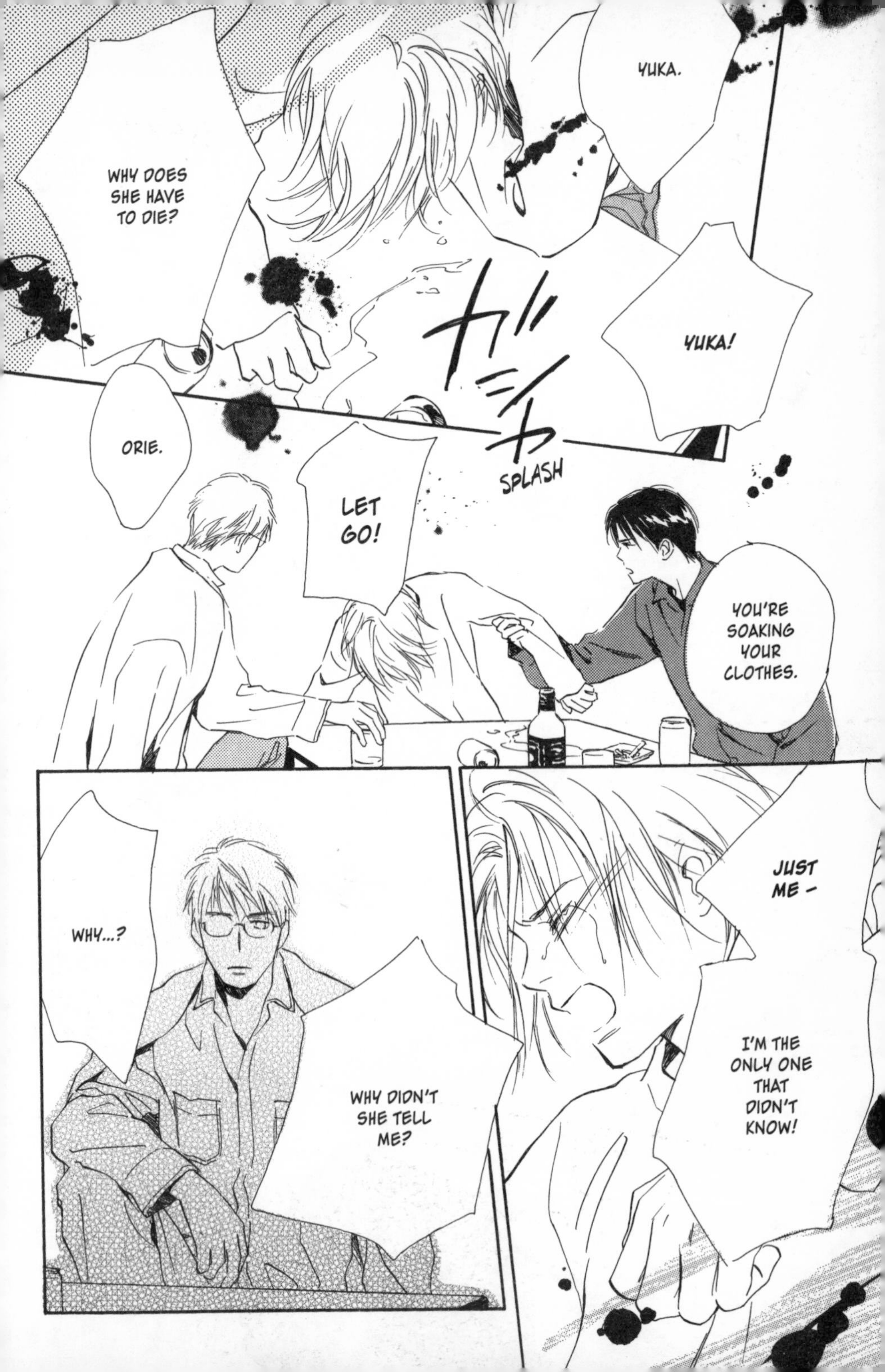
YUKA.
WHY DOES SHE HAVE TO DIE?
YUKA!
SPLASH
YOU'RE SOAKING YOUR CLOTHES.
LET GO!
ORIE.
JUST ME -
I'M THE ONLY ONE THAT DIDN'T KNOW!
WHY...?
WHY DIDN'T SHE TELL ME?

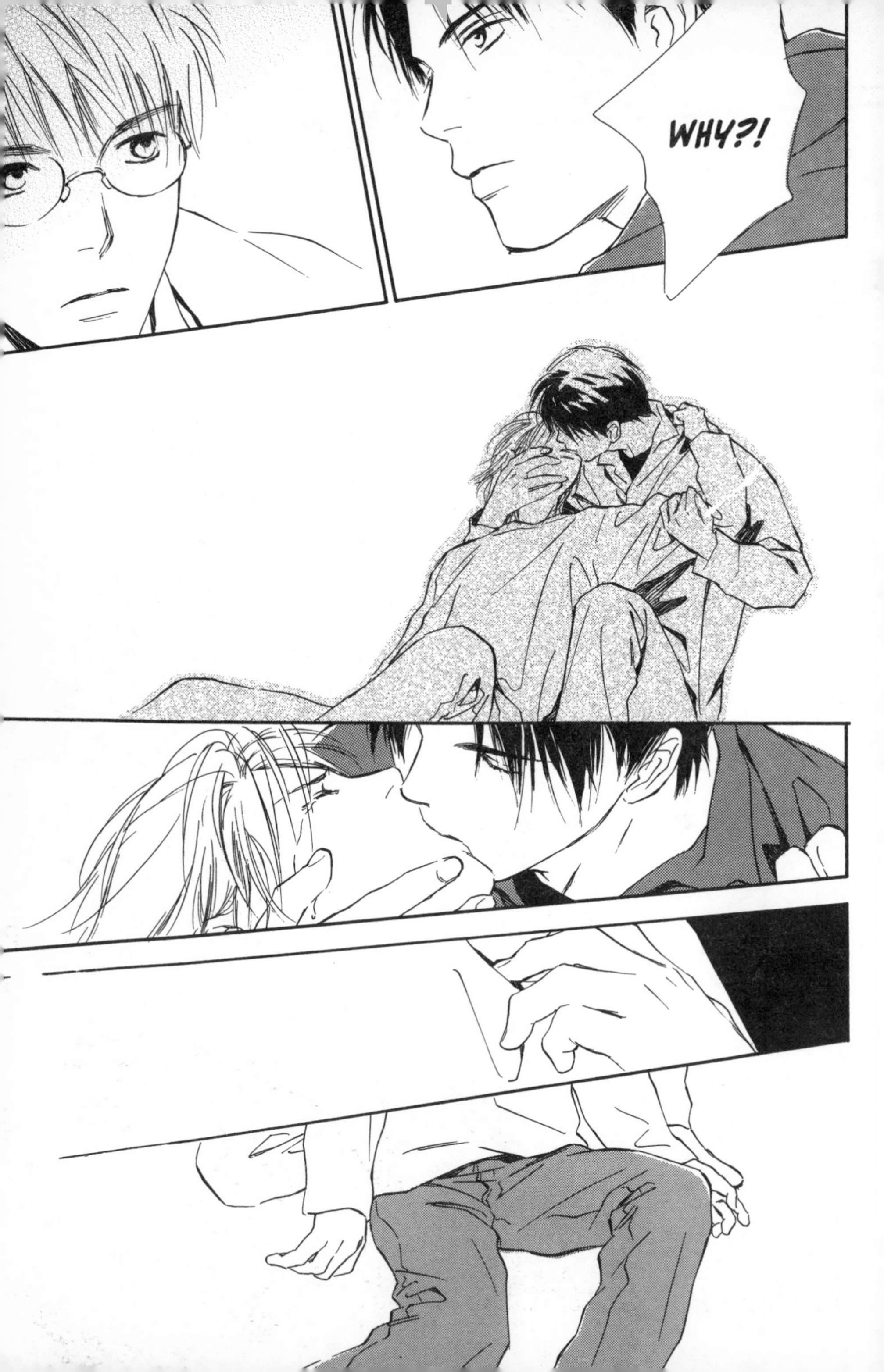
WHY?!

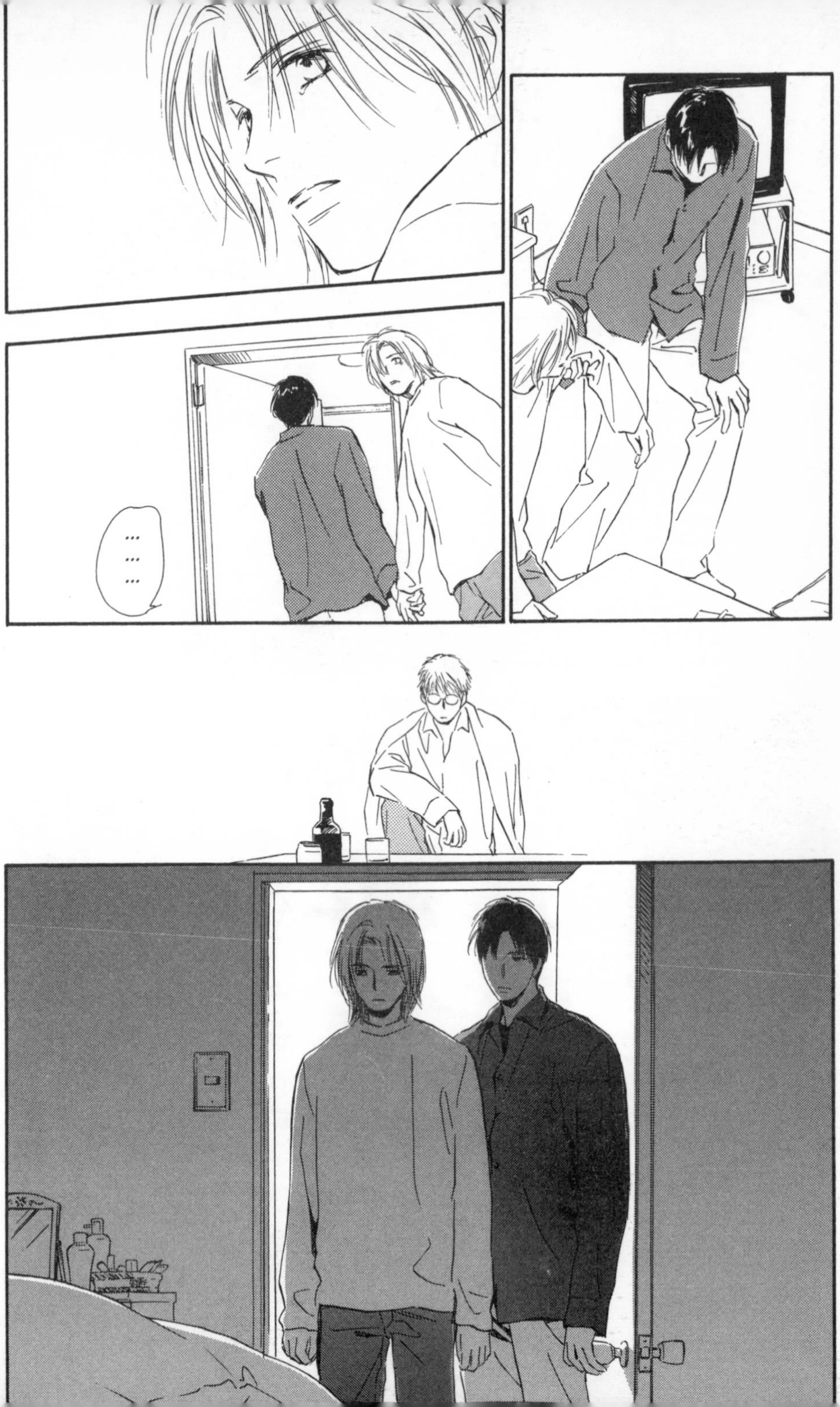
………

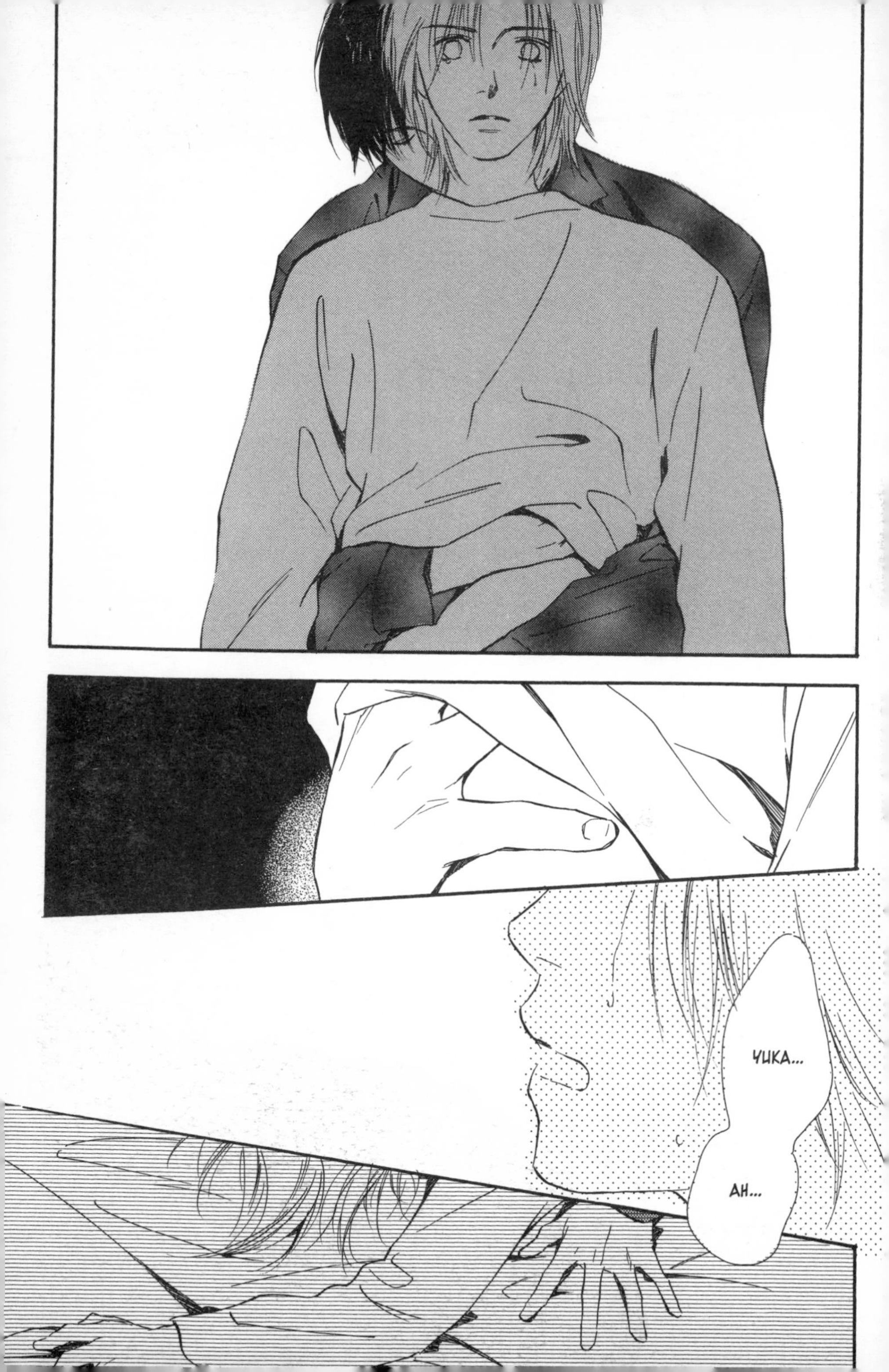
YUKA...
AH...

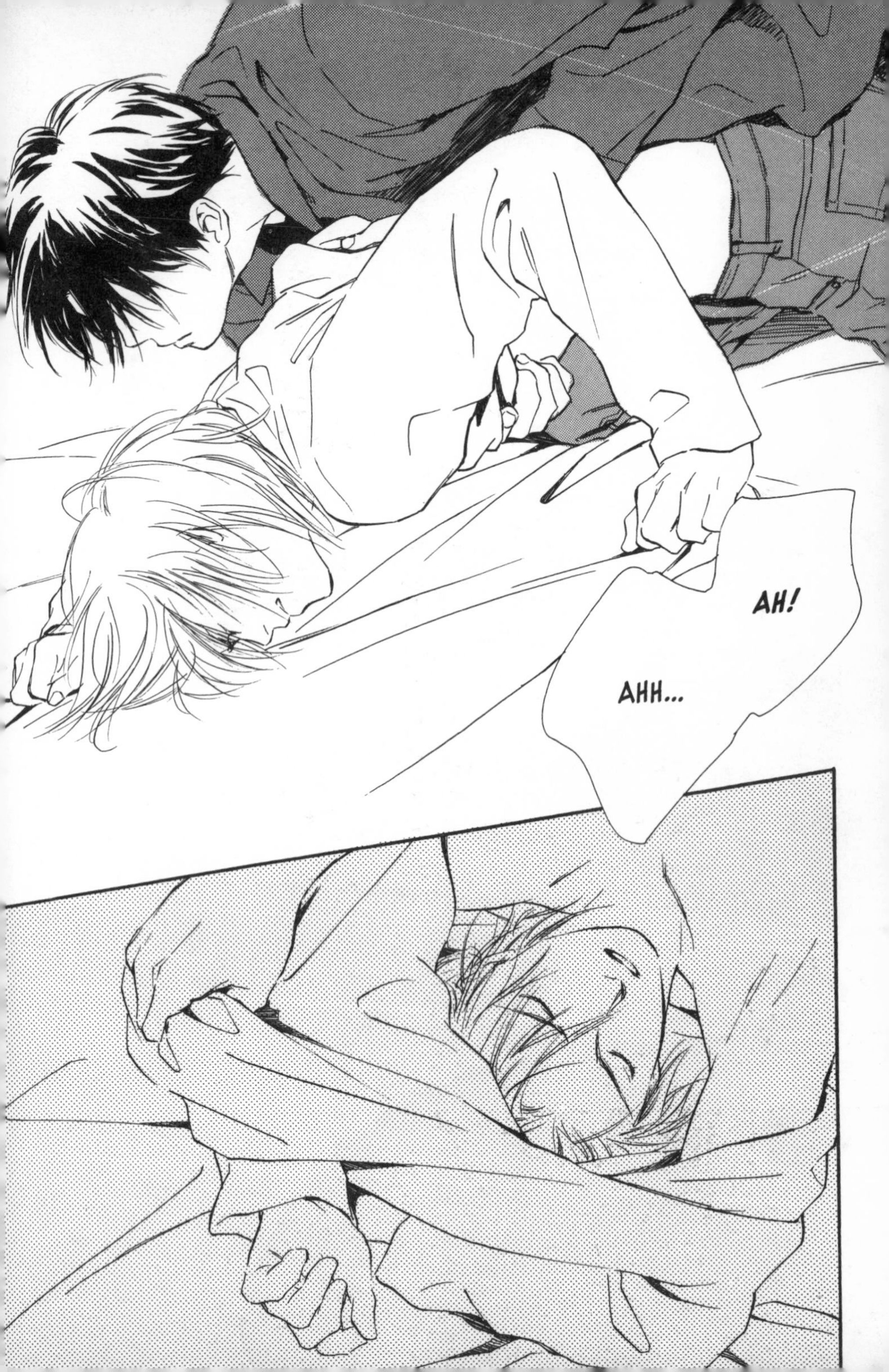
AH!
AHH...

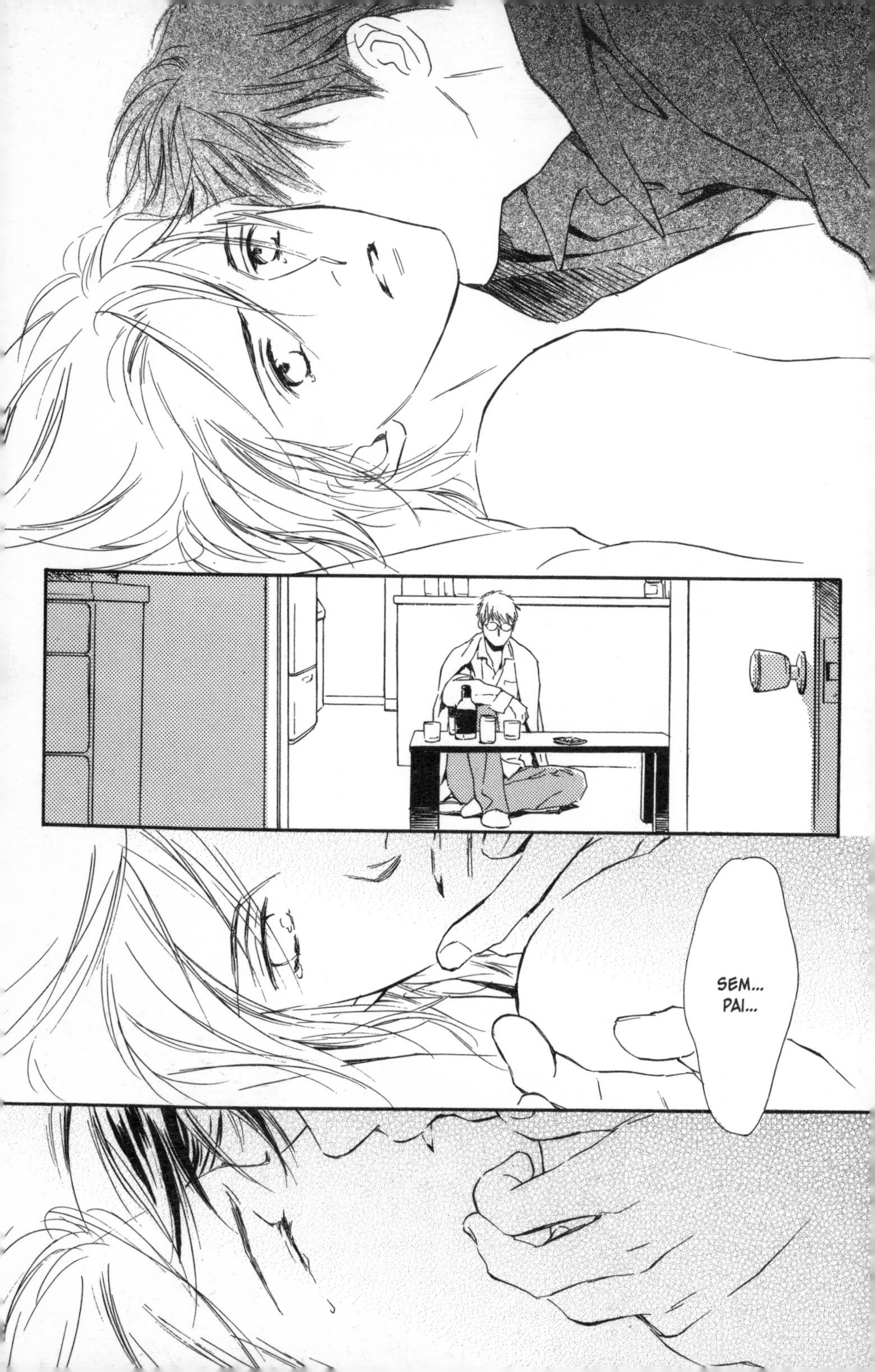
SEM... PAI...

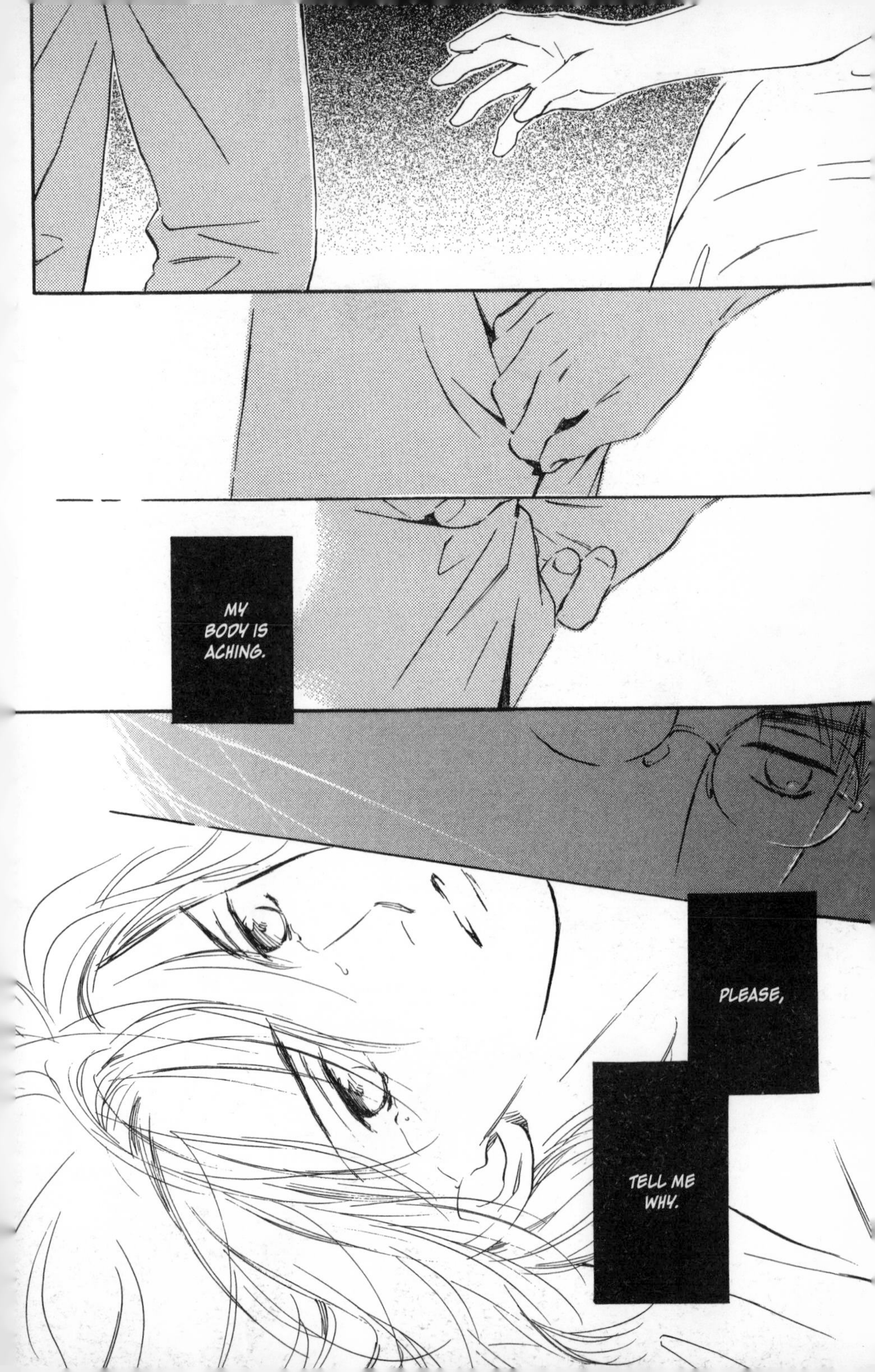
MY BODY IS ACHING.
PLEASE,
TELL ME WHY.

CHAPTER 4

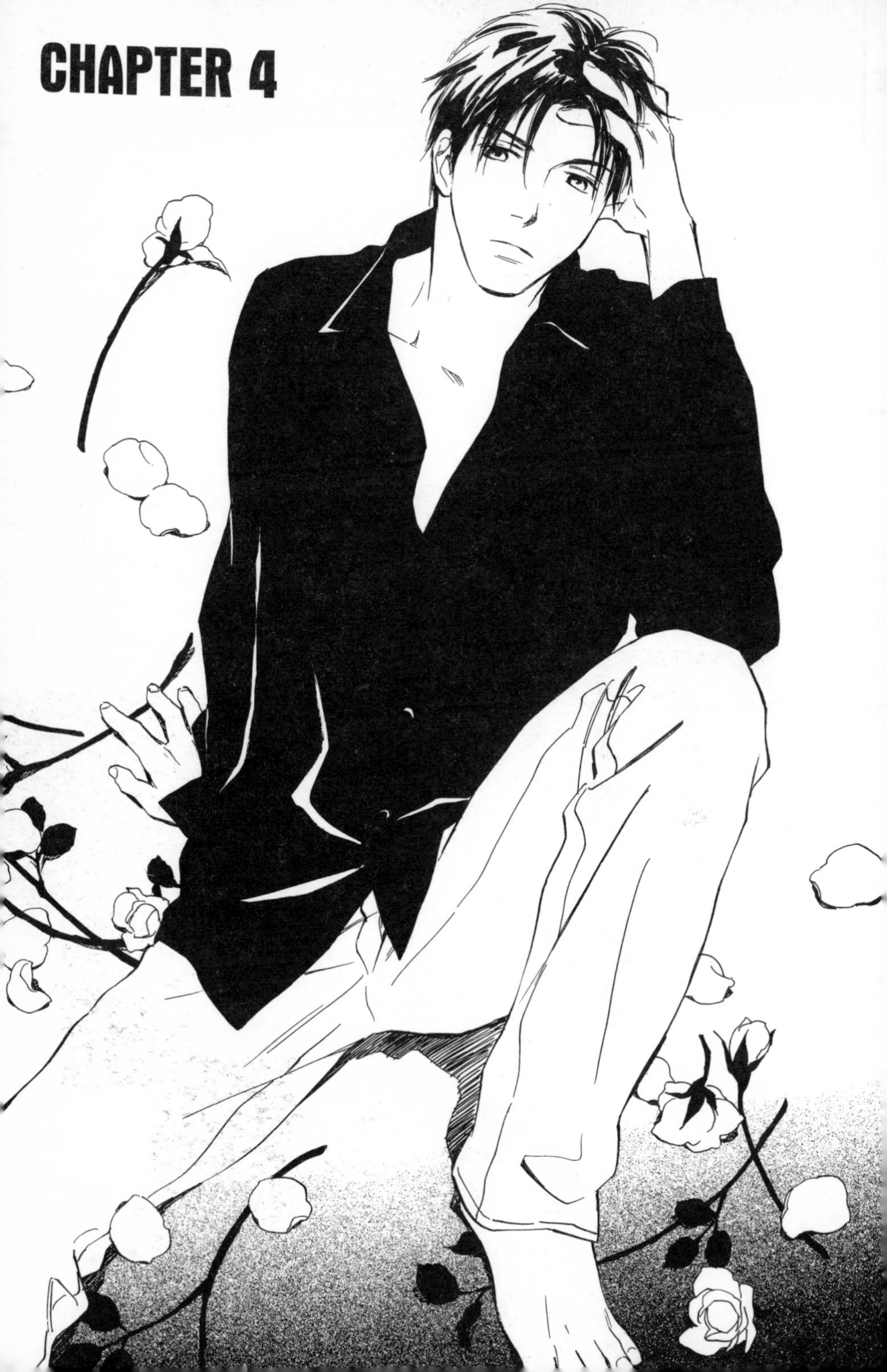

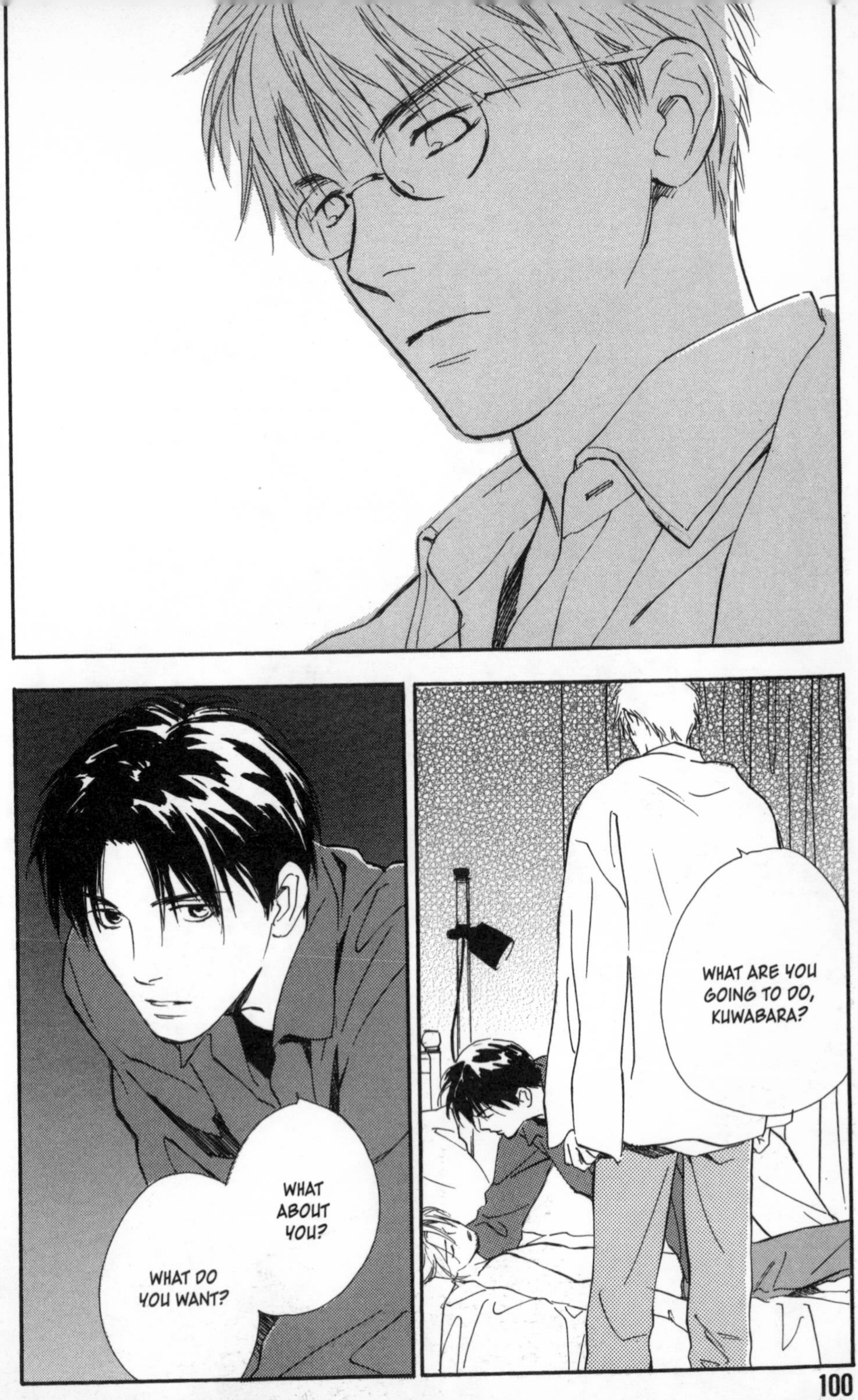
WHAT ARE YOU GOING TO DO, KUWABARA?
WHAT ABOUT YOU?
WHAT DO YOU WANT?

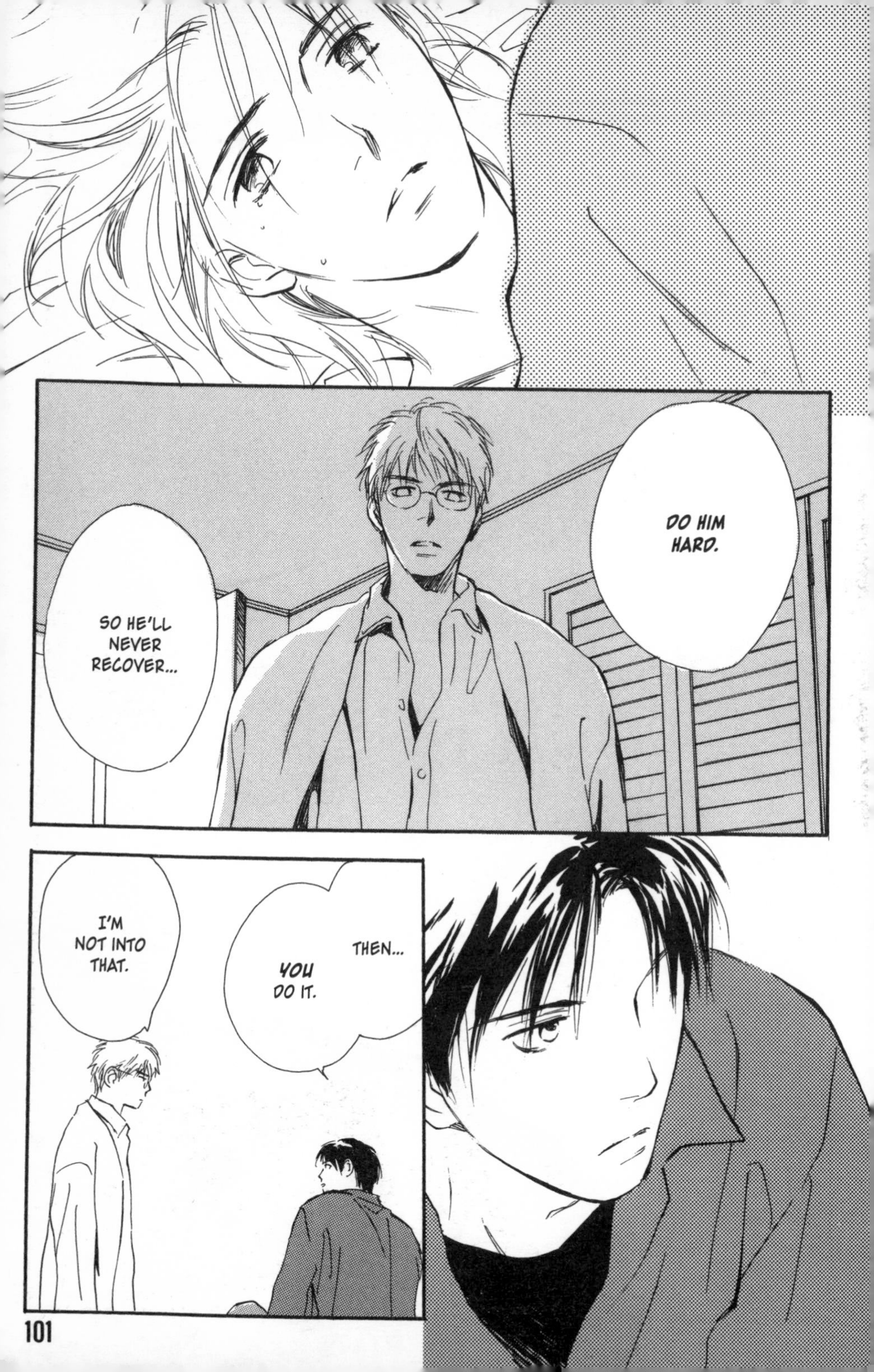
DO HIM HARD.
SO HE'LL NEVER RECOVER...
THEN... YOU DO IT.
I'M NOT INTO THAT.

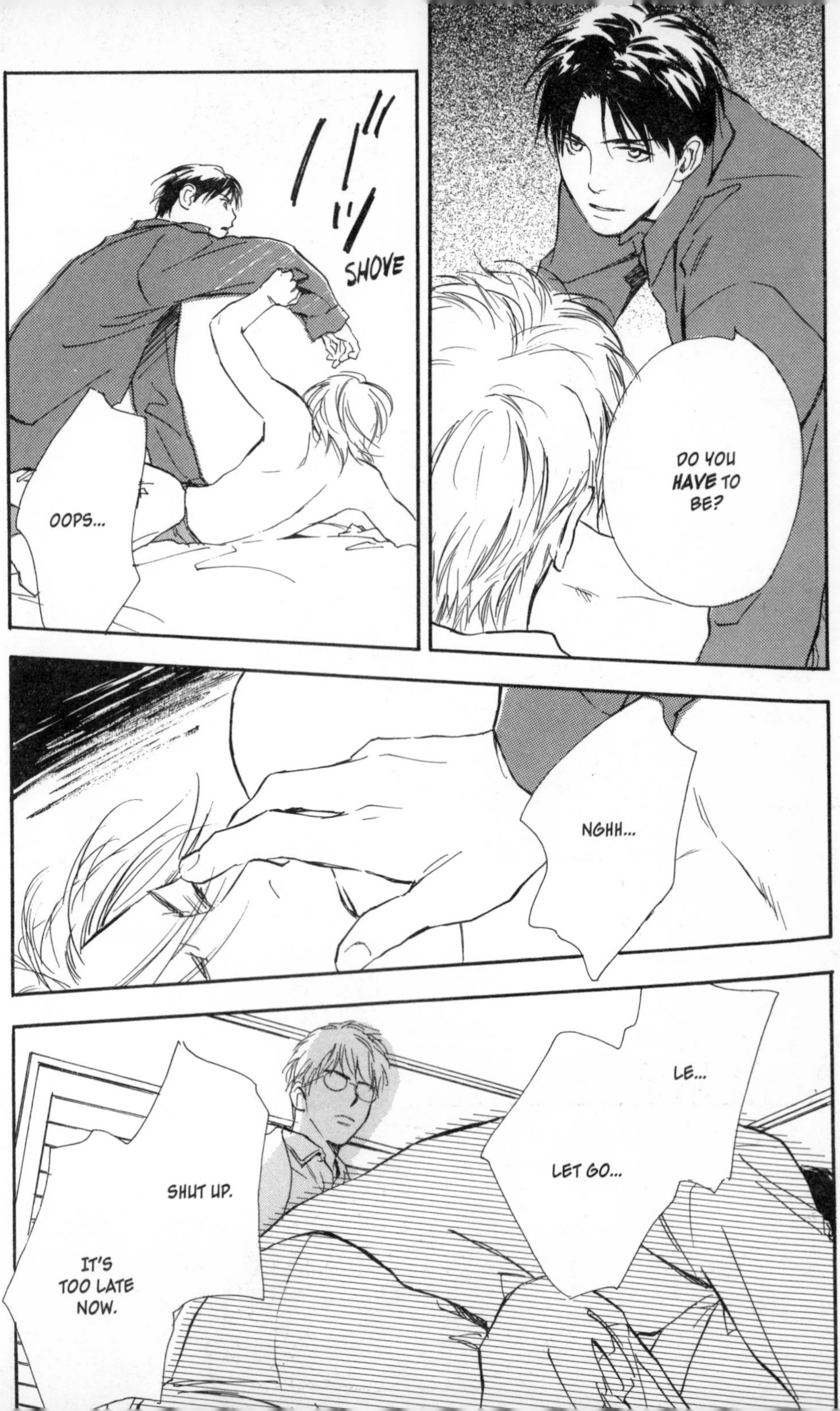
DO YOU **HAVE** TO BE?
SHOVE
OOPS...
NGHH...
LE...
LET GO...
SHUT UP.
IT'S TOO LATE NOW.

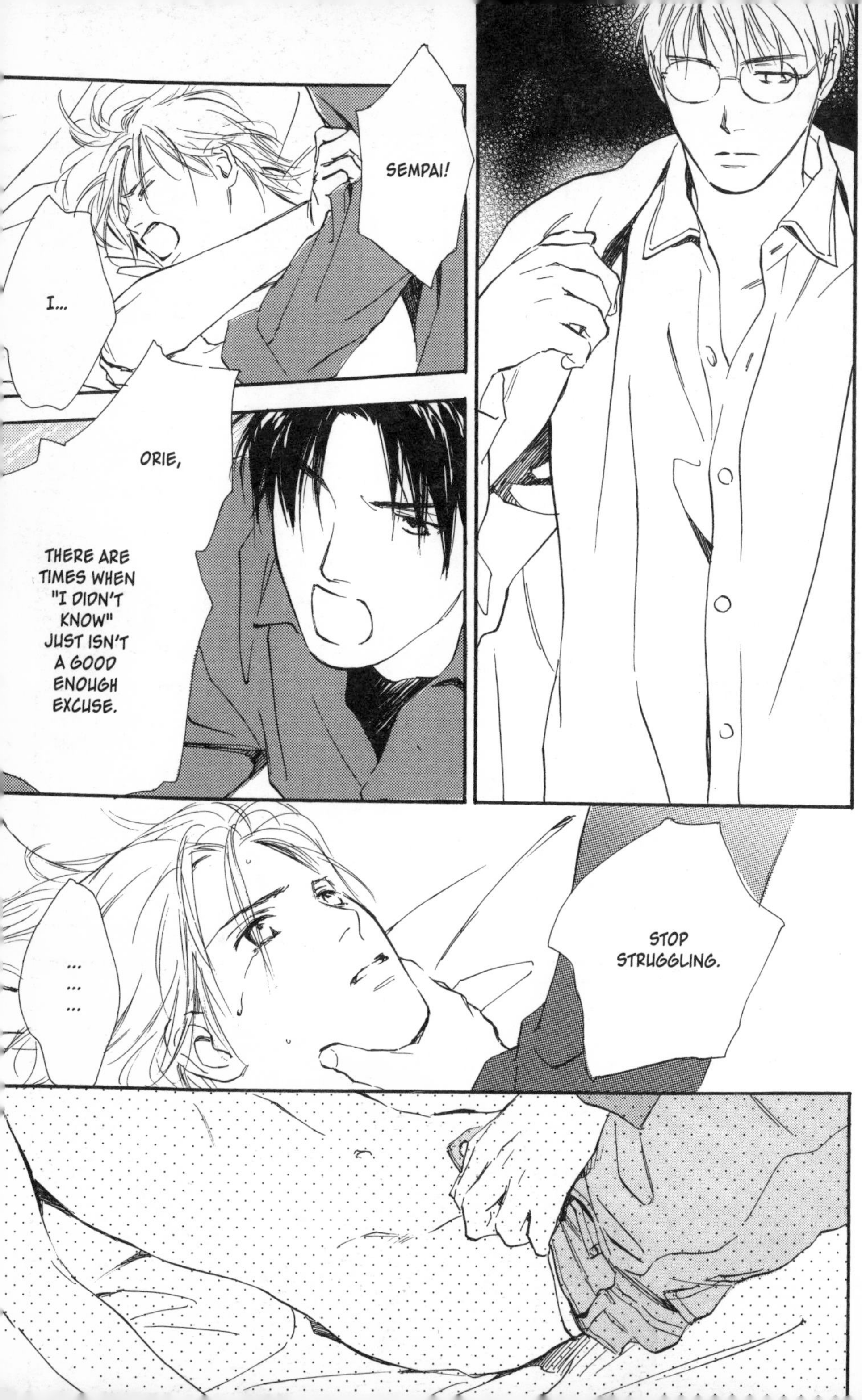
SEMPAI!
I...
ORIE,
THERE ARE TIMES WHEN "I DIDN'T KNOW" JUST ISN'T A GOOD ENOUGH EXCUSE.
STOP STRUGGLING.
... ...

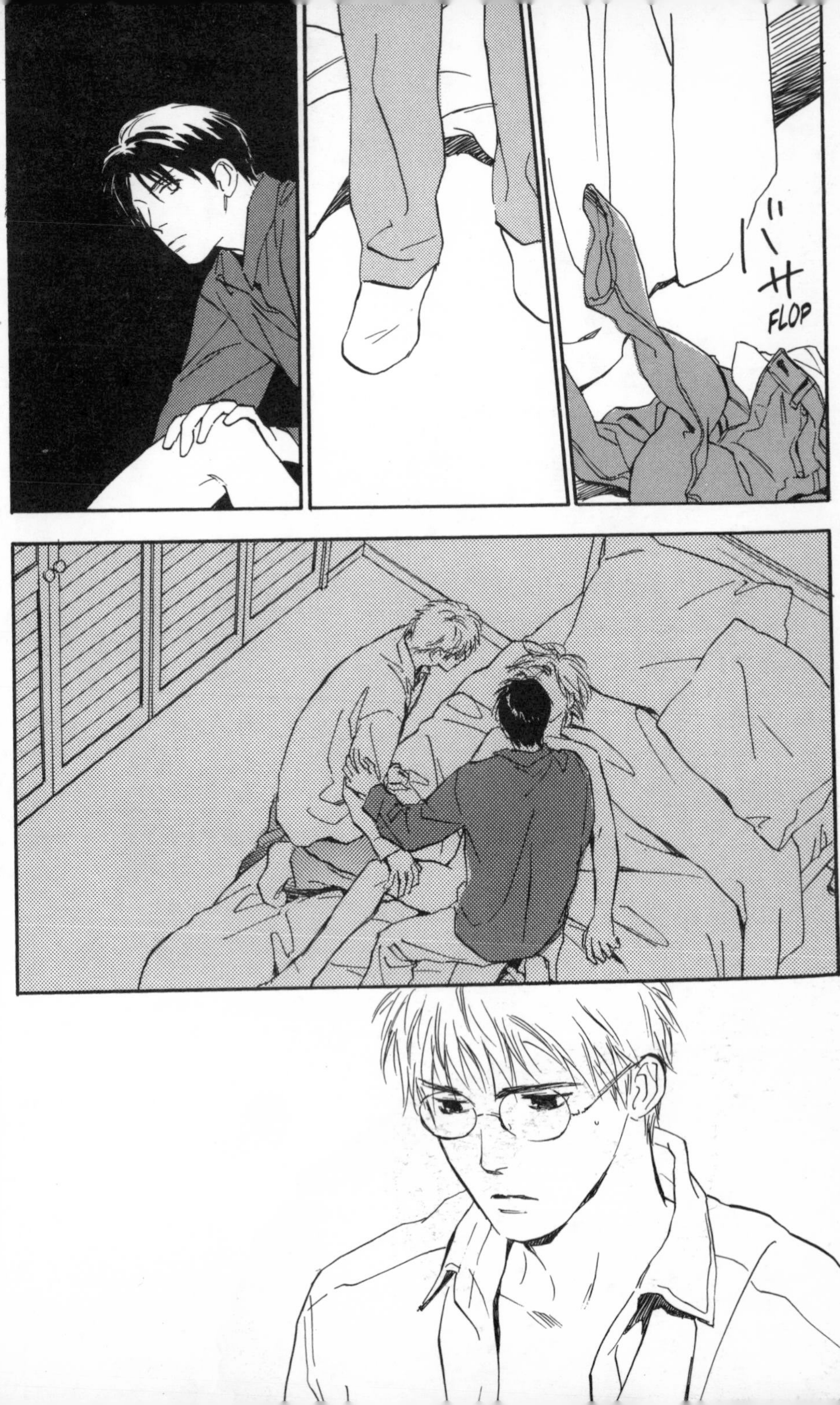
バサ
FLOP

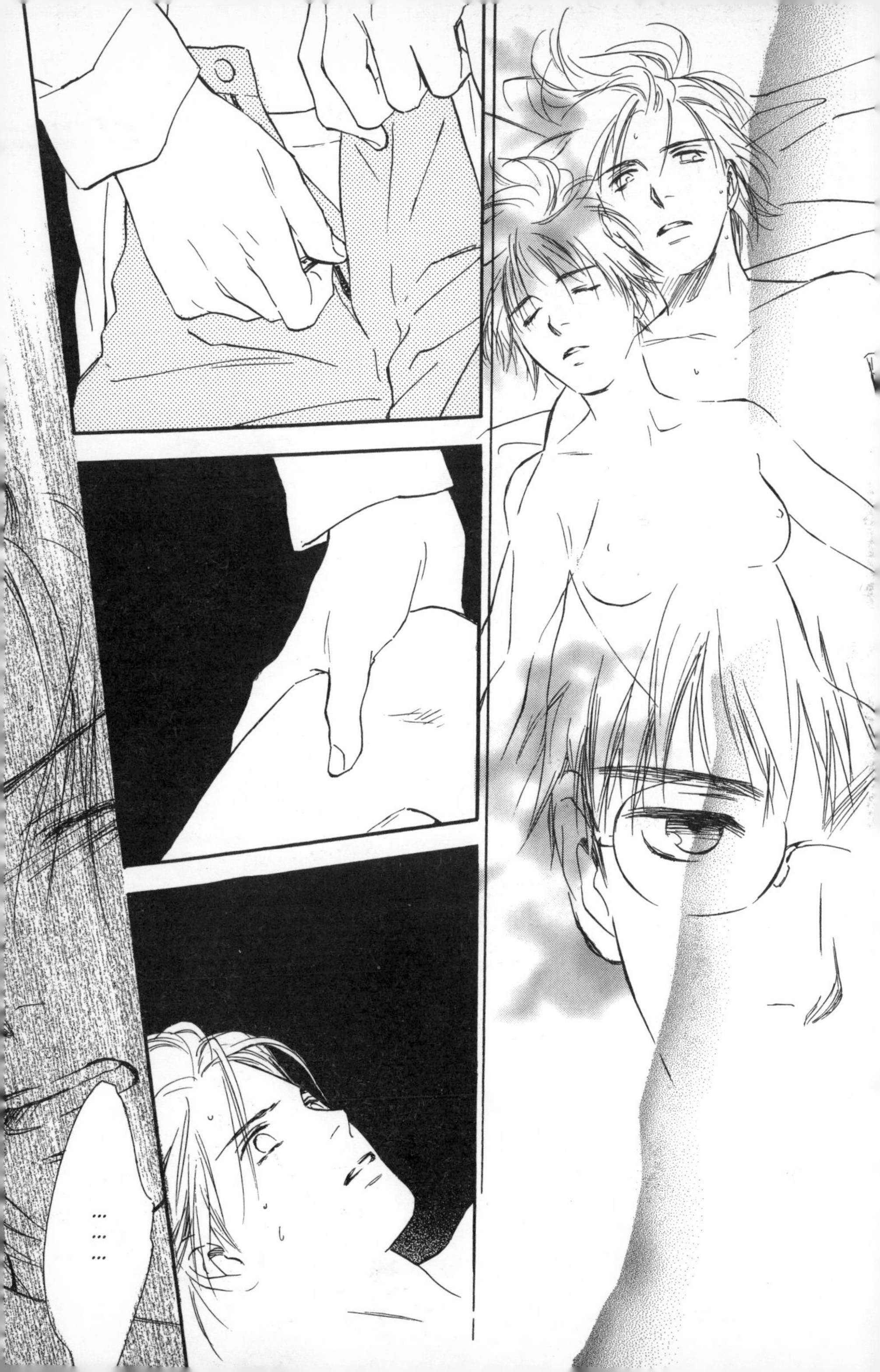
………

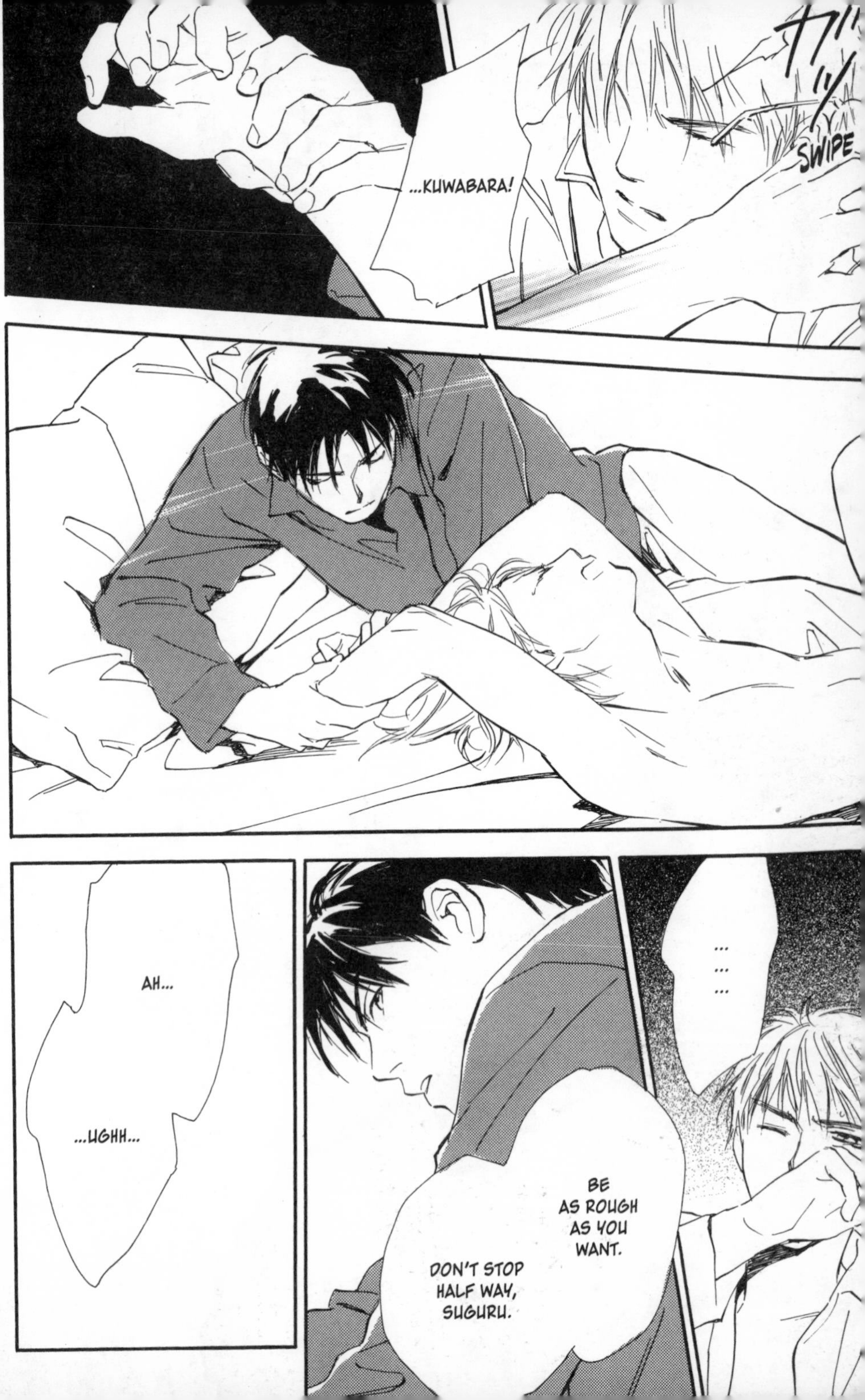
SWIPE
...KUWABARA!
...
...
...
BE AS ROUGH AS YOU WANT.
DON'T STOP HALF WAY, SUGURU.
AH...
...UGHH...

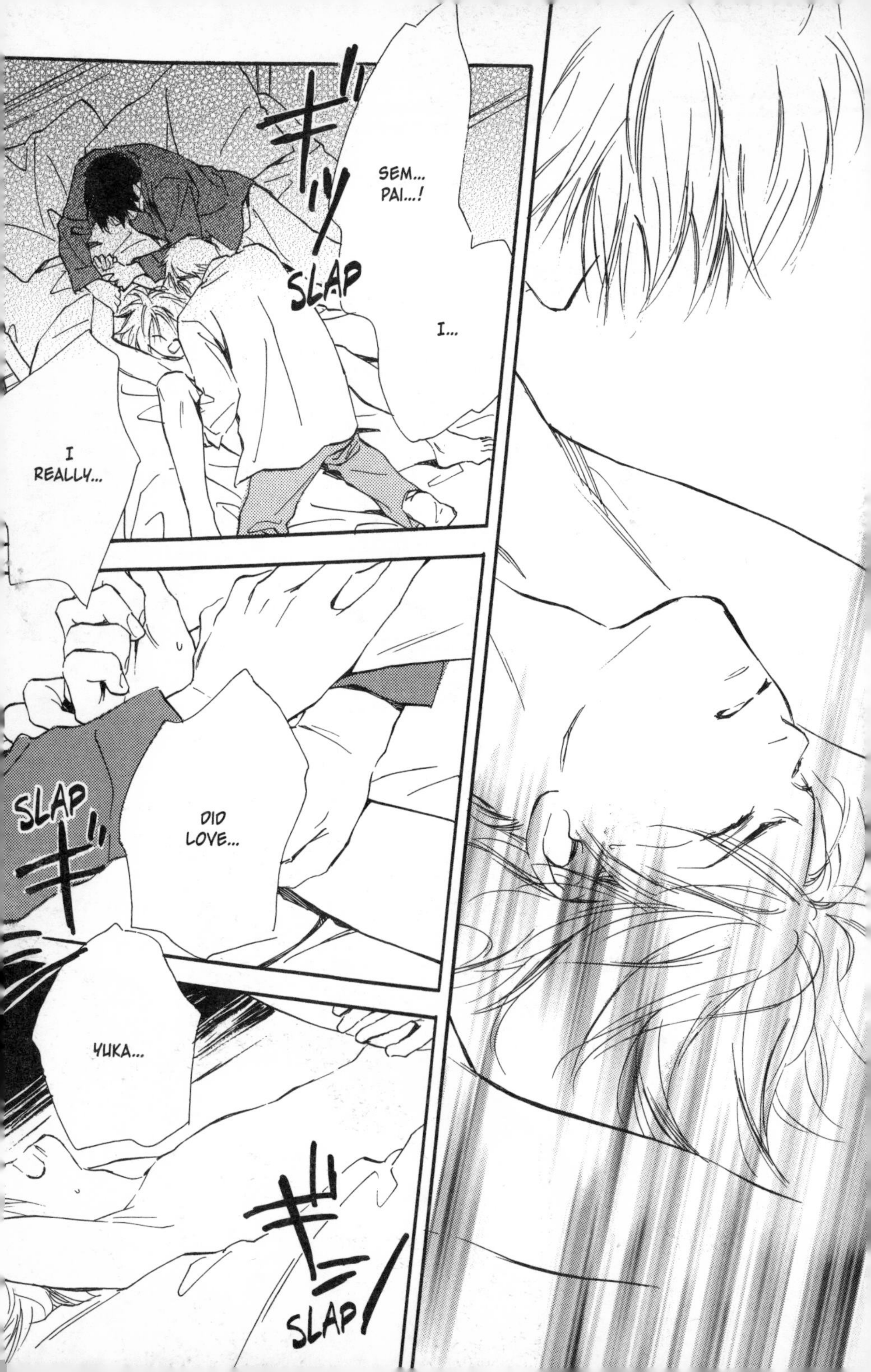
SEM... PAI...!
ギッ
SLAP
I...
I REALLY...
DID LOVE...
ギ
SLAP
YUKA...
ギー
SLAP

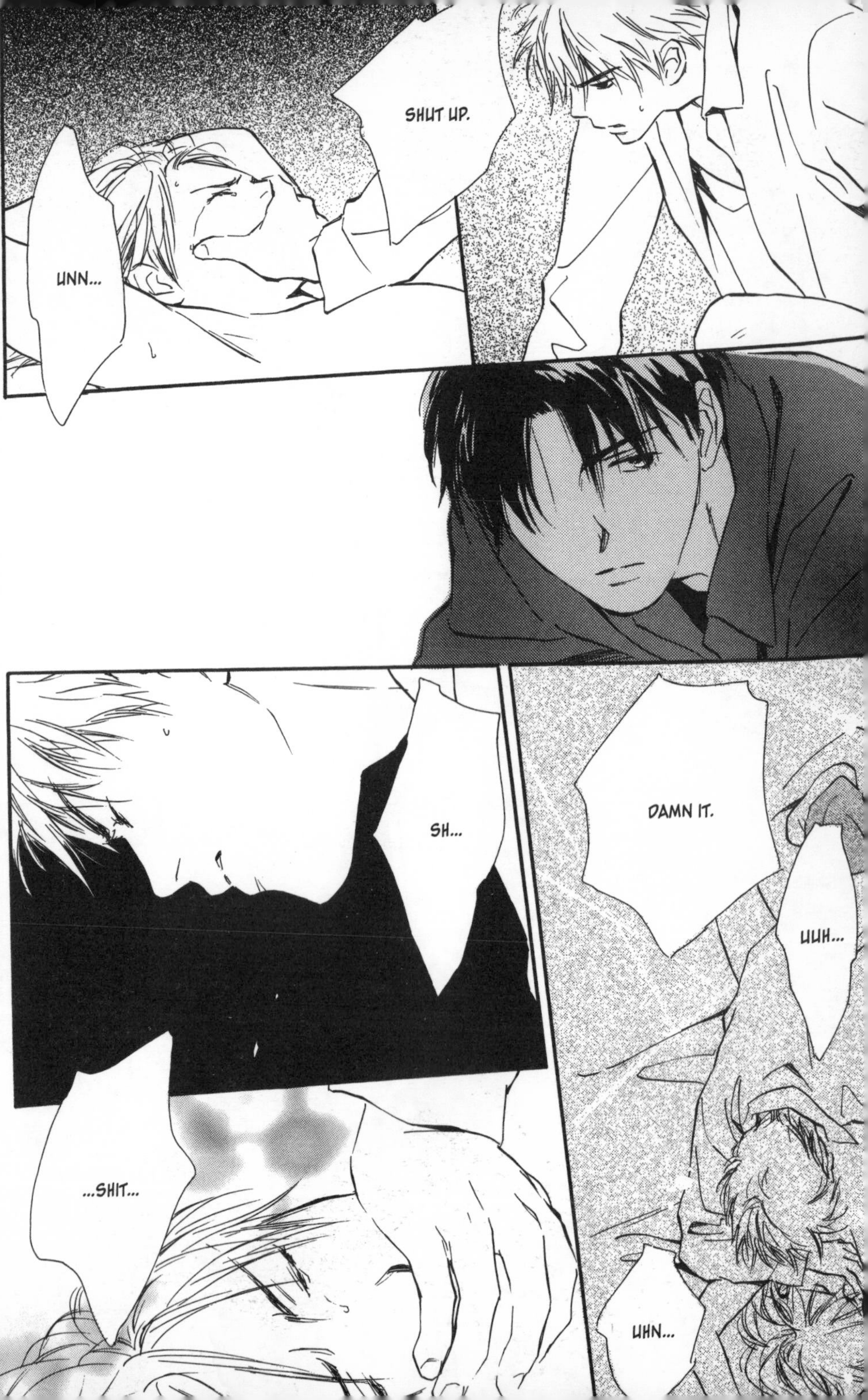
SHUT UP.
UNN...
DAMN IT.
UUH...
UHN...
SH...
...SHIT...

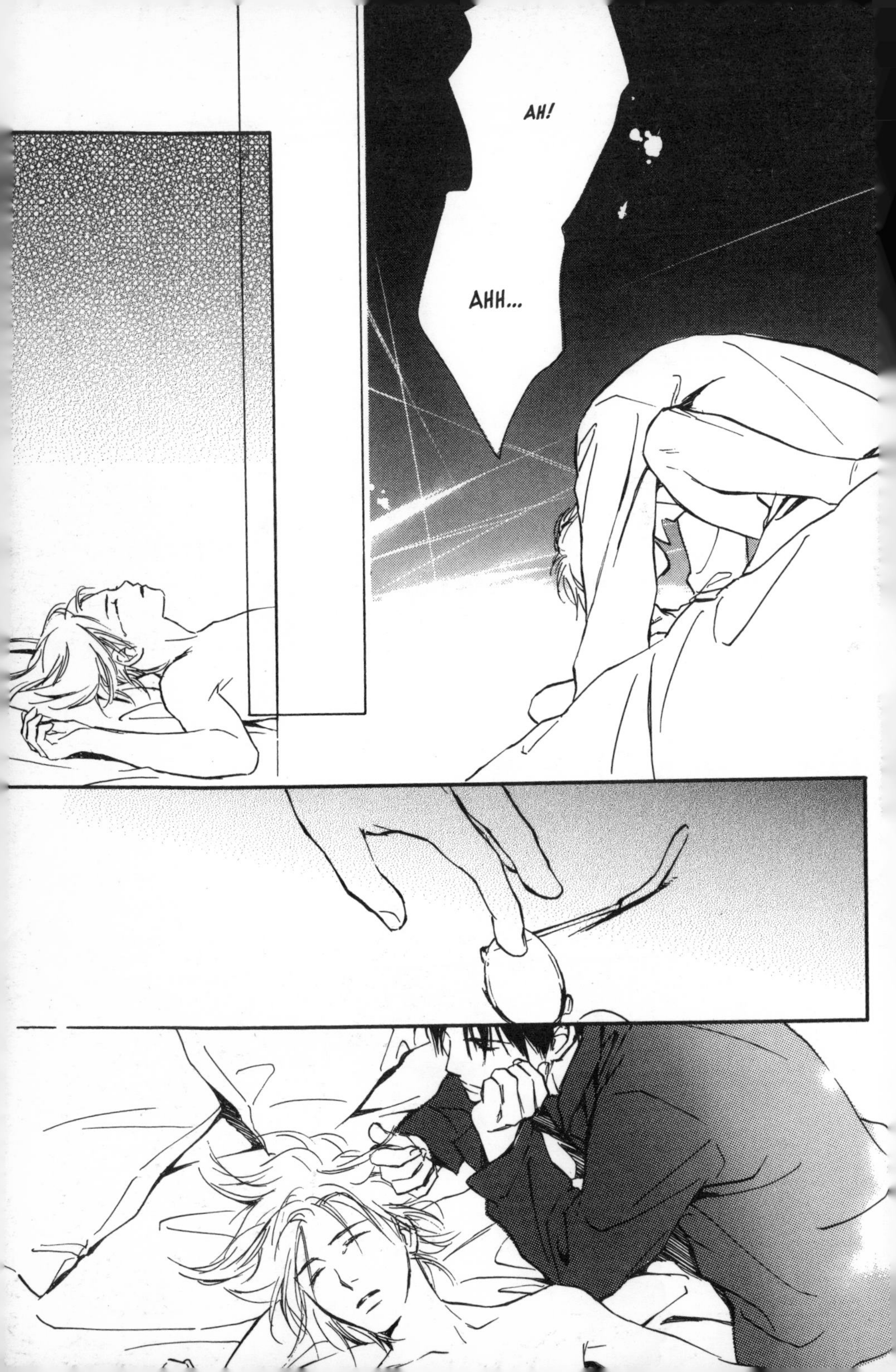
AH!
AHH...

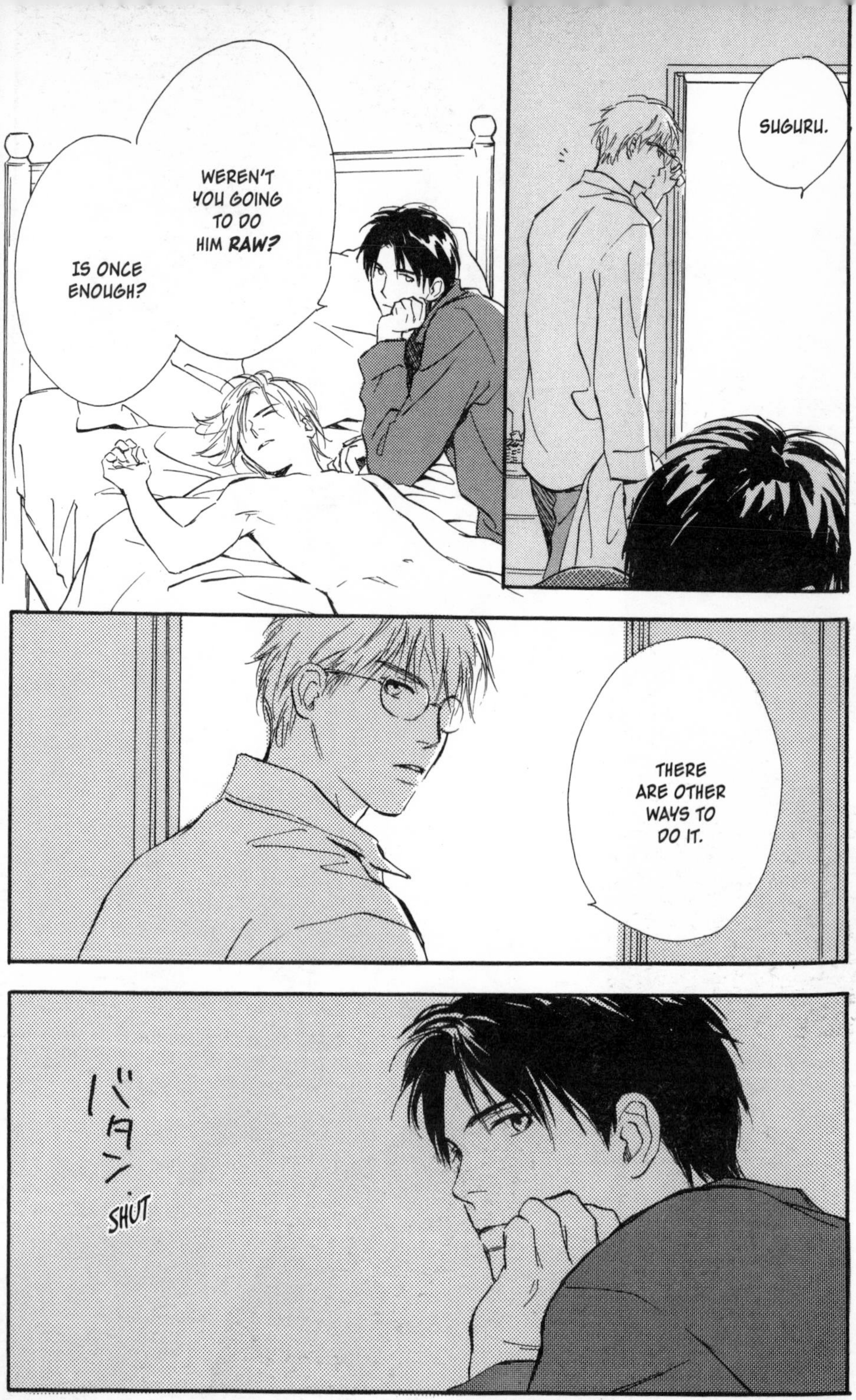
SUGURU.
WEREN'T YOU GOING TO DO HIM RAW?
IS ONCE ENOUGH?
THERE ARE OTHER WAYS TO DO IT.
バタン
SHUT

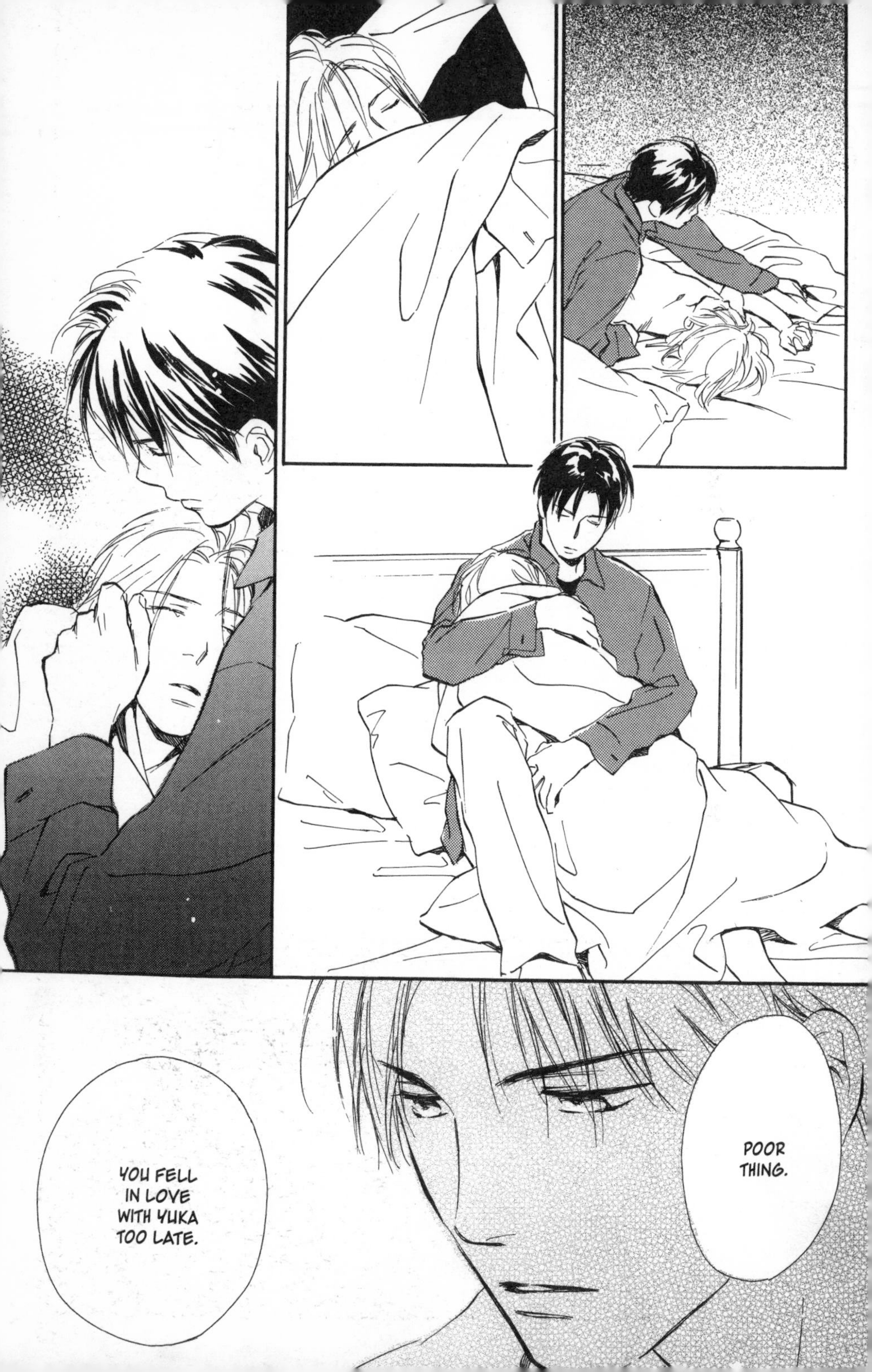
POOR THING.
YOU FELL IN LOVE WITH YUKA TOO LATE.

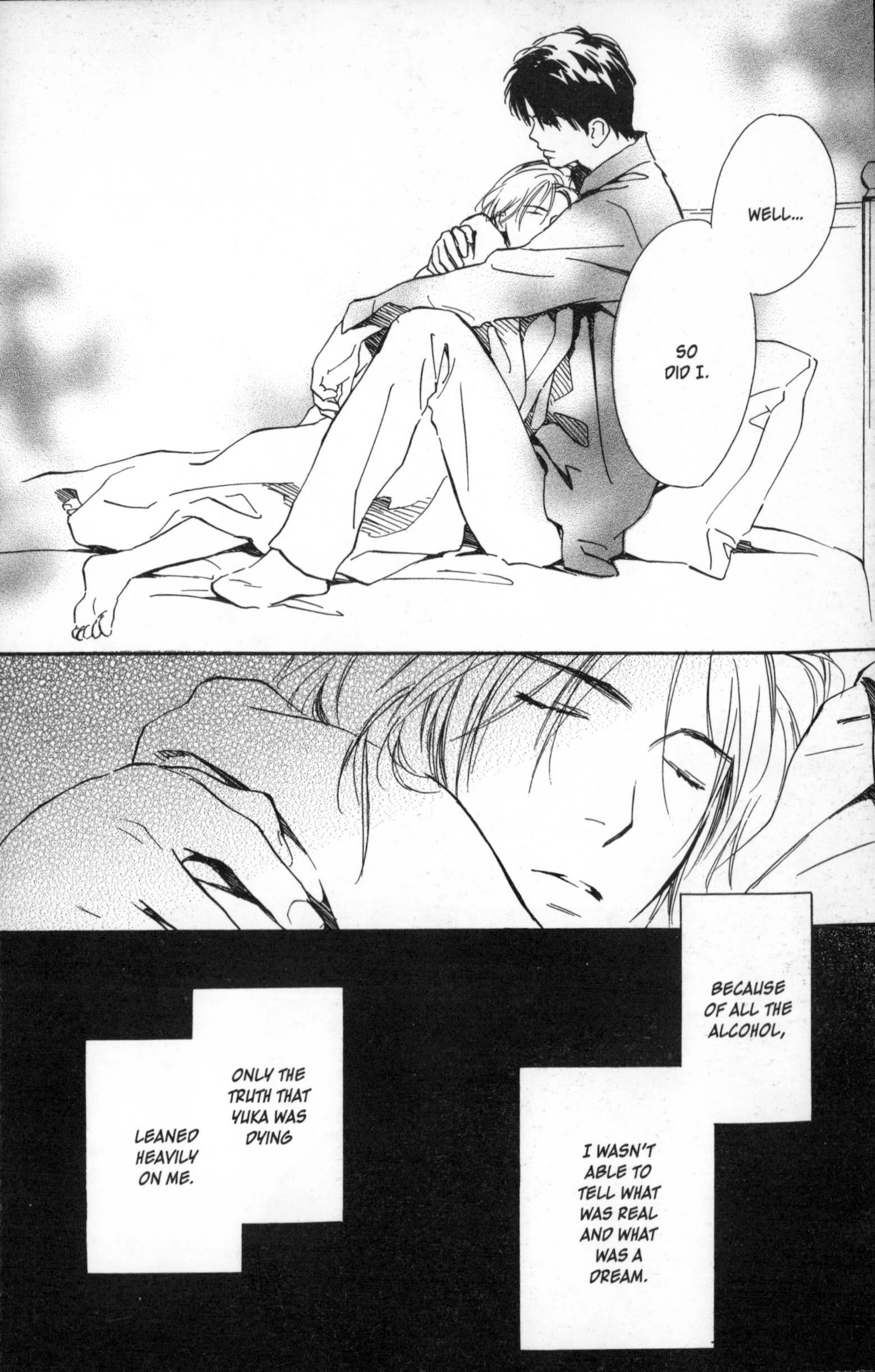
WELL...
SO DID I.
BECAUSE OF ALL THE ALCOHOL,
I WASN'T ABLE TO TELL WHAT WAS REAL AND WHAT WAS A DREAM.
ONLY THE TRUTH THAT YUKA WAS DYING
LEANED HEAVILY ON ME.

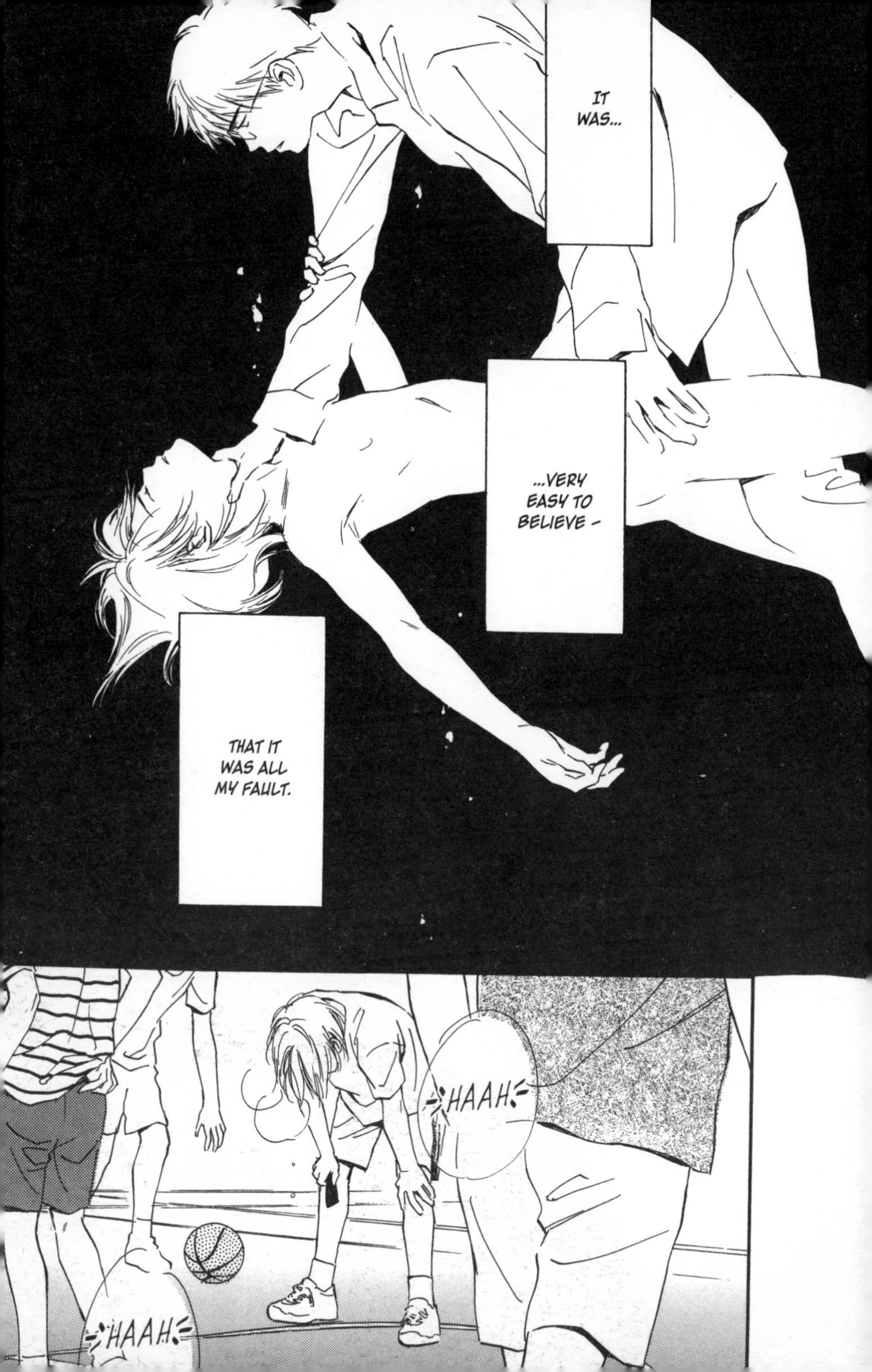
IT WAS...
...VERY EASY TO BELIEVE -
THAT IT WAS ALL MY FAULT.
HAAH
HAAH

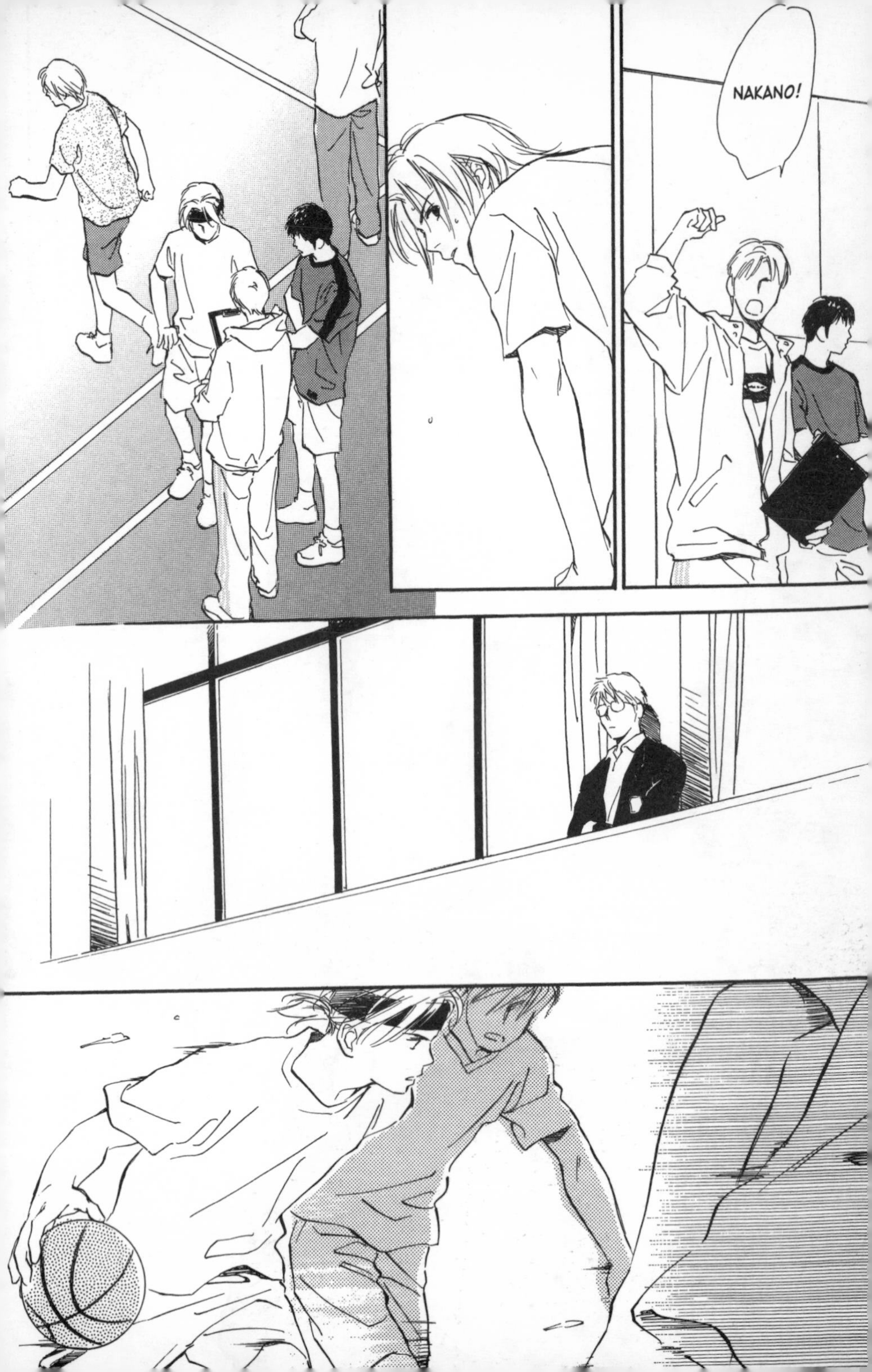
NAKANO!

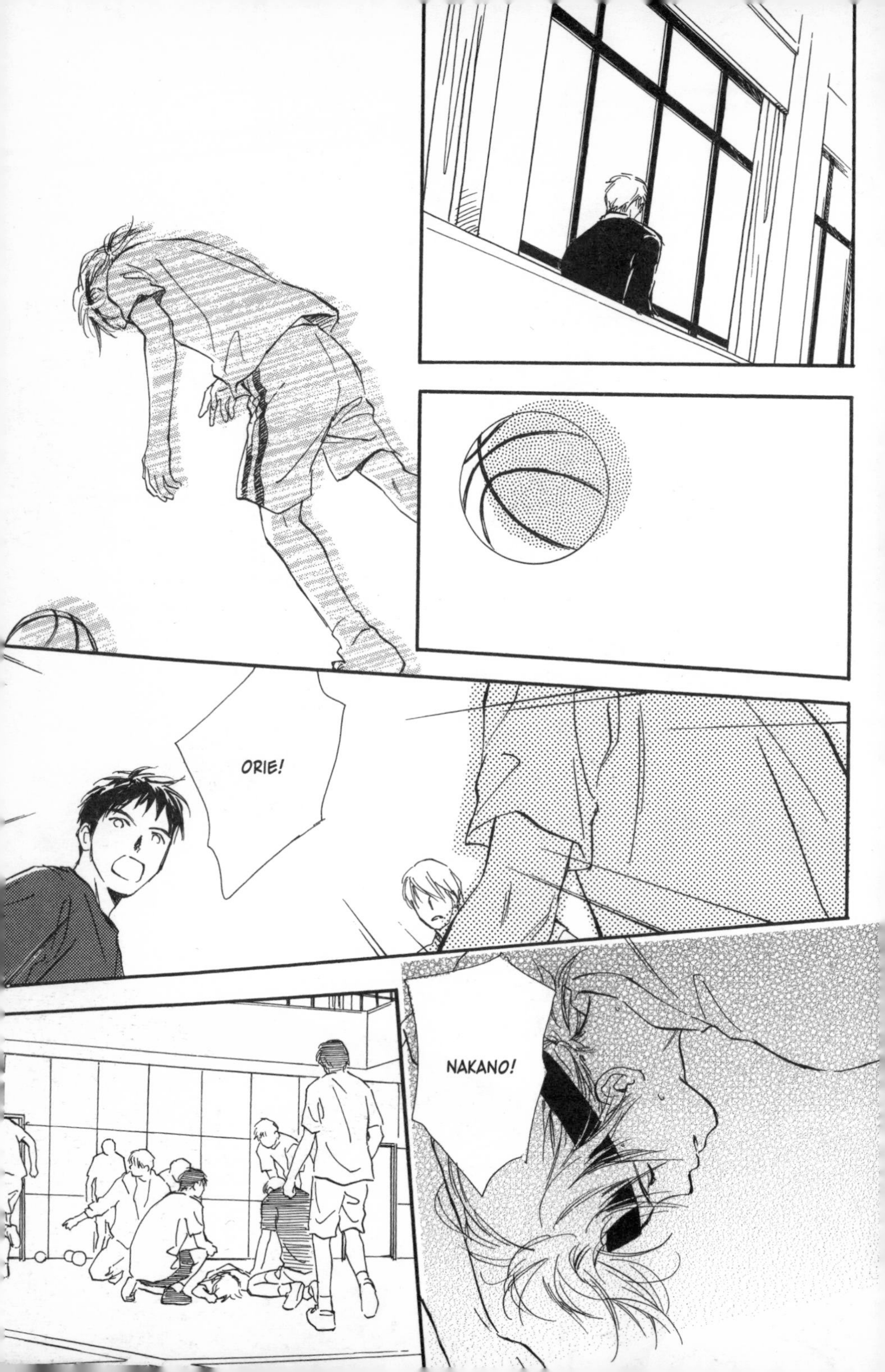
ORIE!
NAKANO!

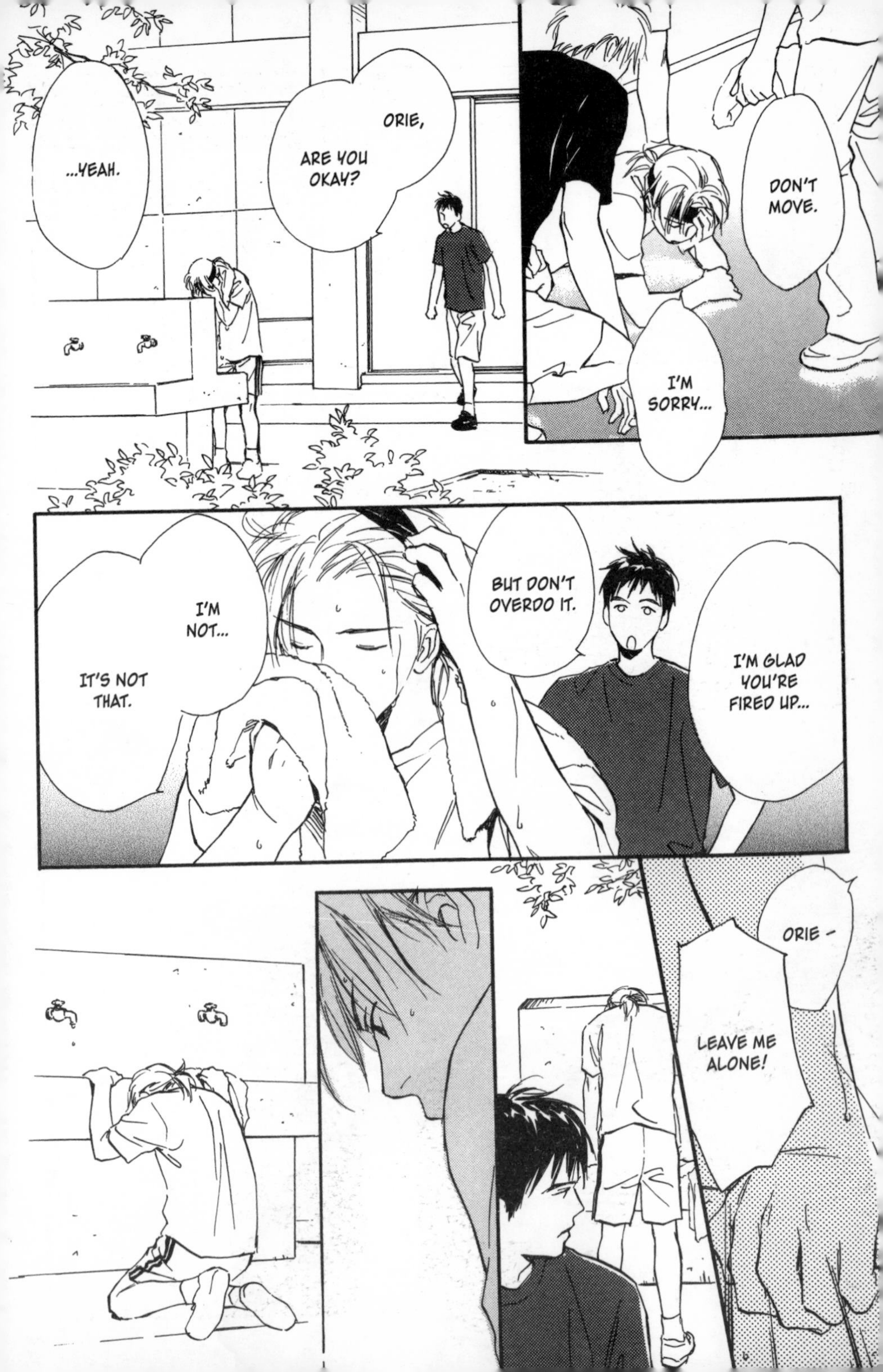
DON'T MOVE.
I'M SORRY...
ORIE,
ARE YOU OKAY?
...YEAH.
I'M GLAD YOU'RE FIRED UP...
BUT DON'T OVERDO IT.
I'M NOT...
IT'S NOT THAT.
ORIE -
LEAVE ME ALONE!

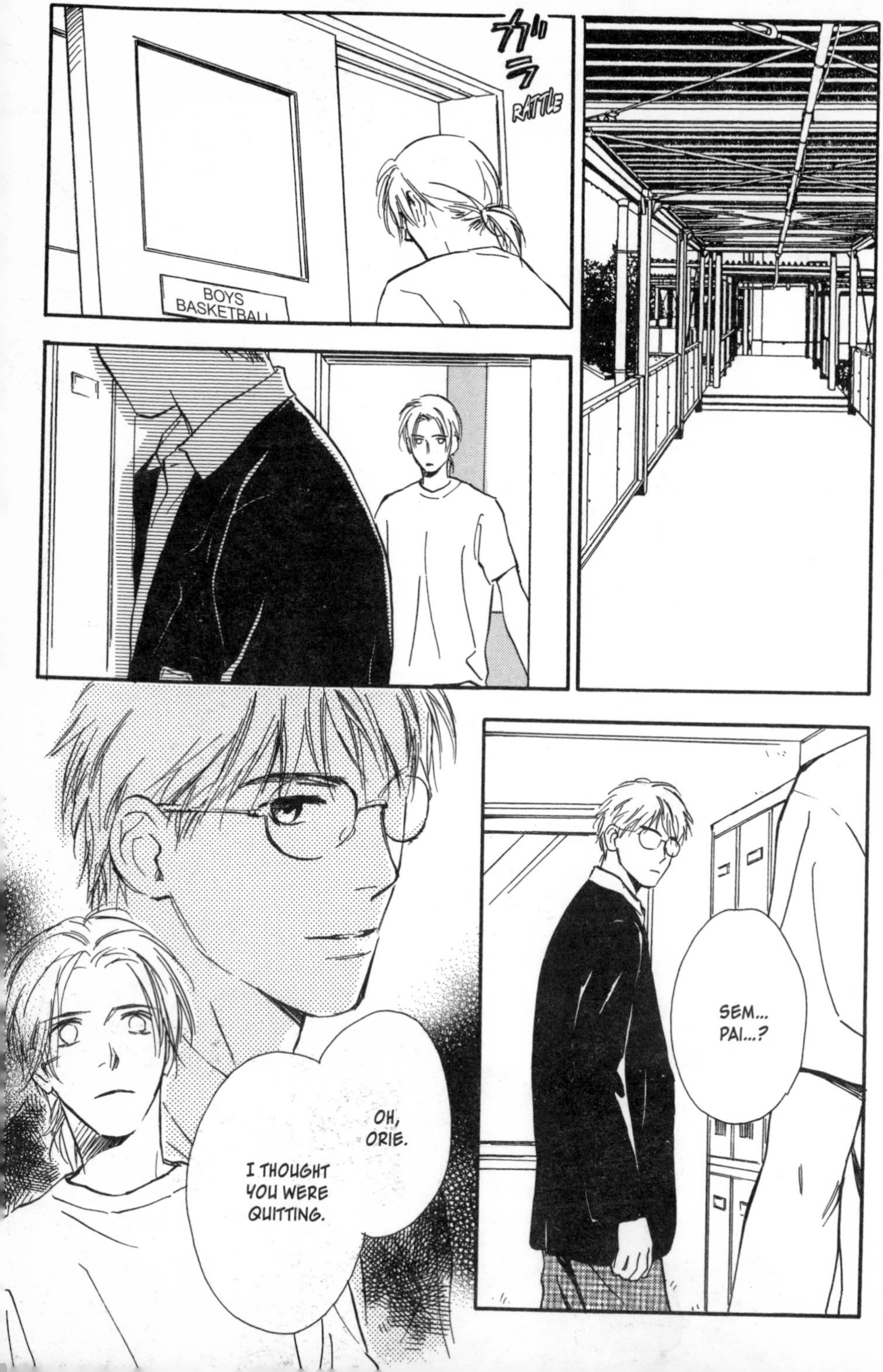
RATTLE
BOYS BASKETBALL
SEM... PAI...?
OH, ORIE.
I THOUGHT YOU WERE QUITTING.

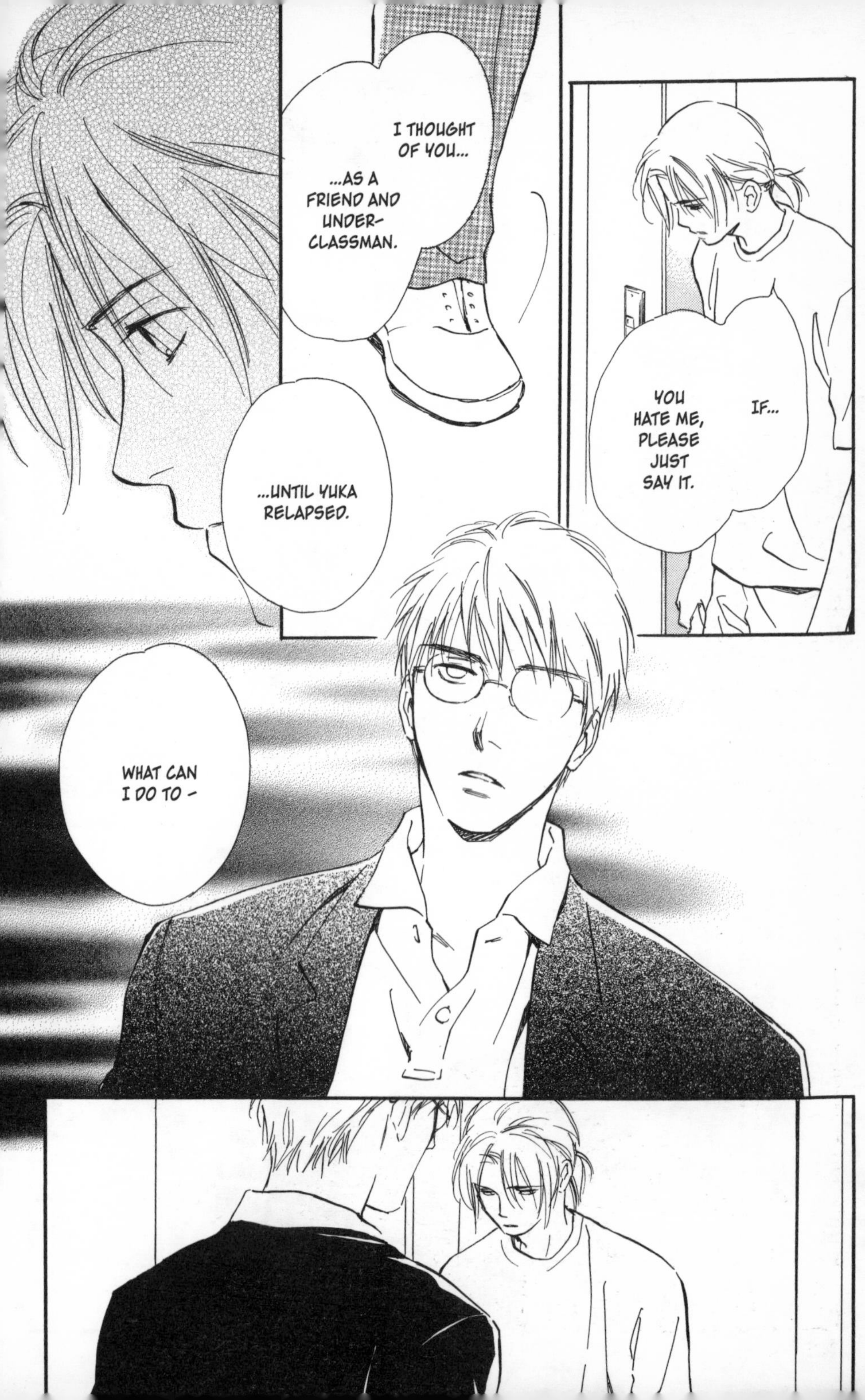
IF... YOU HATE ME, PLEASE JUST SAY IT.
I THOUGHT OF YOU...
...AS A FRIEND AND UNDER-CLASSMAN.
...UNTIL YUKA RELAPSED.
WHAT CAN I DO TO -

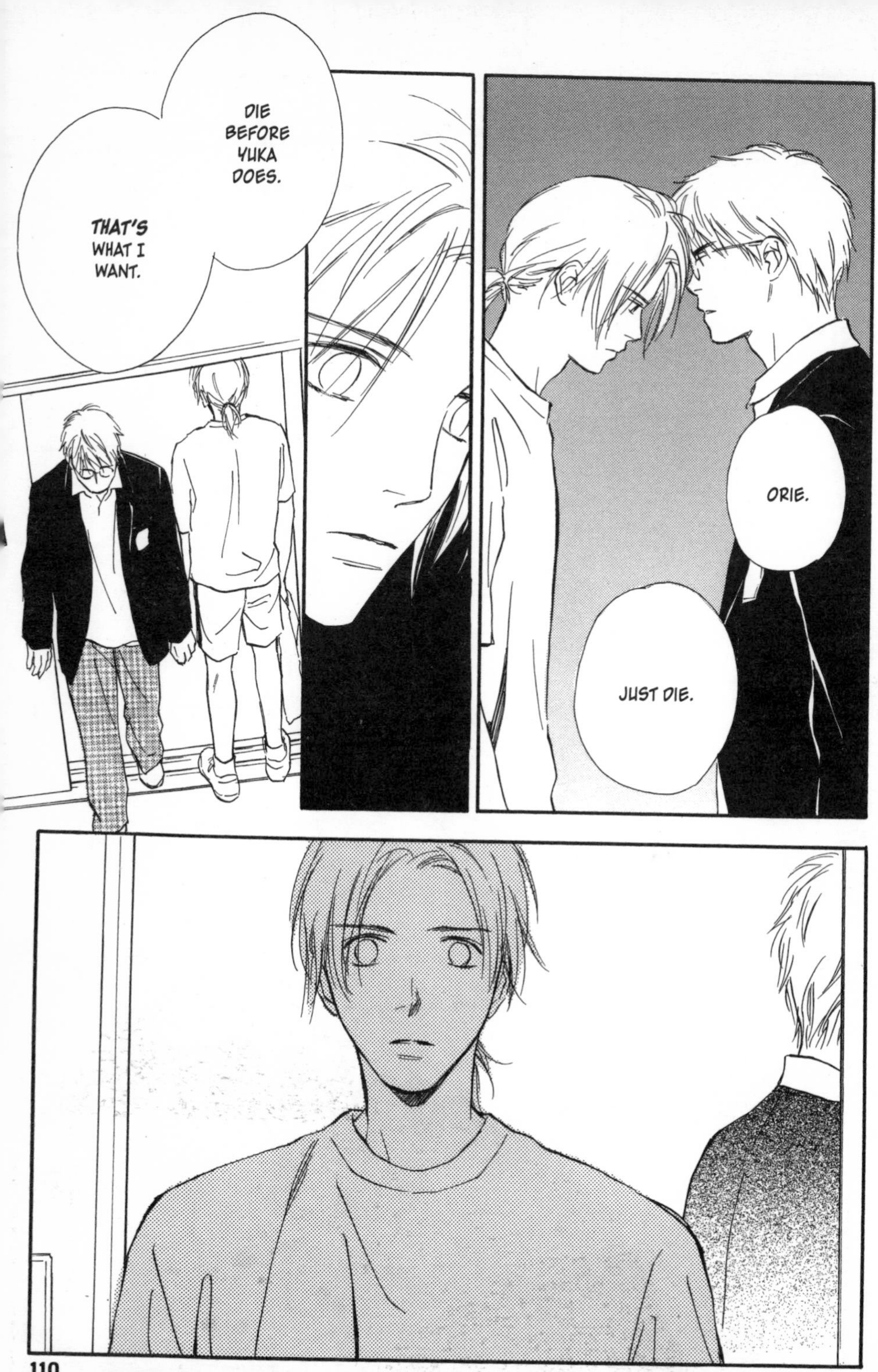
ORIE.
JUST DIE.
DIE BEFORE YUKA DOES.
THAT'S WHAT I WANT.

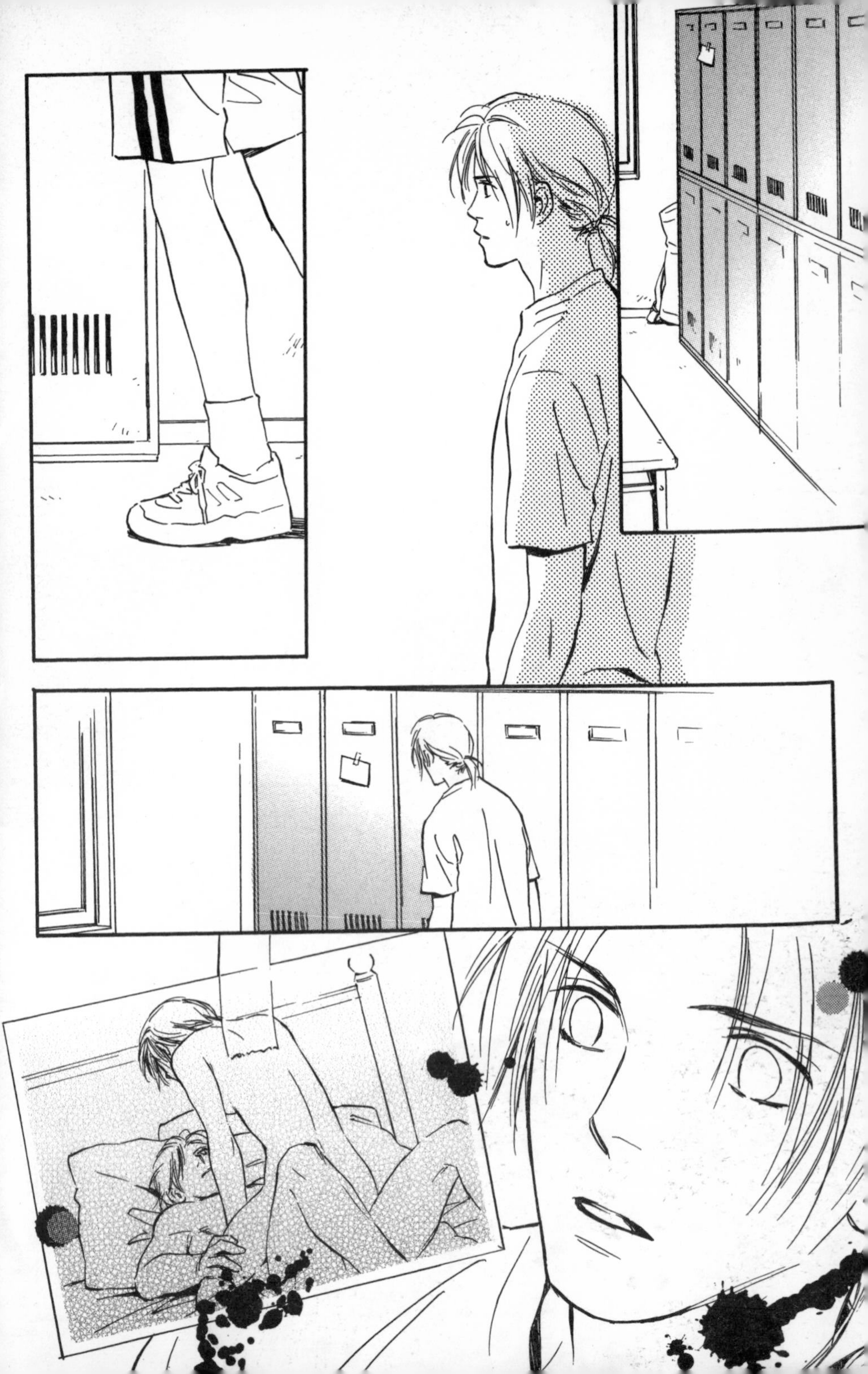

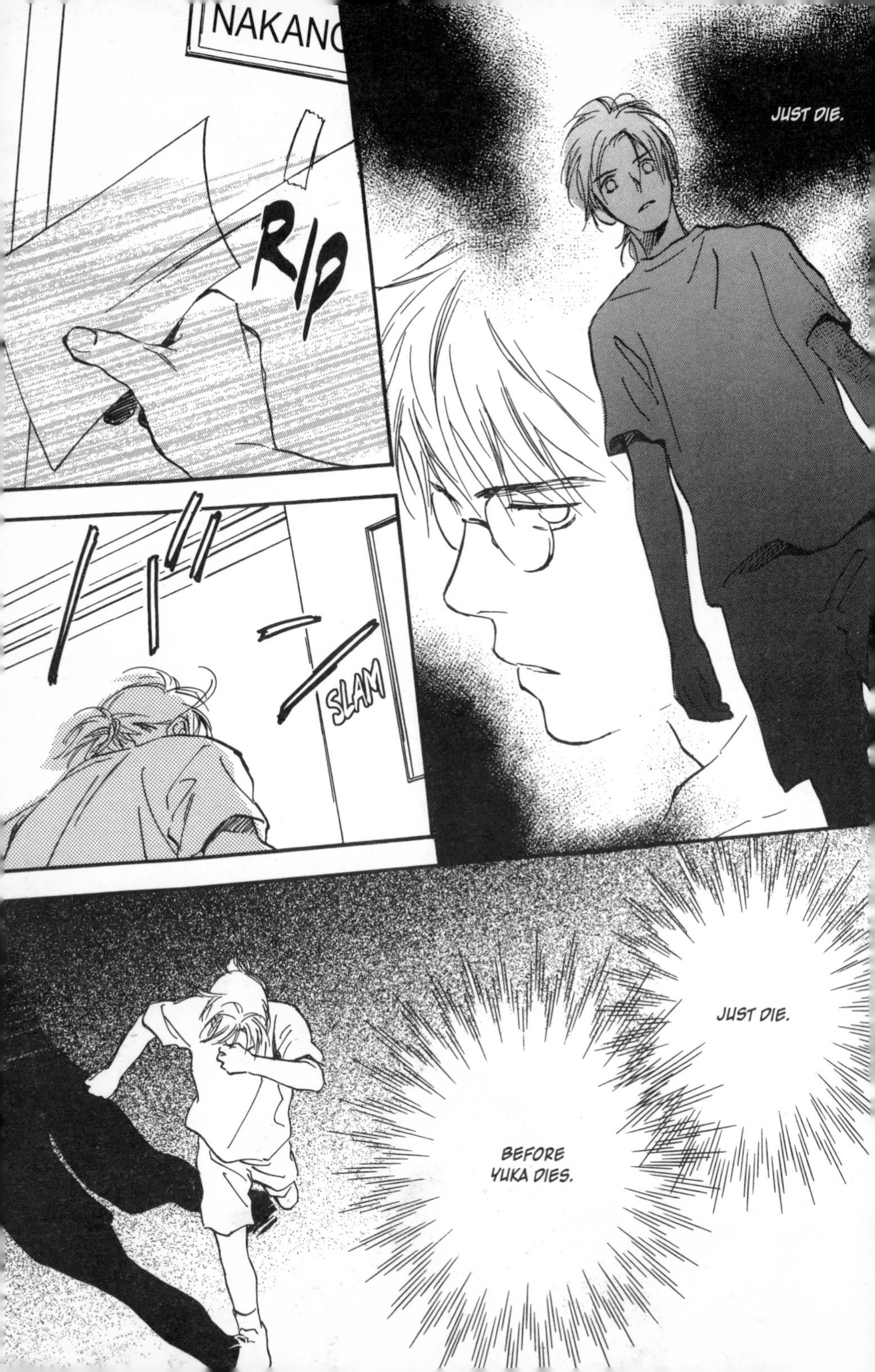
JUST DIE.
NAKANO
RIP
SLAM
JUST DIE.
BEFORE YUKA DIES.

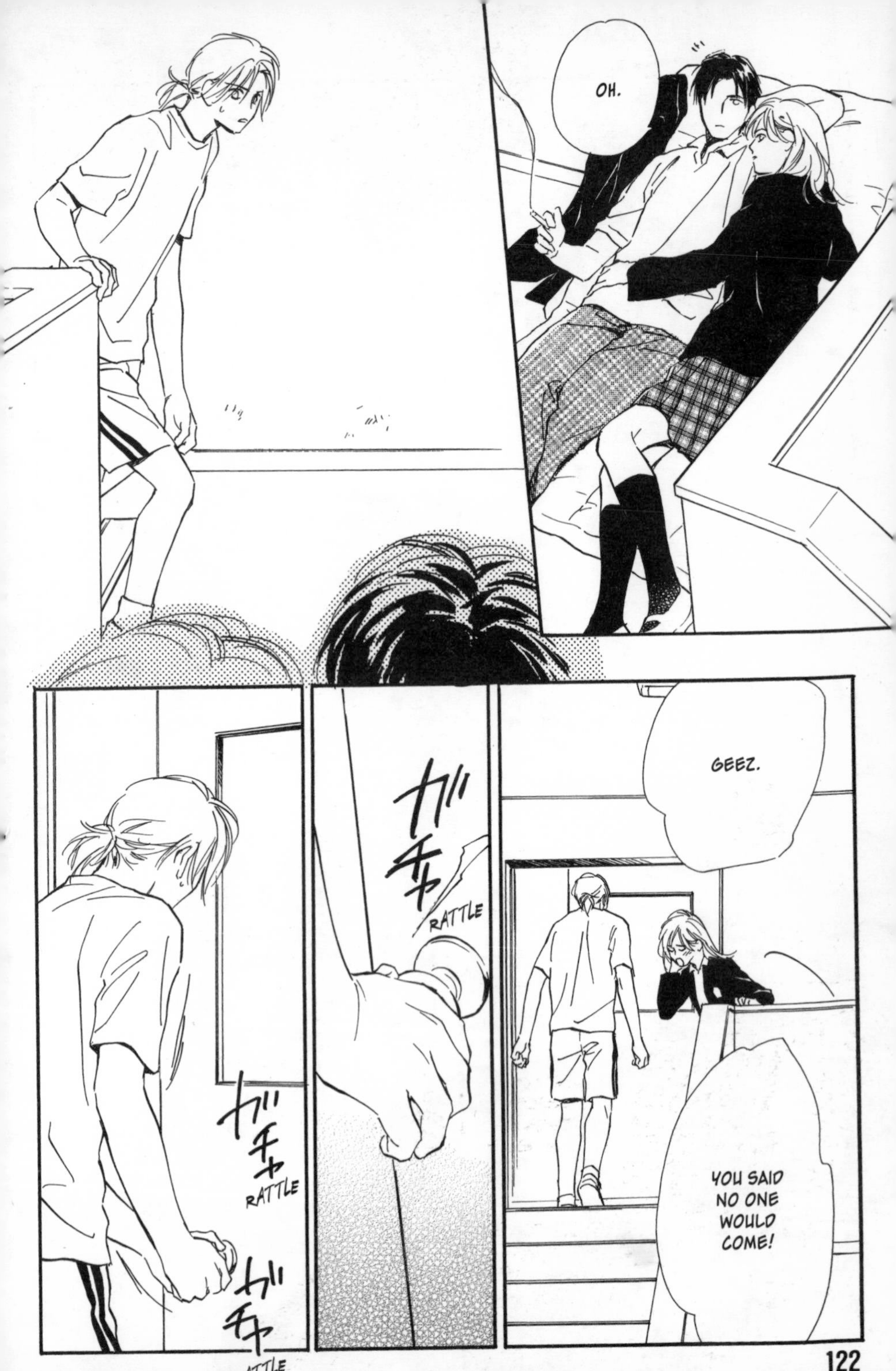
OH.
GEEZ.
YOU SAID NO ONE WOULD COME!
ガチャ
RATTLE
ガチャ
RATTLE
ガチャ
RATTLE

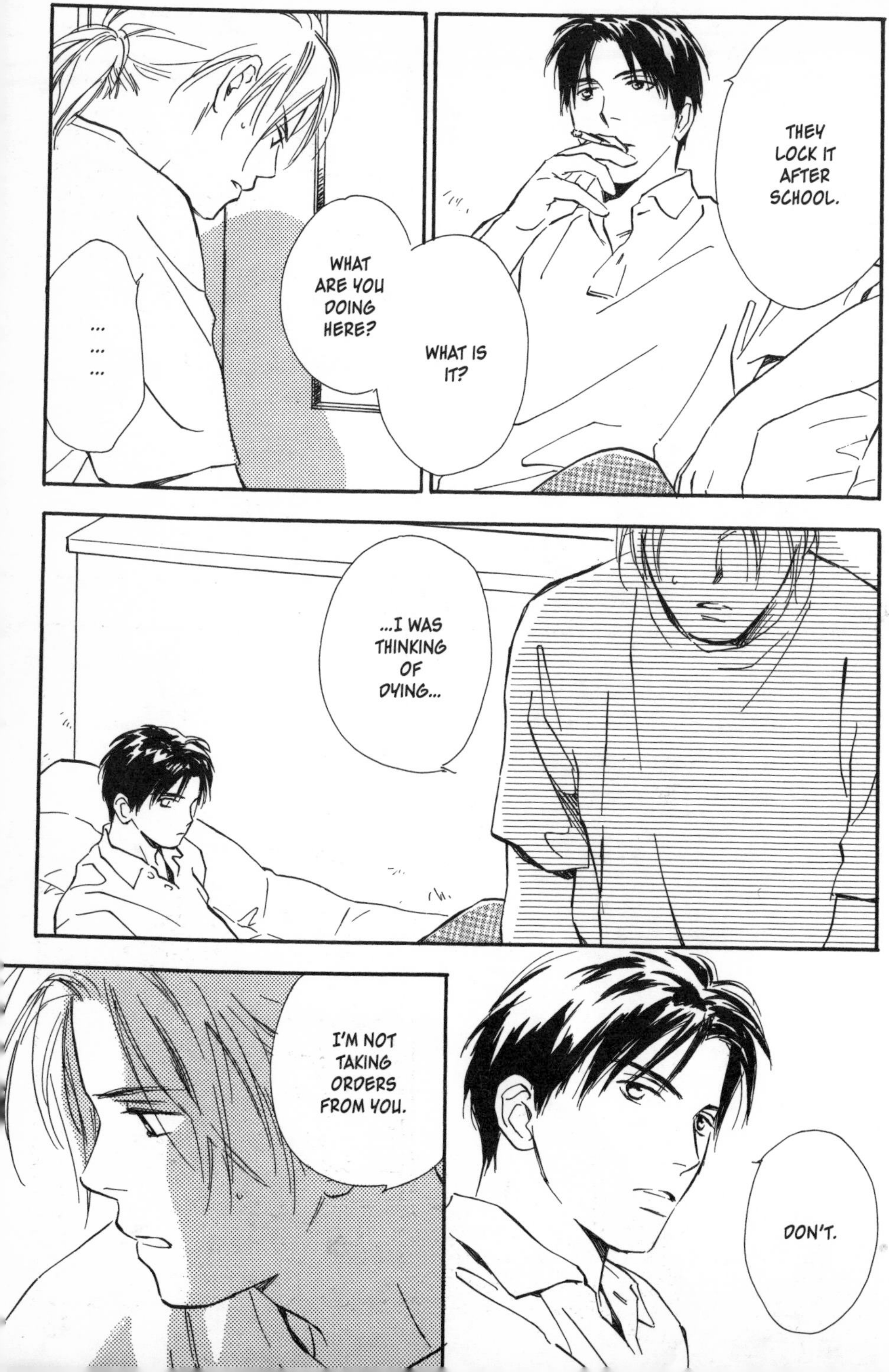
THEY LOCK IT AFTER SCHOOL.
WHAT ARE YOU DOING HERE?
WHAT IS IT?
... ...
...I WAS THINKING OF DYING...
DON'T.
I'M NOT TAKING ORDERS FROM YOU.

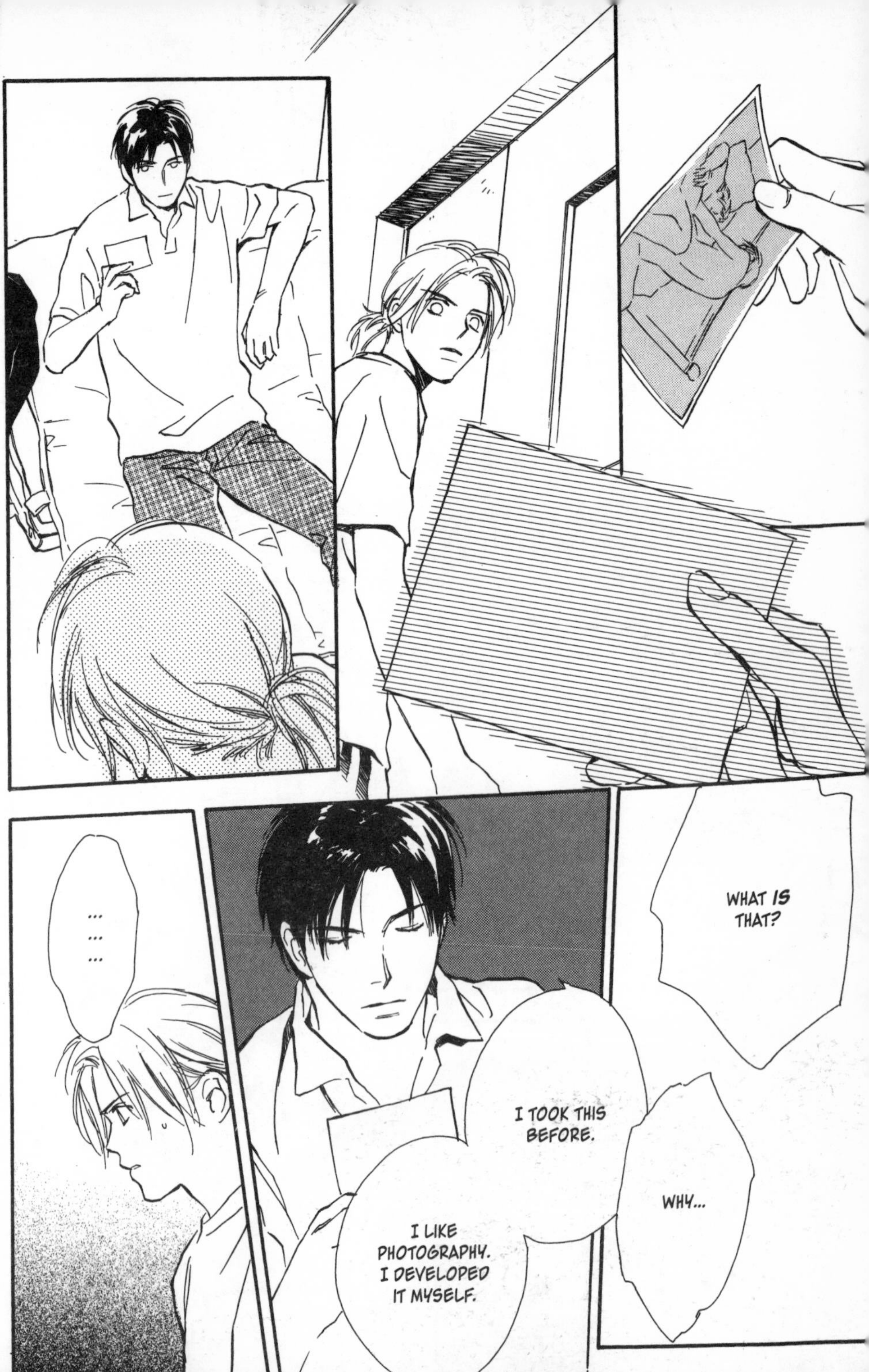
WHAT *IS* THAT?
WHY...
I TOOK THIS BEFORE.
I LIKE PHOTOGRAPHY. I DEVELOPED IT MYSELF.
... ...

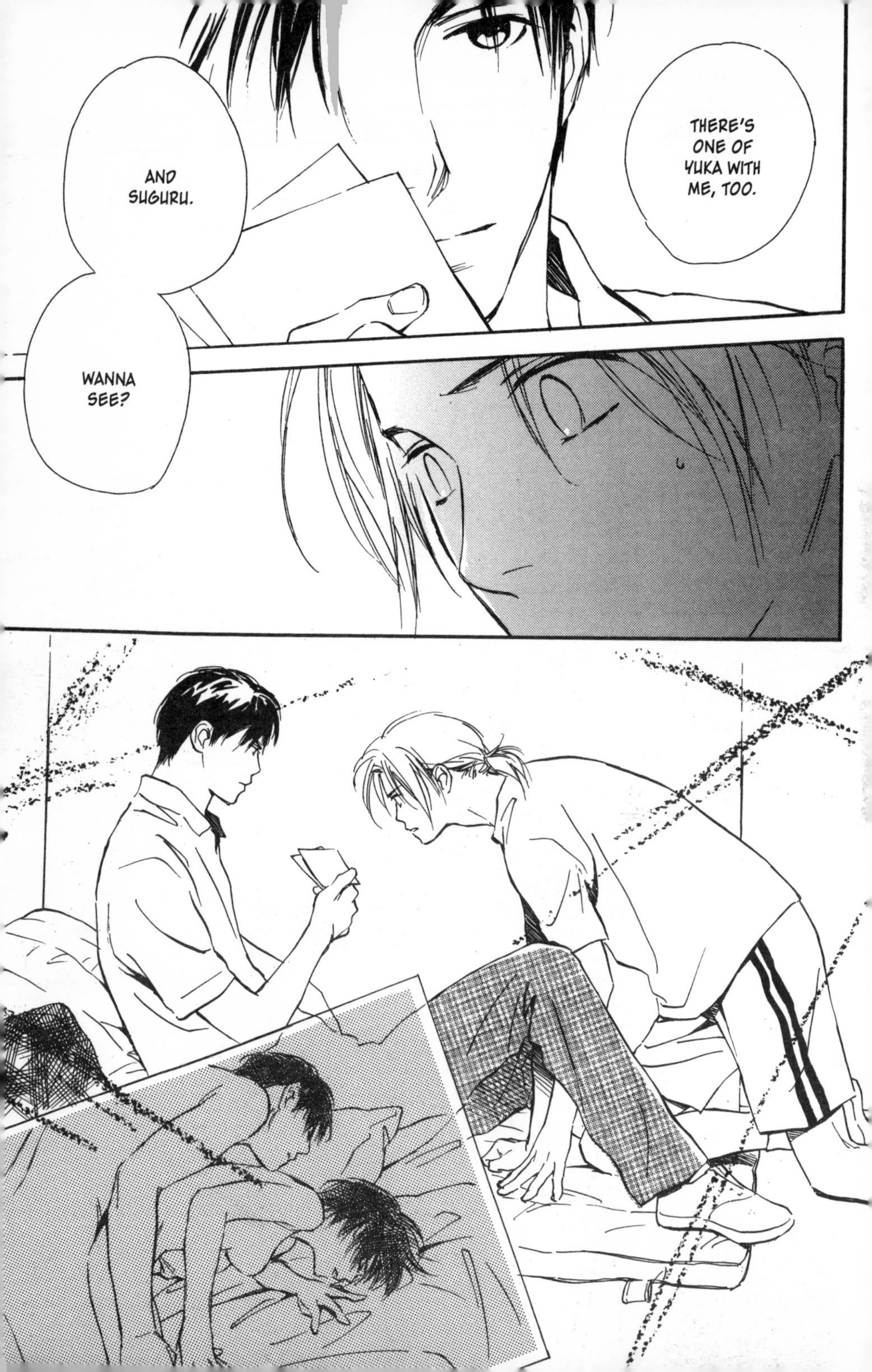
THERE'S ONE OF YUKA WITH ME, TOO.
AND SUGURU.
WANNA SEE?

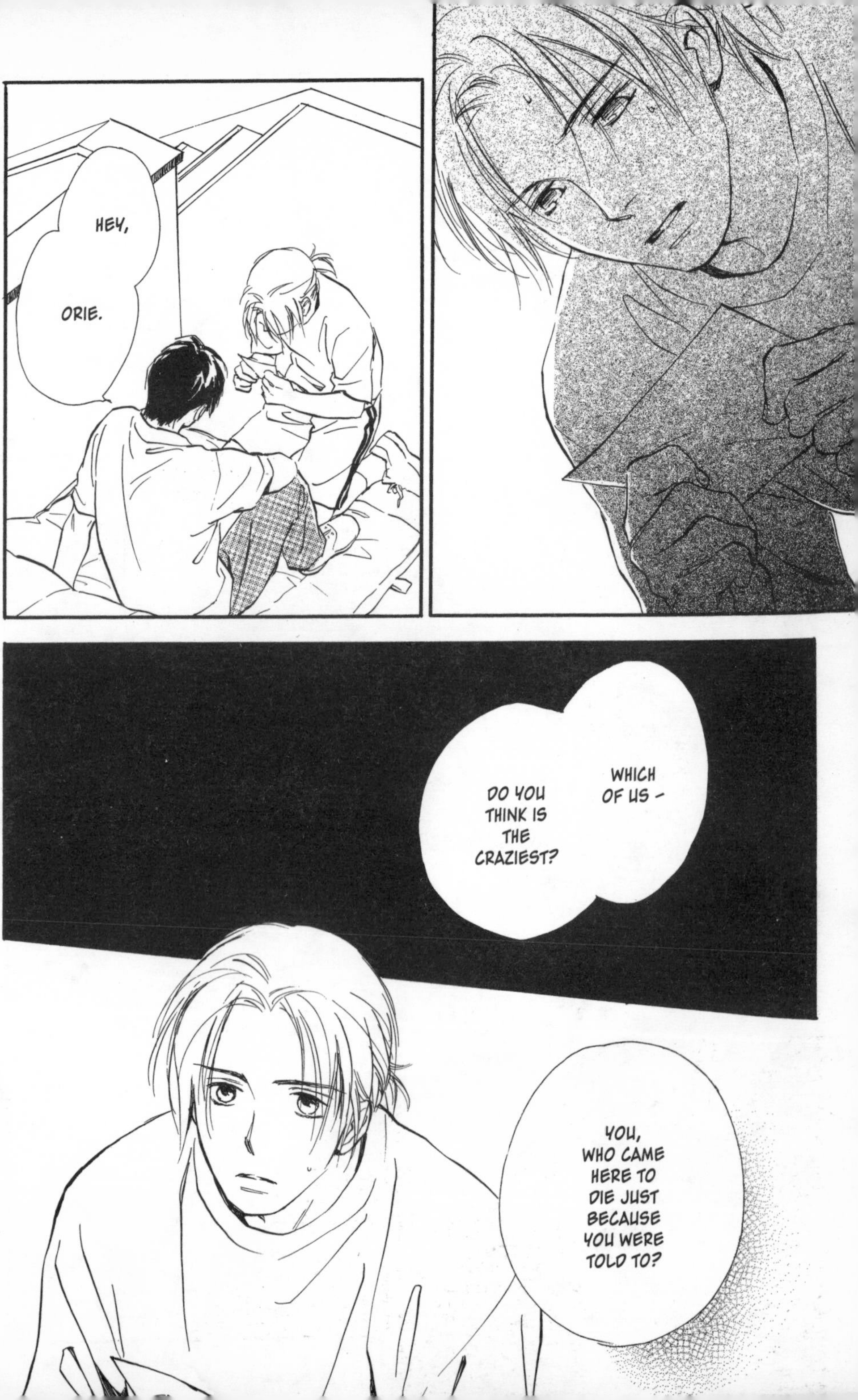
HEY,
ORIE.
WHICH OF US -
DO YOU THINK IS THE CRAZIEST?
YOU, WHO CAME HERE TO DIE JUST BECAUSE YOU WERE TOLD TO?

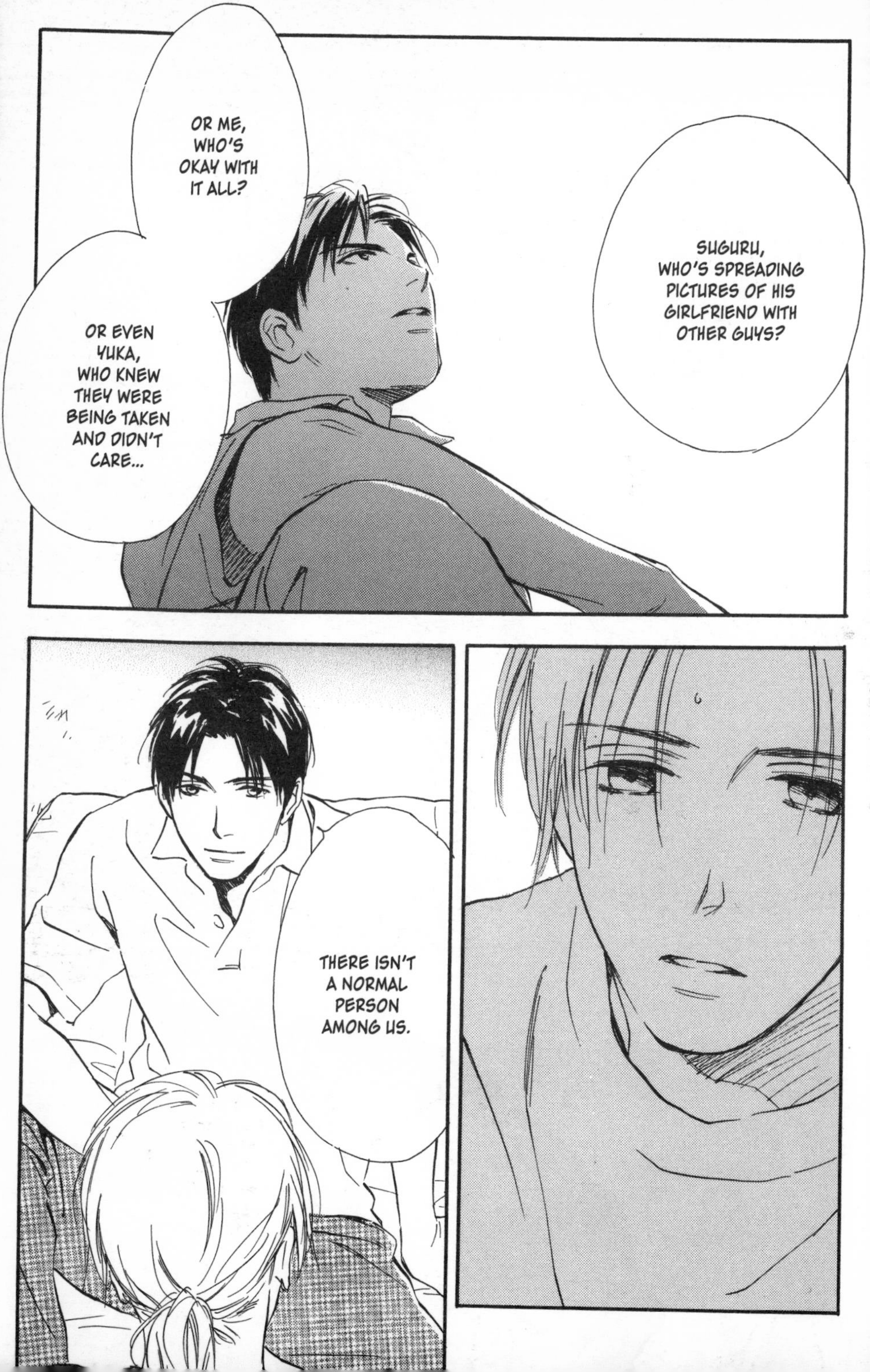
SUGURU, WHO'S SPREADING PICTURES OF HIS GIRLFRIEND WITH OTHER GUYS?
OR ME, WHO'S OKAY WITH IT ALL?
OR EVEN YUKA, WHO KNEW THEY WERE BEING TAKEN AND DIDN'T CARE...
THERE ISN'T A NORMAL PERSON AMONG US.

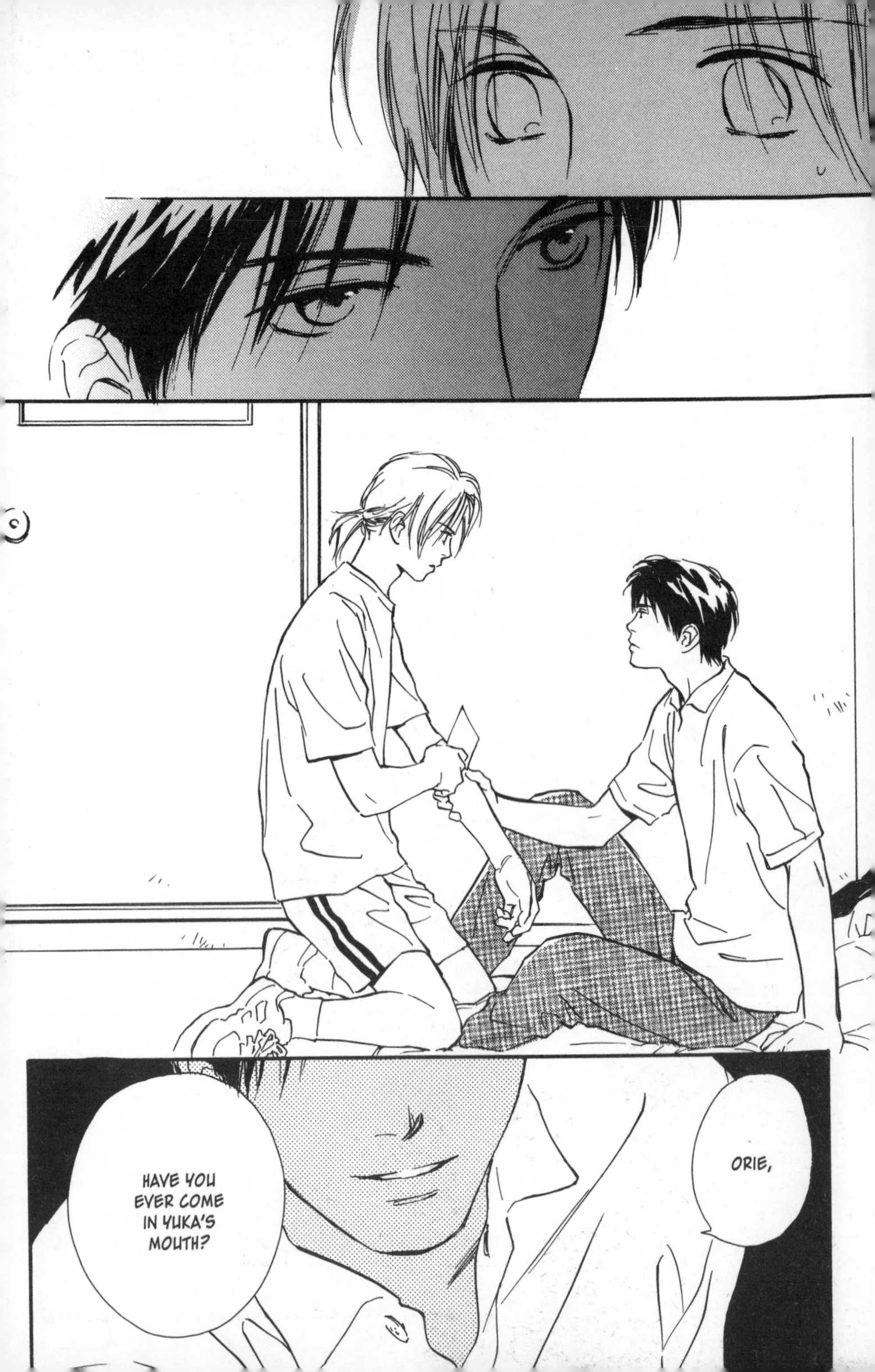
ORIE,
HAVE YOU EVER COME IN YUKA'S MOUTH?

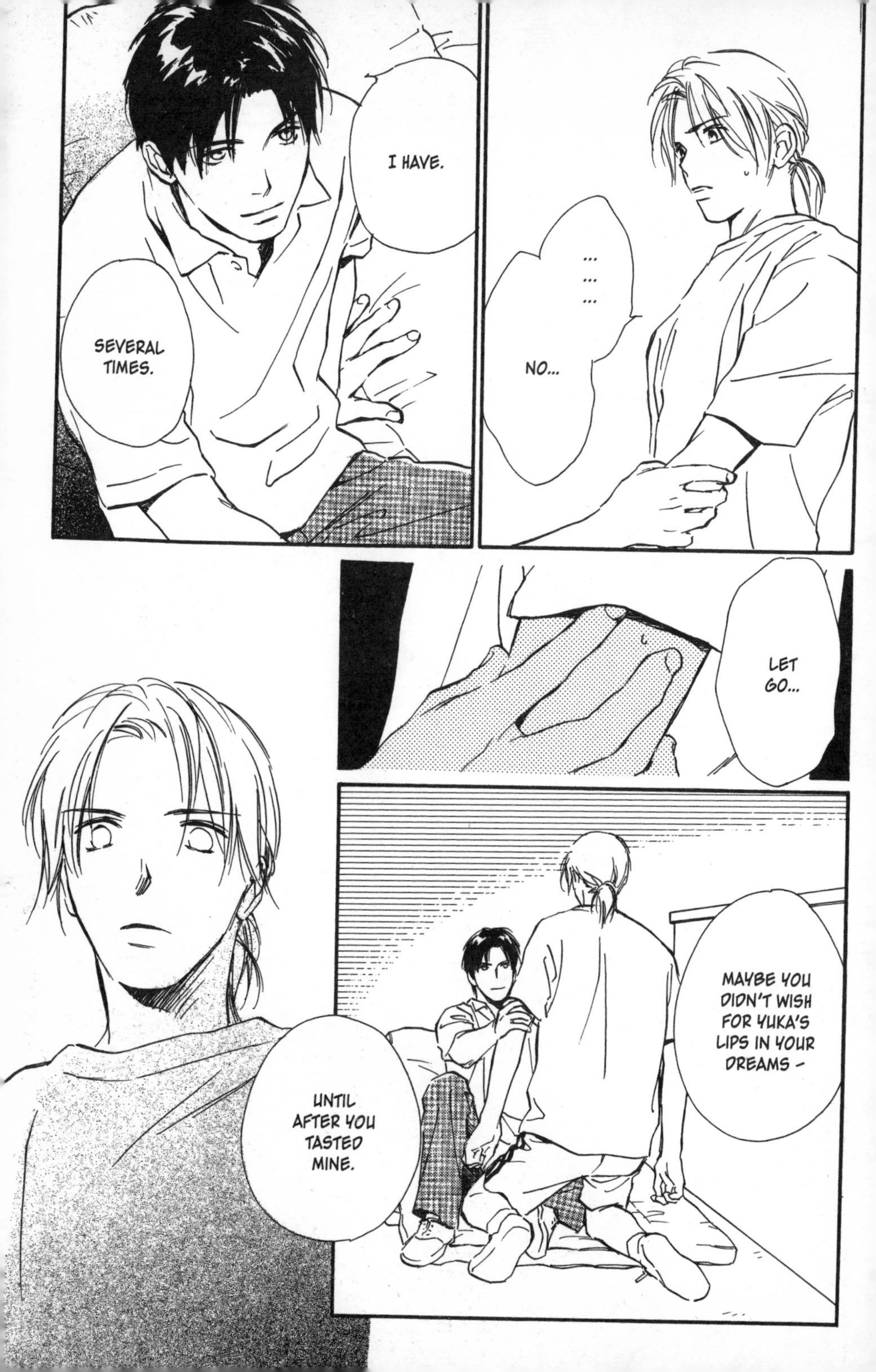

... ... NO...
I HAVE.
SEVERAL TIMES.
LET GO...
MAYBE YOU DIDN'T WISH FOR YUKA'S LIPS IN YOUR DREAMS -
UNTIL AFTER YOU TASTED MINE.

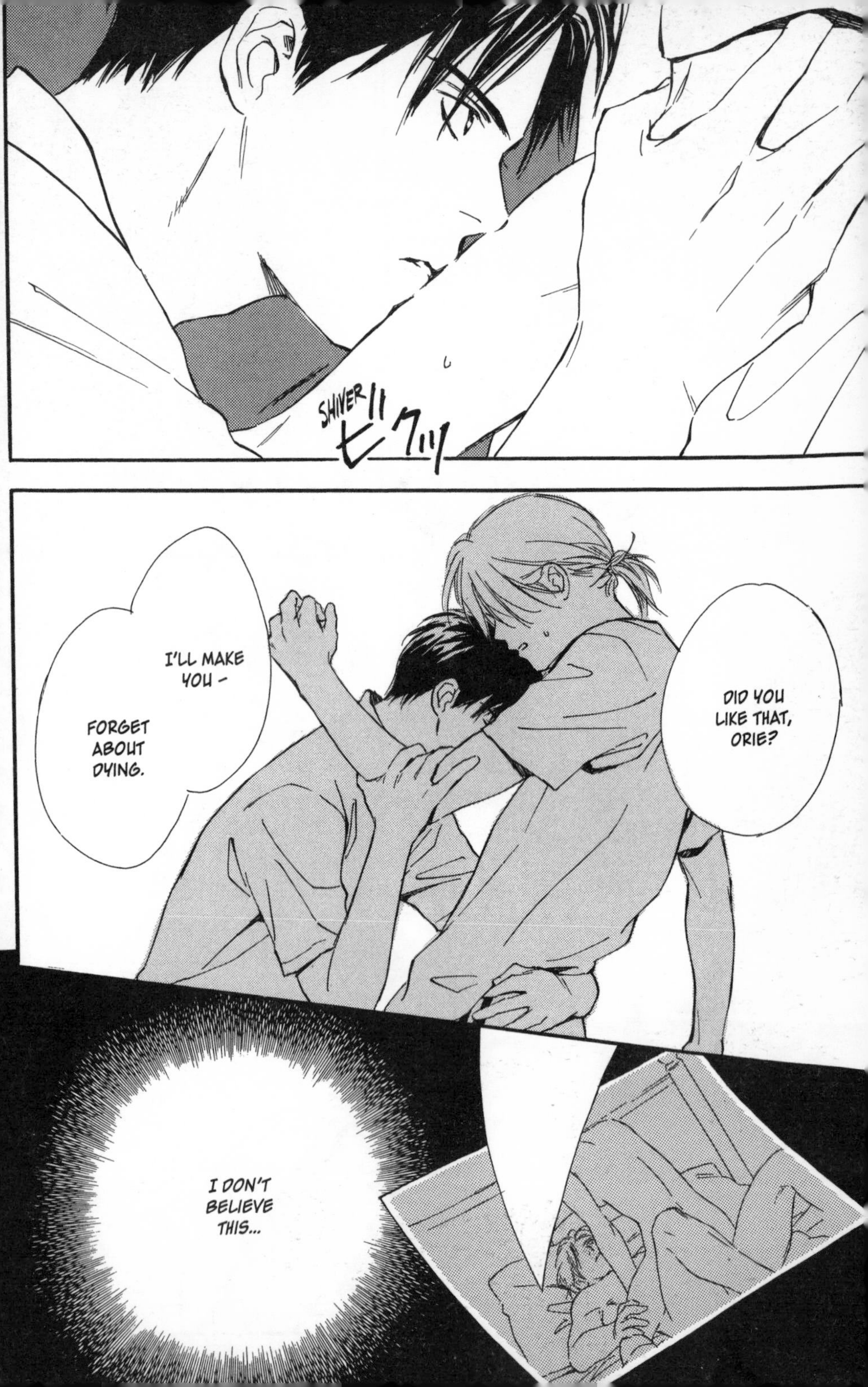
SHIVER
ビクッ
DID YOU LIKE THAT, ORIE?
I'LL MAKE YOU -
FORGET ABOUT DYING.
I DON'T BELIEVE THIS...

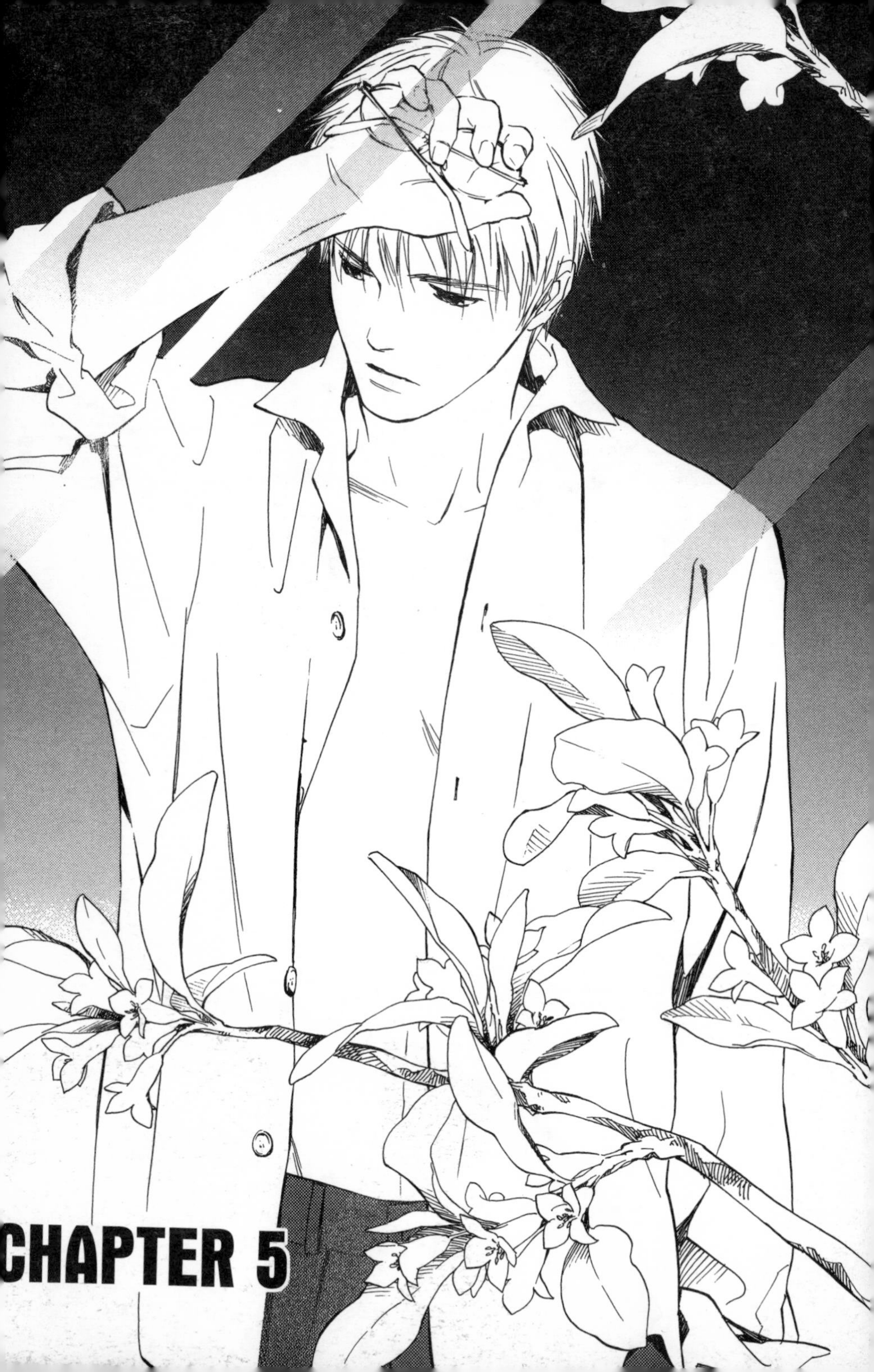
CHAPTER 5

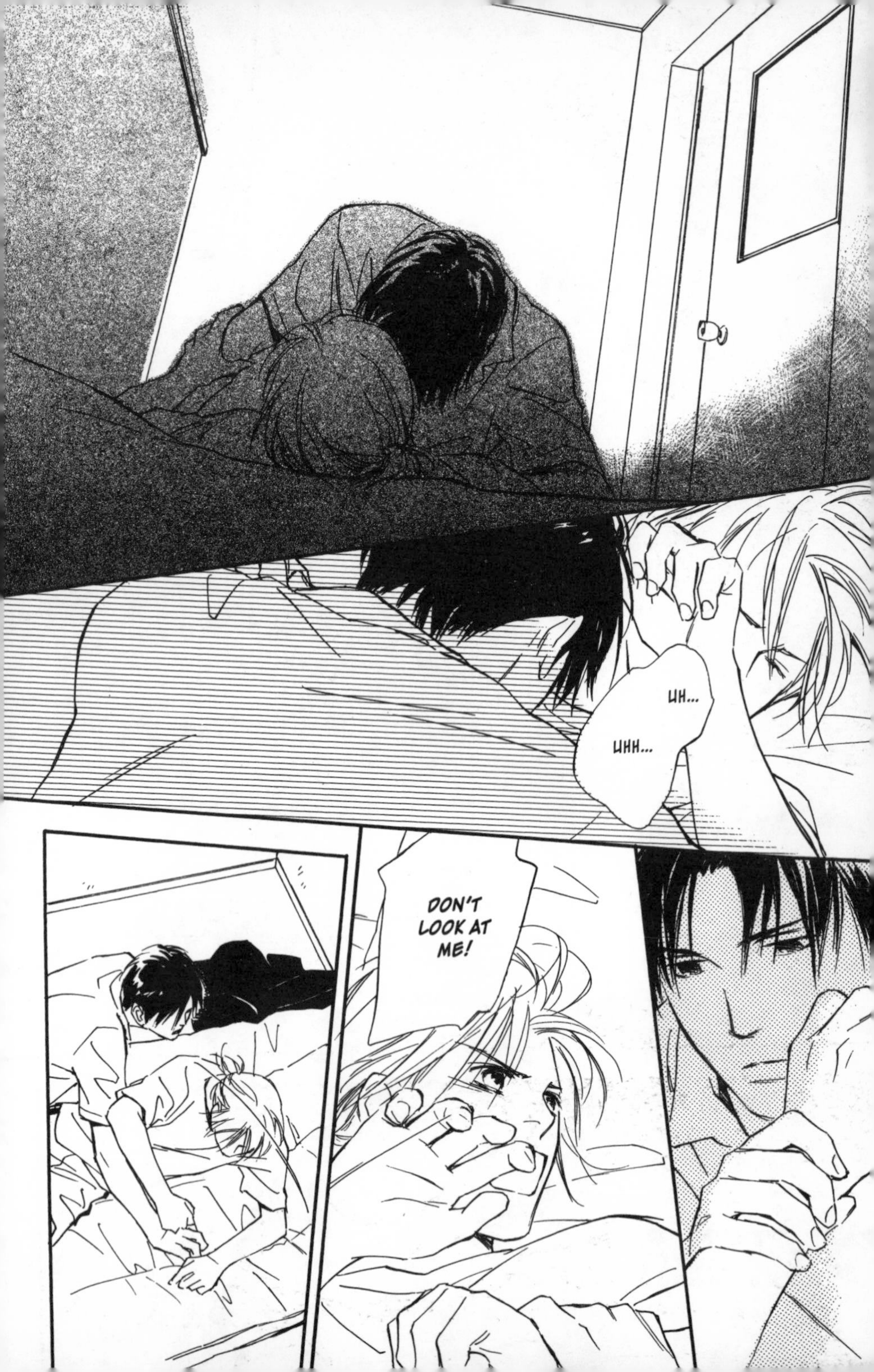
UH...
UHH...
DON'T LOOK AT ME!

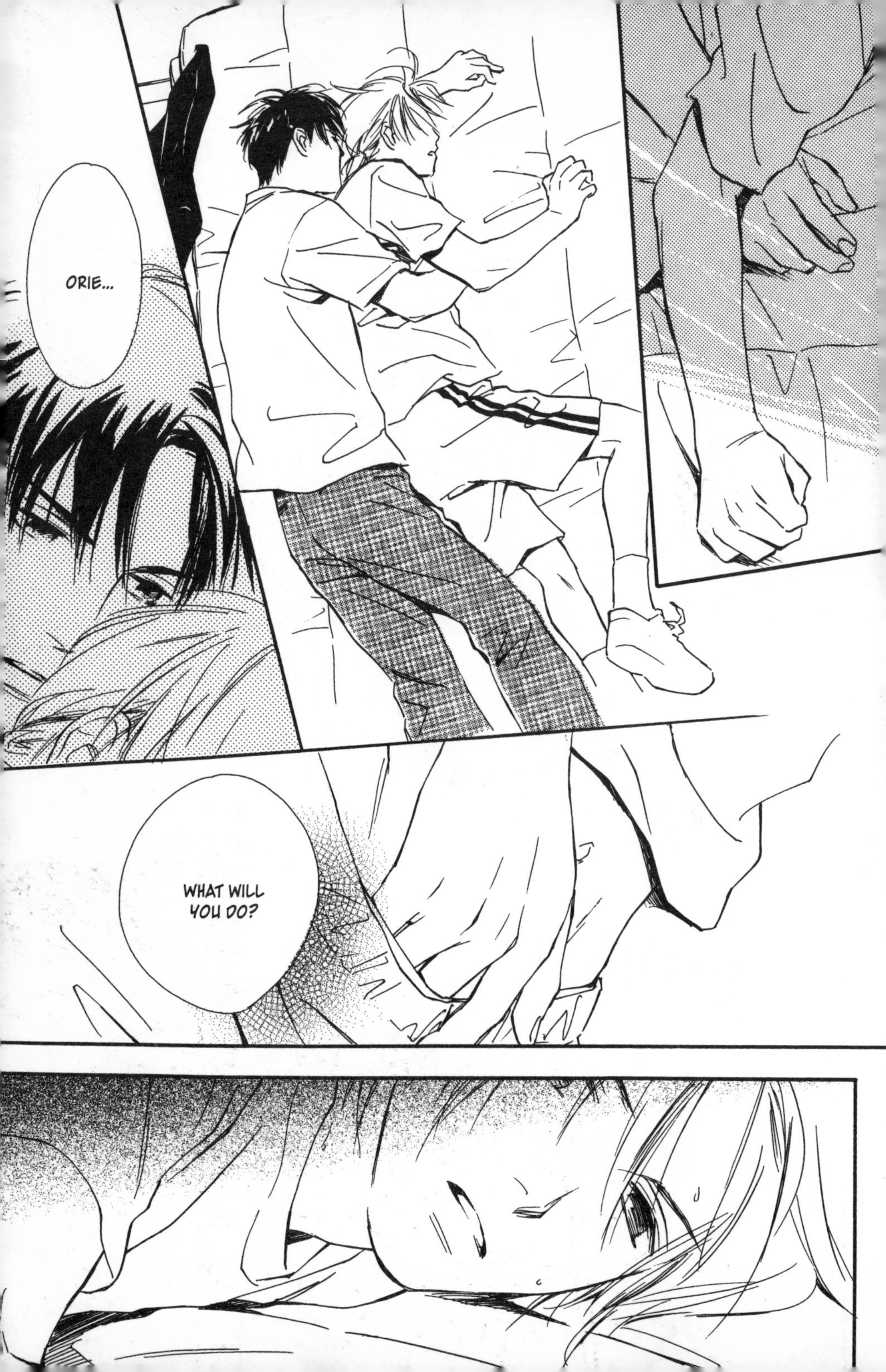
ORIE...
WHAT WILL YOU DO?

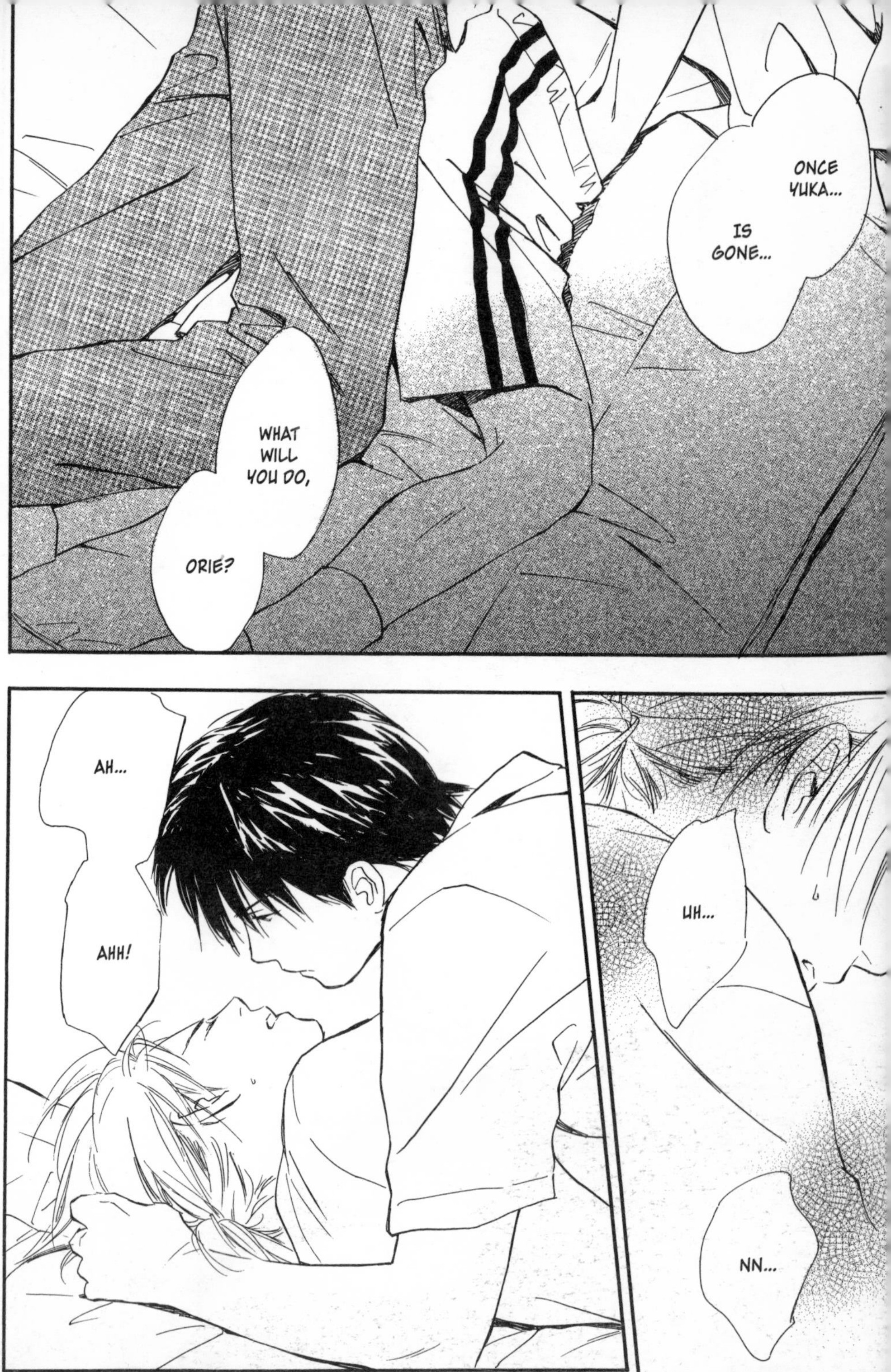
ONCE YUKA...
IS GONE...
WHAT WILL YOU DO,
ORIE?
UH...
NN...
AH...
AHH!

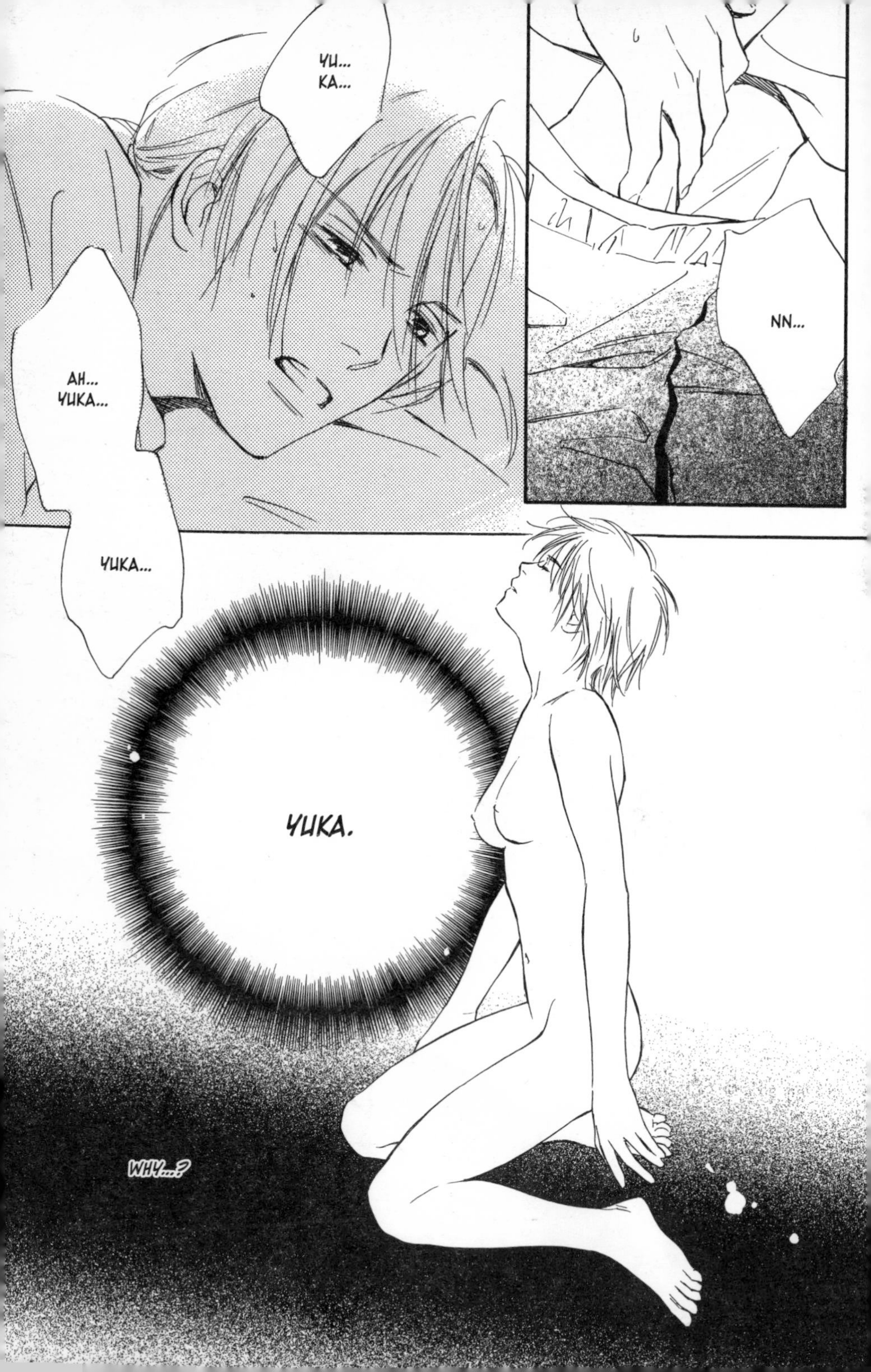
NN...
YU... KA...
AH... YUKA...
YUKA...
YUKA.
WHY...?

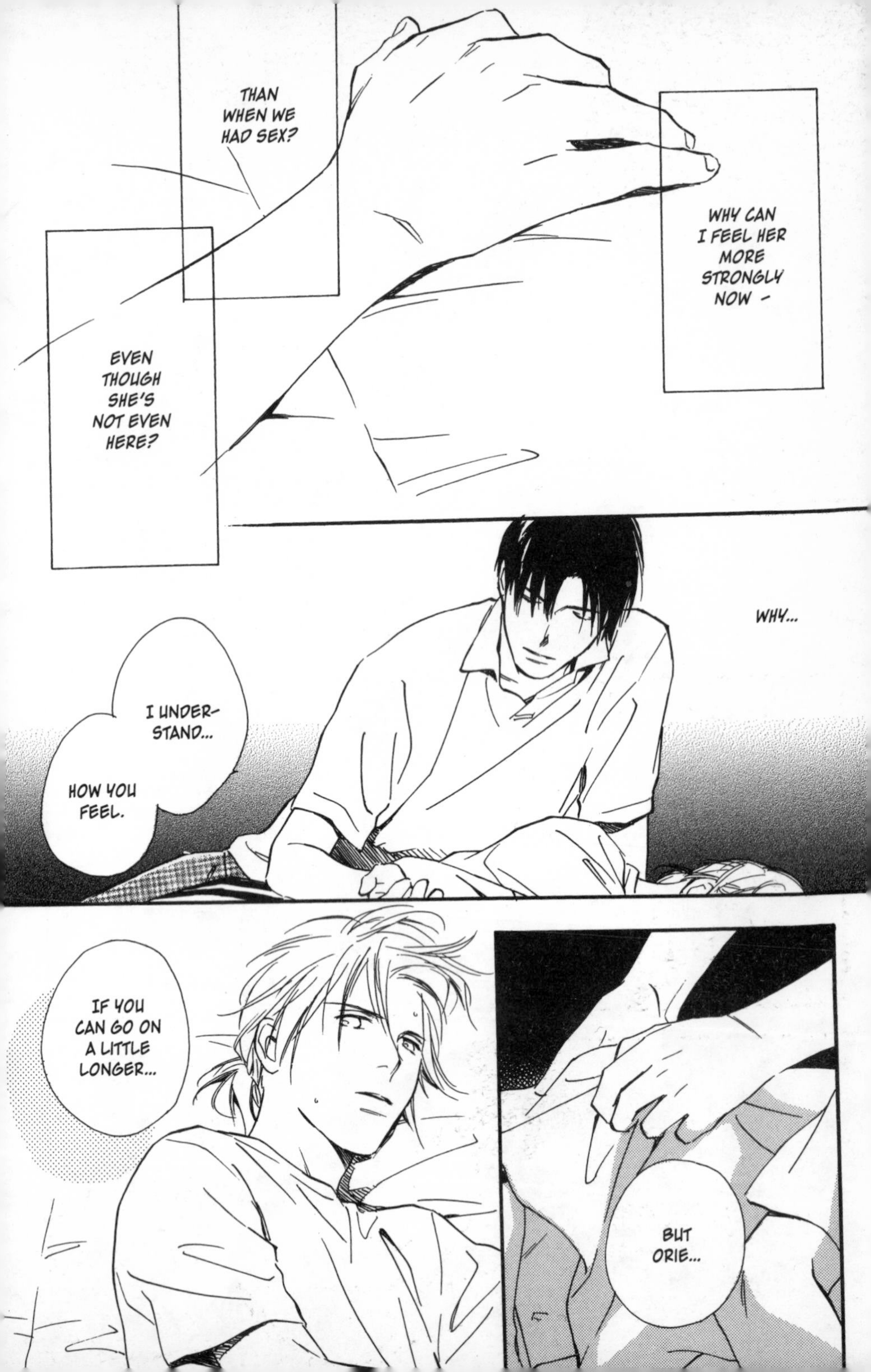
WHY CAN I FEEL HER MORE STRONGLY NOW -
THAN WHEN WE HAD SEX?
EVEN THOUGH SHE'S NOT EVEN HERE?
WHY...
I UNDER-STAND...
HOW YOU FEEL.
BUT ORIE...
IF YOU CAN GO ON A LITTLE LONGER...

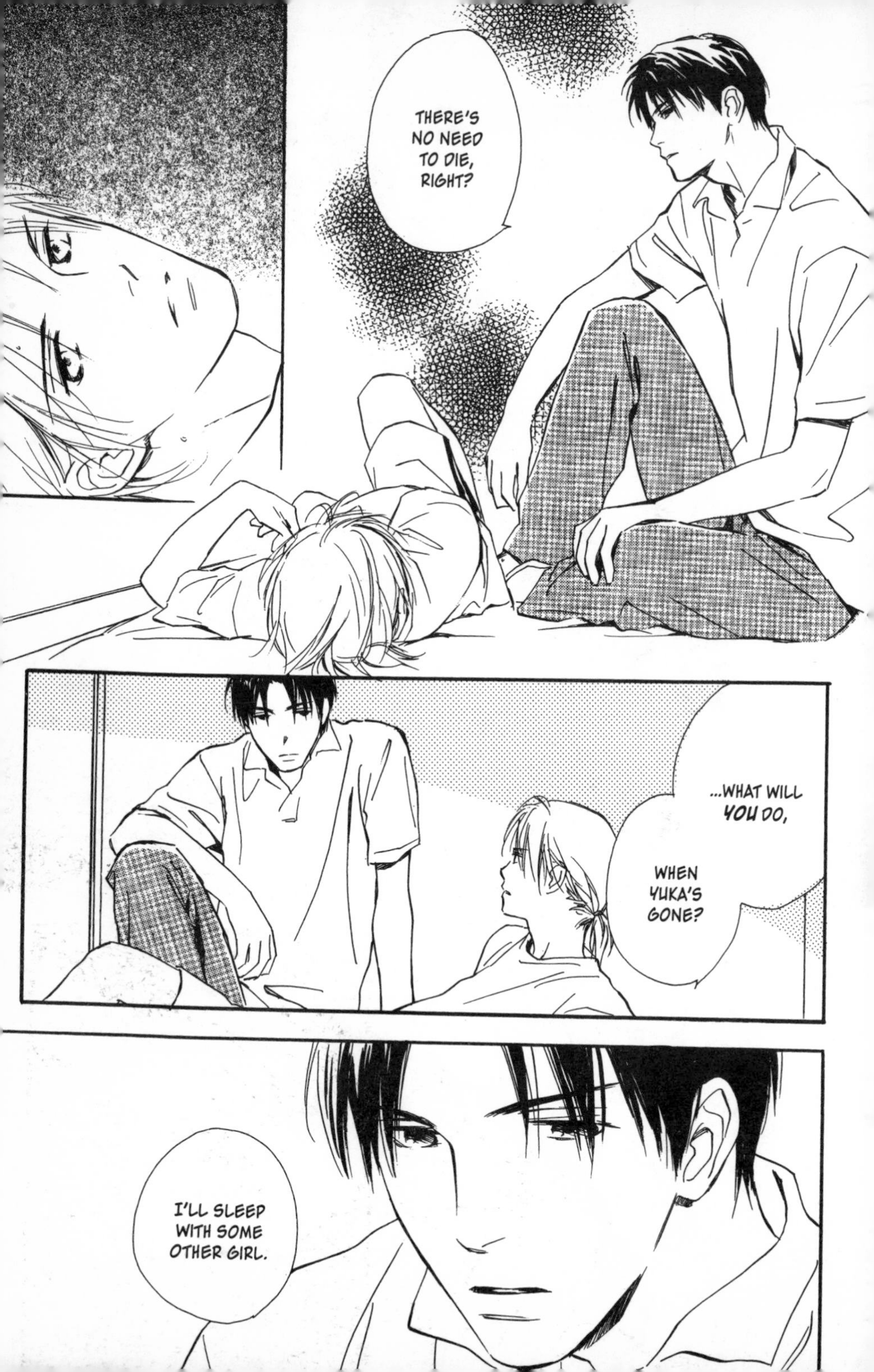
THERE'S NO NEED TO DIE, RIGHT?
...WHAT WILL *YOU* DO, WHEN YUKA'S GONE?
I'LL SLEEP WITH SOME OTHER GIRL.

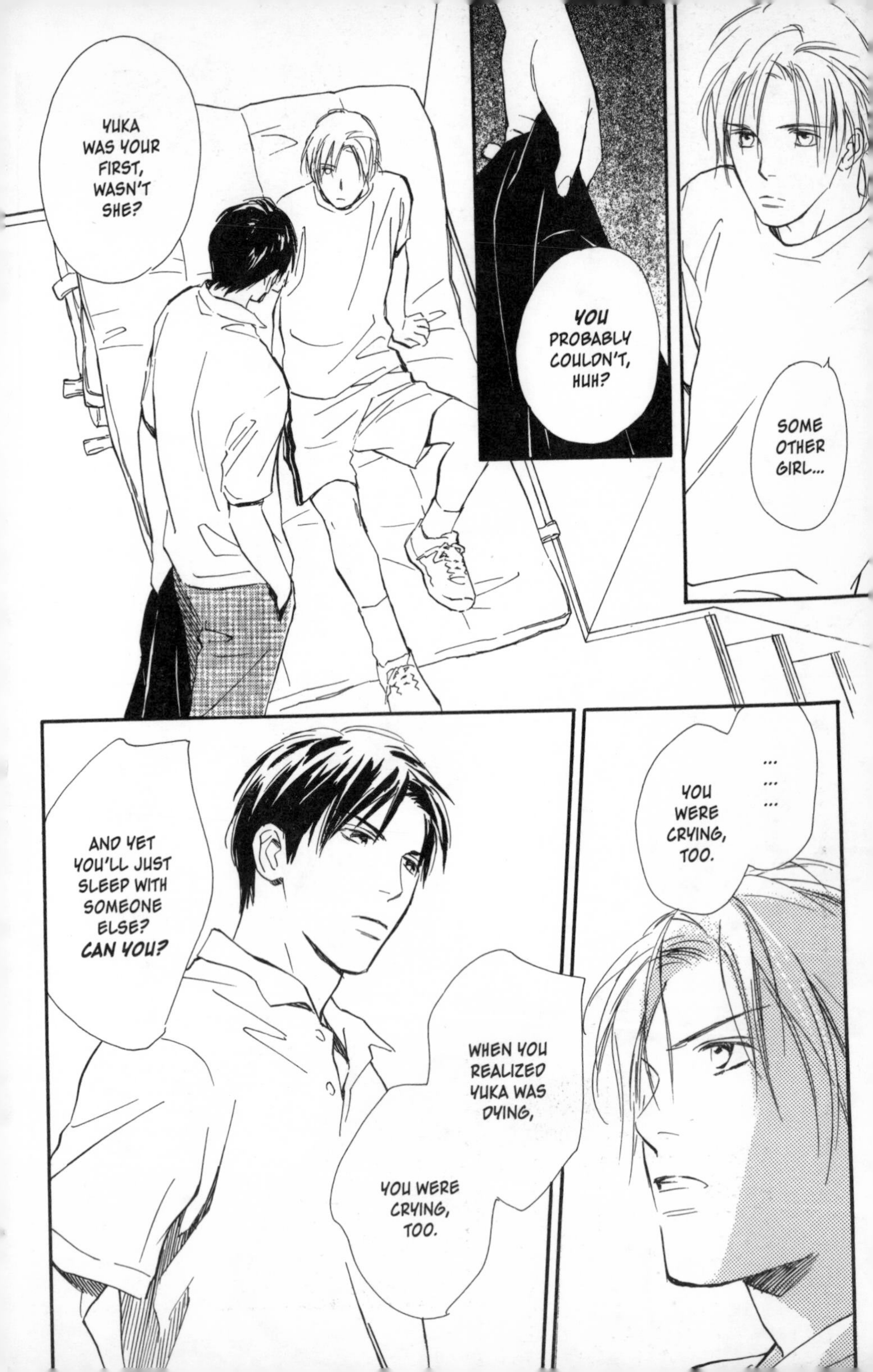
SOME OTHER GIRL...
YOU PROBABLY COULDN'T, HUH?
YUKA WAS YOUR FIRST, WASN'T SHE?
... ...
YOU WERE CRYING, TOO.
AND YET YOU'LL JUST SLEEP WITH SOMEONE ELSE? CAN YOU?
WHEN YOU REALIZED YUKA WAS DYING,
YOU WERE CRYING, TOO.

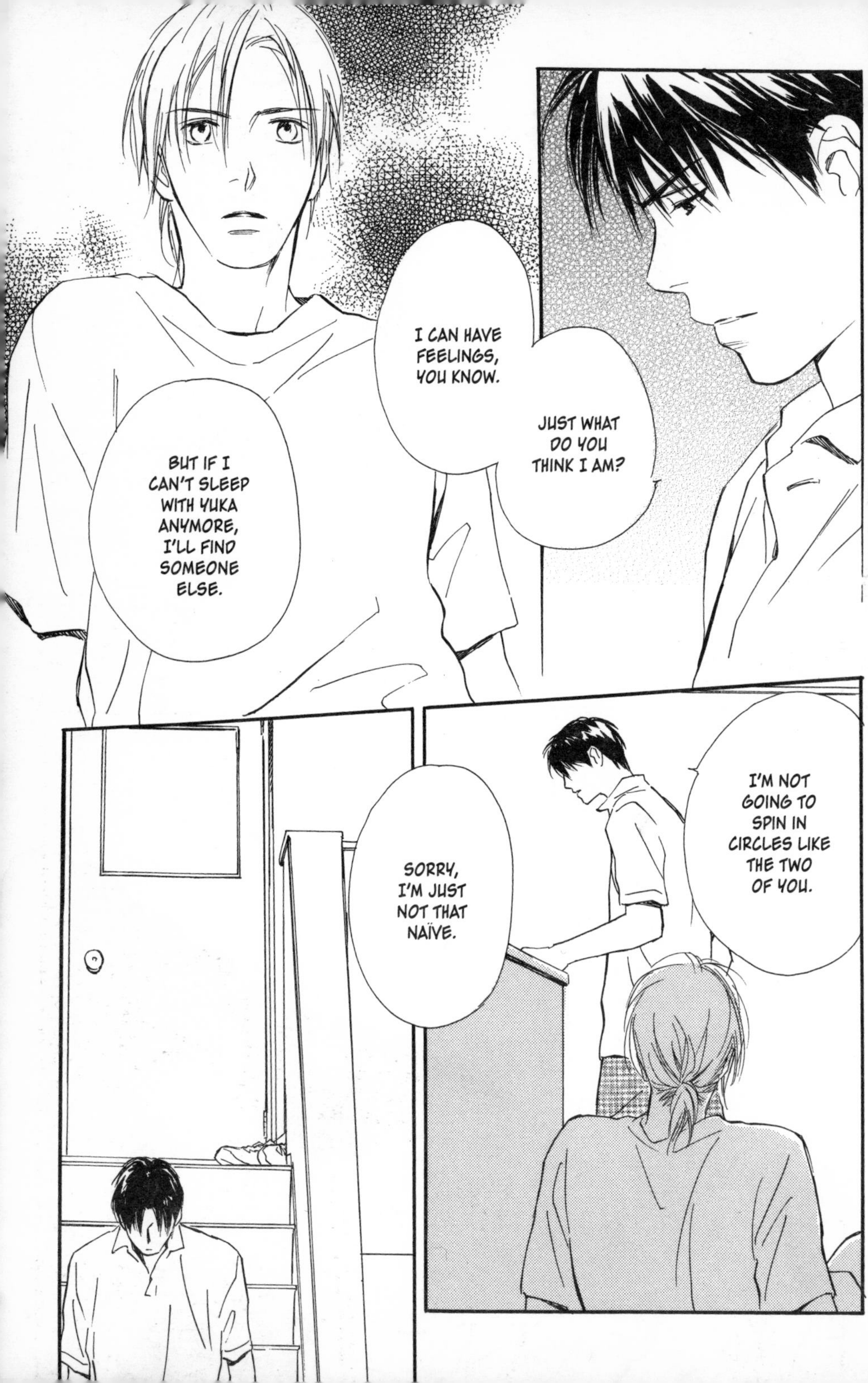
I CAN HAVE FEELINGS, YOU KNOW.
JUST WHAT DO YOU THINK I AM?
BUT IF I CAN'T SLEEP WITH YUKA ANYMORE, I'LL FIND SOMEONE ELSE.
I'M NOT GOING TO SPIN IN CIRCLES LIKE THE TWO OF YOU.
SORRY, I'M JUST NOT THAT NAÏVE.

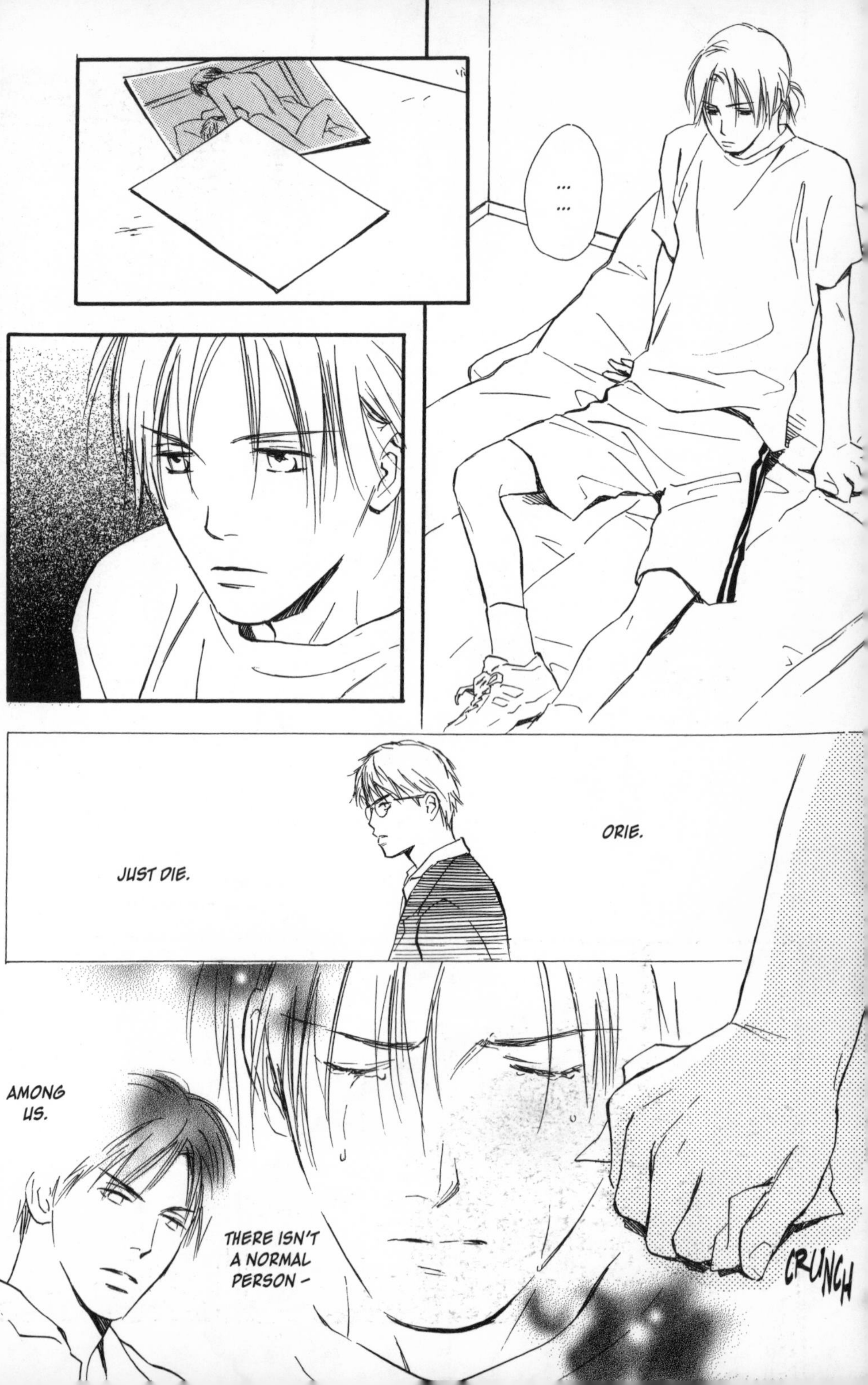
...
...
ORIE.
JUST DIE.
CRUNCH
THERE ISN'T A NORMAL PERSON –
AMONG US.

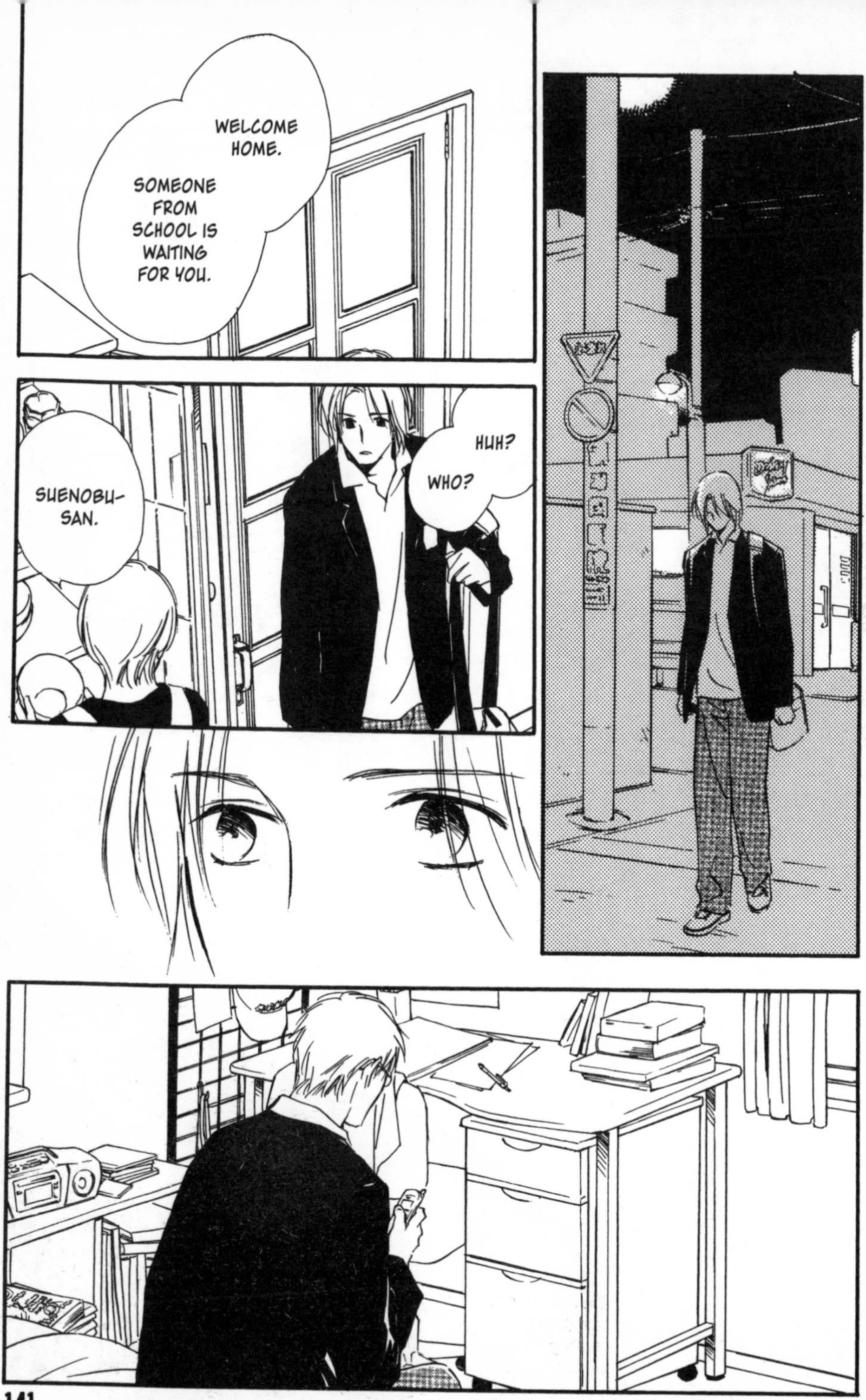
WELCOME HOME.
SOMEONE FROM SCHOOL IS WAITING FOR YOU.
HUH?
WHO?
SUENOBU-SAN.

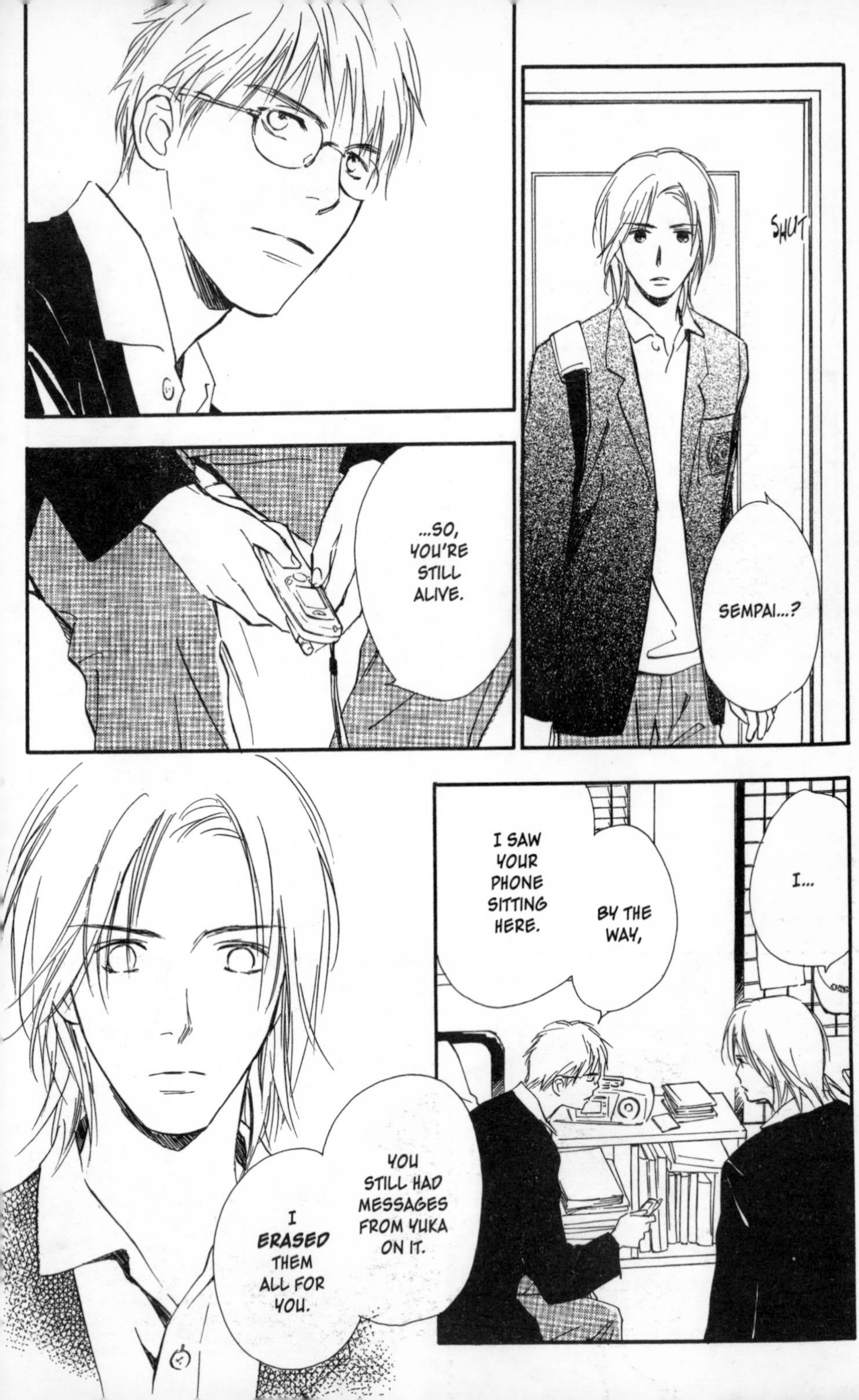
SHUT
SEMPAI...?
...SO, YOU'RE STILL ALIVE.
I...
BY THE WAY,
I SAW YOUR PHONE SITTING HERE.
YOU STILL HAD MESSAGES FROM YUKA ON IT.
I ERASED THEM ALL FOR YOU.

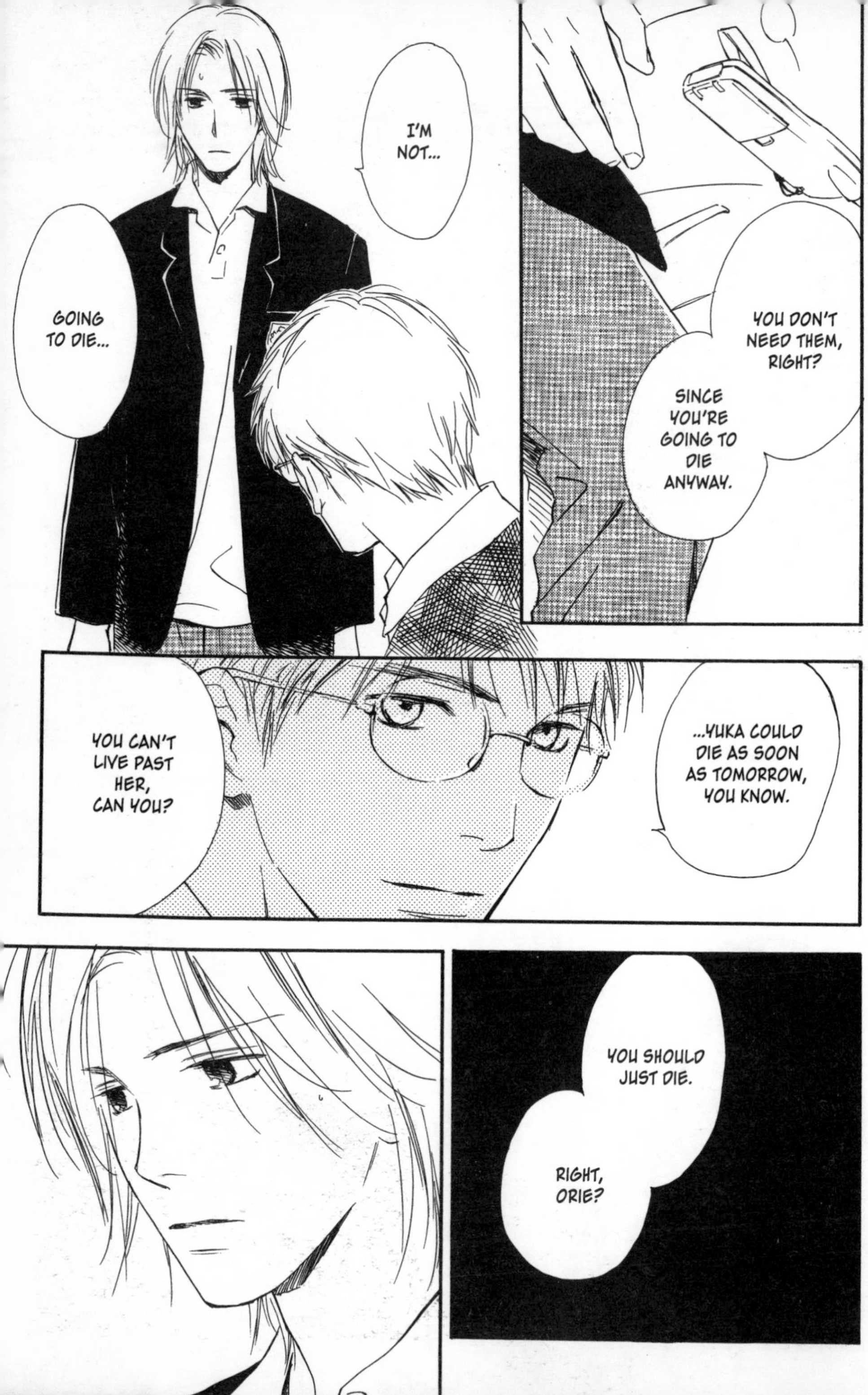
YOU DON'T NEED THEM, RIGHT?
SINCE YOU'RE GOING TO DIE ANYWAY.
I'M NOT...
GOING TO DIE...
...YUKA COULD DIE AS SOON AS TOMORROW, YOU KNOW.
YOU CAN'T LIVE PAST HER, CAN YOU?
YOU SHOULD JUST DIE.
RIGHT, ORIE?

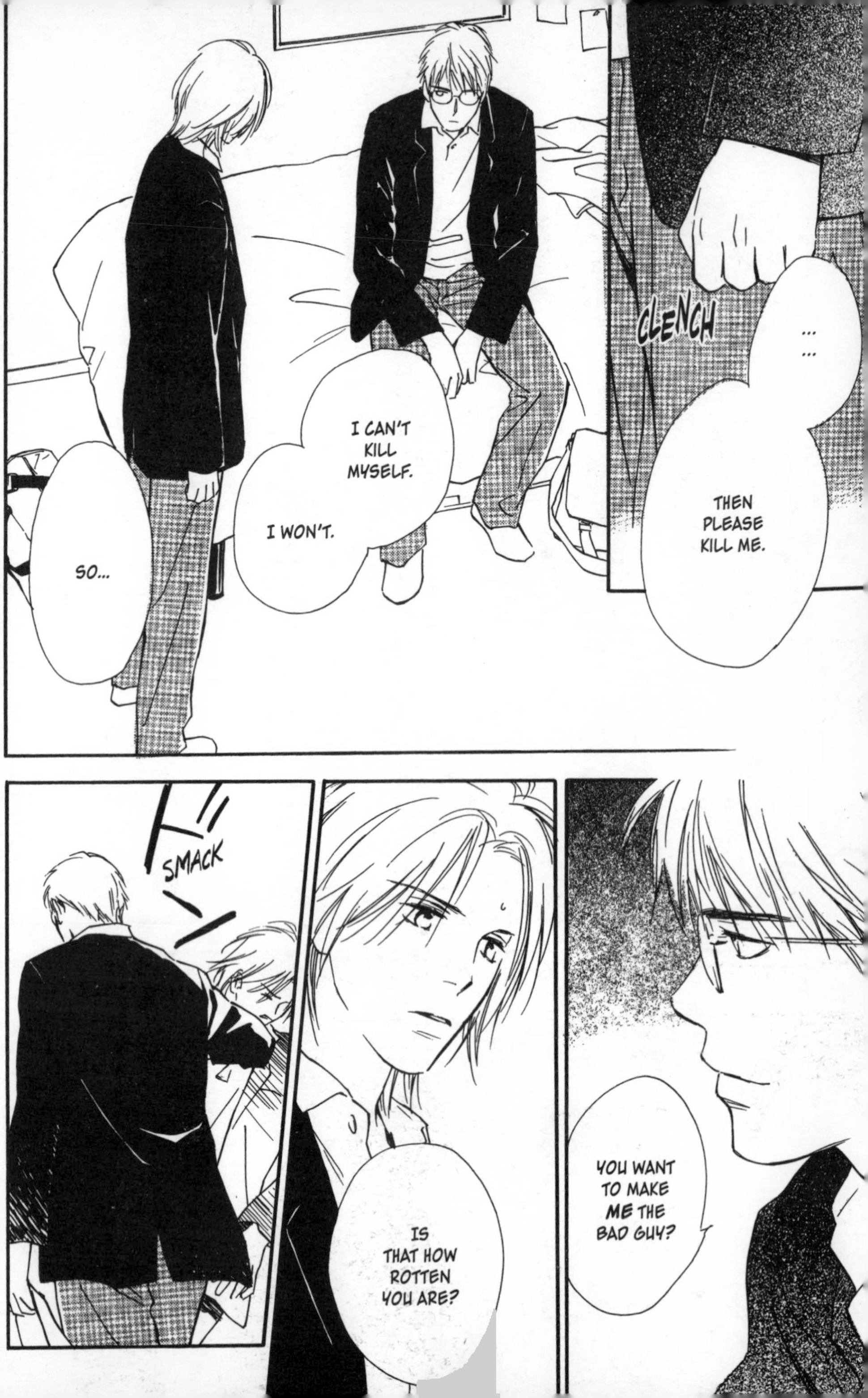
CLENCH
...
...
THEN PLEASE KILL ME.
I CAN'T KILL MYSELF.
I WON'T.
SO...
YOU WANT TO MAKE ME THE BAD GUY?
IS THAT HOW ROTTEN YOU ARE?
SMACK

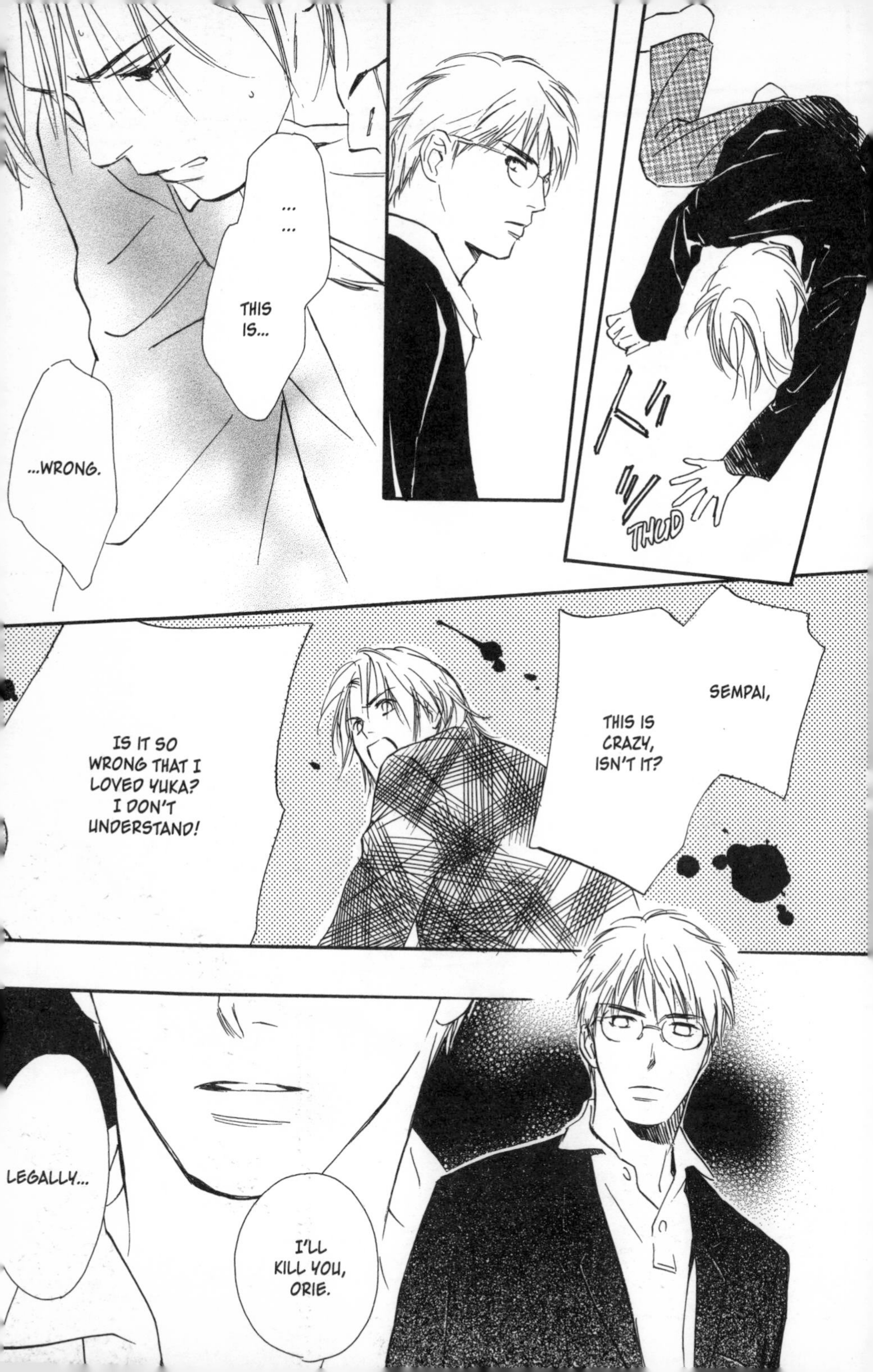
THUD
......
THIS IS...
...WRONG.
SEMPAI, THIS IS CRAZY, ISN'T IT?
IS IT SO WRONG THAT I LOVED YUKA? I DON'T UNDERSTAND!
LEGALLY...
I'LL KILL YOU, ORIE.

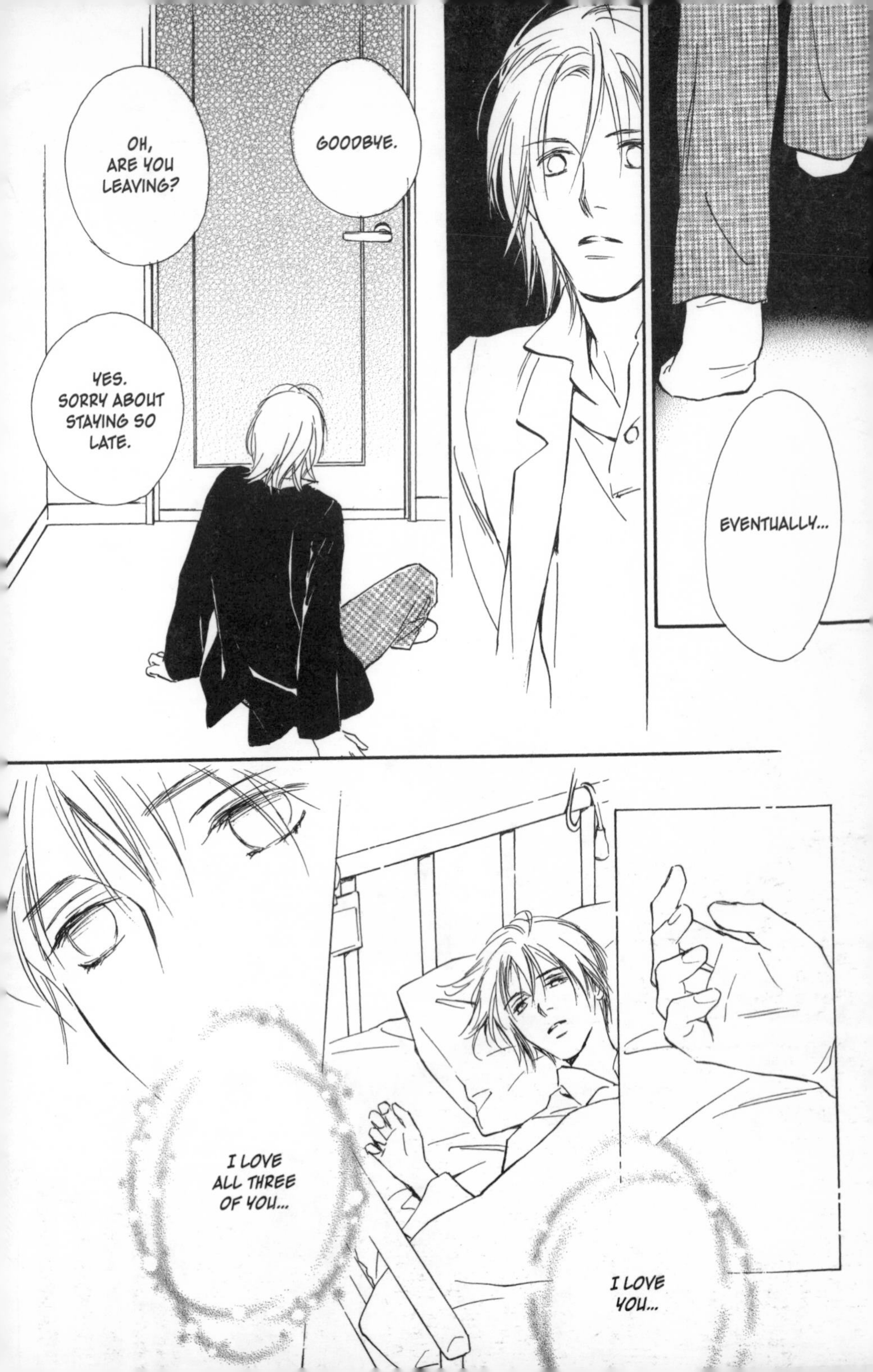
EVENTUALLY...
GOODBYE.
OH, ARE YOU LEAVING?
YES. SORRY ABOUT STAYING SO LATE.
I LOVE YOU...
I LOVE ALL THREE OF YOU...

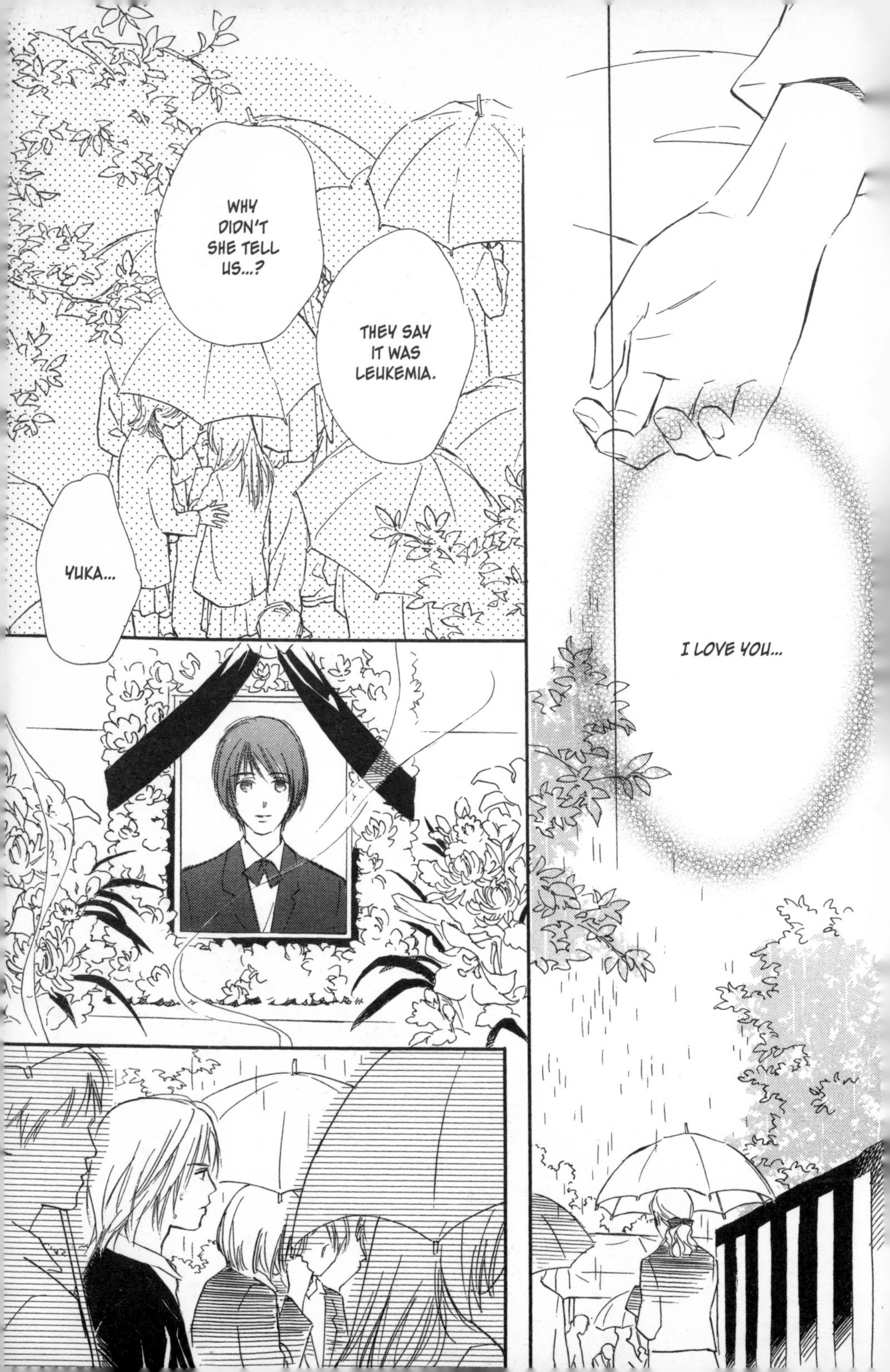
I LOVE YOU...
WHY DIDN'T SHE TELL US...?
THEY SAY IT WAS LEUKEMIA.
YUKA...

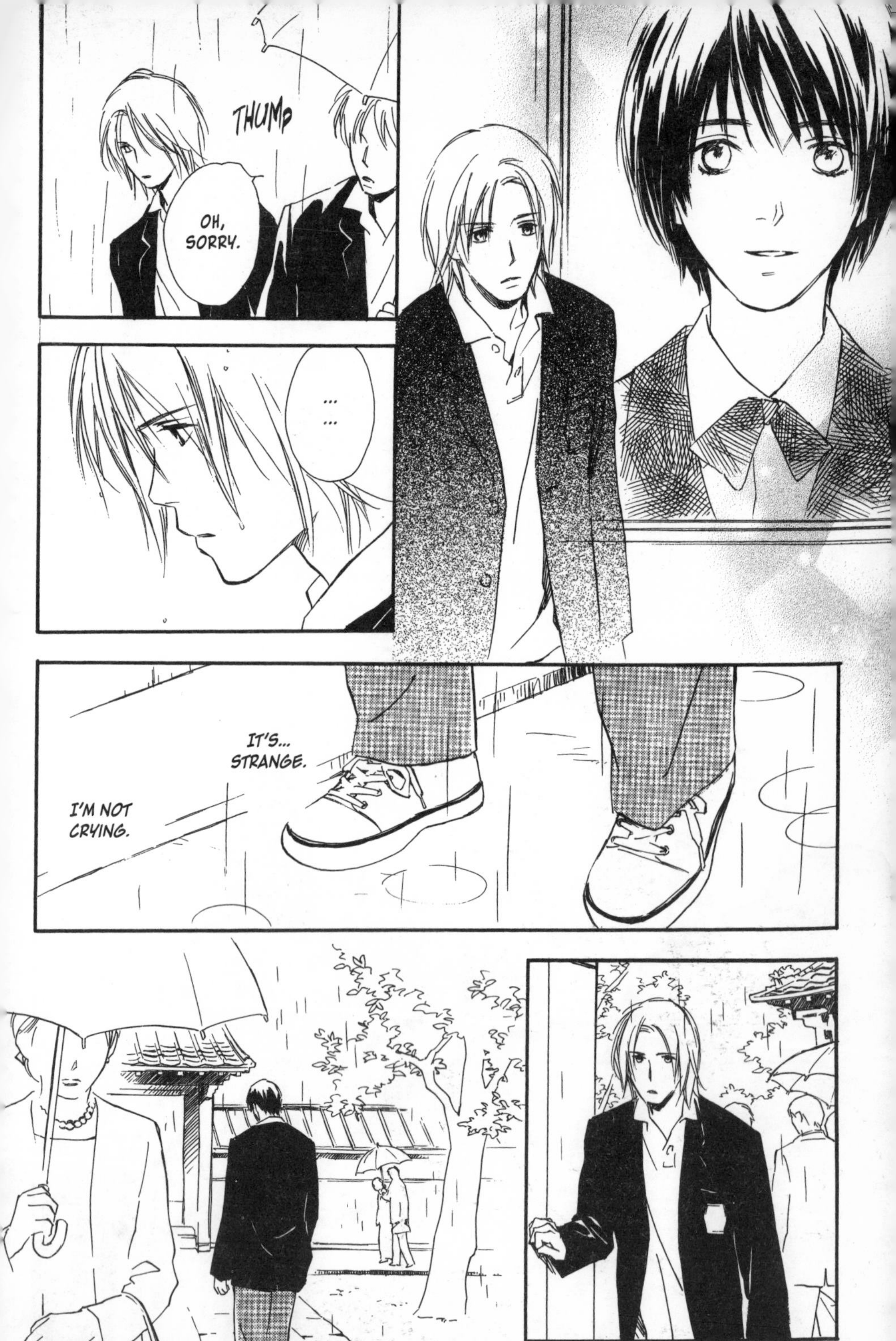
THUMP
OH, SORRY.
... ...
IT'S... STRANGE.
I'M NOT CRYING.

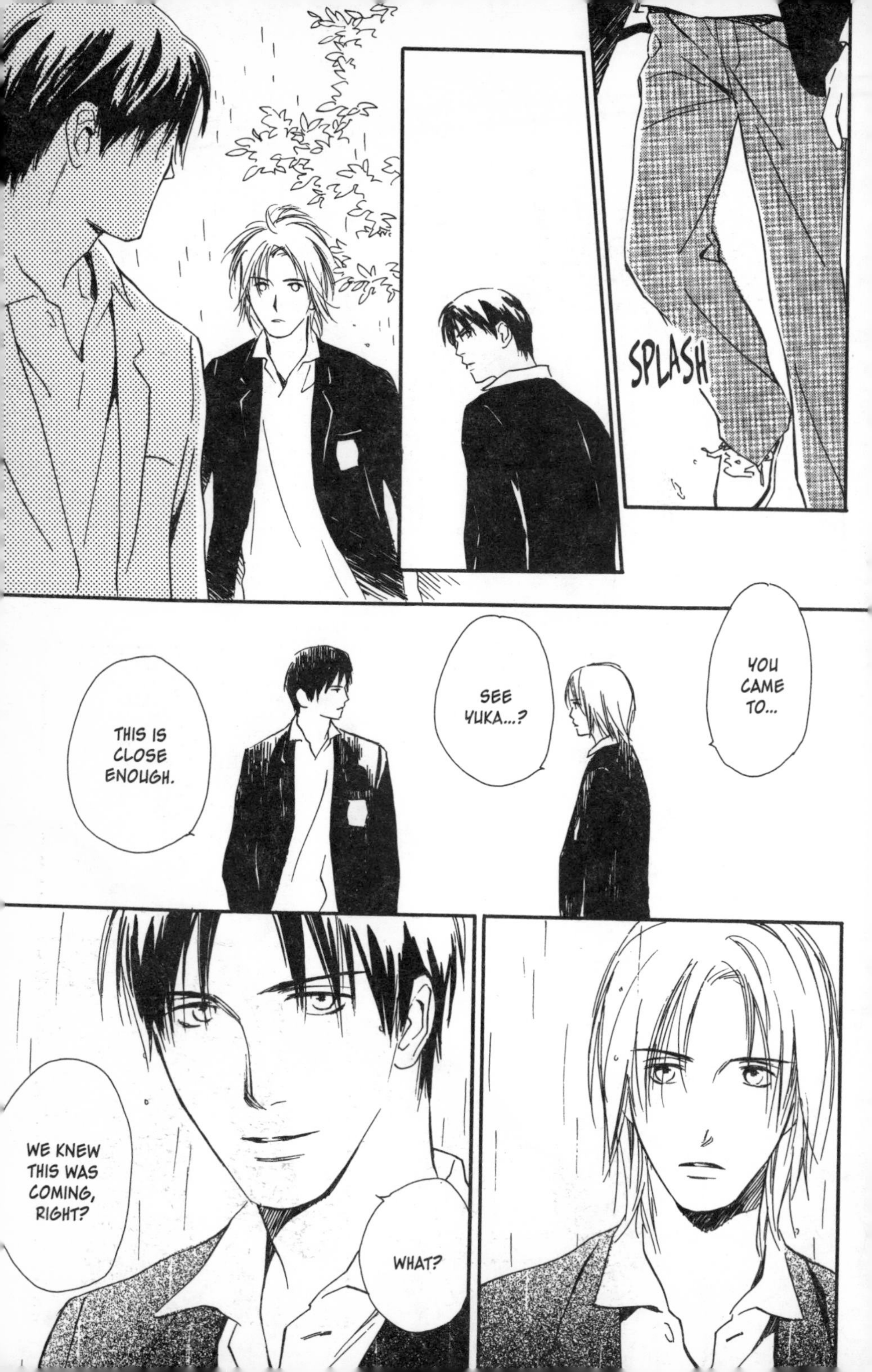
SPLASH
YOU CAME TO...
SEE YUKA...?
THIS IS CLOSE ENOUGH.
WHAT?
WE KNEW THIS WAS COMING, RIGHT?

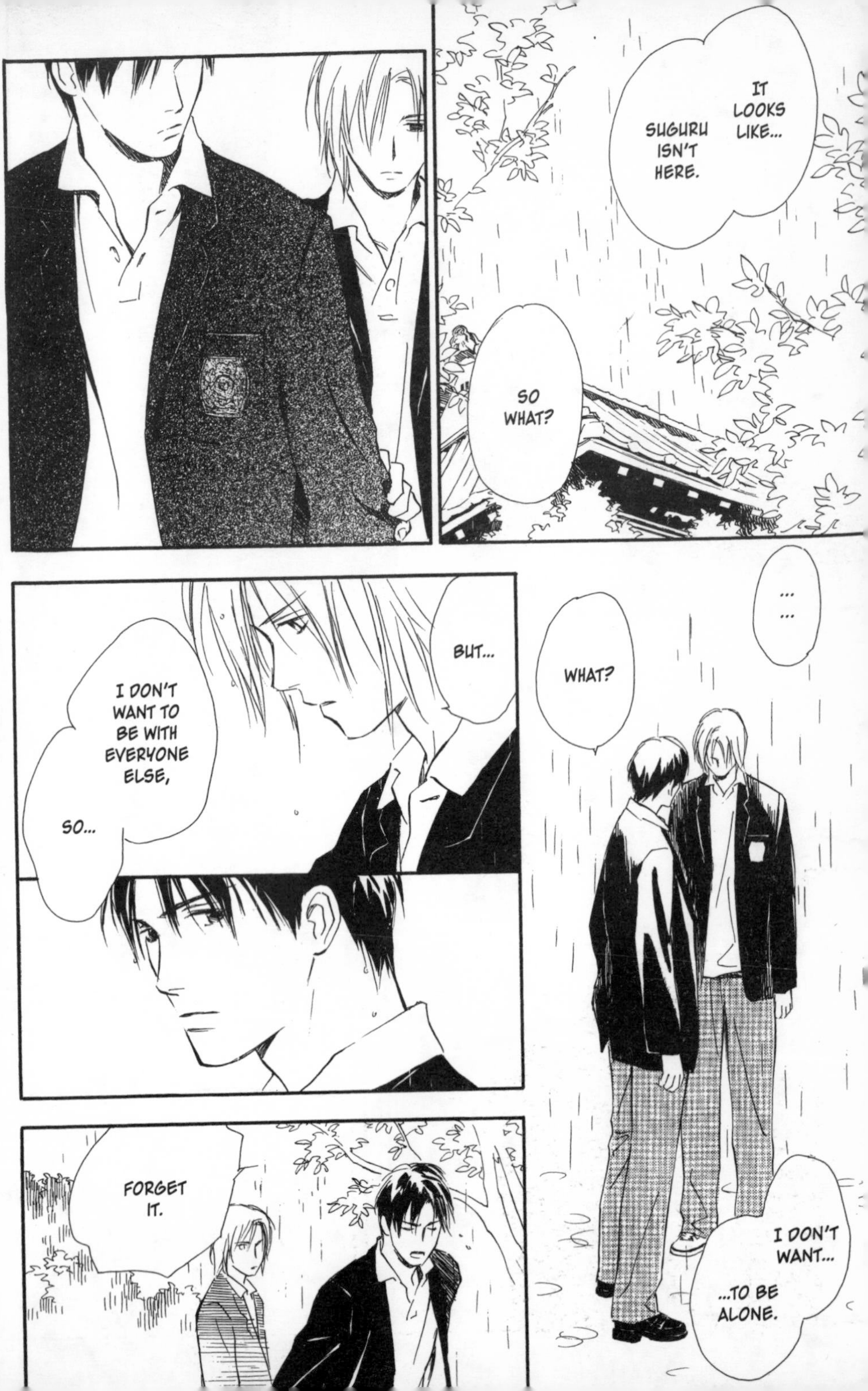
IT LOOKS LIKE... SUGURU ISN'T HERE.
SO WHAT?
... ...
WHAT?
I DON'T WANT...
...TO BE ALONE.
BUT...
I DON'T WANT TO BE WITH EVERYONE ELSE,
SO...
FORGET IT.

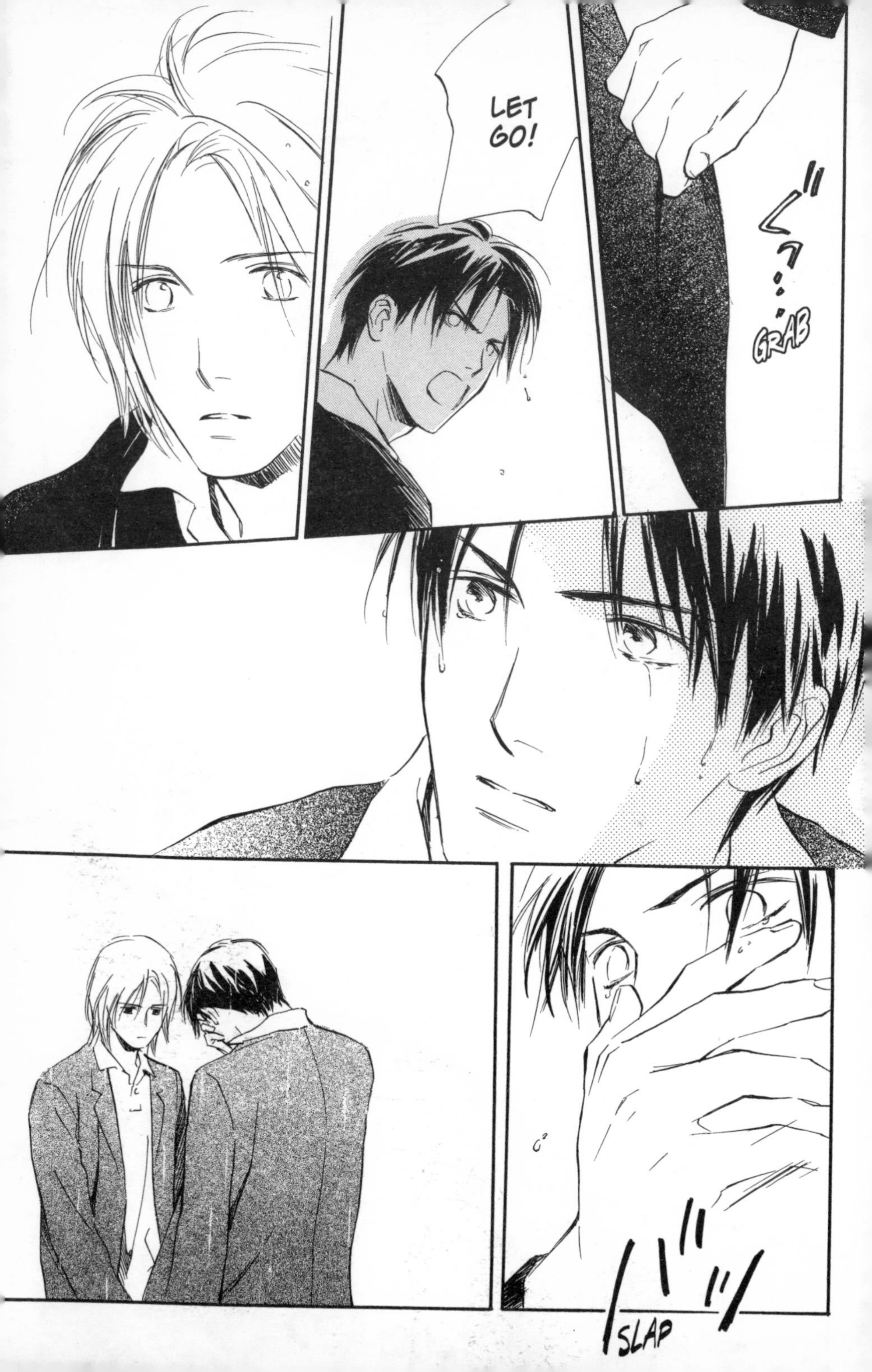
GRAB
LET GO!
SLAP

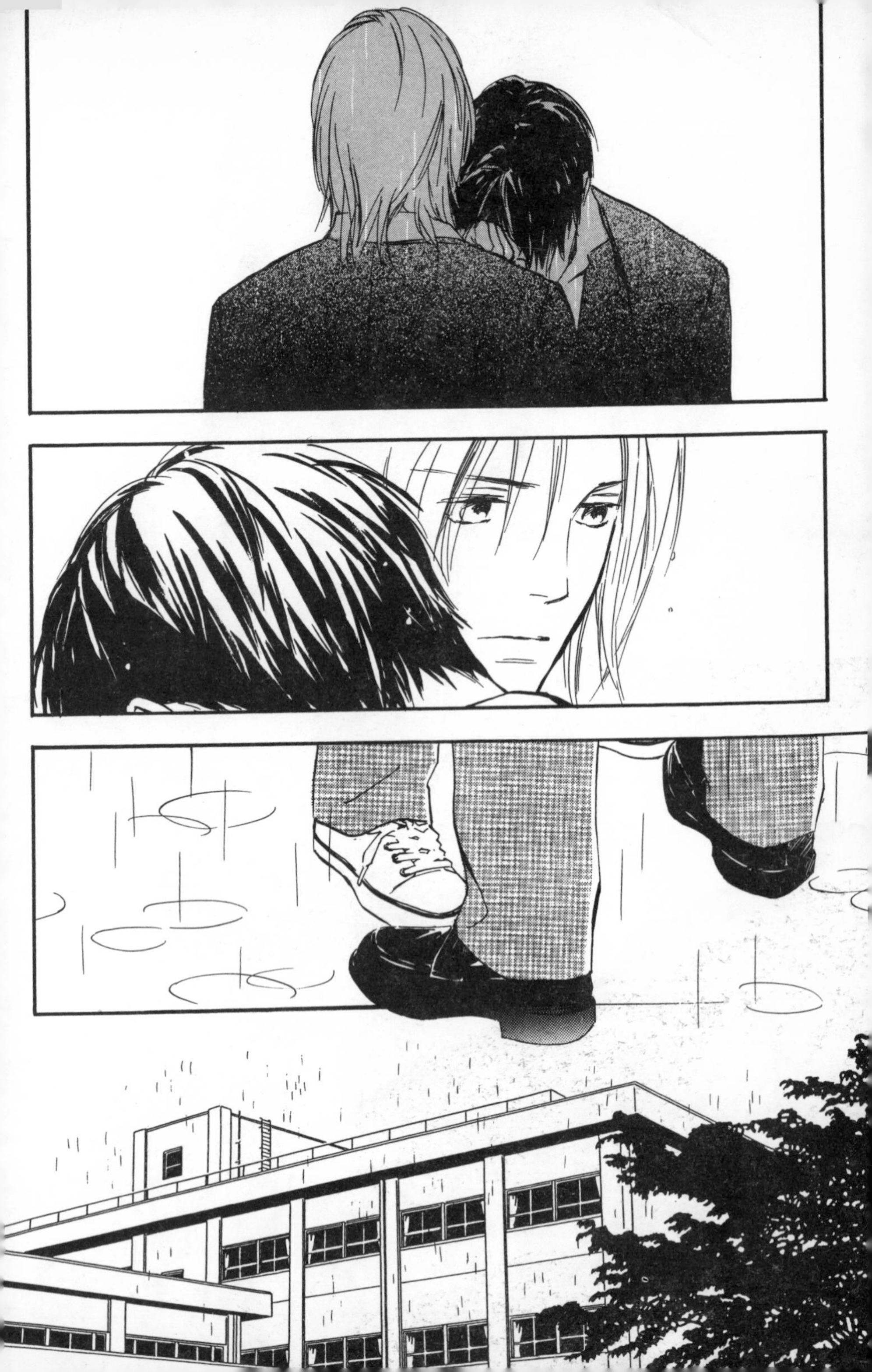

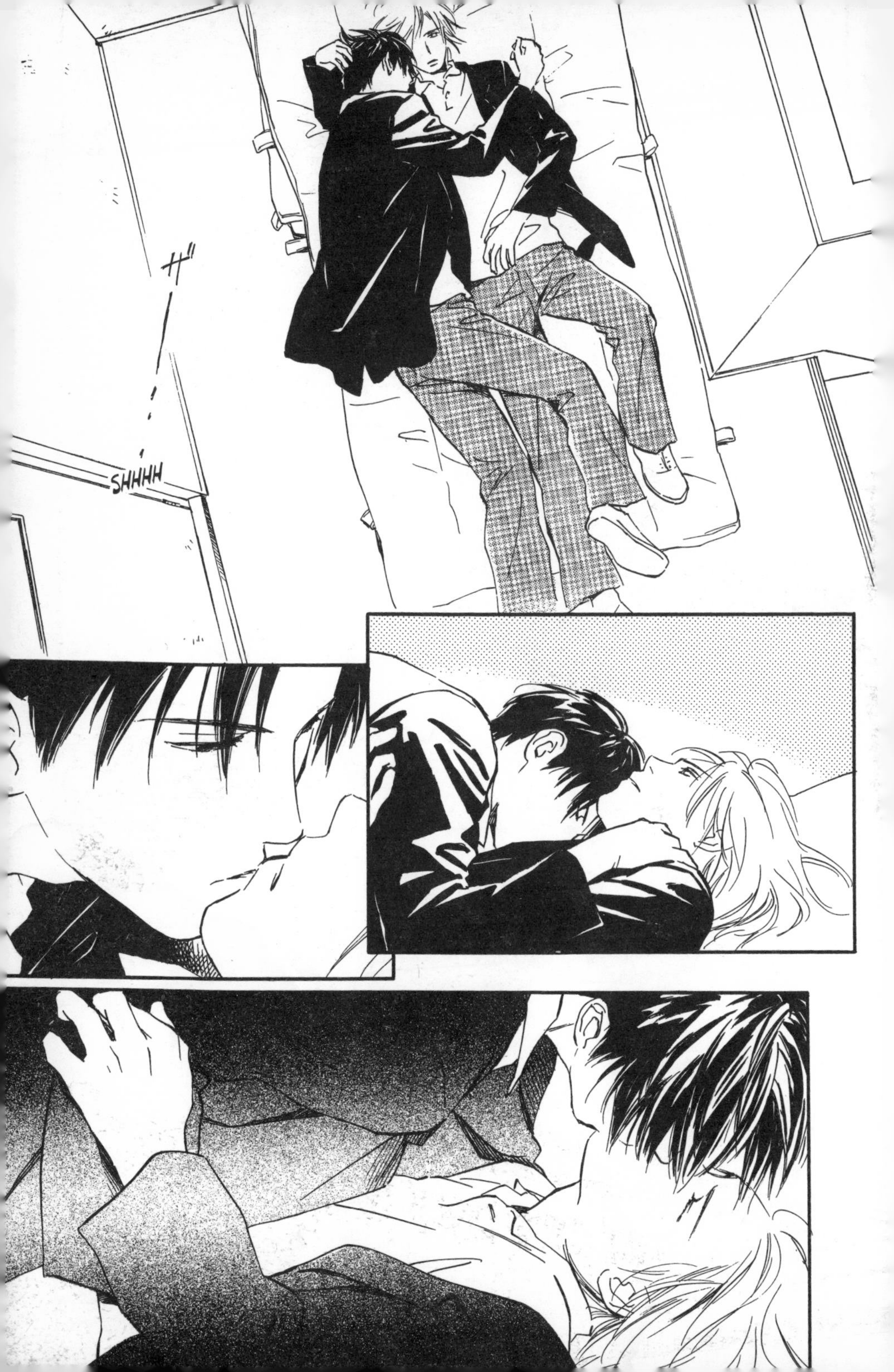
ザ
SHHHH

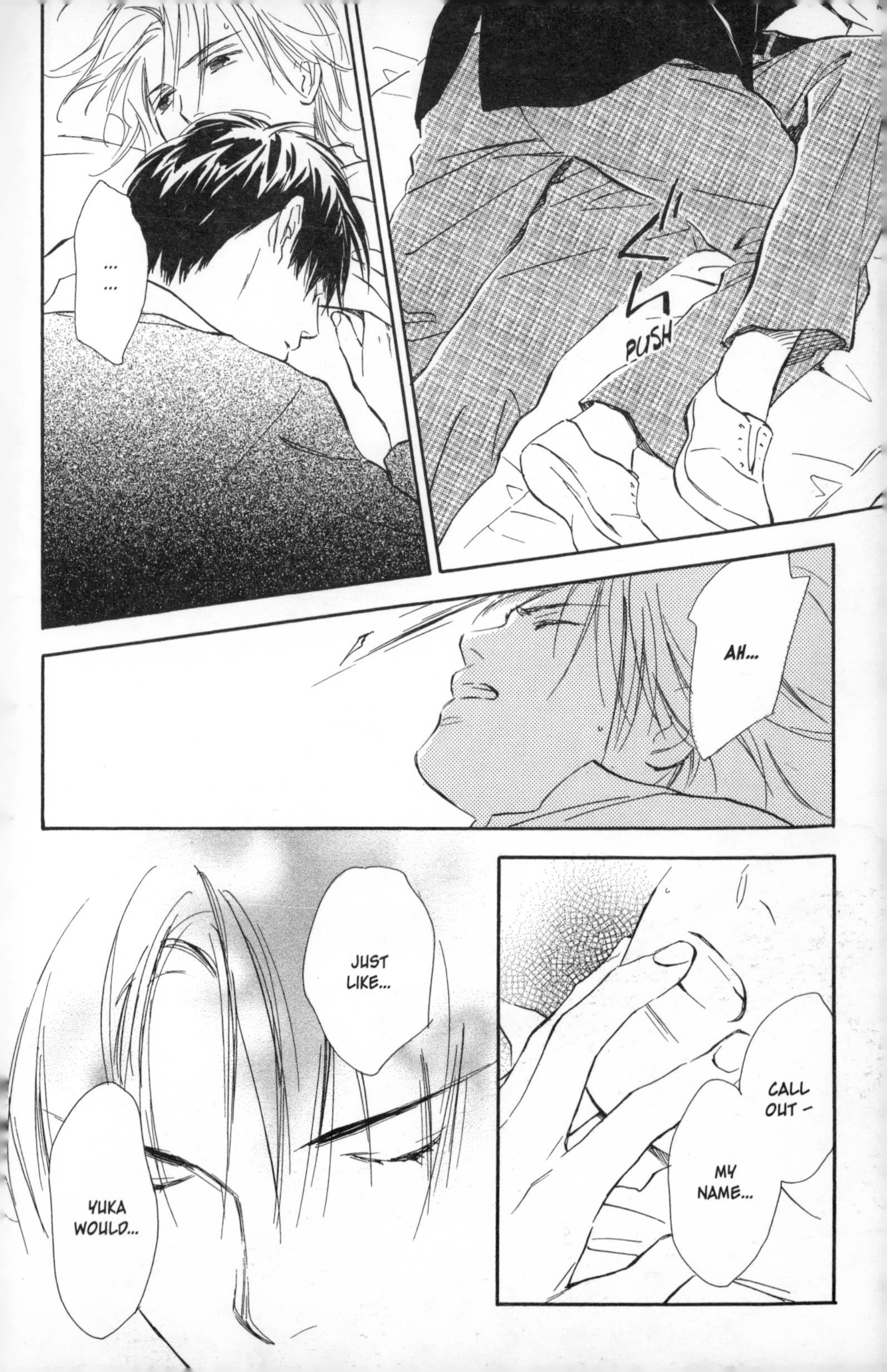
PUSH
...
...
AH...
CALL OUT -
MY NAME...
JUST LIKE...
YUKA WOULD...

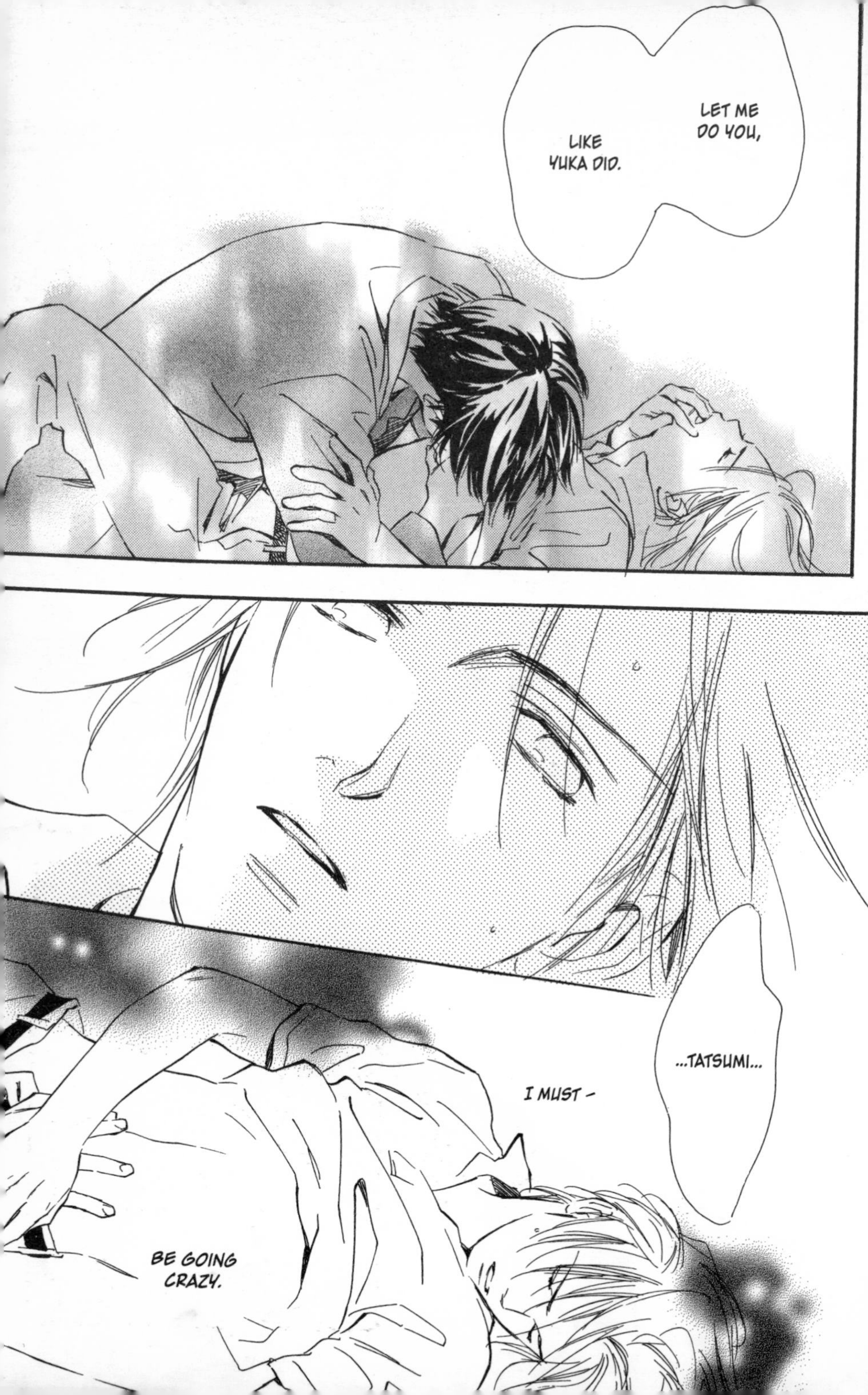
LET ME DO YOU,
LIKE YUKA DID.
...TATSUMI...
I MUST -
BE GOING CRAZY.

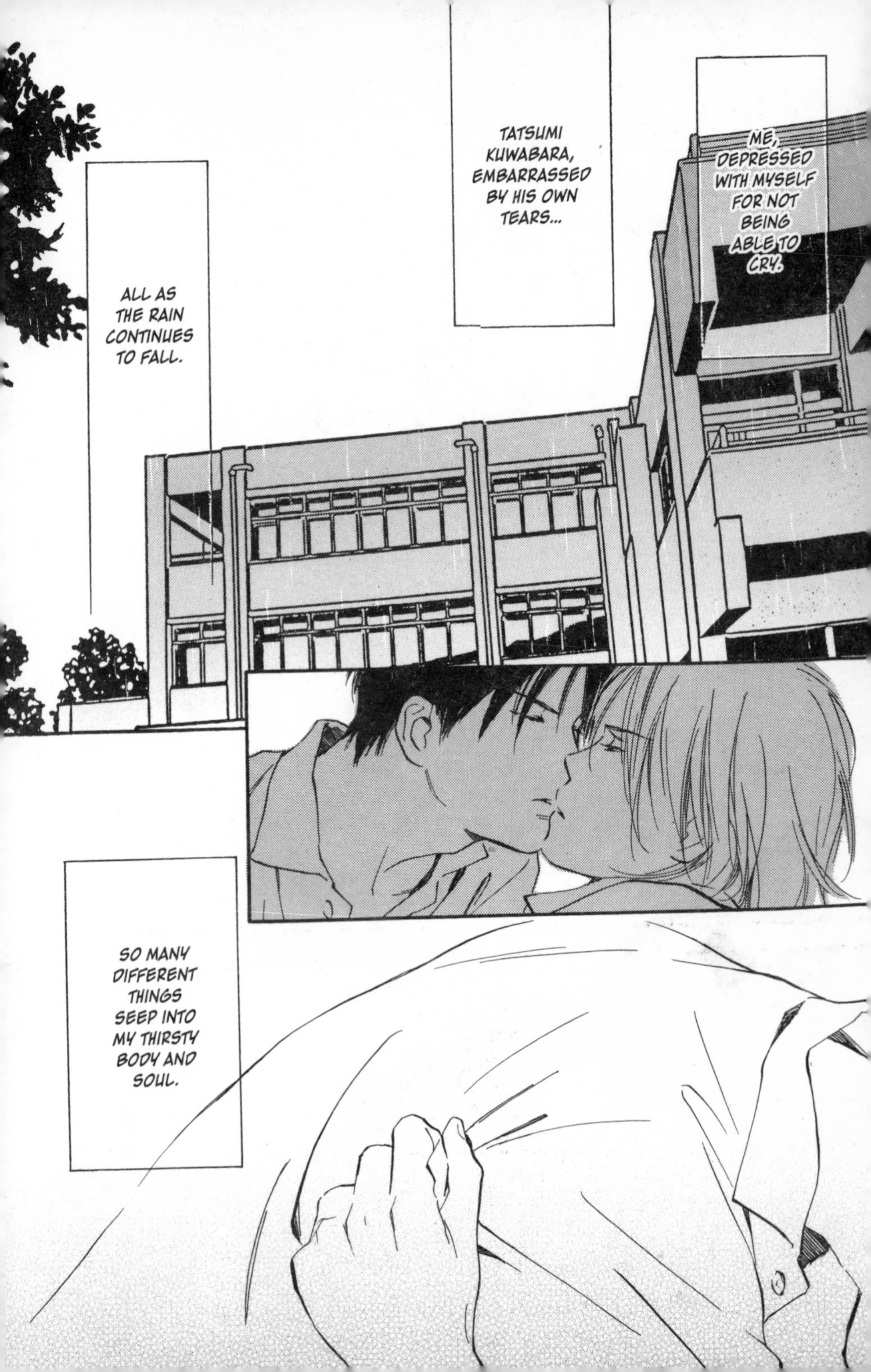
ME, DEPRESSED WITH MYSELF FOR NOT BEING ABLE TO CRY.
TATSUMI KUWABARA, EMBARRASSED BY HIS OWN TEARS...
ALL AS THE RAIN CONTINUES TO FALL.
SO MANY DIFFERENT THINGS SEEP INTO MY THIRSTY BODY AND SOUL.

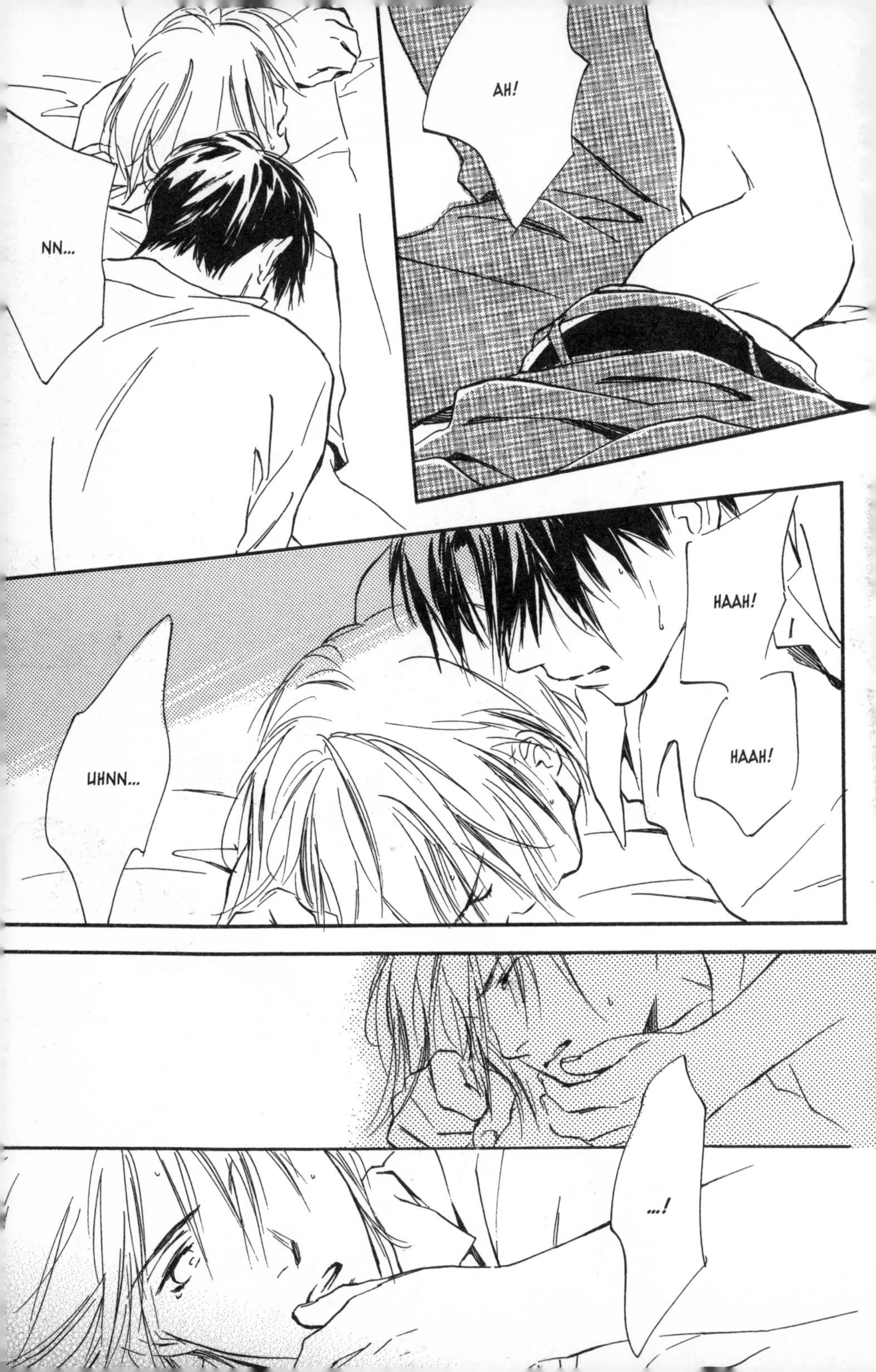
AH!
NN...
HAAH!
HAAH!
UHNN...
...!

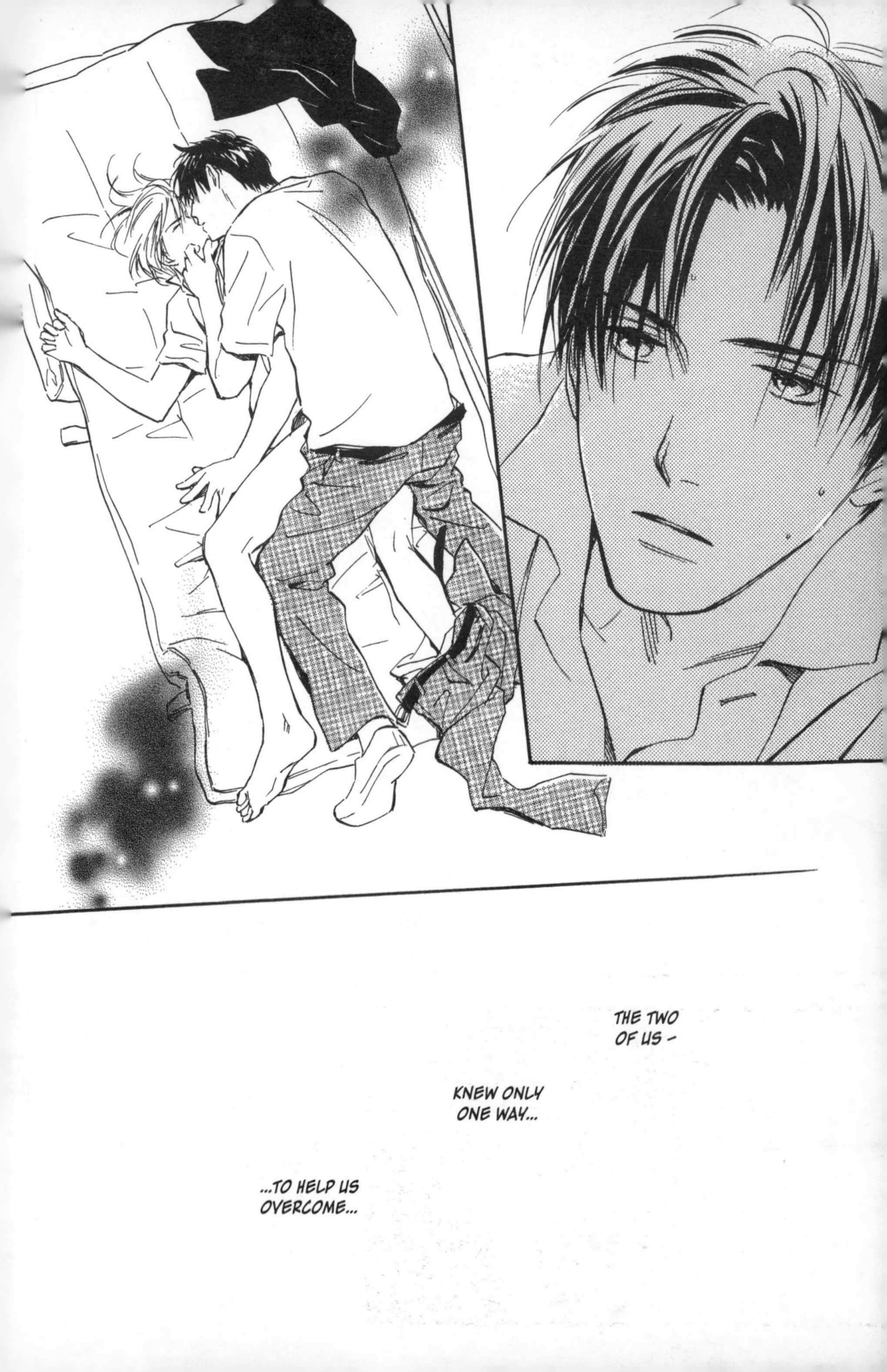
THE TWO OF US -
KNEW ONLY ONE WAY...
...TO HELP US OVERCOME...

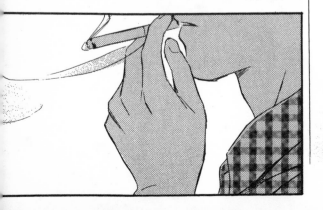

YUKA'S DEATH.

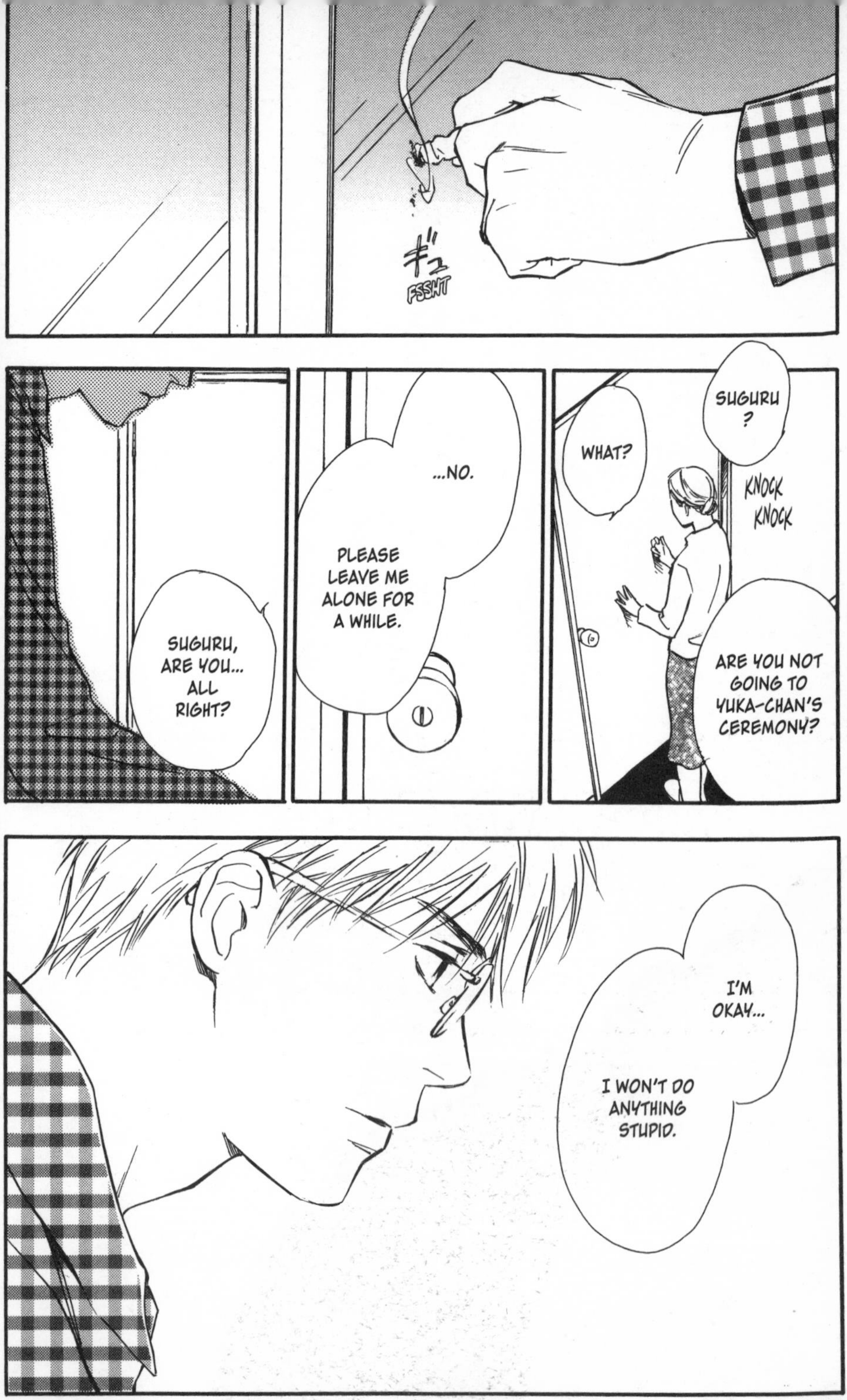
ギュ
FSSHT
SUGURU ?
KNOCK KNOCK
ARE YOU NOT GOING TO YUKA-CHAN'S CEREMONY?
WHAT?
...NO.
PLEASE LEAVE ME ALONE FOR A WHILE.
SUGURU, ARE YOU... ALL RIGHT?
I'M OKAY...
I WON'T DO ANYTHING STUPID.

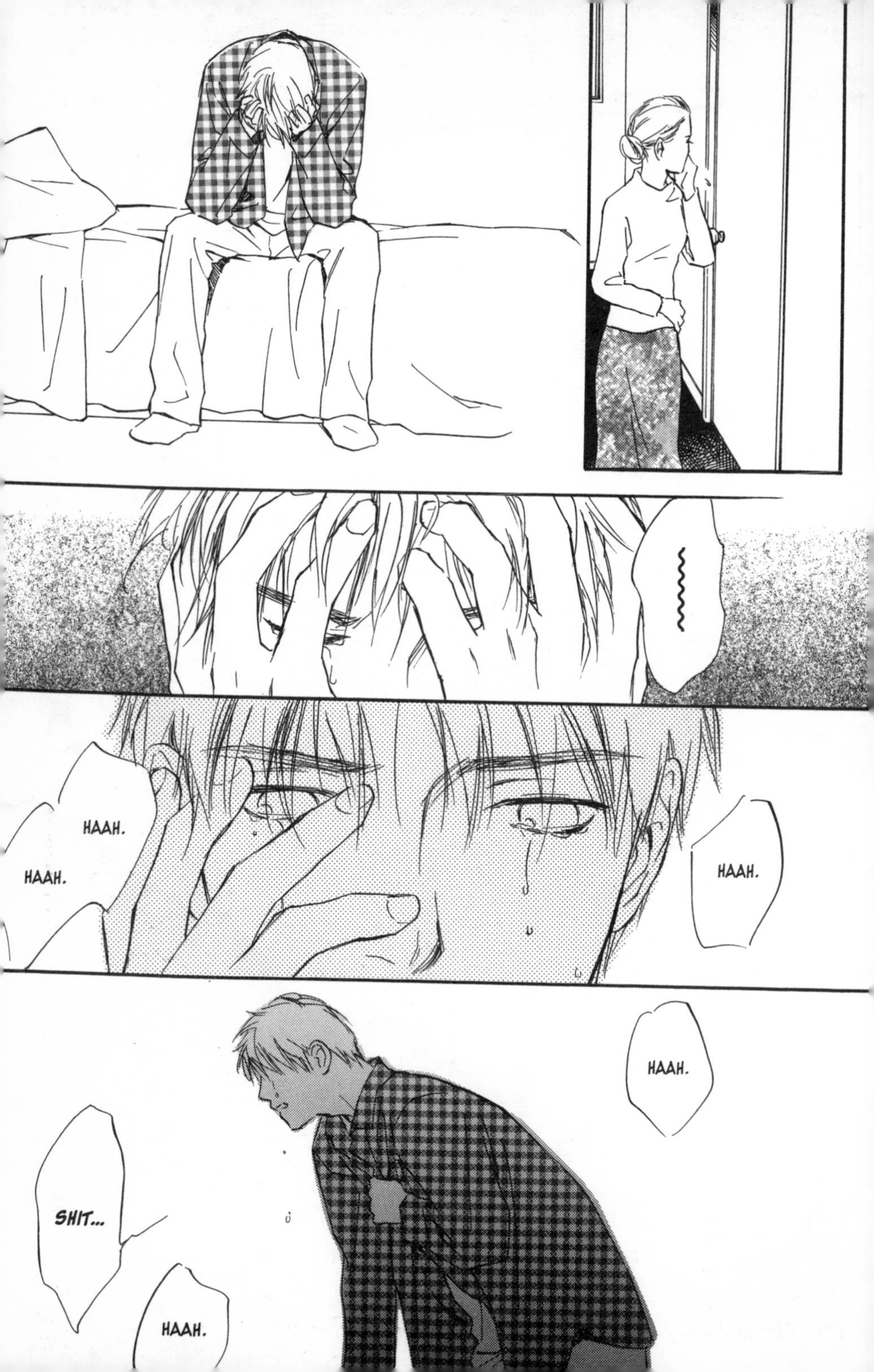
HAAH.
HAAH.
HAAH.
HAAH.
SHIT...
HAAH.

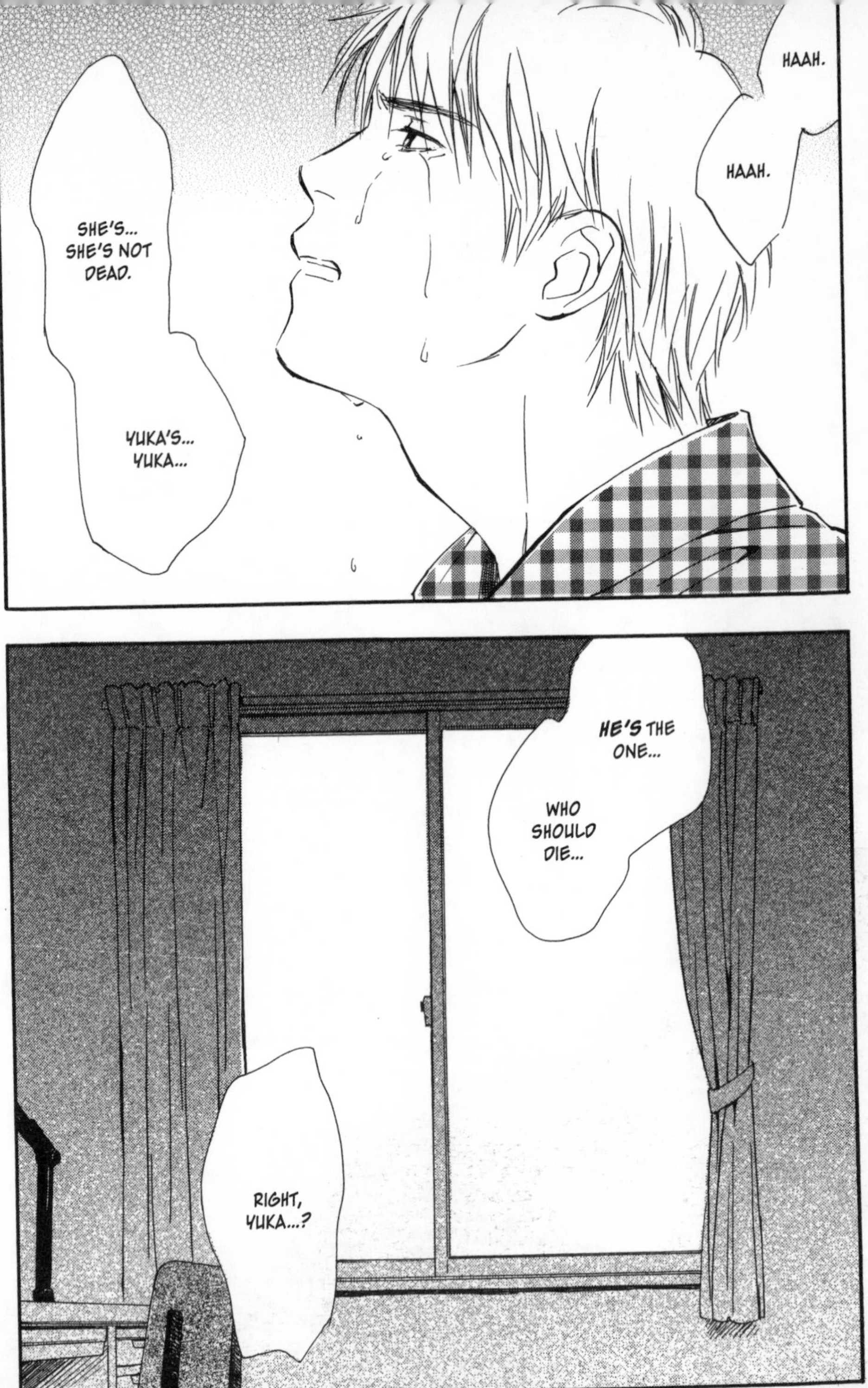
HAAH.
HAAH.
SHE'S... SHE'S NOT DEAD.
YUKA'S... YUKA...
HE'S THE ONE...
WHO SHOULD DIE...
RIGHT, YUKA...?

CHAPTER 6

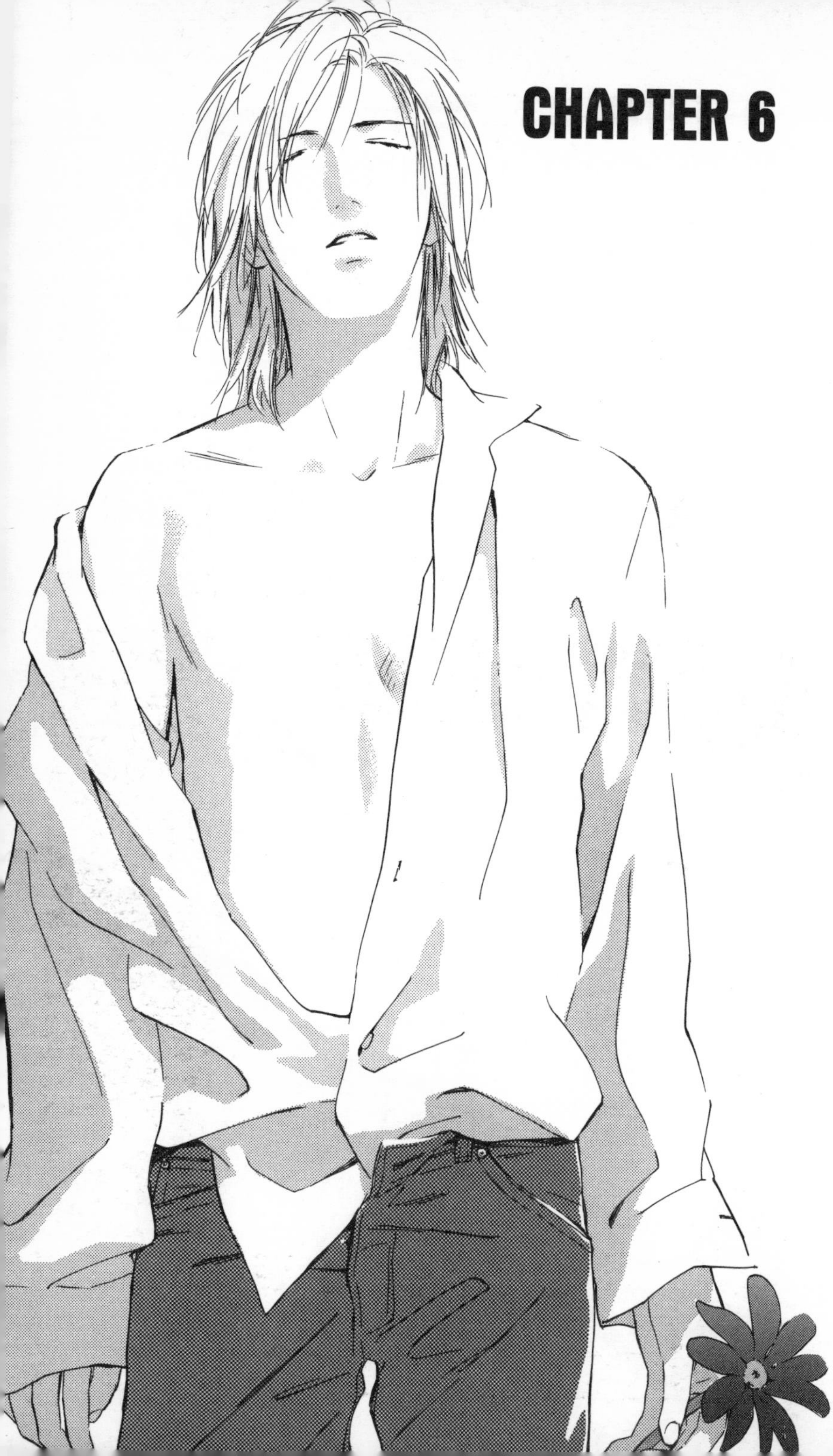

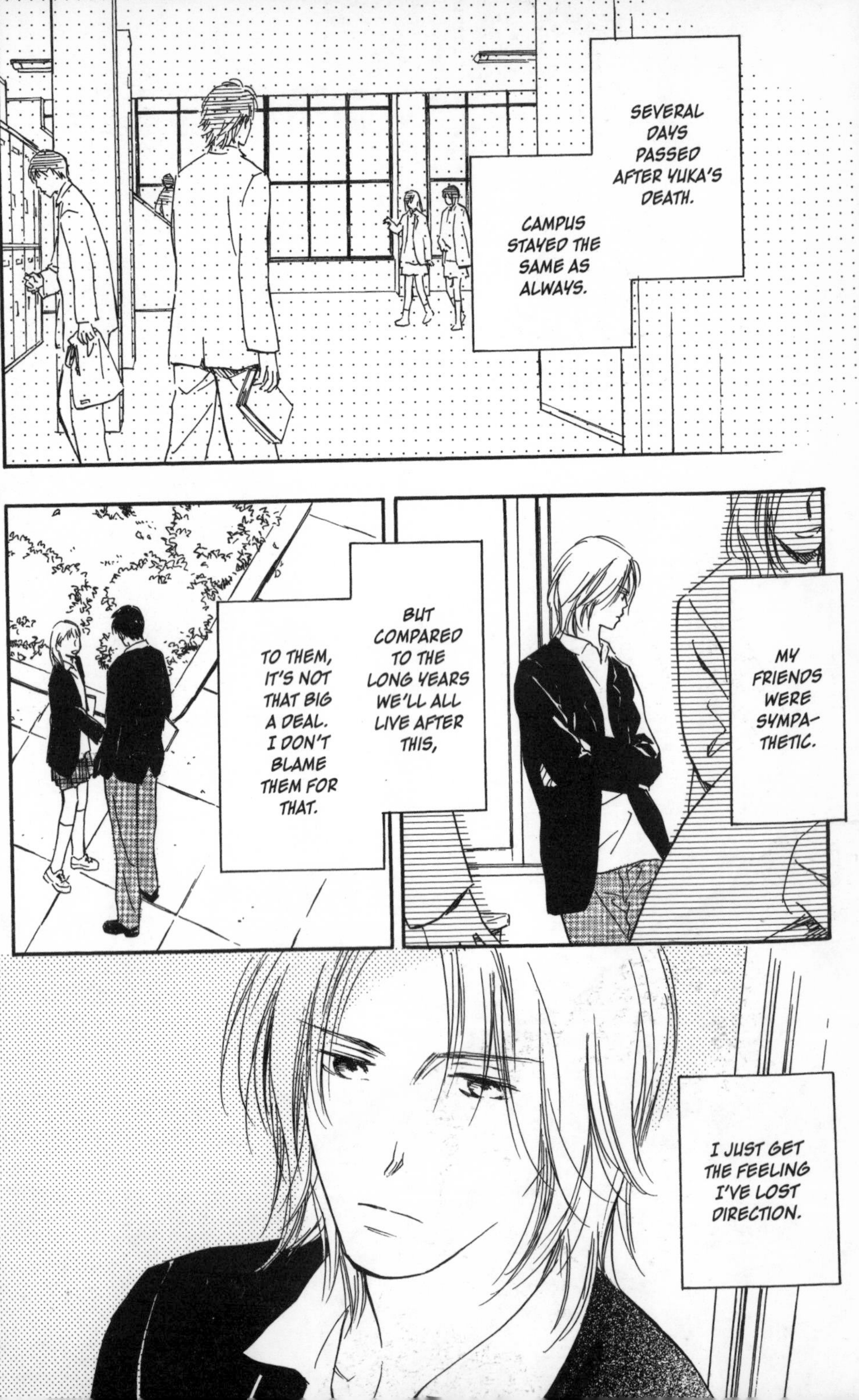
SEVERAL DAYS PASSED AFTER YUKA'S DEATH.
CAMPUS STAYED THE SAME AS ALWAYS.
MY FRIENDS WERE SYMPA-THETIC.
BUT COMPARED TO THE LONG YEARS WE'LL ALL LIVE AFTER THIS,
TO THEM, IT'S NOT THAT BIG A DEAL. I DON'T BLAME THEM FOR THAT.
I JUST GET THE FEELING I'VE LOST DIRECTION.

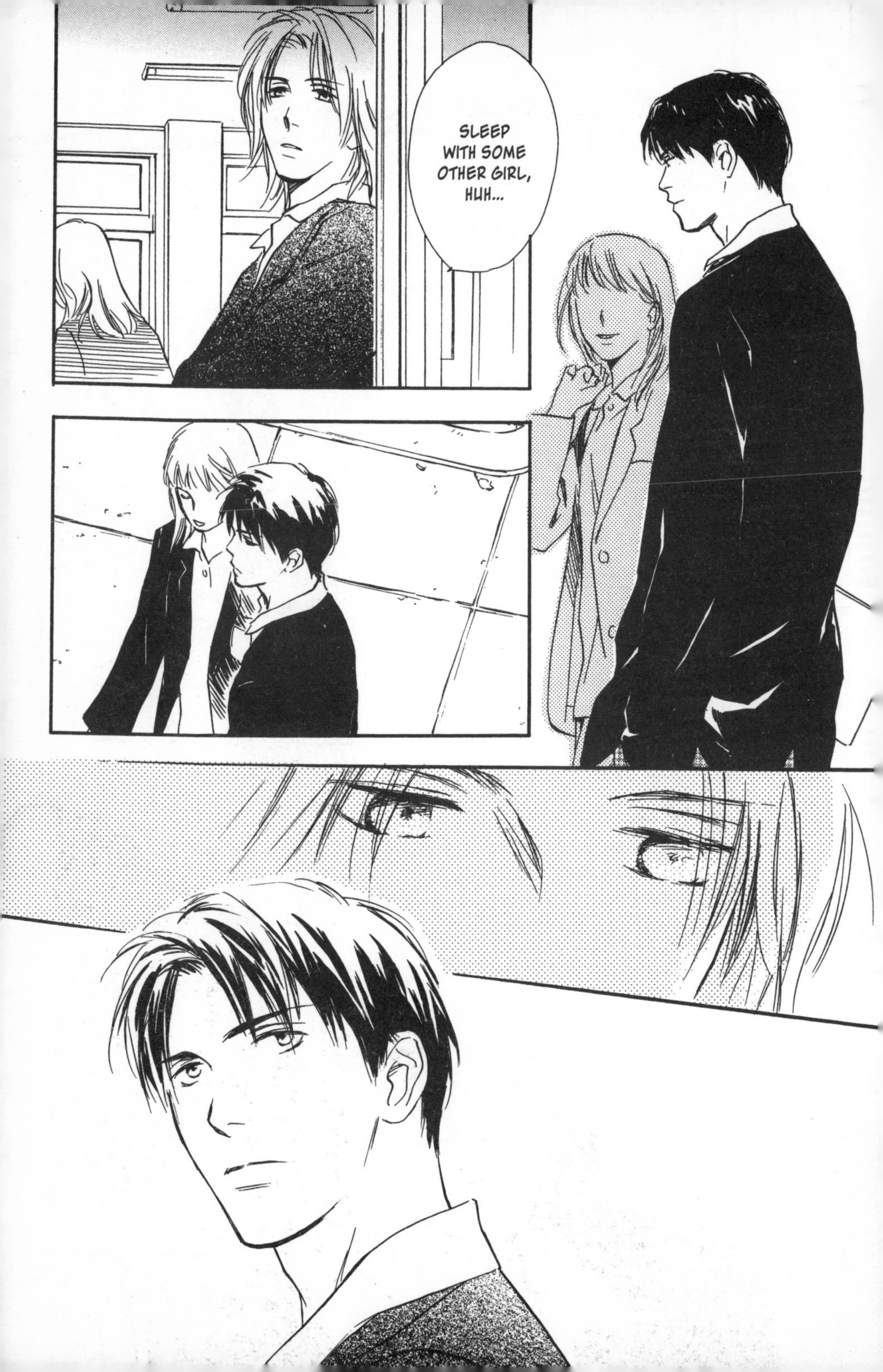
SLEEP WITH SOME OTHER GIRL, HUH...

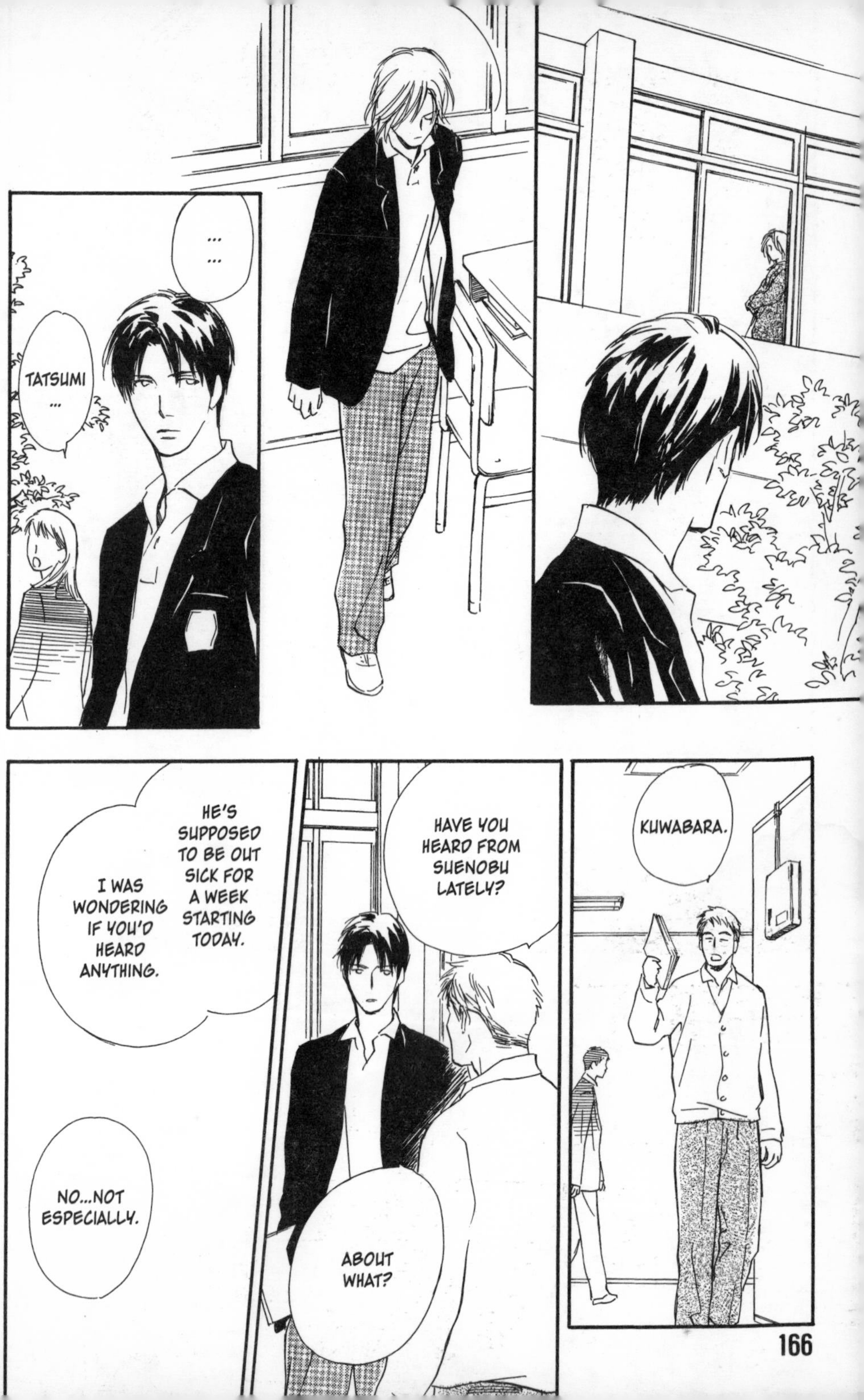
......
TATSUMI ...
KUWABARA.
HAVE YOU HEARD FROM SUENOBU LATELY?
ABOUT WHAT?
HE'S SUPPOSED TO BE OUT SICK FOR A WEEK STARTING TODAY.
I WAS WONDERING IF YOU'D HEARD ANYTHING.
NO...NOT ESPECIALLY.

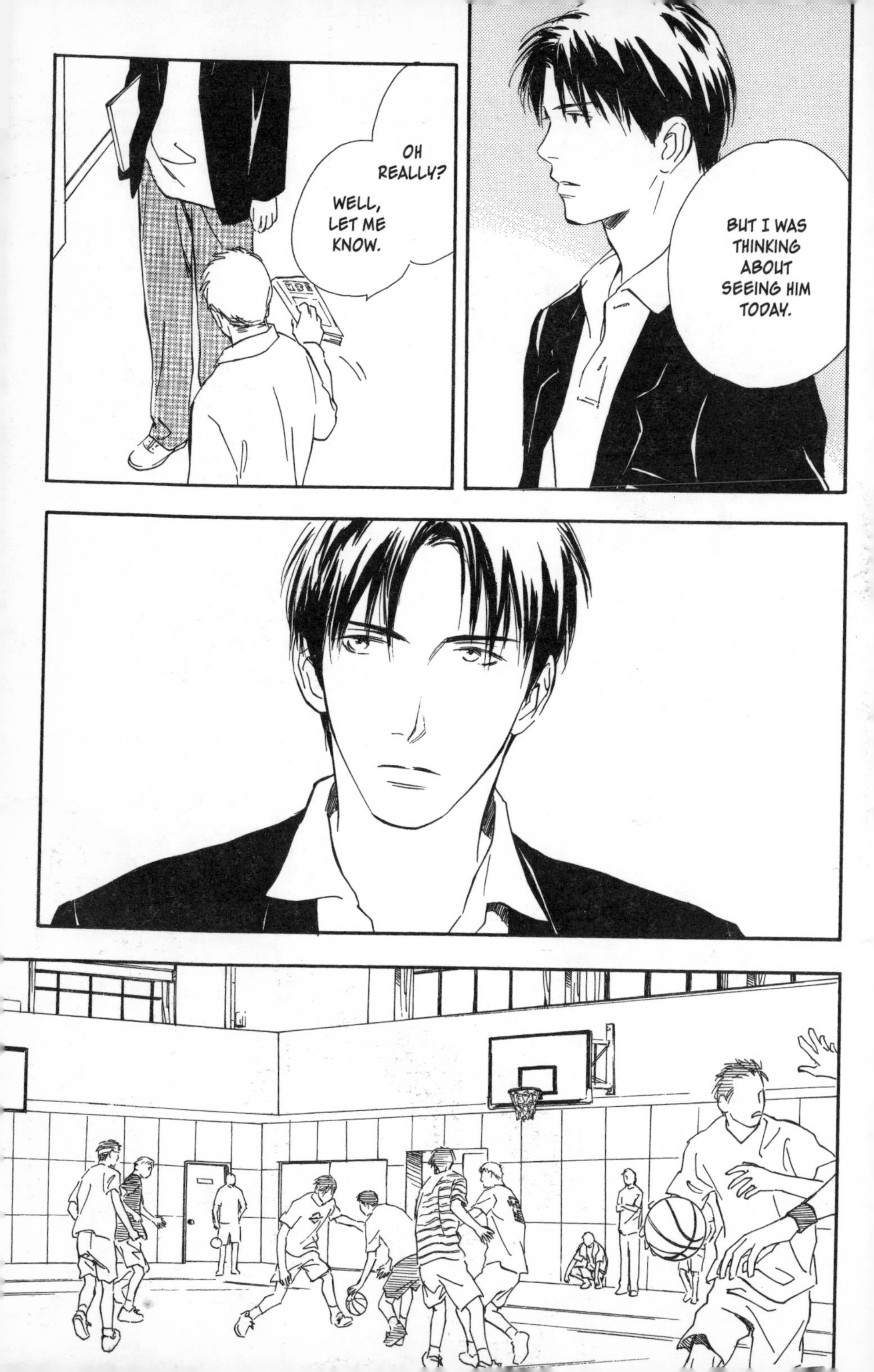
BUT I WAS THINKING ABOUT SEEING HIM TODAY.
OH REALLY?
WELL, LET ME KNOW.

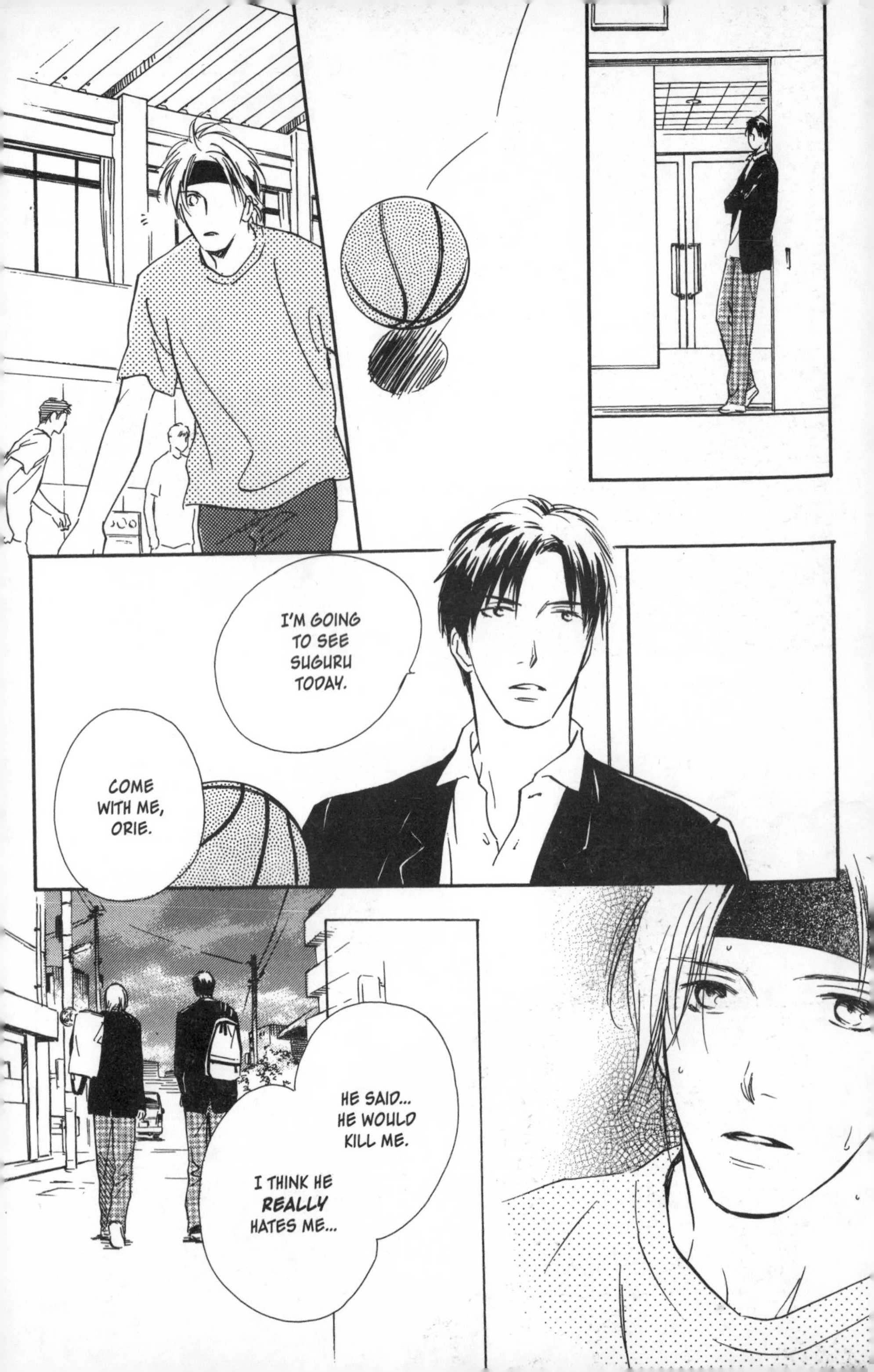
I'M GOING TO SEE SUGURU TODAY.
COME WITH ME, ORIE.
HE SAID... HE WOULD KILL ME.
I THINK HE REALLY HATES ME...

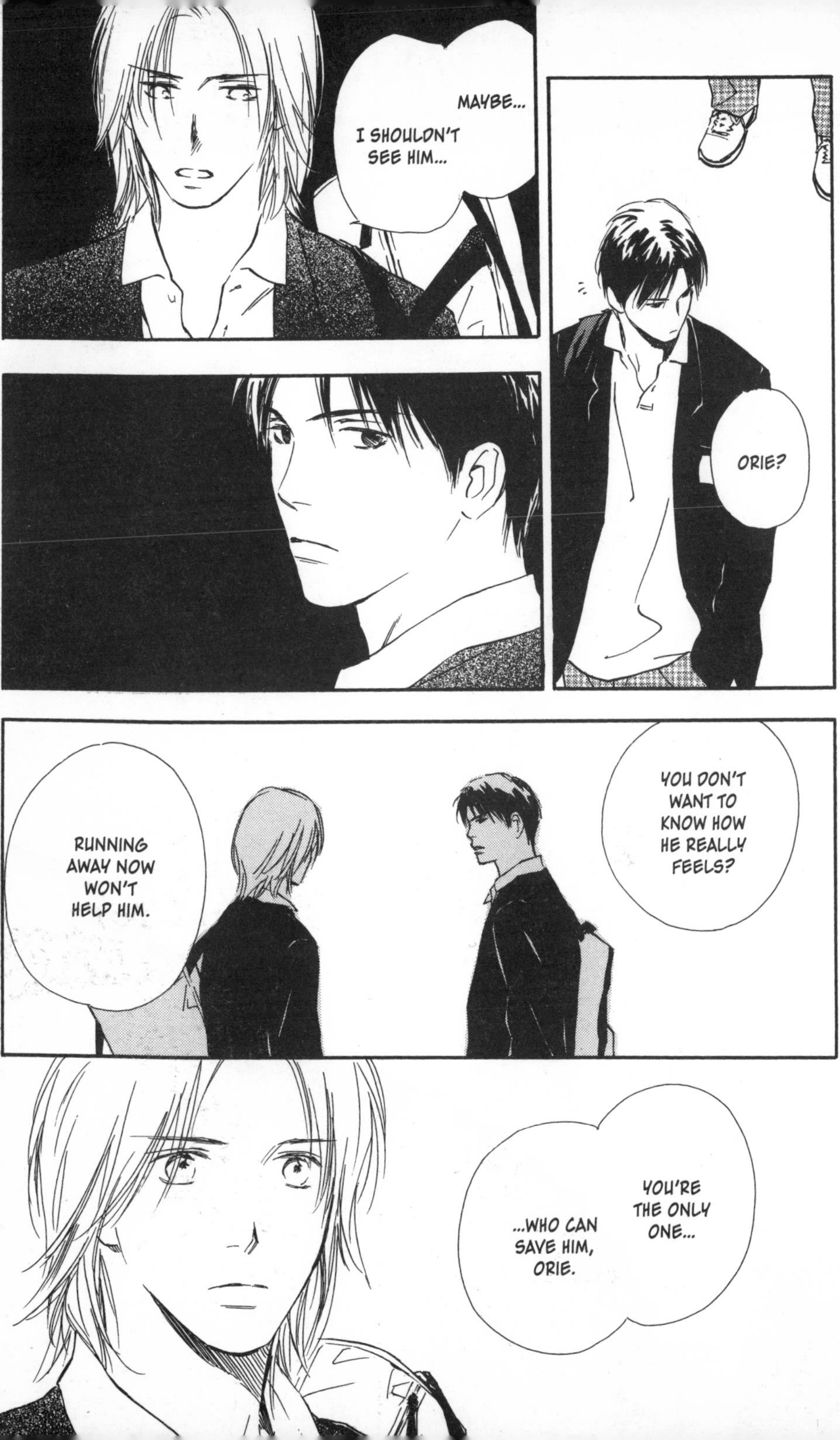
ORIE?
MAYBE...
I SHOULDN'T SEE HIM...
YOU DON'T WANT TO KNOW HOW HE REALLY FEELS?
RUNNING AWAY NOW WON'T HELP HIM.
YOU'RE THE ONLY ONE...
...WHO CAN SAVE HIM, ORIE.

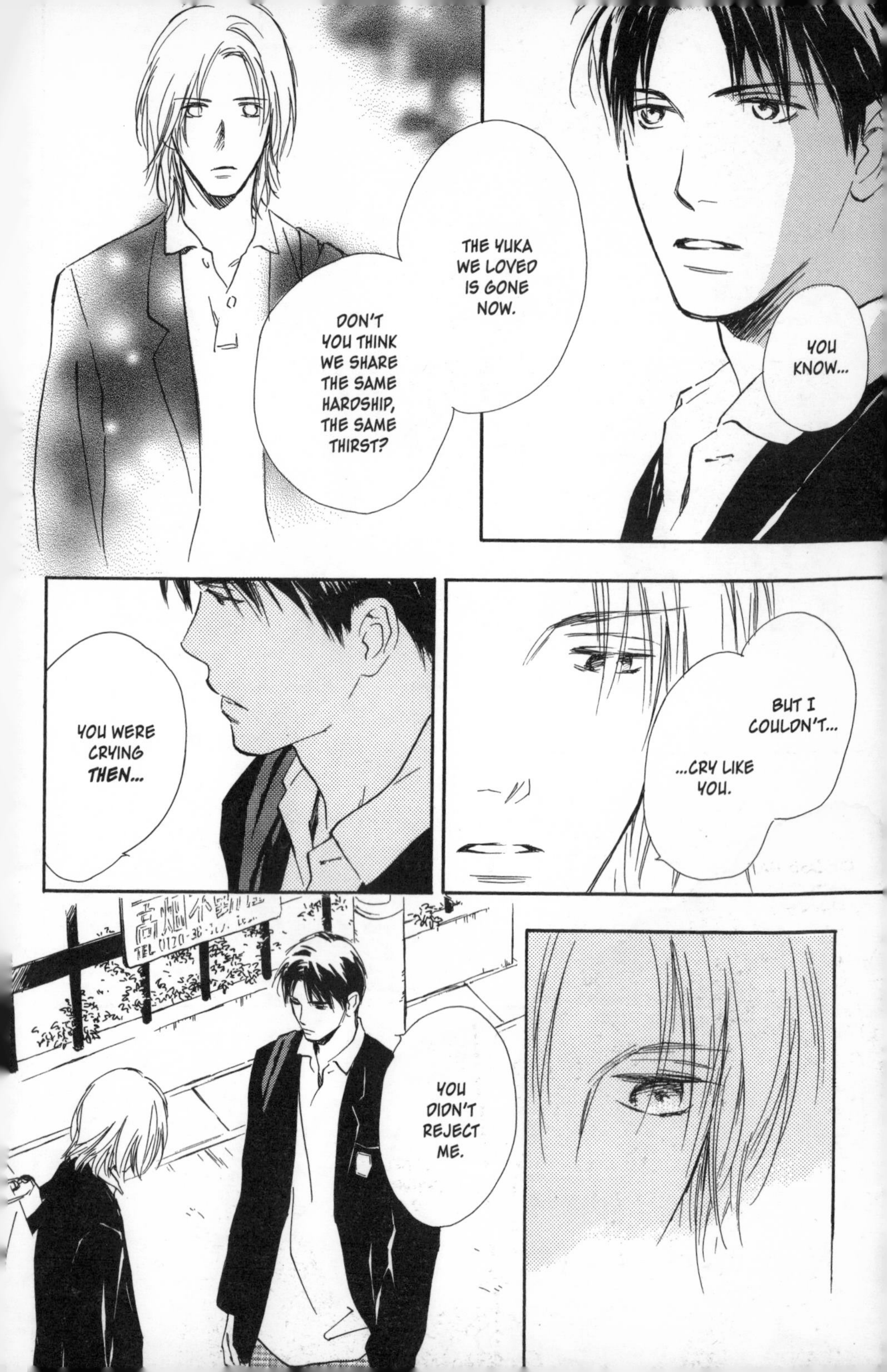
YOU KNOW...
THE YUKA WE LOVED IS GONE NOW.
DON'T YOU THINK WE SHARE THE SAME HARDSHIP, THE SAME THIRST?
BUT I COULDN'T...
...CRY LIKE YOU.
YOU WERE CRYING THEN...
YOU DIDN'T REJECT ME.

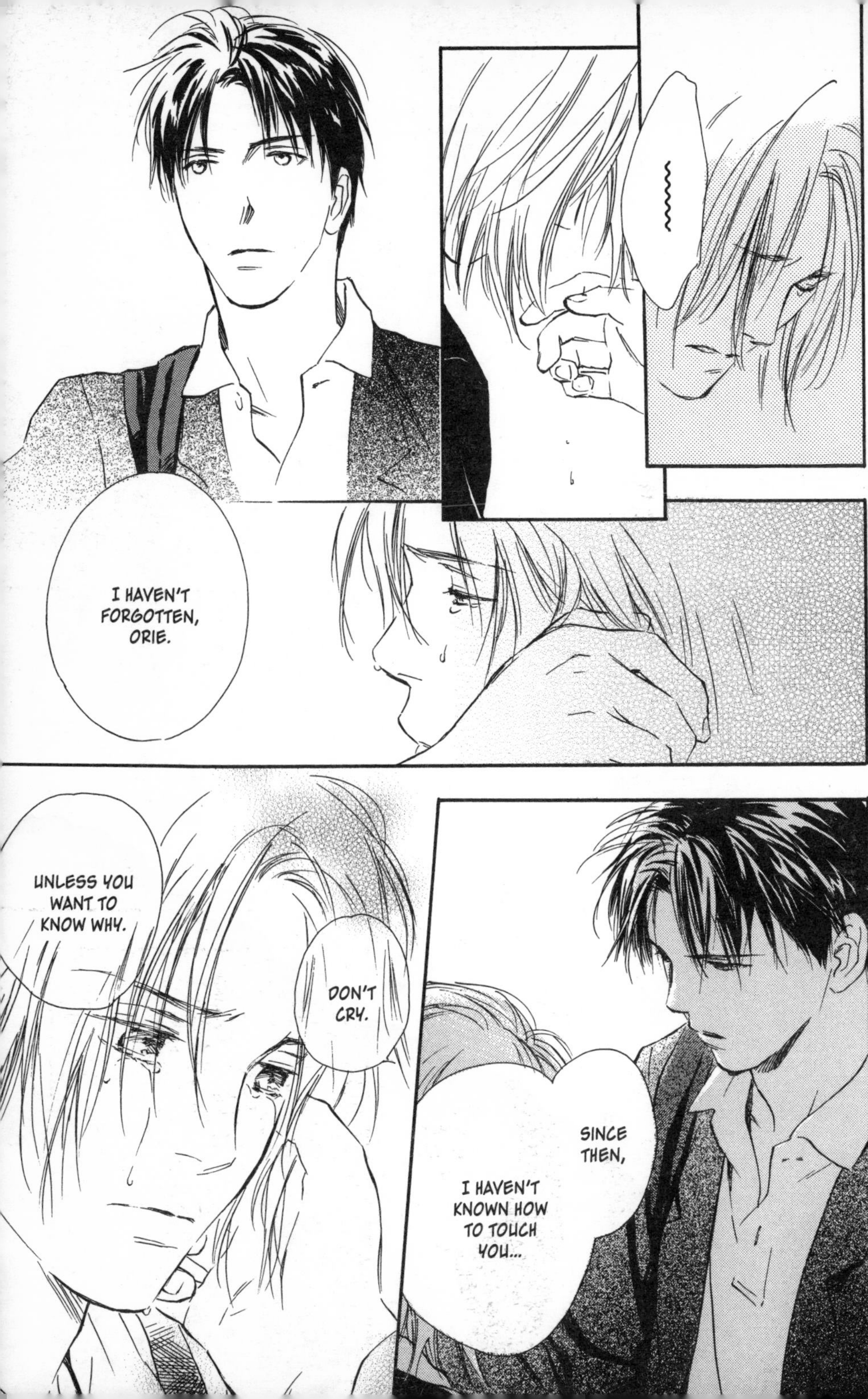
I HAVEN'T FORGOTTEN, ORIE.
SINCE THEN,
I HAVEN'T KNOWN HOW TO TOUCH YOU...
DON'T CRY.
UNLESS YOU WANT TO KNOW WHY.

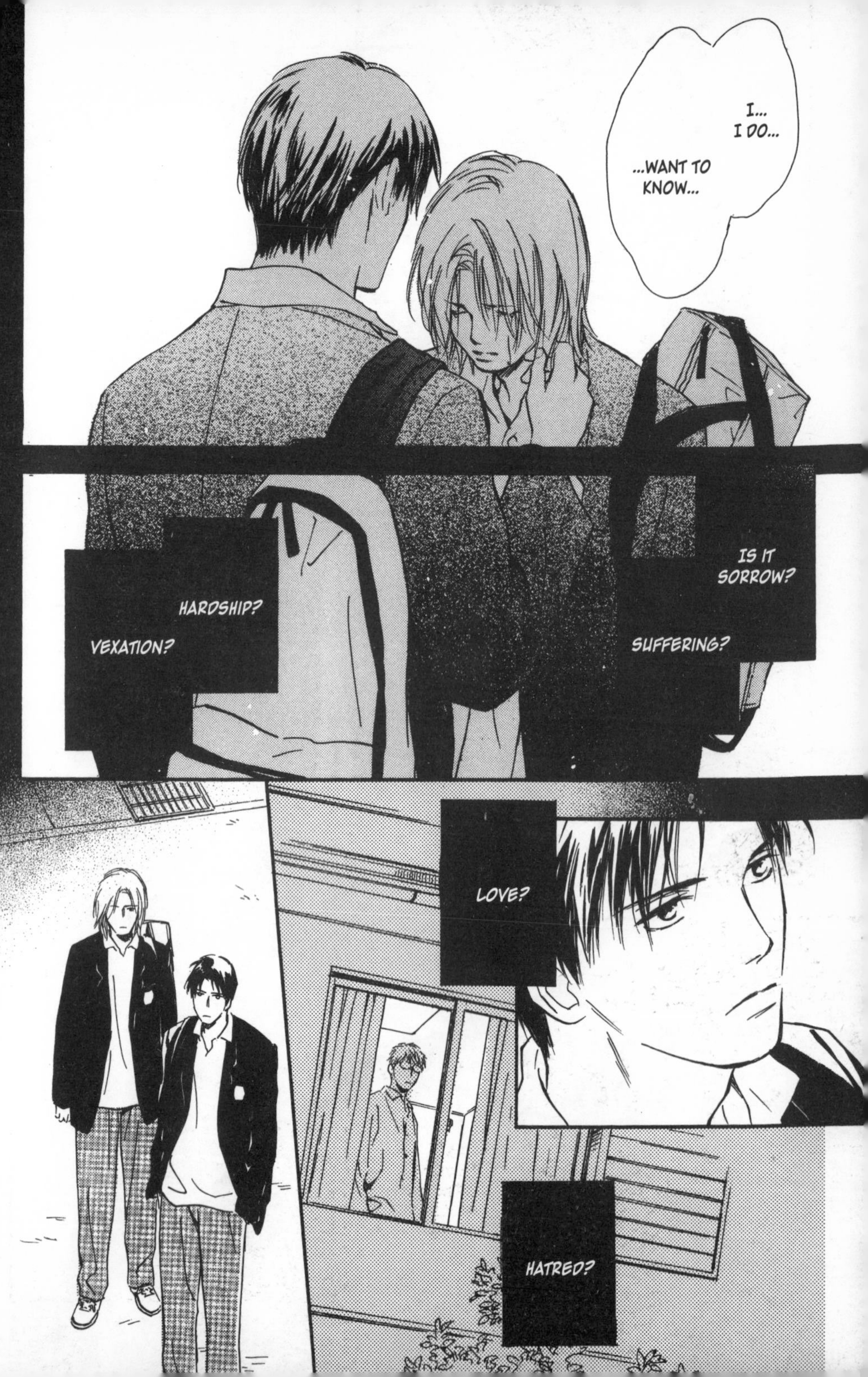
I...
I DO...
...WANT TO
KNOW...
IS IT
SORROW?
SUFFERING?
HARDSHIP?
VEXATION?
LOVE?
HATRED?

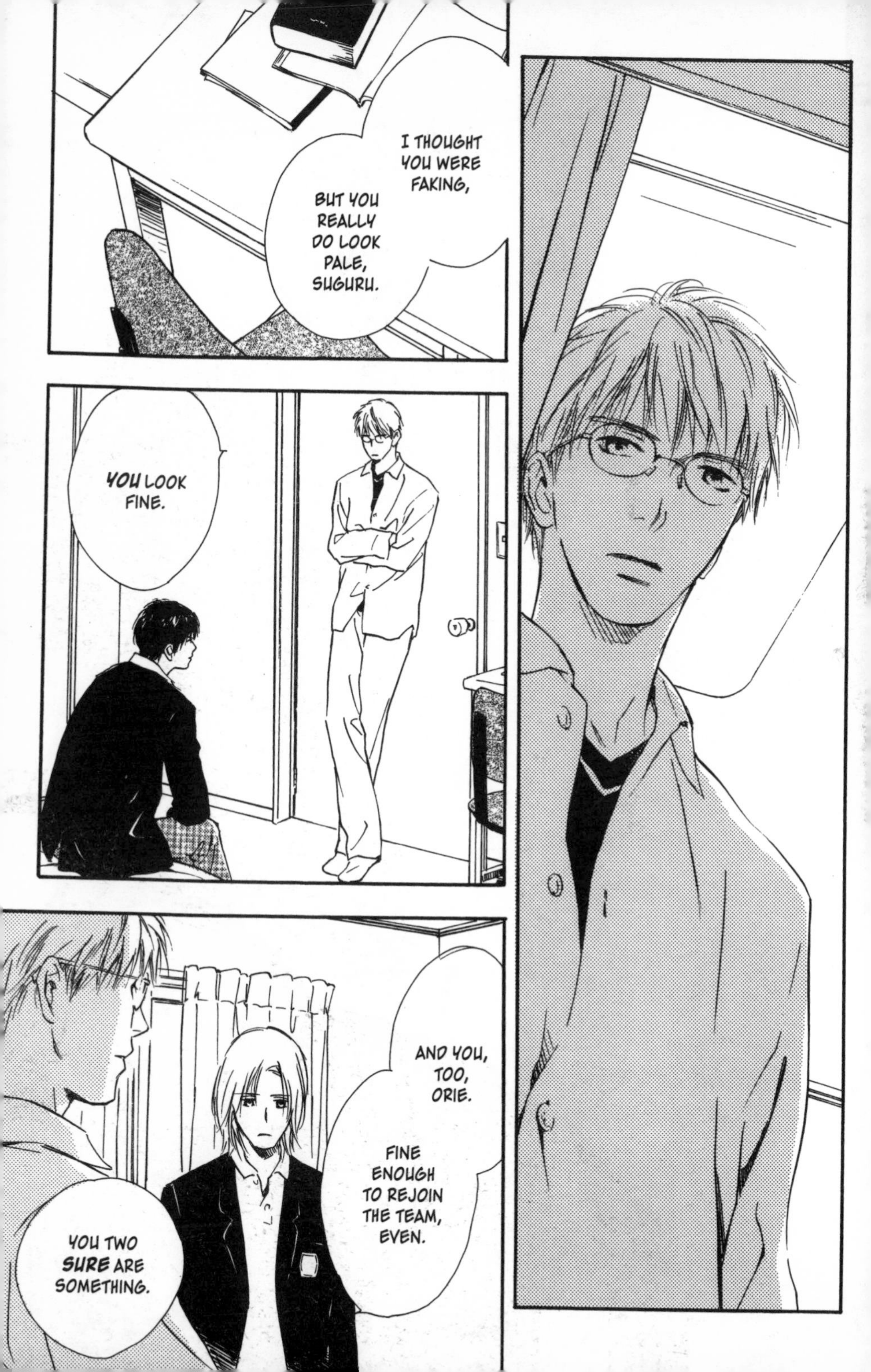
I THOUGHT YOU WERE FAKING,
BUT YOU REALLY DO LOOK PALE, SUGURU.
YOU LOOK FINE.
AND YOU, TOO, ORIE.
FINE ENOUGH TO REJOIN THE TEAM, EVEN.
YOU TWO SURE ARE SOMETHING.

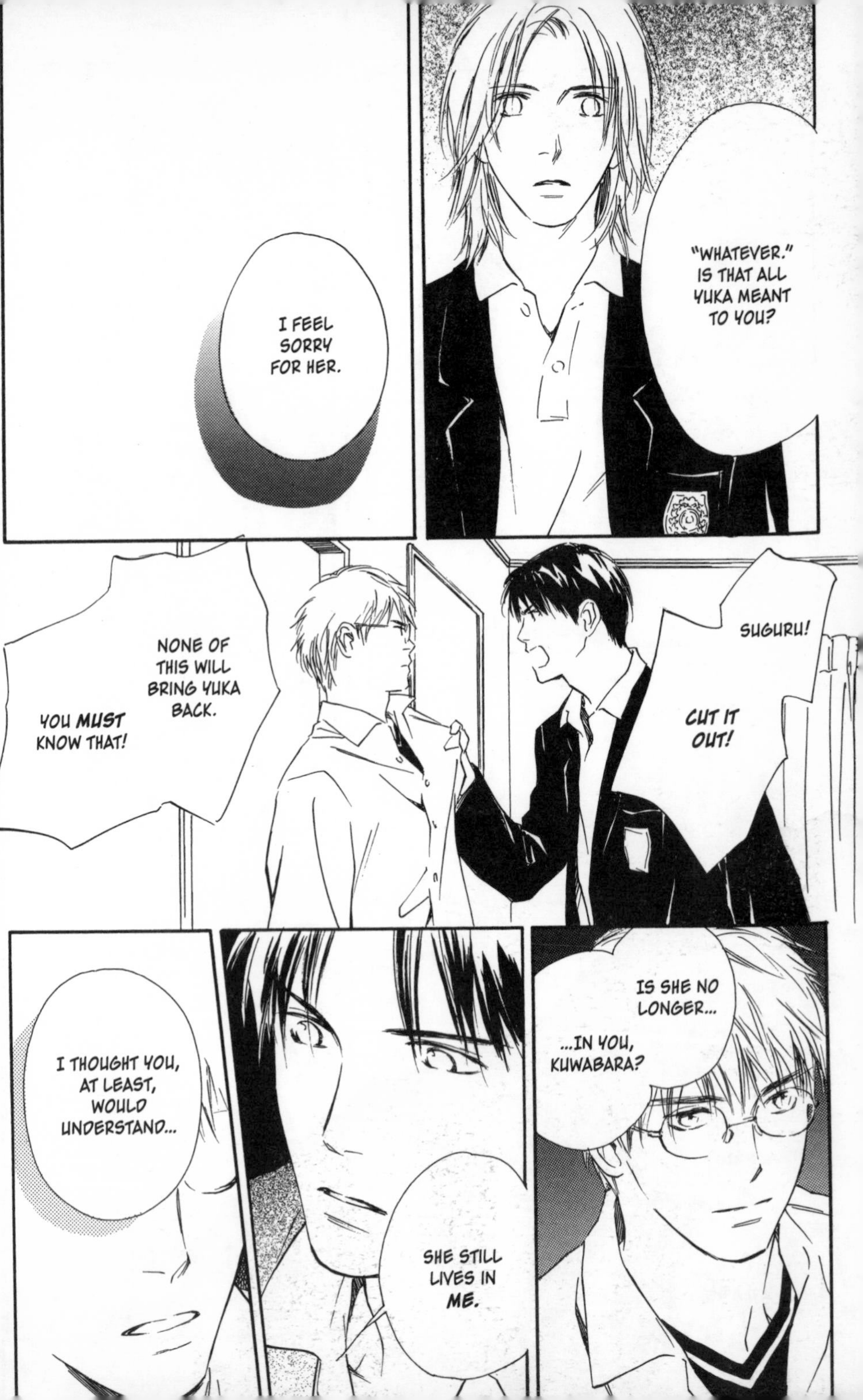
"WHATEVER." IS THAT ALL YUKA MEANT TO YOU?
I FEEL SORRY FOR HER.
SUGURU!
CUT IT OUT!
NONE OF THIS WILL BRING YUKA BACK.
YOU **MUST** KNOW THAT!
IS SHE NO LONGER...
...IN YOU, KUWABARA?
SHE STILL LIVES IN **ME**.
I THOUGHT YOU, AT LEAST, WOULD UNDERSTAND...

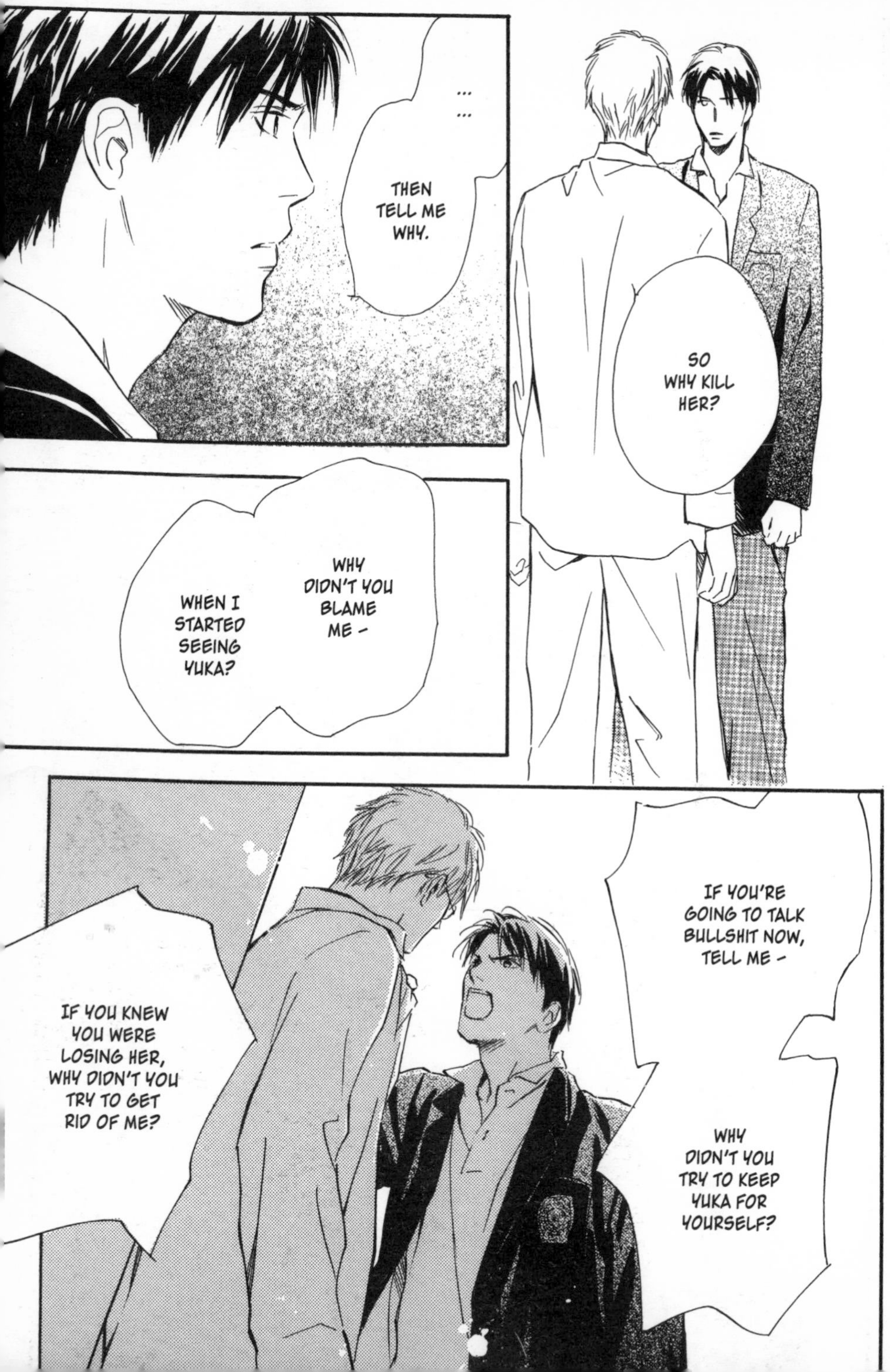
SO WHY KILL HER?
...
...
THEN TELL ME WHY.
WHY DIDN'T YOU BLAME ME - WHEN I STARTED SEEING YUKA?
IF YOU'RE GOING TO TALK BULLSHIT NOW, TELL ME -
WHY DIDN'T YOU TRY TO KEEP YUKA FOR YOURSELF?
IF YOU KNEW YOU WERE LOSING HER, WHY DIDN'T YOU TRY TO GET RID OF ME?

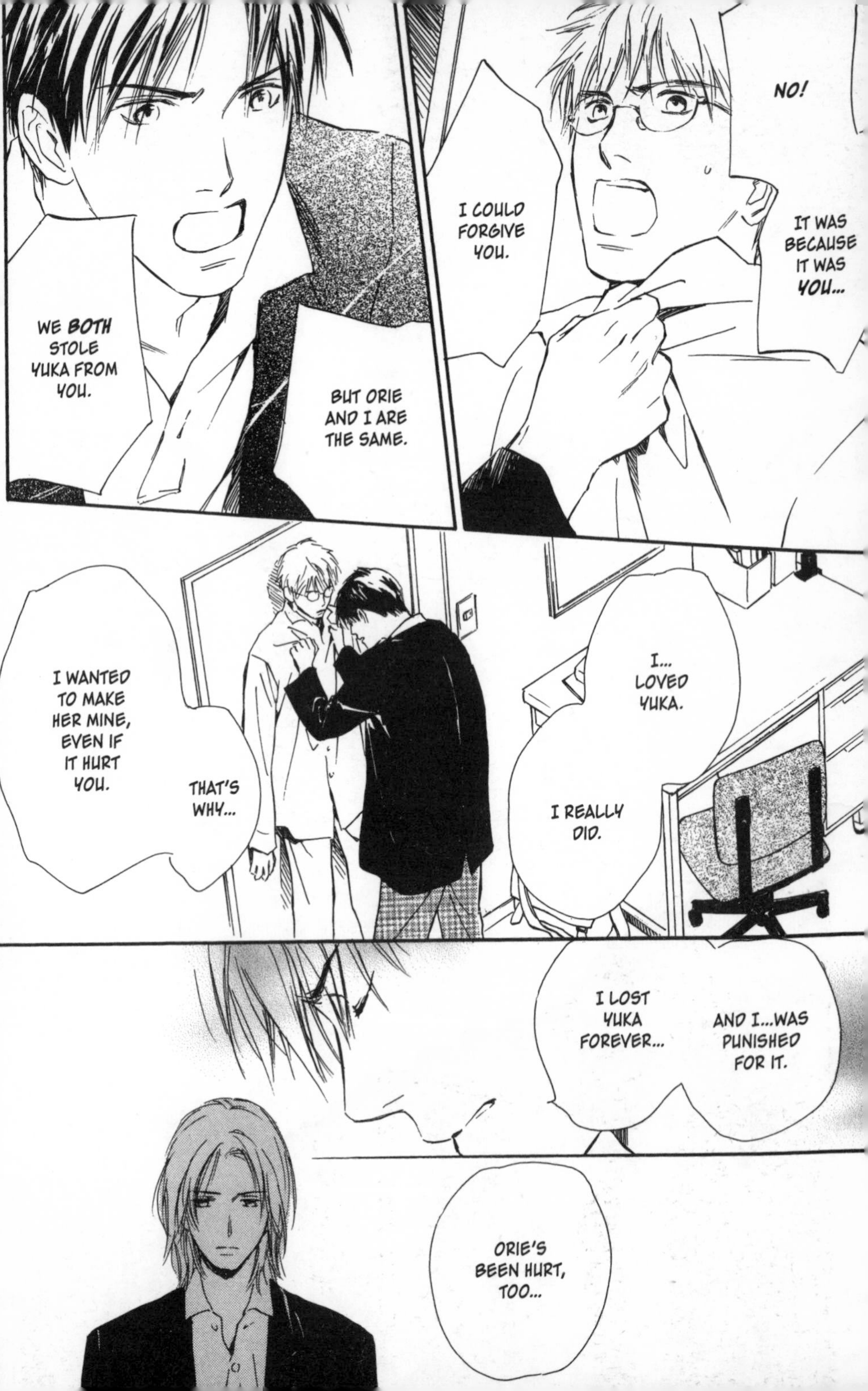
NO!
IT WAS BECAUSE IT WAS YOU...
I COULD FORGIVE YOU.
BUT ORIE AND I ARE THE SAME.
WE BOTH STOLE YUKA FROM YOU.
I... LOVED YUKA.
I REALLY DID.
THAT'S WHY...
I WANTED TO MAKE HER MINE, EVEN IF IT HURT YOU.
AND I...WAS PUNISHED FOR IT.
I LOST YUKA FOREVER...
ORIE'S BEEN HURT, TOO...

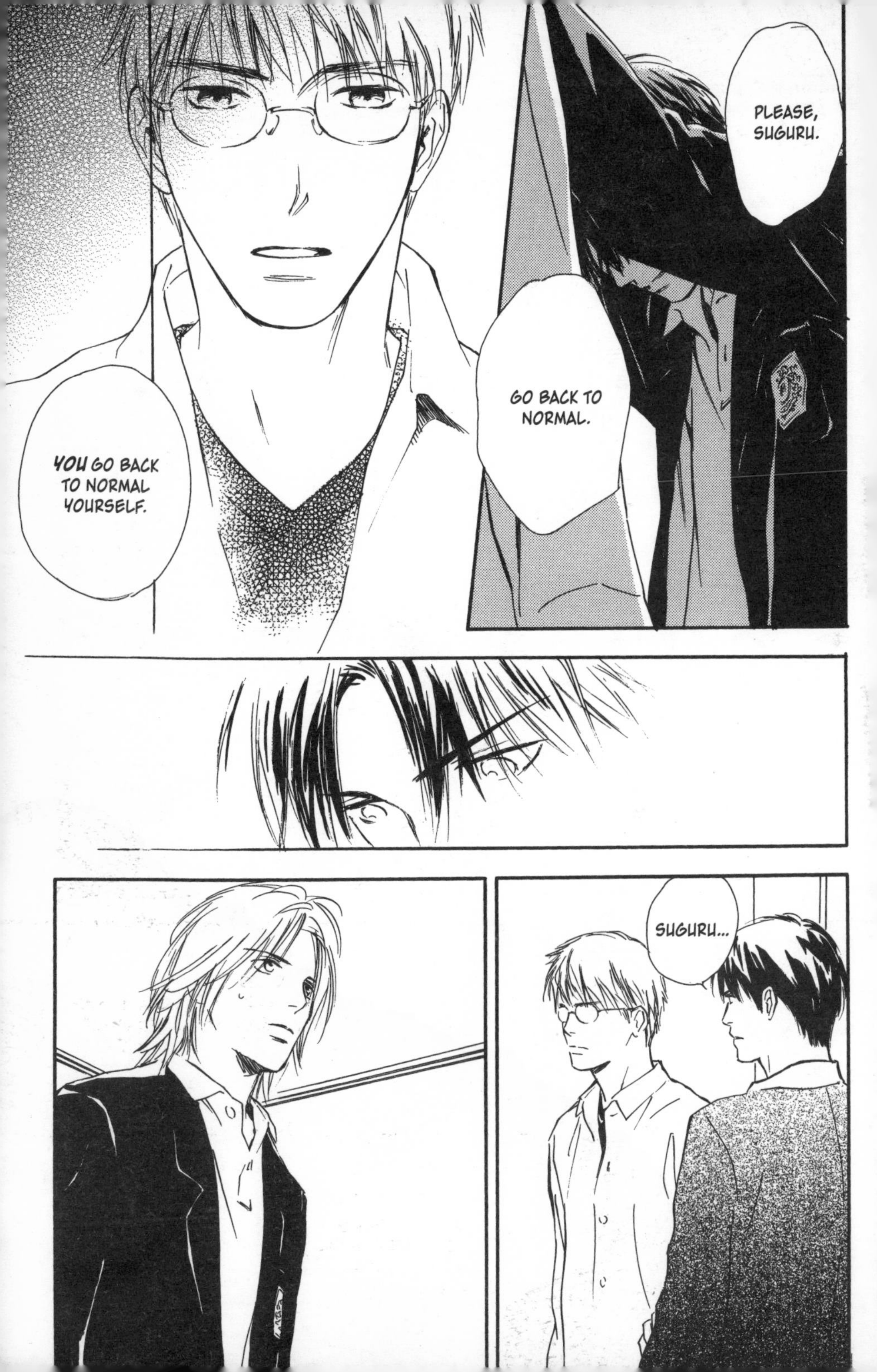
PLEASE, SUGURU.
GO BACK TO NORMAL.
YOU GO BACK TO NORMAL YOURSELF.
SUGURU...

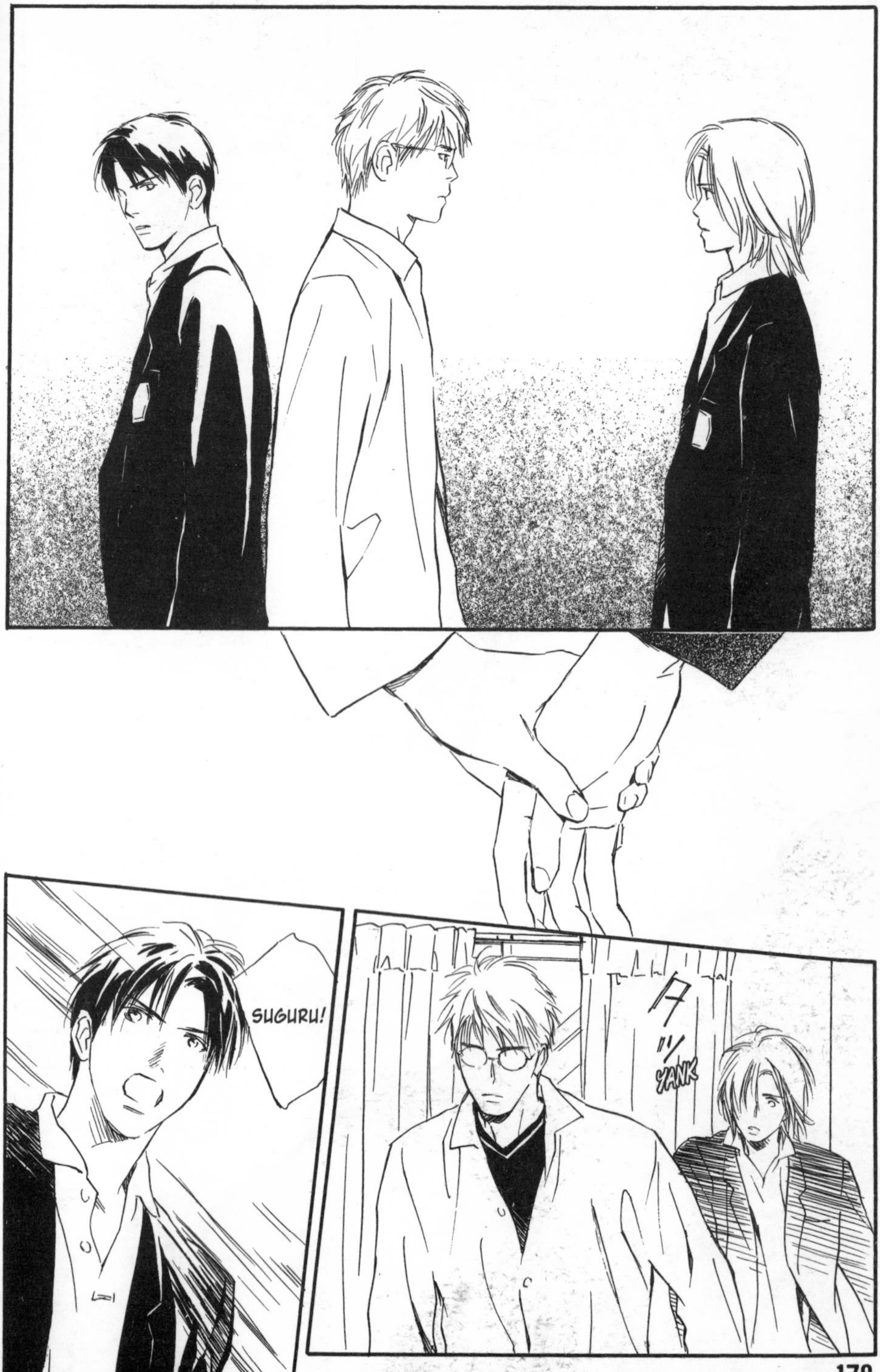
タッ
YANK
SUGURU!

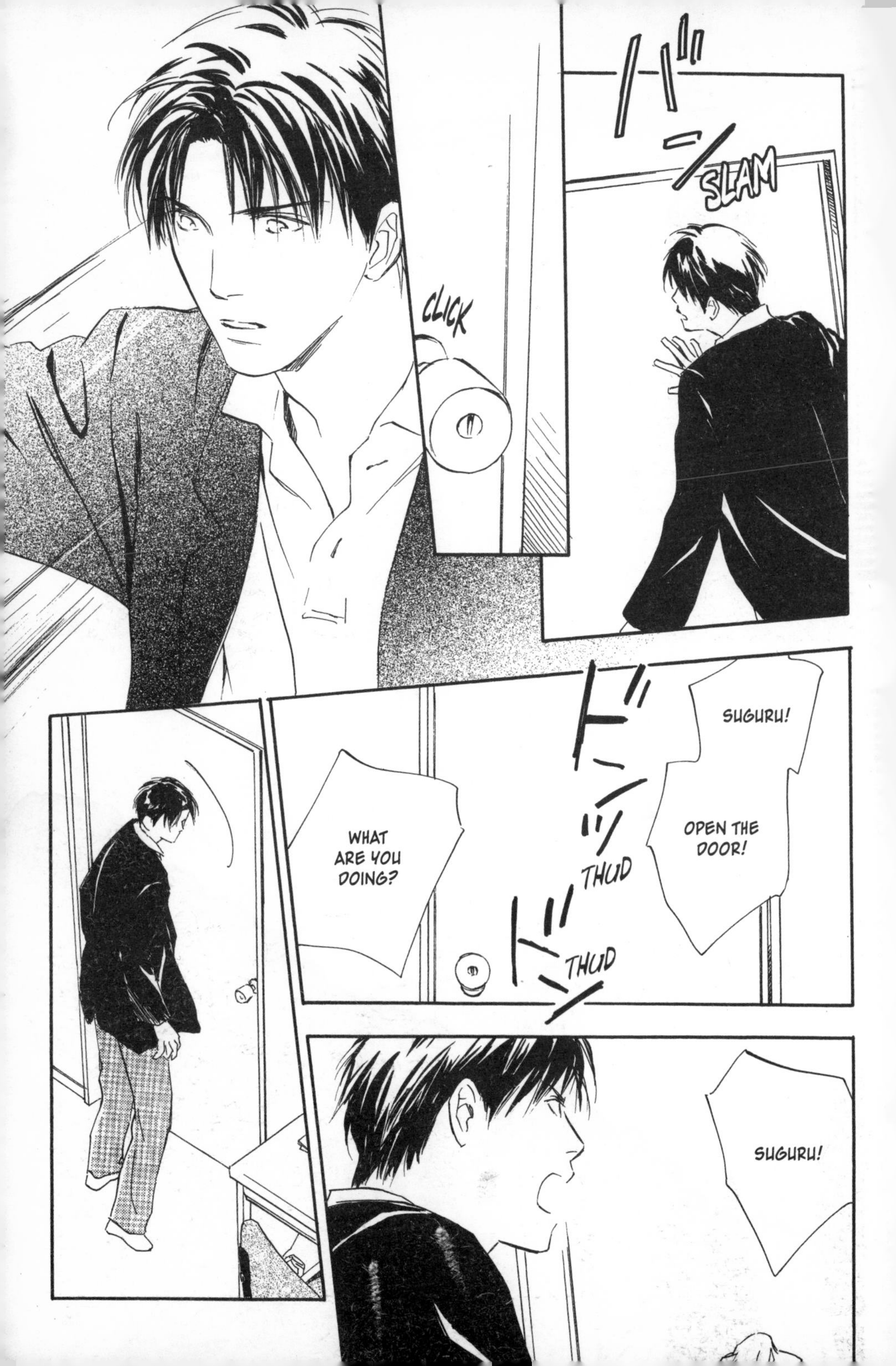
SLAM
CLICK
SUGURU!
OPEN THE DOOR!
THUD
THUD
WHAT ARE YOU DOING?
SUGURU!

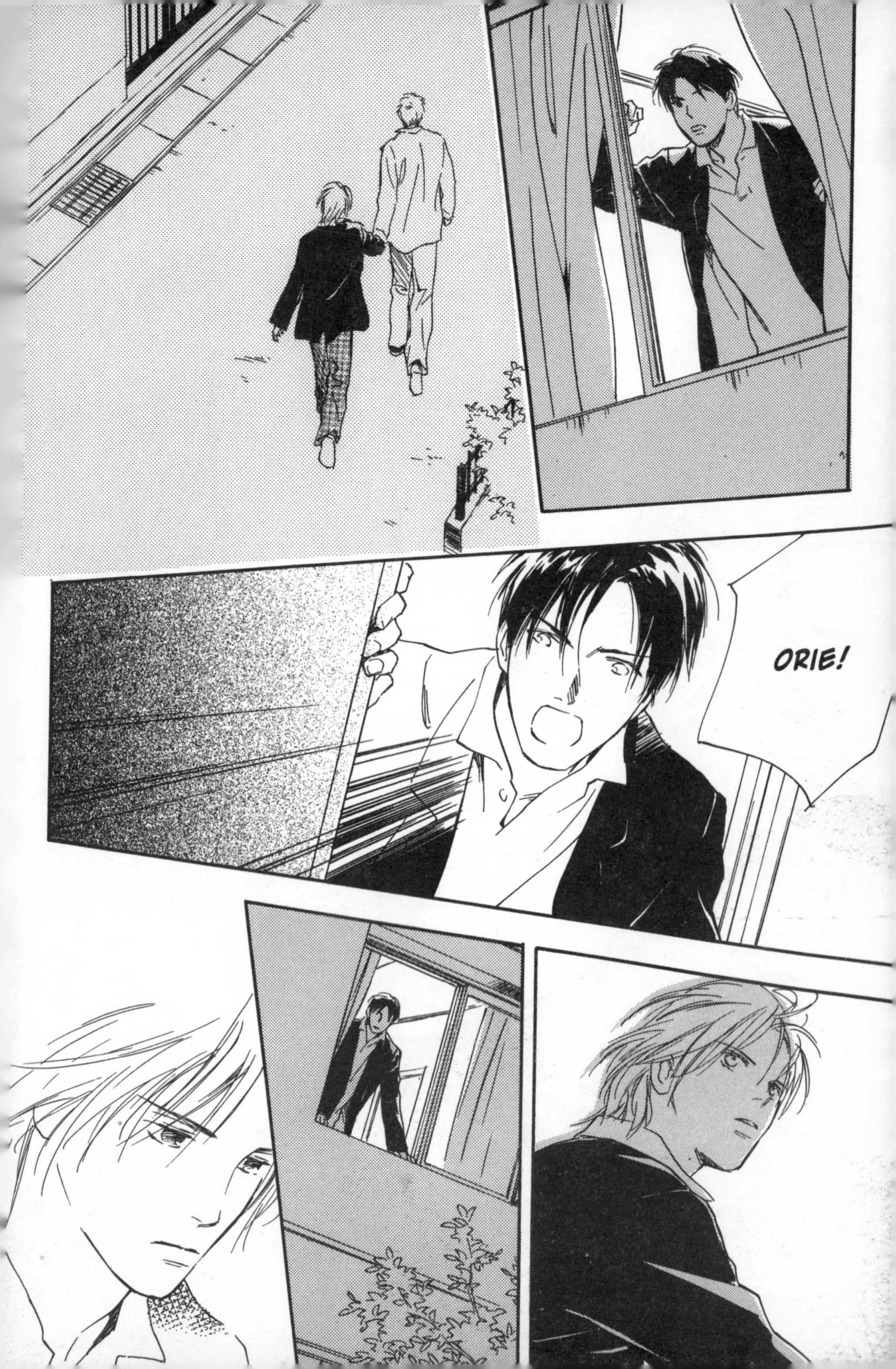
ORIE!

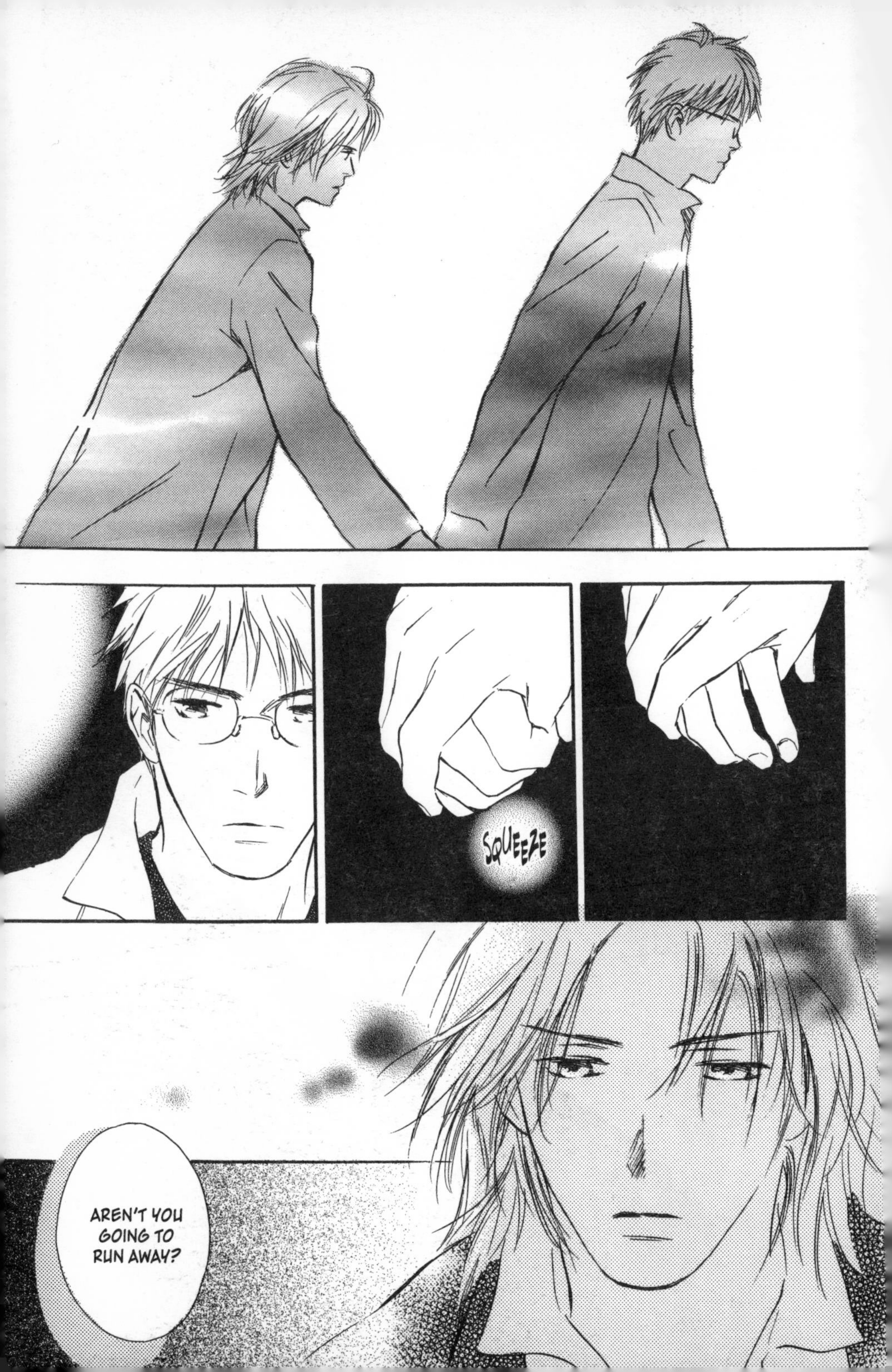
SQUEEZE
AREN'T YOU GOING TO RUN AWAY?

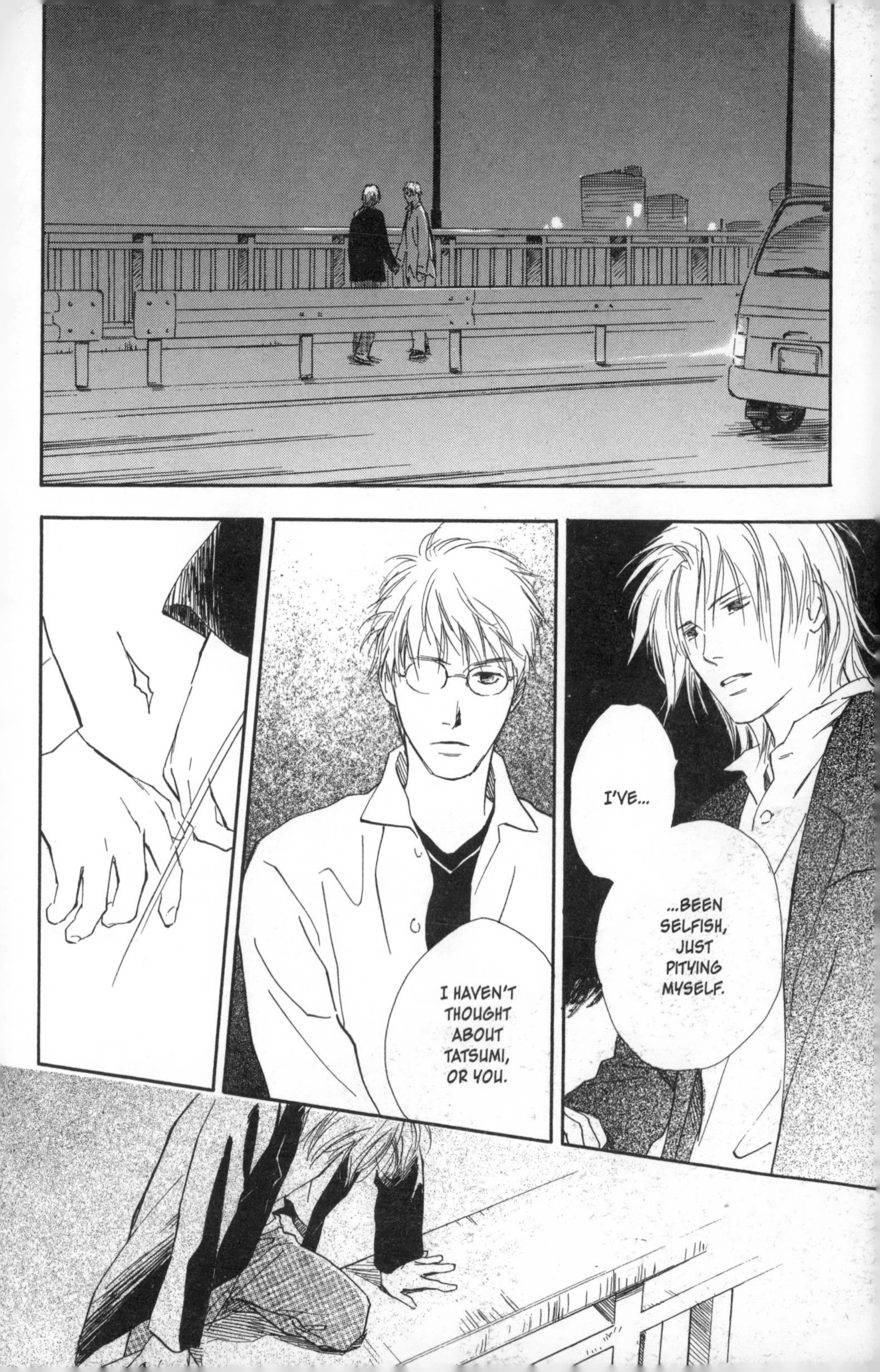
I'VE...
...BEEN SELFISH, JUST PITYING MYSELF.
I HAVEN'T THOUGHT ABOUT TATSUMI, OR YOU.

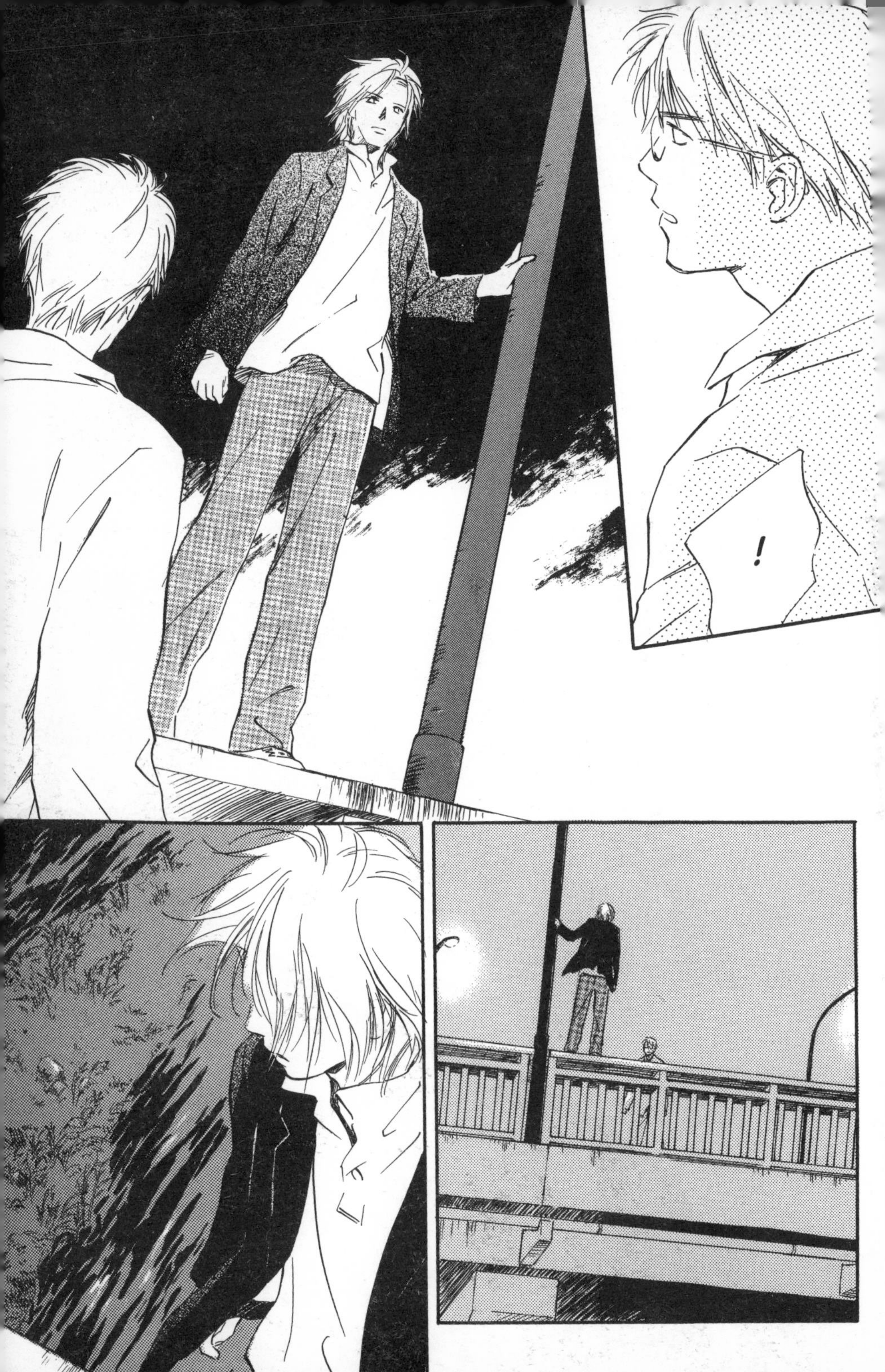
!

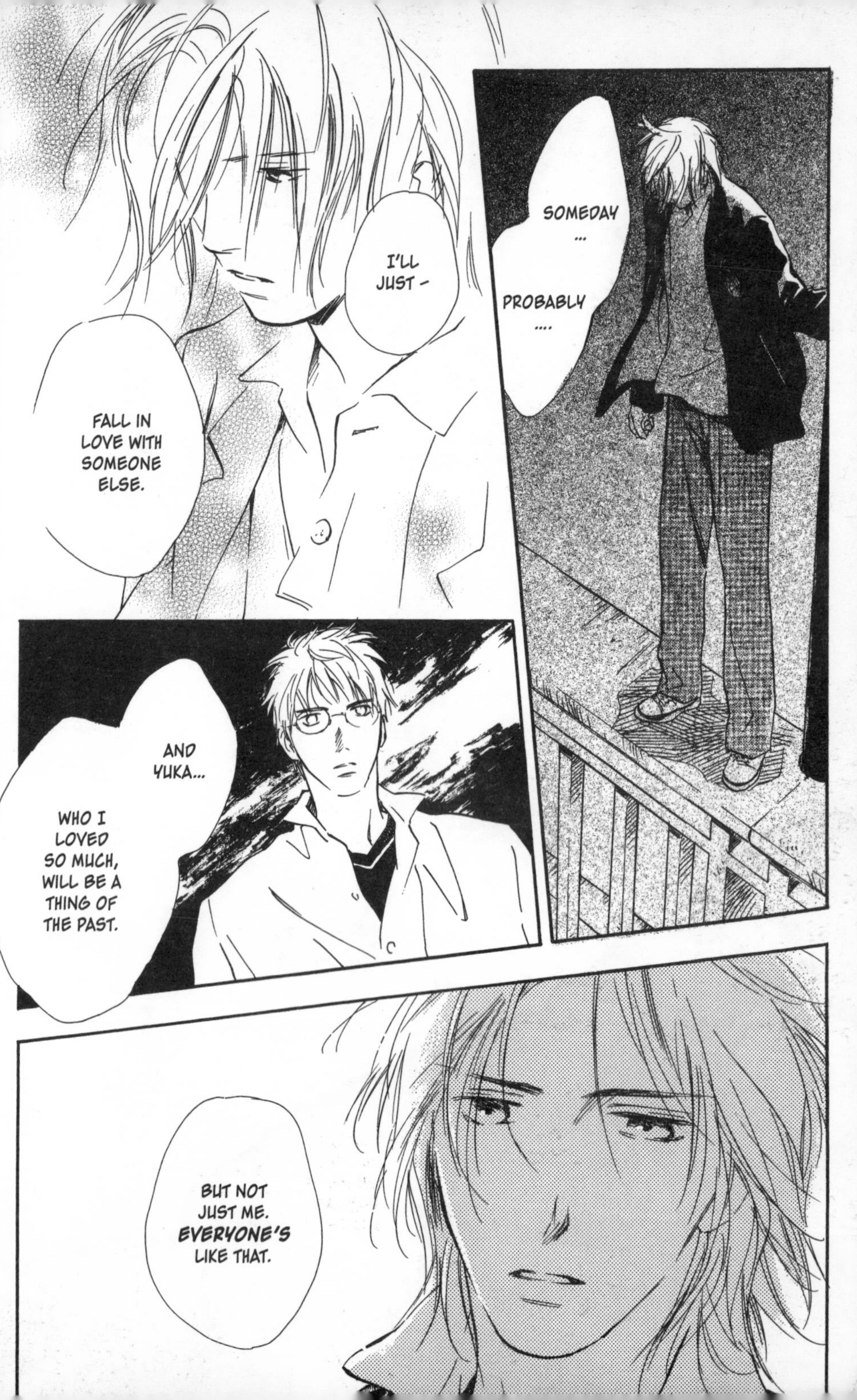
SOMEDAY ...
PROBABLY ....
I'LL JUST -
FALL IN LOVE WITH SOMEONE ELSE.
AND YUKA...
WHO I LOVED SO MUCH, WILL BE A THING OF THE PAST.
BUT NOT JUST ME. EVERYONE'S LIKE THAT.

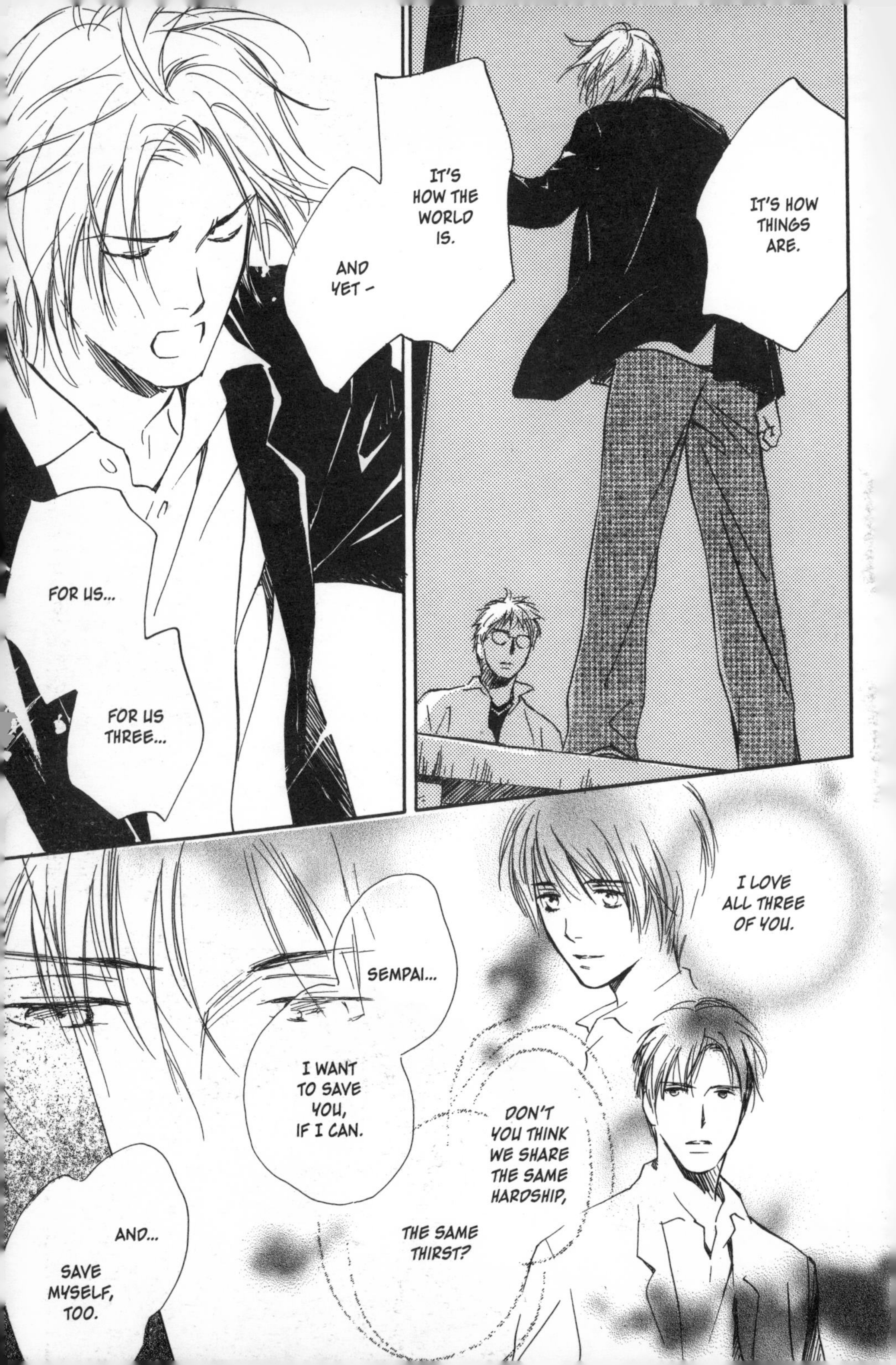
IT'S HOW THINGS ARE.
IT'S HOW THE WORLD IS.
AND YET -
FOR US...
FOR US THREE...
I LOVE ALL THREE OF YOU.
SEMPAI...
DON'T YOU THINK WE SHARE THE SAME HARDSHIP,
THE SAME THIRST?
I WANT TO SAVE YOU, IF I CAN.
AND...
SAVE MYSELF, TOO.

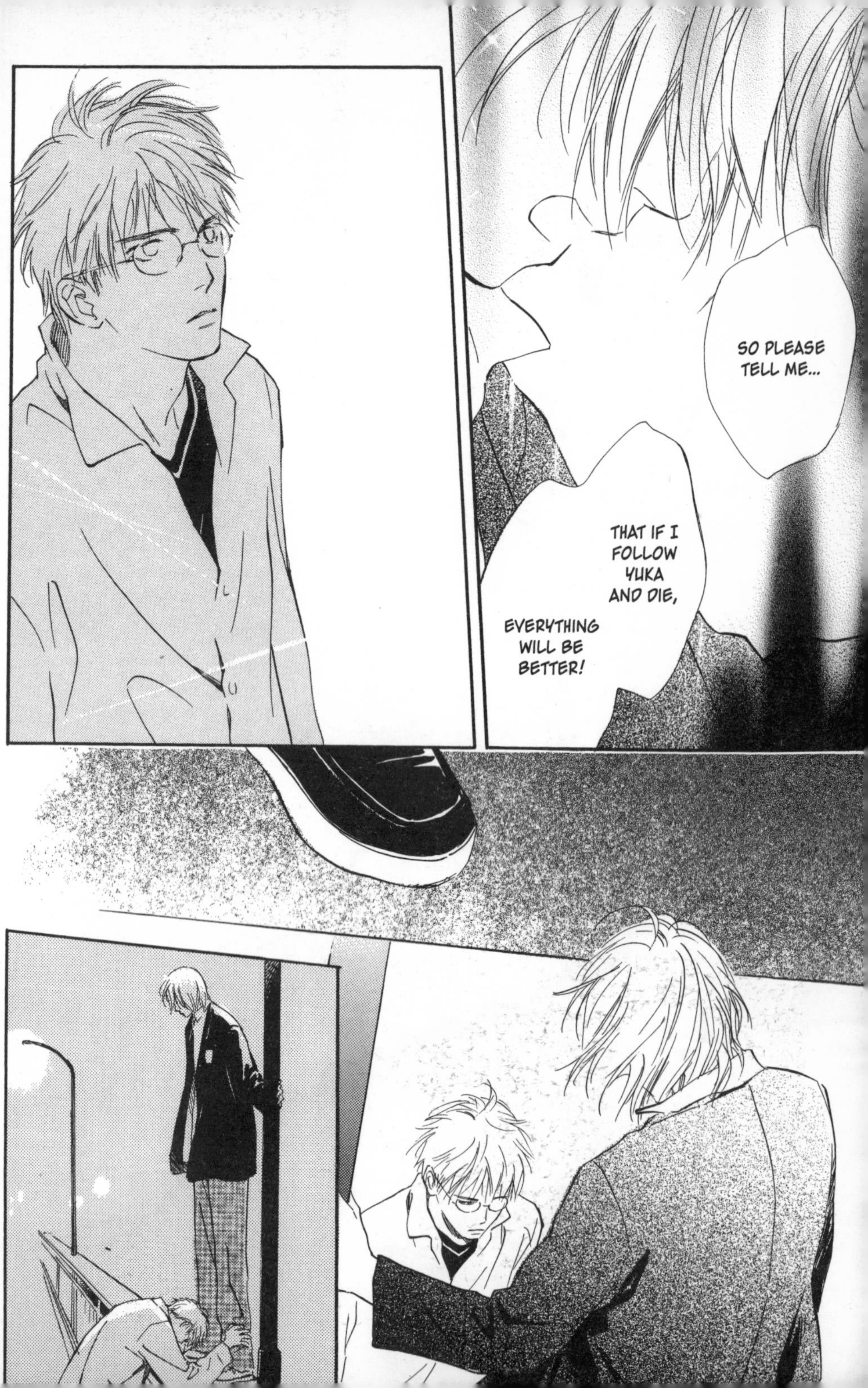
SO PLEASE TELL ME...
THAT IF I FOLLOW YUKA AND DIE,
EVERYTHING WILL BE BETTER!

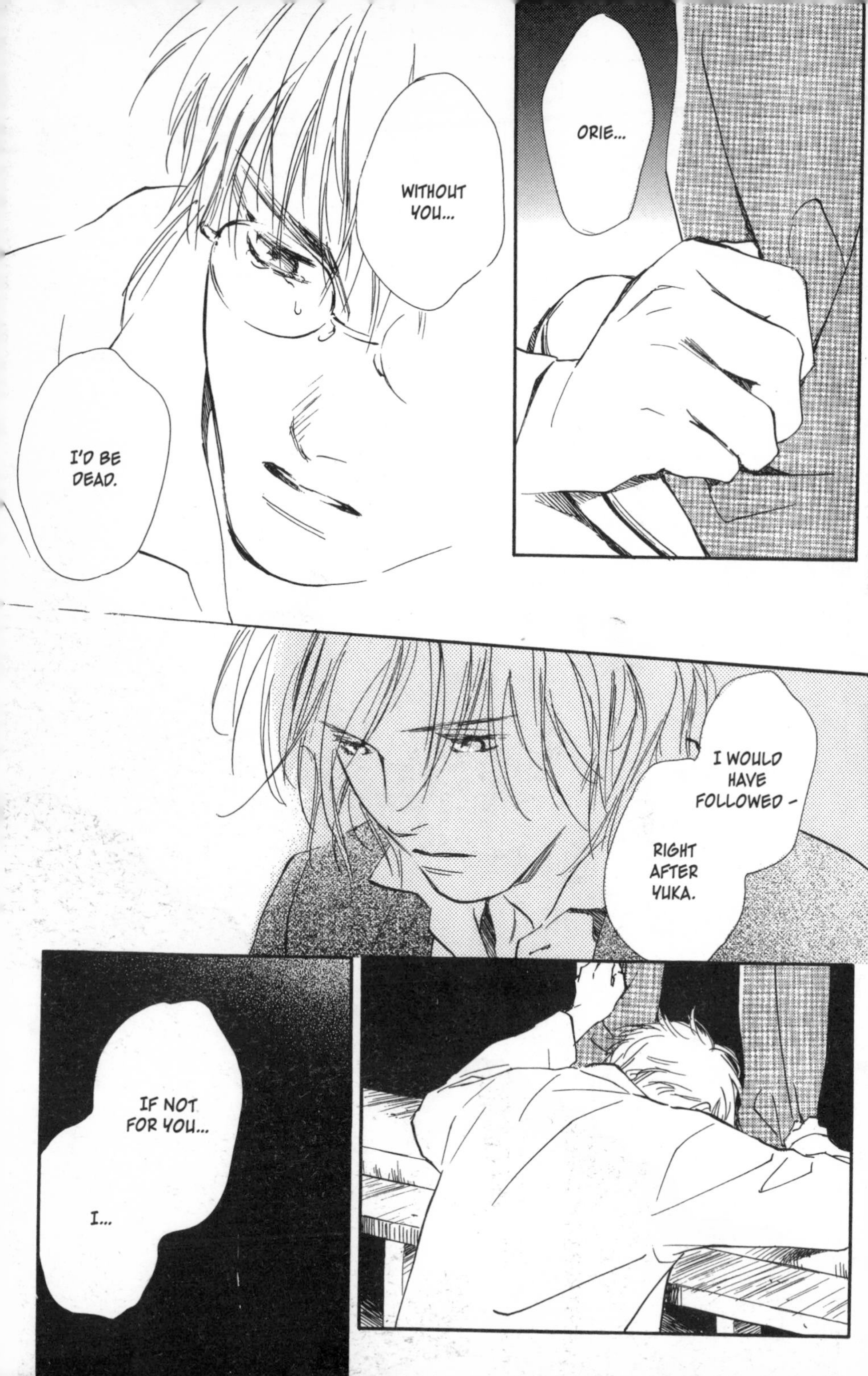
ORIE...
WITHOUT YOU...
I'D BE DEAD.
I WOULD HAVE FOLLOWED -
RIGHT AFTER YUKA.
IF NOT FOR YOU...
I...

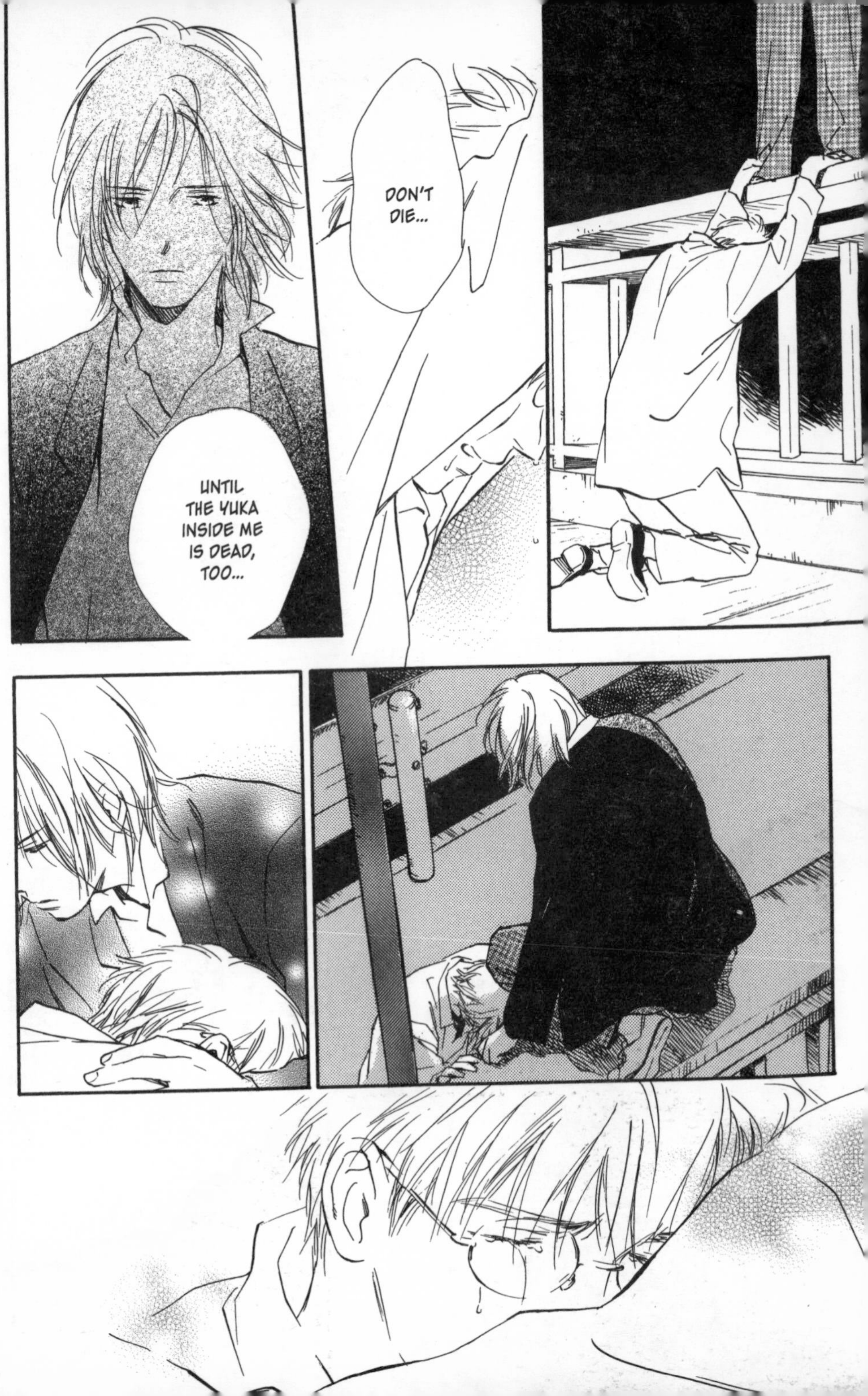
DON'T DIE...
UNTIL THE YUKA INSIDE ME IS DEAD, TOO...

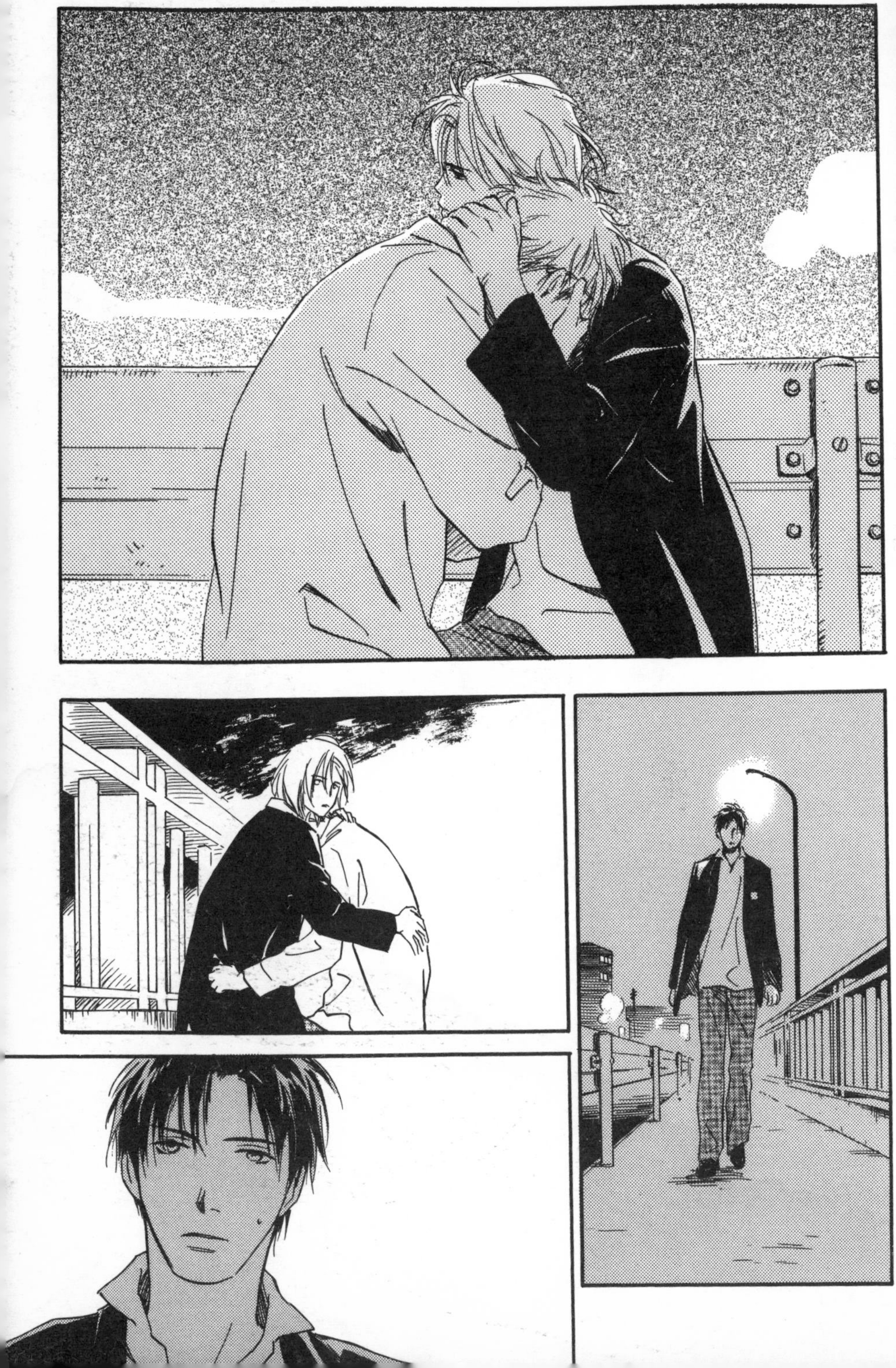

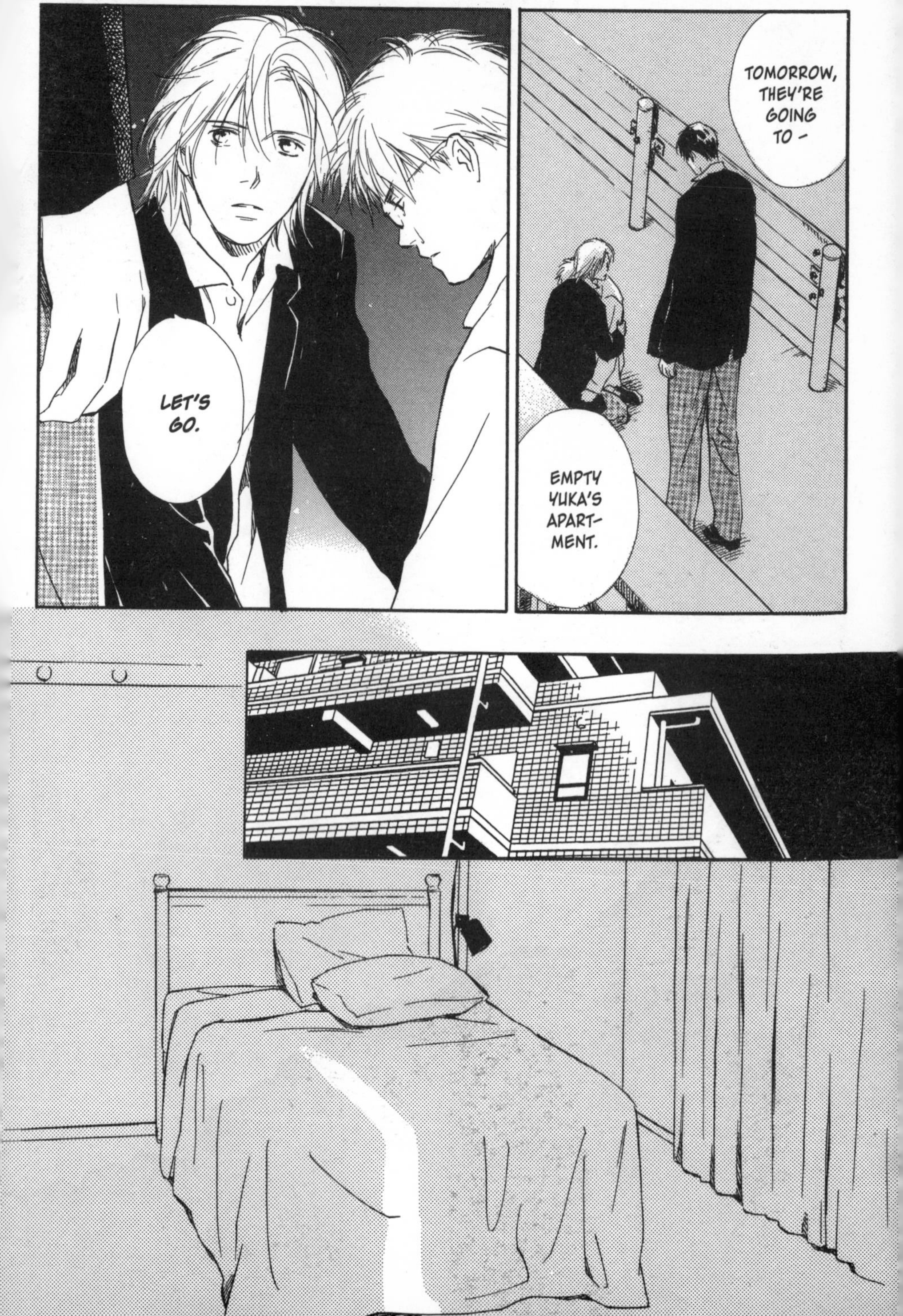
TOMORROW, THEY'RE GOING TO -
EMPTY YUKA'S APART-MENT.
LET'S GO.

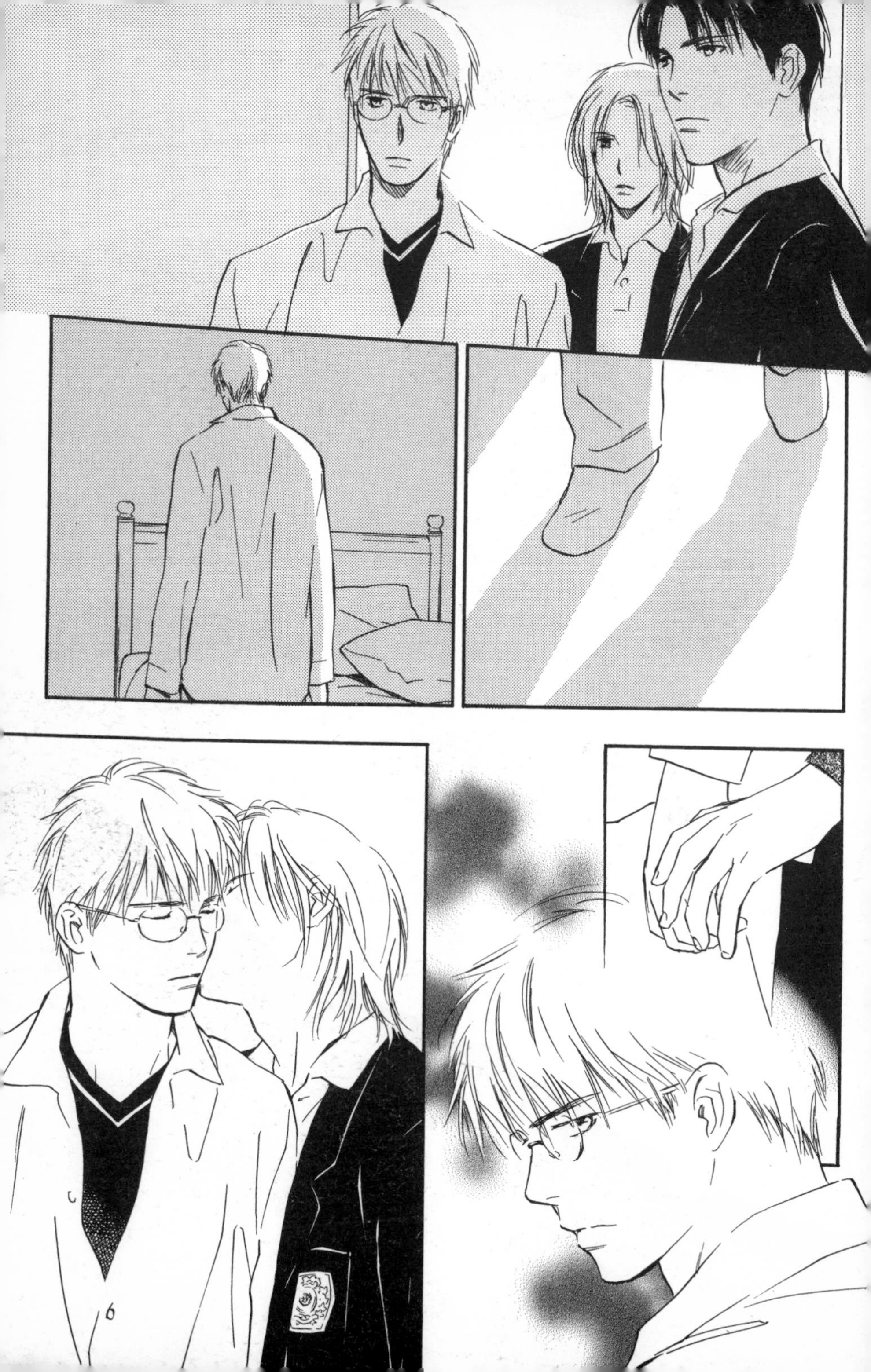

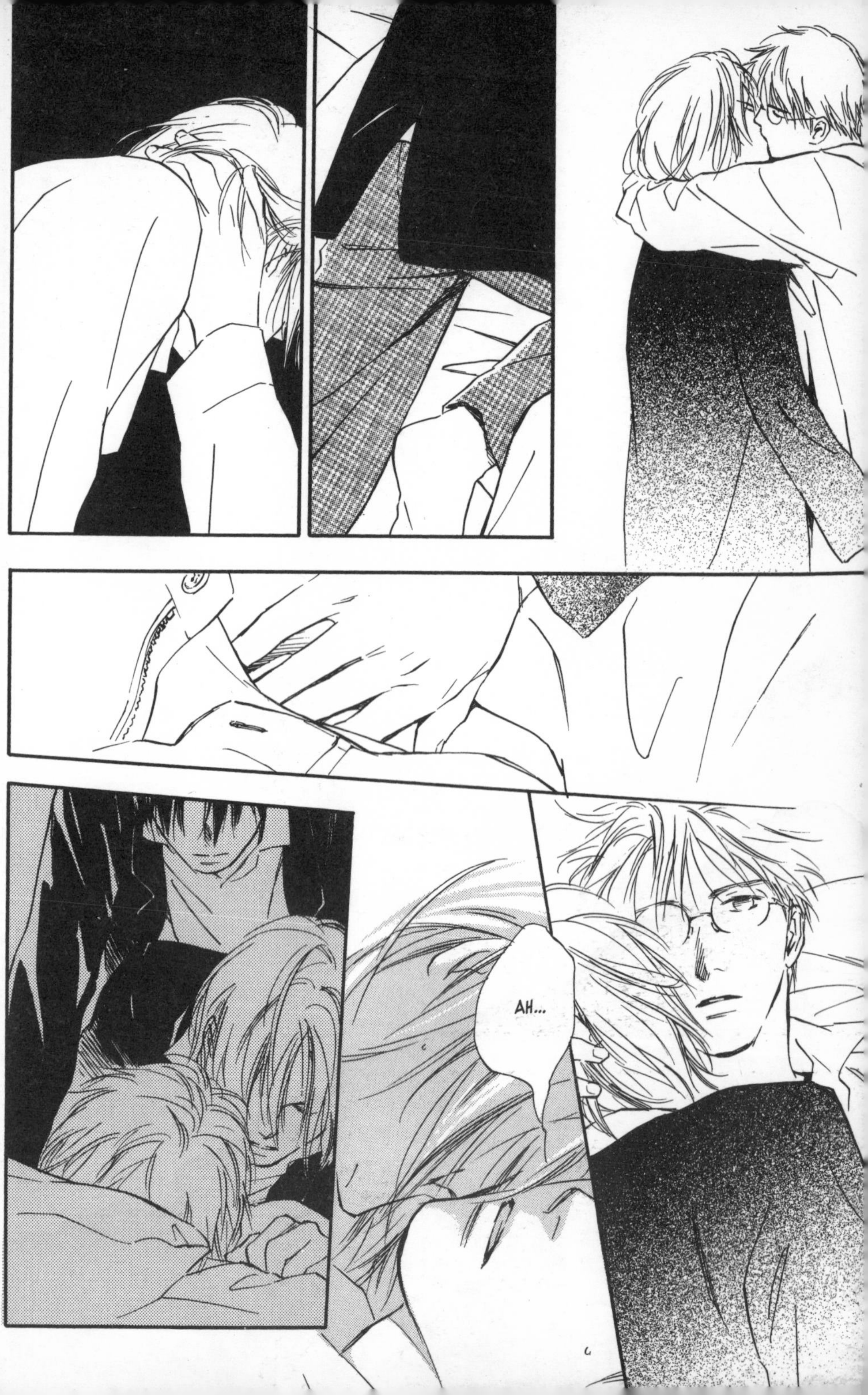
AH...

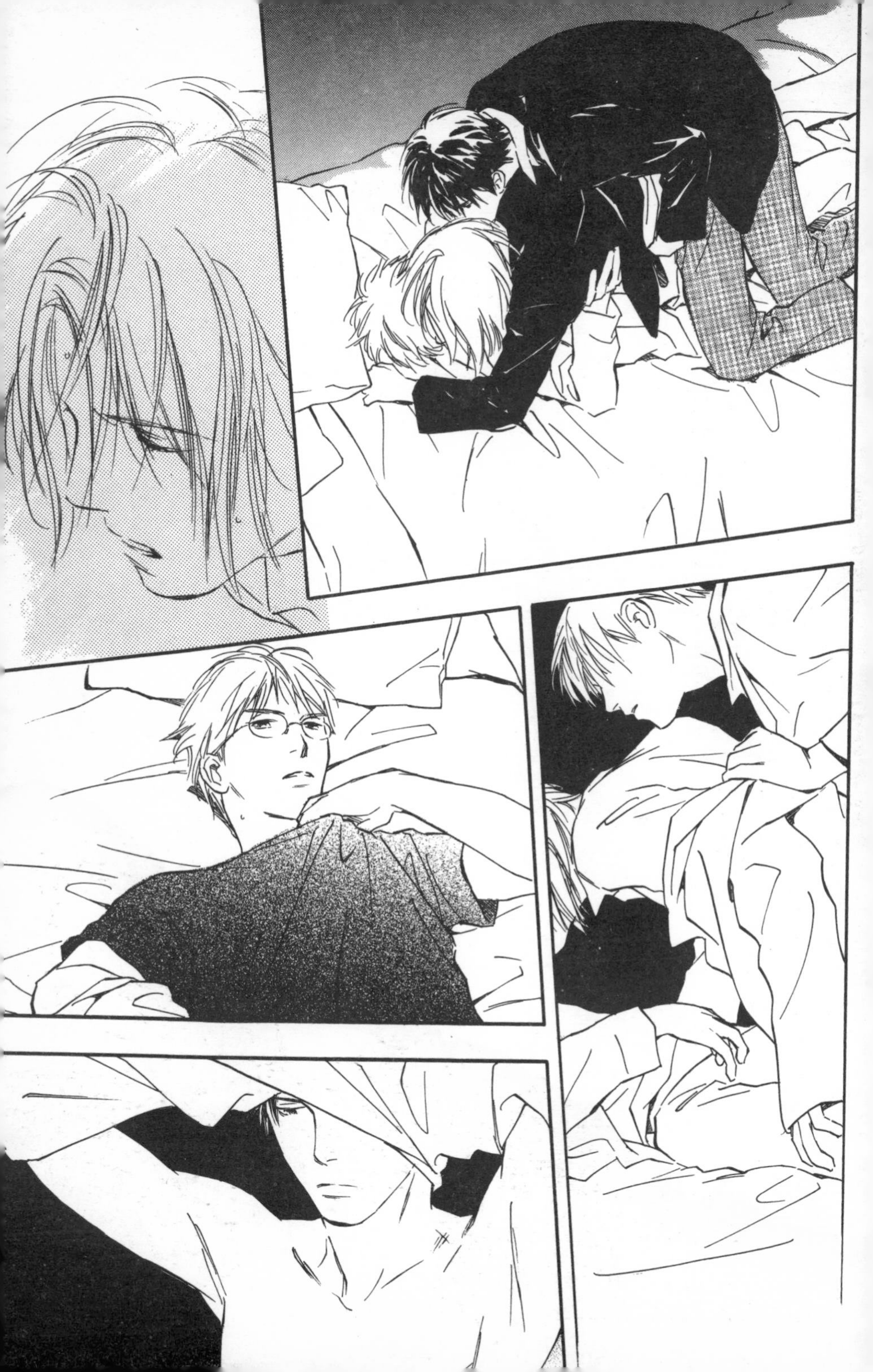

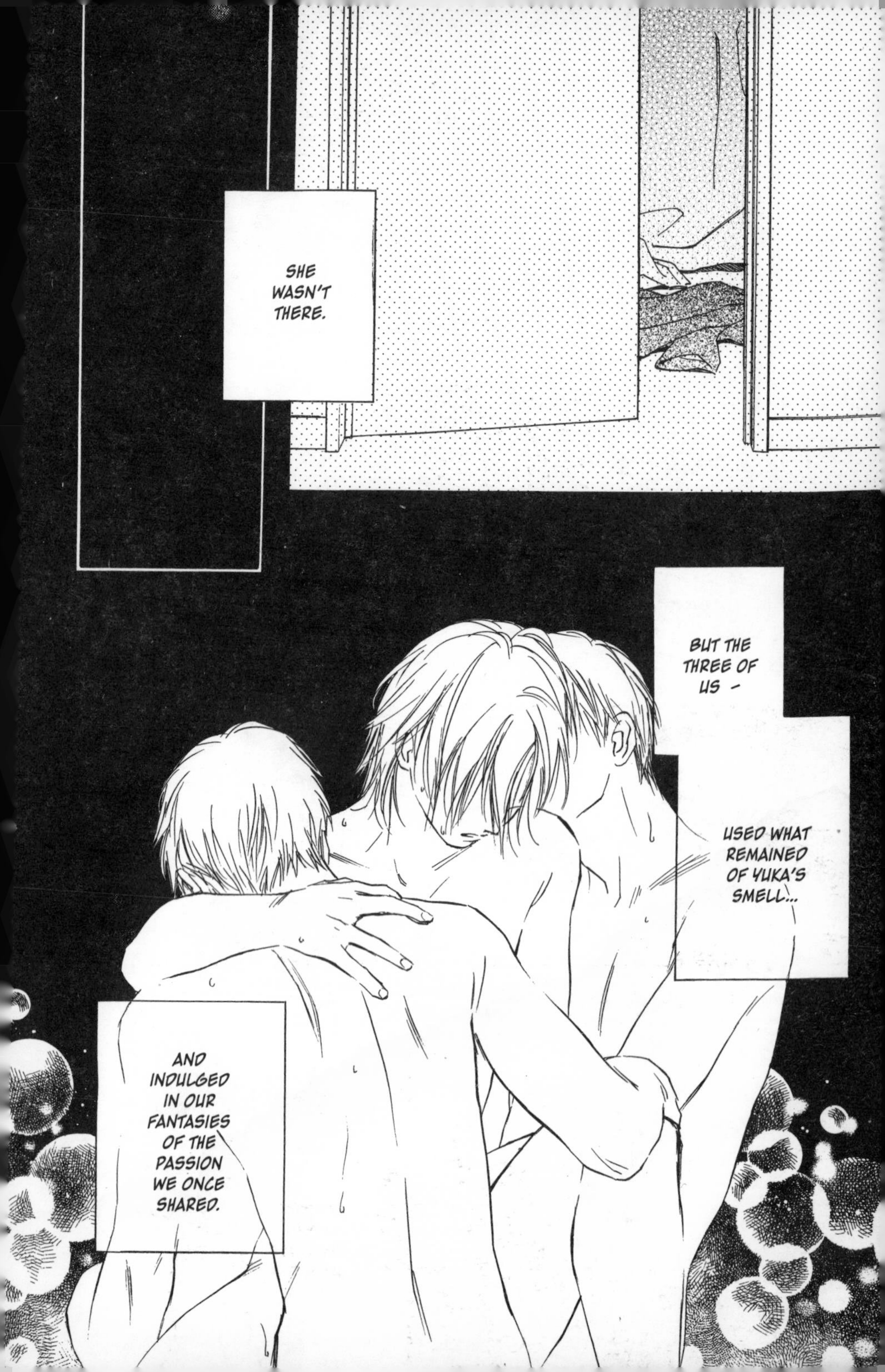

SHE WASN'T THERE.
BUT THE THREE OF US -
USED WHAT REMAINED OF YUKA'S SMELL...
AND INDULGED IN OUR FANTASIES OF THE PASSION WE ONCE SHARED.

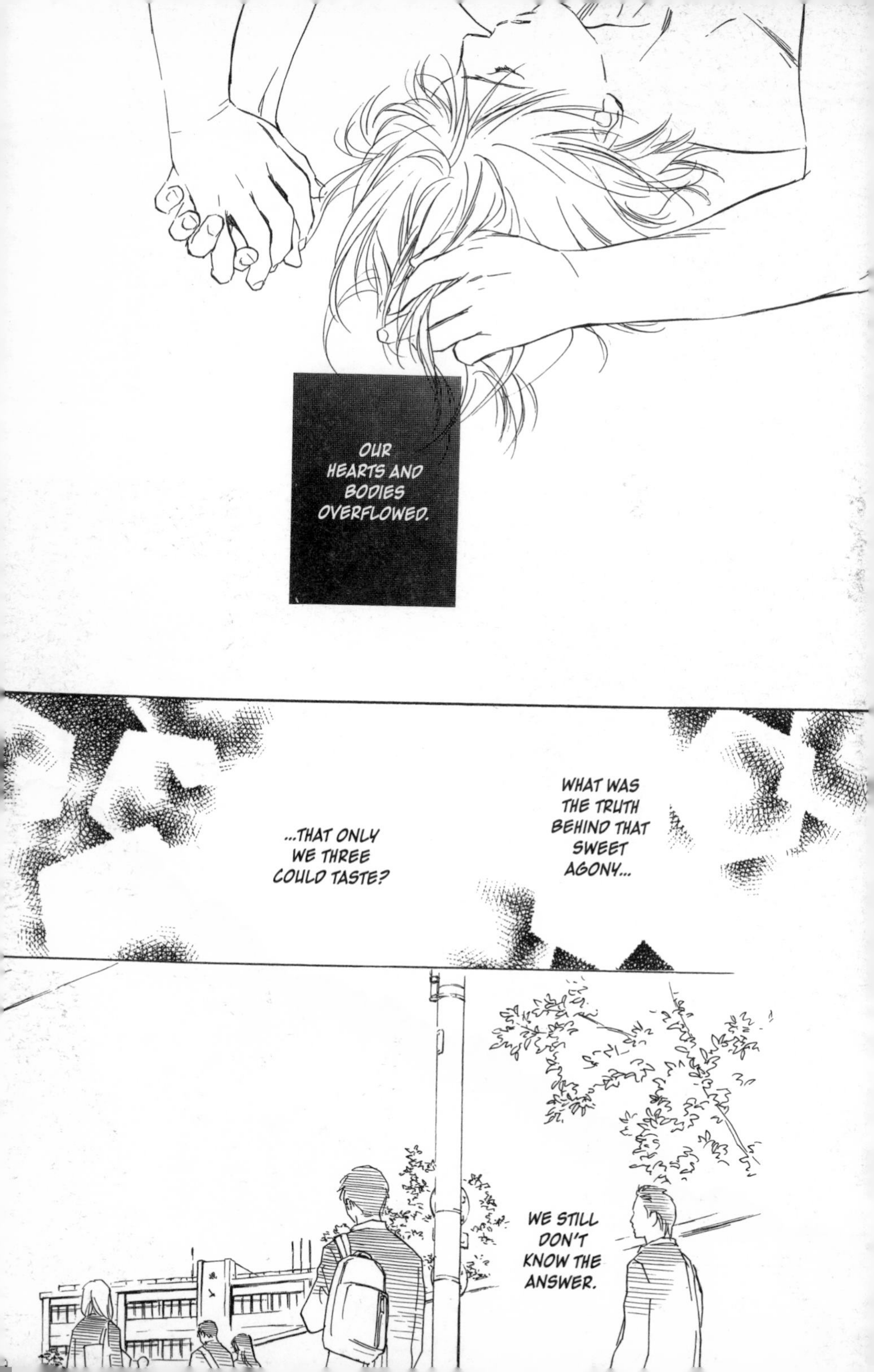
OUR HEARTS AND BODIES OVERFLOWED.
WHAT WAS THE TRUTH BEHIND THAT SWEET AGONY...
...THAT ONLY WE THREE COULD TASTE?
WE STILL DON'T KNOW THE ANSWER.

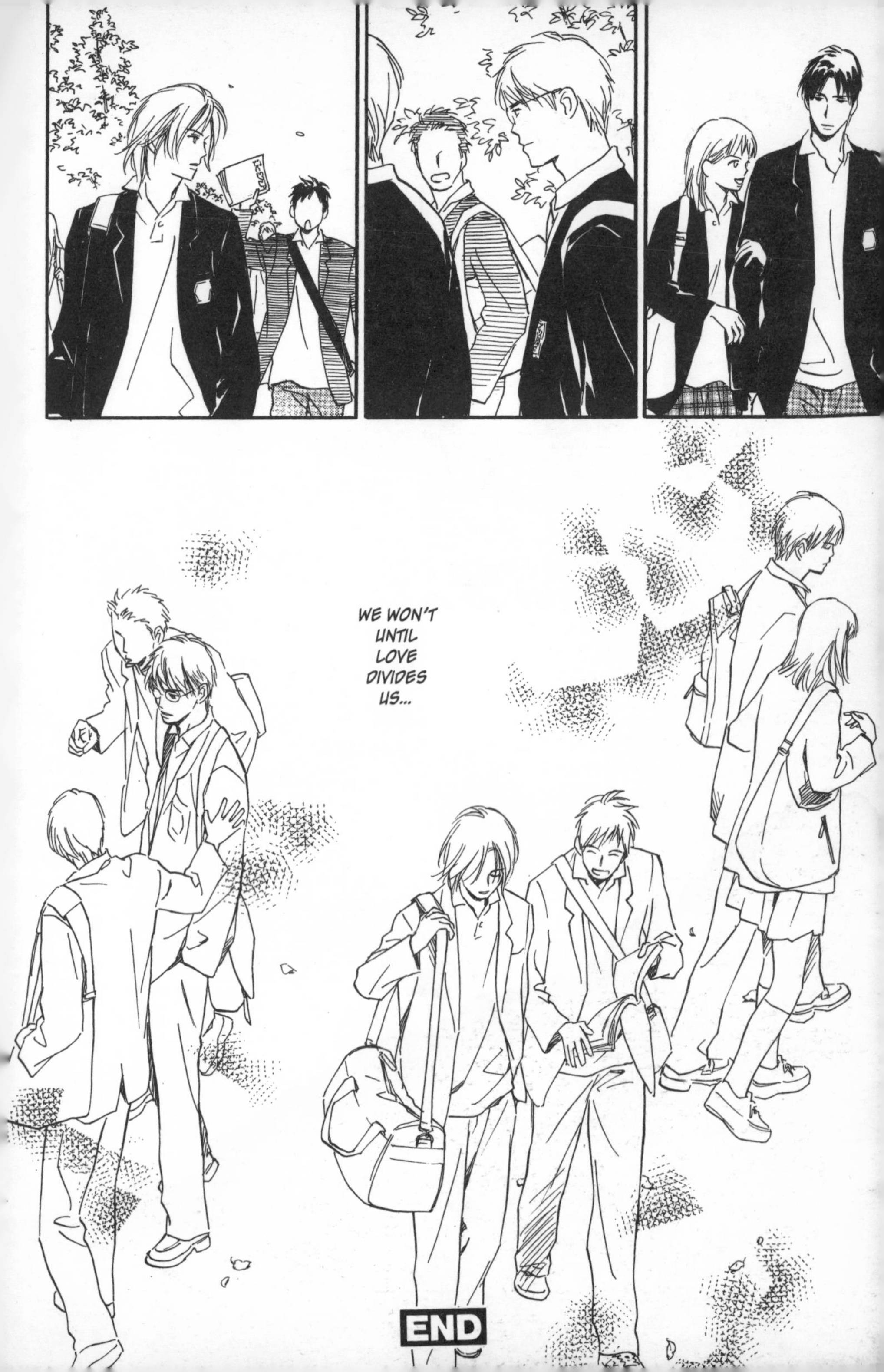
WE WON'T
UNTIL
LOVE
DIVIDES
US...
END

EXTRAS XXX

HELLO TO THOSE OF YOU WHO HAVE FINISHED READING, AND THOSE WHO ARE READING THE EXTRAS FIRST. THIS IS HONAMI.

THOUGH I MUST APOLOGIZE EVERY TIME TO MY MANUSCRIPT WRITERS FOR MY HAVING SUCH POOR SKILL, I WORK HARD EVERY DAY TO IMPROVE. AND ESPECIALLY THIS TIME, SINCE THE MANUSCRIPT IS COMING FROM A FELLOW MANGA ARTIST. MY NERVOUSNESS TRIPLES IN CASES LIKE THIS. I'D LIKE TO GATHER MY SPIRITS AND SAY, "LEAVE IT TO ME!" BUT TODAY I'M FEELING A LITTLE DOWN, SO I THOUGHT I'D TRY DRAWING ORIE... I'M NOT THAT GOOD AT DRAWING PEOPLE WITH LONG HAIR...

I WONDER IF I'M REALLY ABLE TO CONVEY THE SEXINESS OF TAKAGUCHI'S MANUSCRIPT THROUGH MY DRAWINGS. THIS IS MY FIRST TIME WITH A PIECE THAT'S ENTIRELY SERIOUS, AND IT'S RATHER DIFFICULT. THERE ARE ALMOST NO EXPRESSIONS OF "HAPPINESS" OR "EASE" SO...I HAVE TO PAY SPECIAL ATTENTION TO THE EYEBROWS. THERE'S BEEN A LOT OF "THIS! THIS IS THE ANGLE!" AND "MAYBE IF I LOWER THIS BY A FRACTION, HIS EXPRESSION WILL CHANGE...?!" I HOPE YOU WON'T PAY TOO MUCH ATTENTION TO THAT.

BY THE WAY, THE ONLY REASON I DREW THEM WITH SO MANY FLOWERS WAS BECAUSE I WANTED TO SYMBOLIZE "LOVE" AS "FLOWERS." I'M NOT SURE IF IT WAS VERY SUCCESSFUL, BUT OH WELL, IT WAS JUST A SMALL THING.

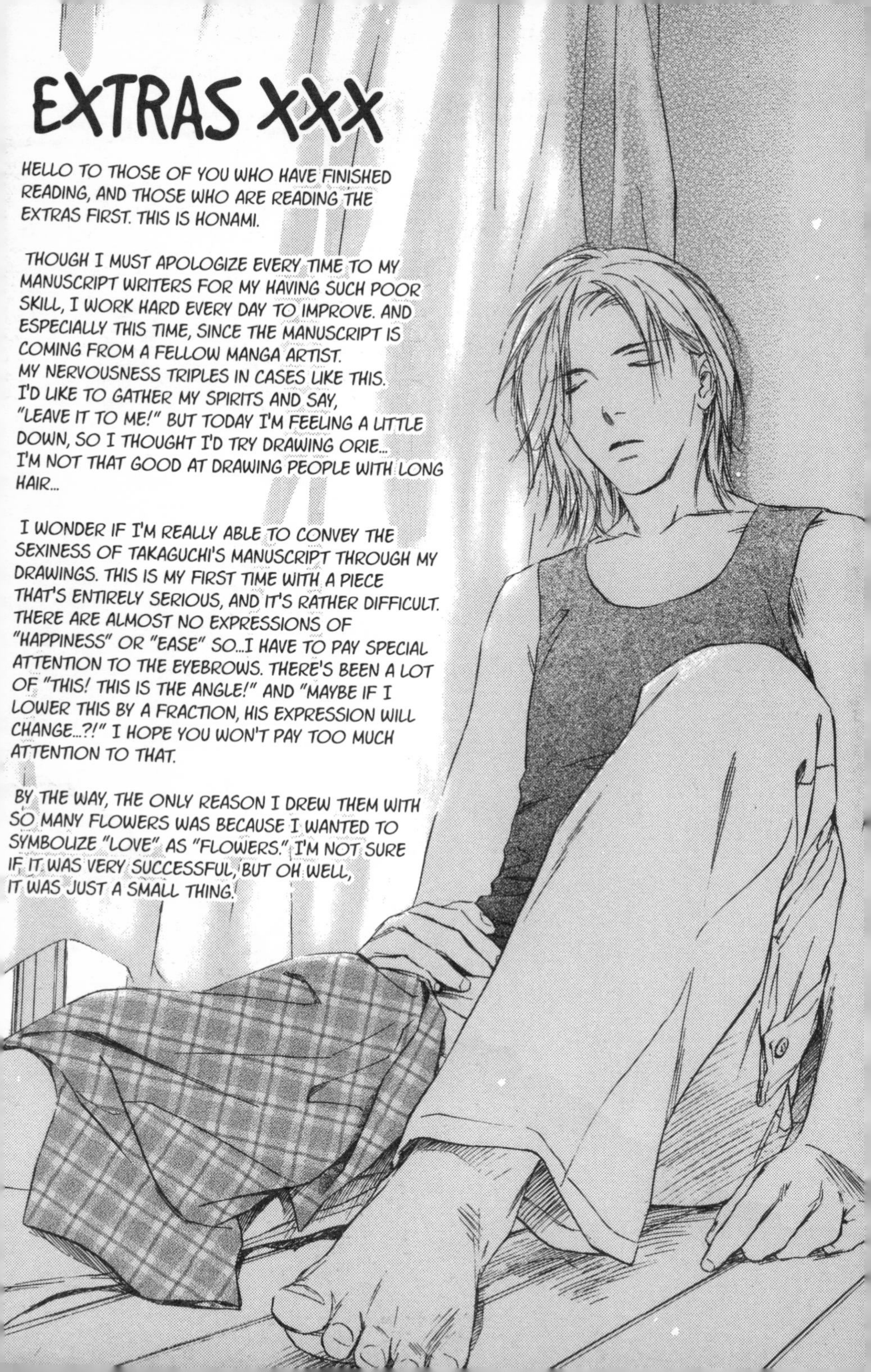

HERE'S THE FIRST SHOT OF THE TWO OLD FRIENDS↓. AT FIRST, I DREW THEM WITH HARDER EXPRESSIONS, AND THOUGHT TO MYSELF, "THESE DON'T LOOK LIKE HIGH SCHOOL KIDS," SO I SECRETLY MADE THEM LOOK YOUNG. BUT OF COURSE, RIGHT AWAY T-NAKA-SAN CAUGHT ON, AND SAID, "WHY DON'T YOU ROUND OUT THE OUTLINE ON THE FACE? THEY CAN LOOK A LITTLE OLDER." THAT'S WHAT HAPPENED. HONESTLY. I FORGOT ABOUT IT LATER, BUT REALLY, THEY'RE HIGH SCHOOL KIDS! ...BESIDES, TATSUMI'S LIFESTYLE DOESN'T REALLY FIT WITH A HIGH SCHOOLER ANYWAY...

IS HE REALLY AN OLDER MAN, TAKAGUCHI-SENSEI?! I LIKE OLDER MEN WELL ENOUGH, BUT I HAVEN'T LEARNED ENOUGH YET TO DRAW ANYONE IN BETWEEN. BUT IF I LEARN TO DRAW THEM SOMEDAY, THEN LET'S DO IT!

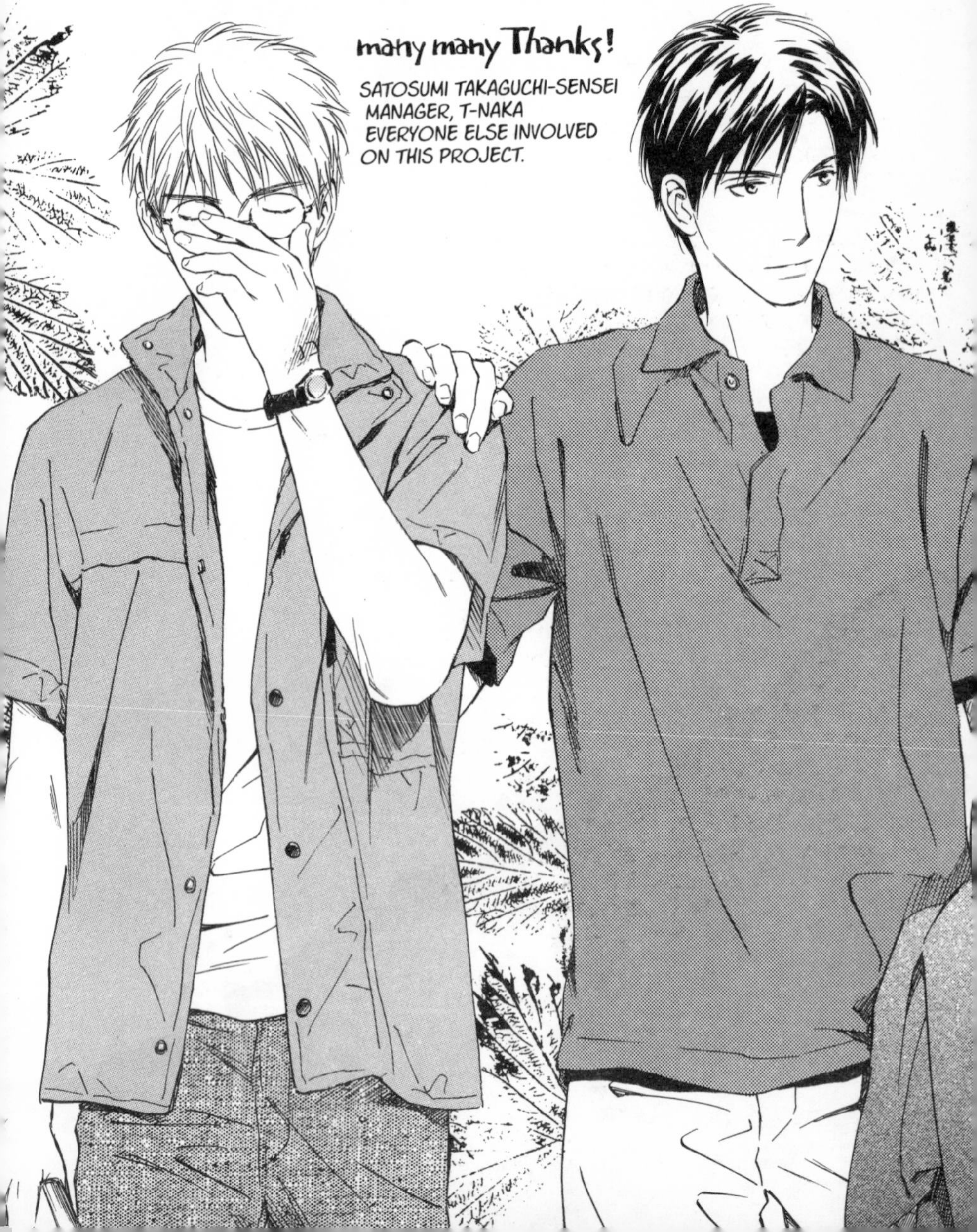
many many Thanks!
SATOSUMI TAKAGUCHI-SENSEI
MANAGER, T-NAKA
EVERYONE ELSE INVOLVED
ON THIS PROJECT.

GOOD WORK, HONAMI-SAN!

THE WELL DONE POSE!
I NEED TO EXERCISE MORE...

WELL NOW...ABOUT TAKAGUCHI AND BL -
I DON'T DO MANY MANUSCRIPTS.
MY TASTE IS A LITTLE OUT THERE...

I DECIDED THAT IF I WAS GOING TO DO A MANUSCRIPT, I WOULD HAVE TO HAVE YUKINE HONAMI! (ALL ON MY OWN). AND THUS, THE GOD OF YAOI APPEARED BEFORE ME! AMAZING...RIGHT?

SO HOW WAS "THIRSTY FOR LOVE"?
I CAN'T IMAGINE HOW CONFUSED YUKINE-SAN MUST HAVE BEEN, READING A TAKAGUCHI MANUSCRIPT FOR THE FIRST TIME!!
(IT'S SCARY...)
SOMEHOW...I THINK MY DEVELOPMENT HAS BEEN RATHER QUICK...
I WANTED TO BE A BIT MORE STUBBORN ABOUT IT.
MY FAVORITE WAS TATSUMI (TOTALLY OBVIOUS).
I'M PRETTY SURE YUKINE-SAN'S WAS SUGURU. I GET THE FEELING SHE SAID "HE'S LOVELY♡" SEVERAL TIMES... (I WONDER WHY...?).
ACTUALLY, I LIKE GUYS WITH GLASSES, TOO!
POOR ORIE, NOT GETTING AS MUCH LOVE FROM THE TWO OF US.
THOUGH I DO LIKE HOW HE LOOKS.
ANYWAY! YUKINE-SAN'S ART IS FANTASTIC! ♡♡
BUT THIS ONE'S ALL YOUNG MEN, SO NEXT TIME,
I WANT HER TO DRAW SOME OLDER MEN -
WOULD YOU LIKE THAT, YUKINE-SAN?!

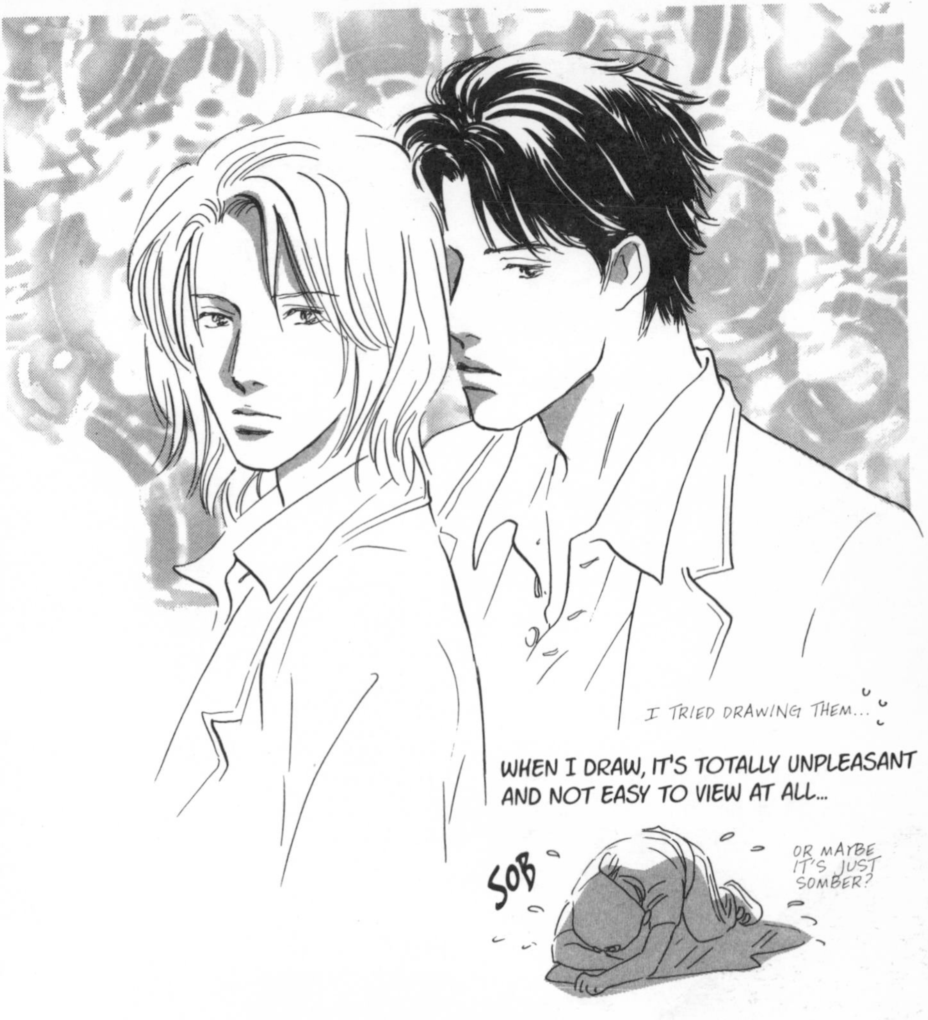
I TRIED DRAWING THEM...
WHEN I DRAW, IT'S TOTALLY UNPLEASANT AND NOT EASY TO VIEW AT ALL...
SOB
OR MAYBE IT'S JUST SOMBER?

ISN'T IT SUPPOSED TO BE A BIT HAPPIER THAN THAT...???
WHEN I THINK ABOUT IT, ISN'T THAT WHY I DECIDED TO MAKE MANUSCRIPTS INSTEAD? (DEEP IN THOUGHT)
I DON'T DO THIS OFTEN...MAYBE IT'S JUST BECAUSE I HAD YUKINE-SAN DOING IT THAT I COULD REMAIN STRONG. (SAD SMILE).
IN ANY CASE, I'M SO GRATEFUL TO HAVE SEEN IT THROUGH TO THE END!
THANK YOU, YUKINE-SAN!
LET'S DO IT AGAIN! (HUH? REALLY?!)

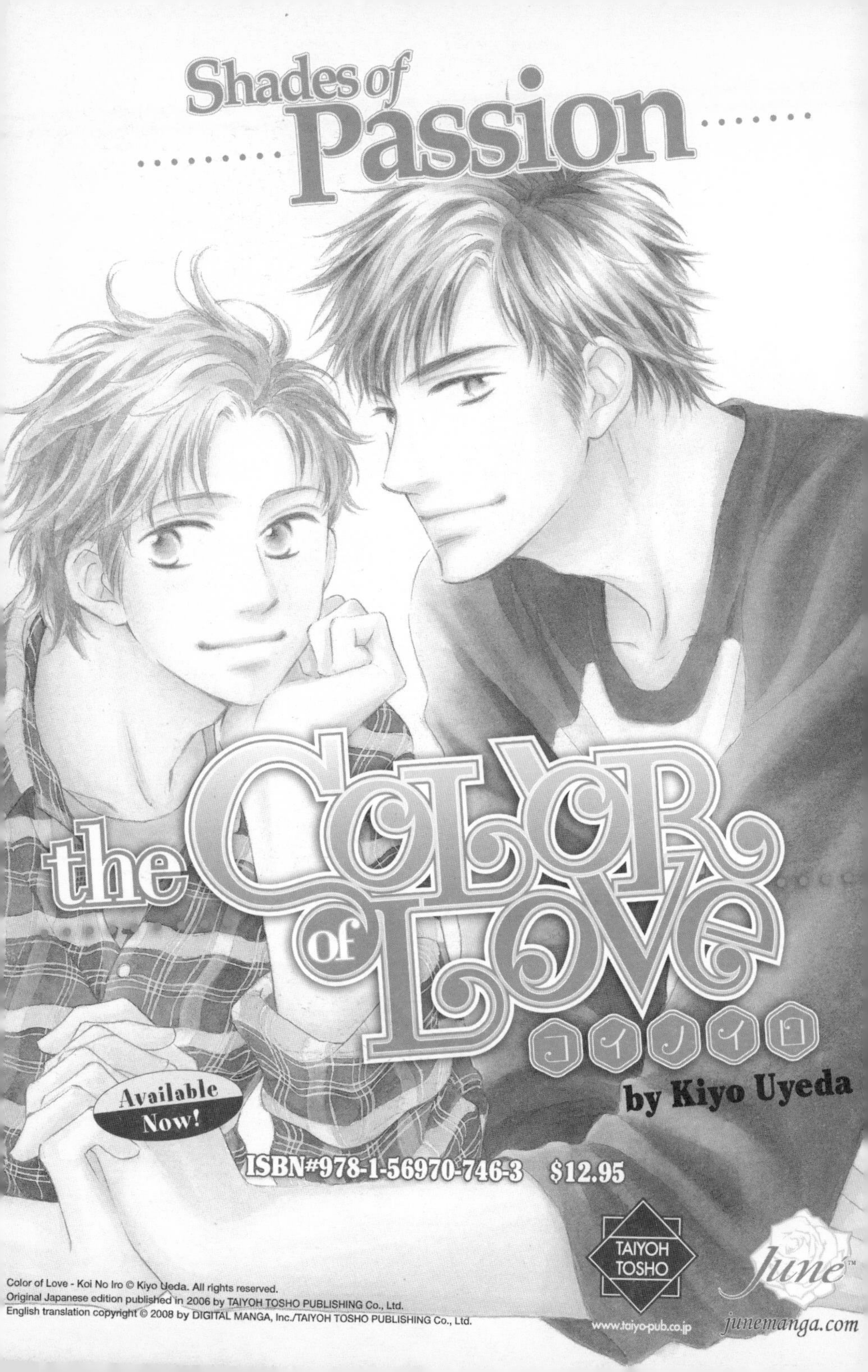
Shades of Passion
the Color of Love
コイノイロ
by Kiyo Uyeda
Available Now!
ISBN#978-1-56970-746-3 $12.95
TAIYOH TOSHO
www.taiyo-pub.co.jp
June™
junemanga.com
Color of Love - Koi No Iro © Kiyo Ueda. All rights reserved.
Original Japanese edition published in 2006 by TAIYOH TOSHO PUBLISHING Co., Ltd.
English translation copyright © 2008 by DIGITAL MANGA, Inc./TAIYOH TOSHO PUBLISHING Co., Ltd.

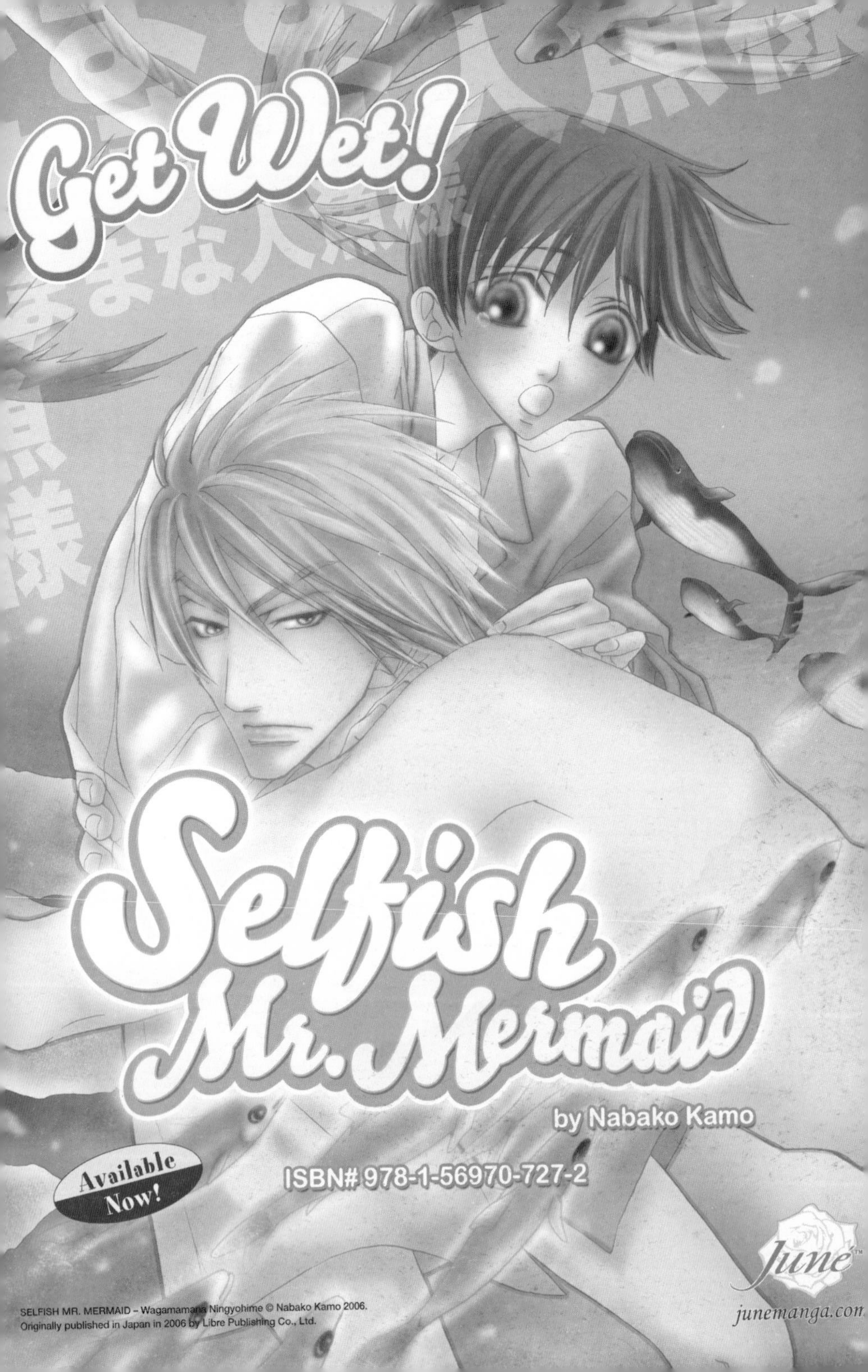
Get Wet!
Selfish Mr. Mermaid
by Nabako Kamo
Available Now!
ISBN# 978-1-56970-727-2
June
junemanga.com
SELFISH MR. MERMAID – Wagamamana Ningyohime © Nabako Kamo 2006.
Originally published in Japan in 2006 by Libre Publishing Co., Ltd.

a life less ordinary

by **Yugi Yamada**

Illustrator of CLOSE THE LAST DOOR

DON'T BLAME ME

俺は悪くない 1

Volume 1
On Sale Now!

Vol. 1 – ISBN# 978-1-56970-741-8 $12.95
Vol. 2 – ISBN# 978-1-56970-740-1 $12.95

June

junemanga.co

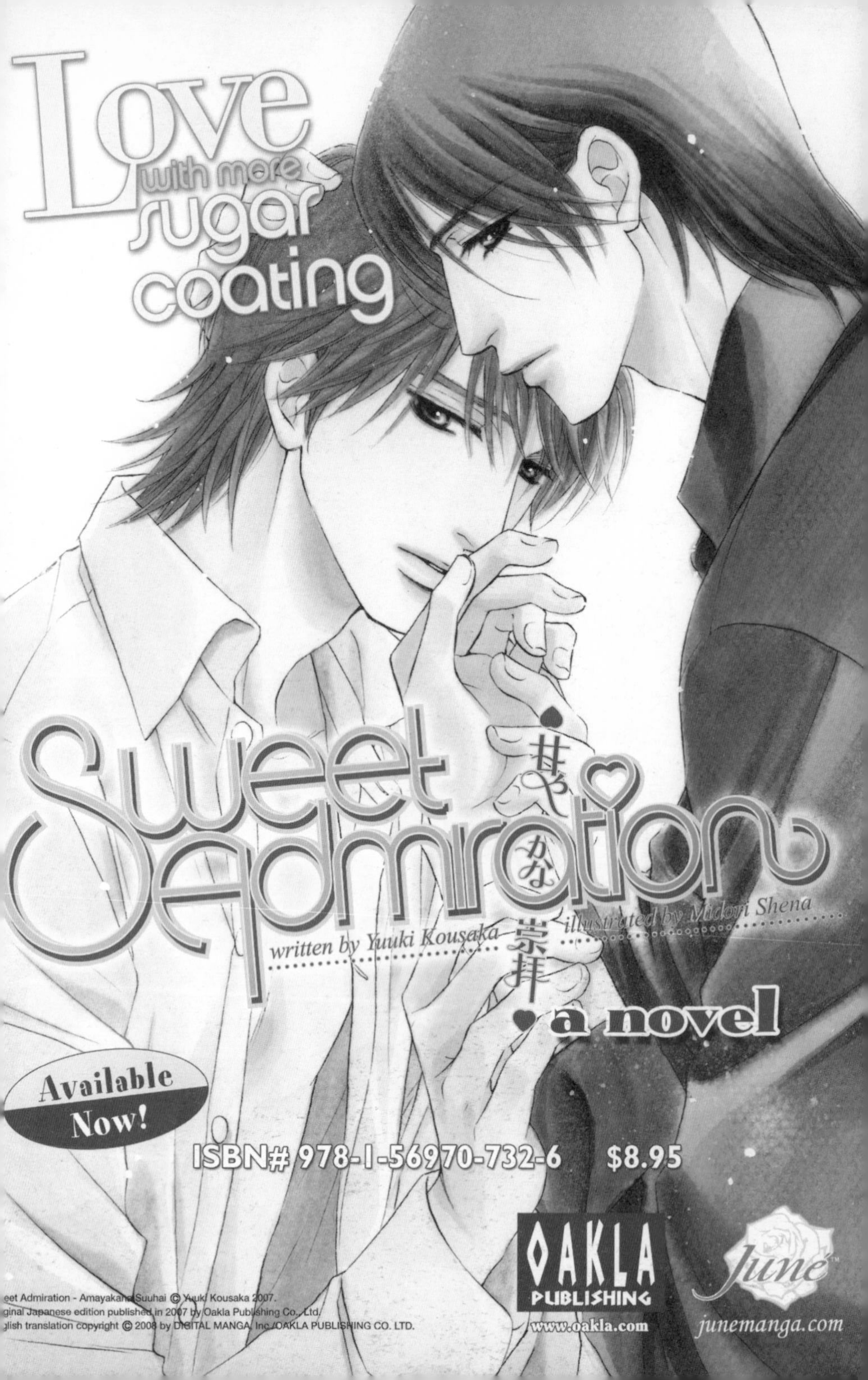
Love
with more
sugar
coating
Sweet Admiration
甘やかな崇拝
written by Yuuki Kousaka
illustrated by Midori Shena
a novel
Available Now!
ISBN# 978-1-56970-732-6
$8.95
OAKLA PUBLISHING
www.oakla.com
June
junemanga.com
eet Admiration - Amayakana Suuhai © Yuuki Kousaka 2007.
ginal Japanese edition published in 2007 by Oakla Publishing Co., Ltd.
glish translation copyright © 2008 by DIGITAL MANGA, Inc./OAKLA PUBLISHING CO. LTD.

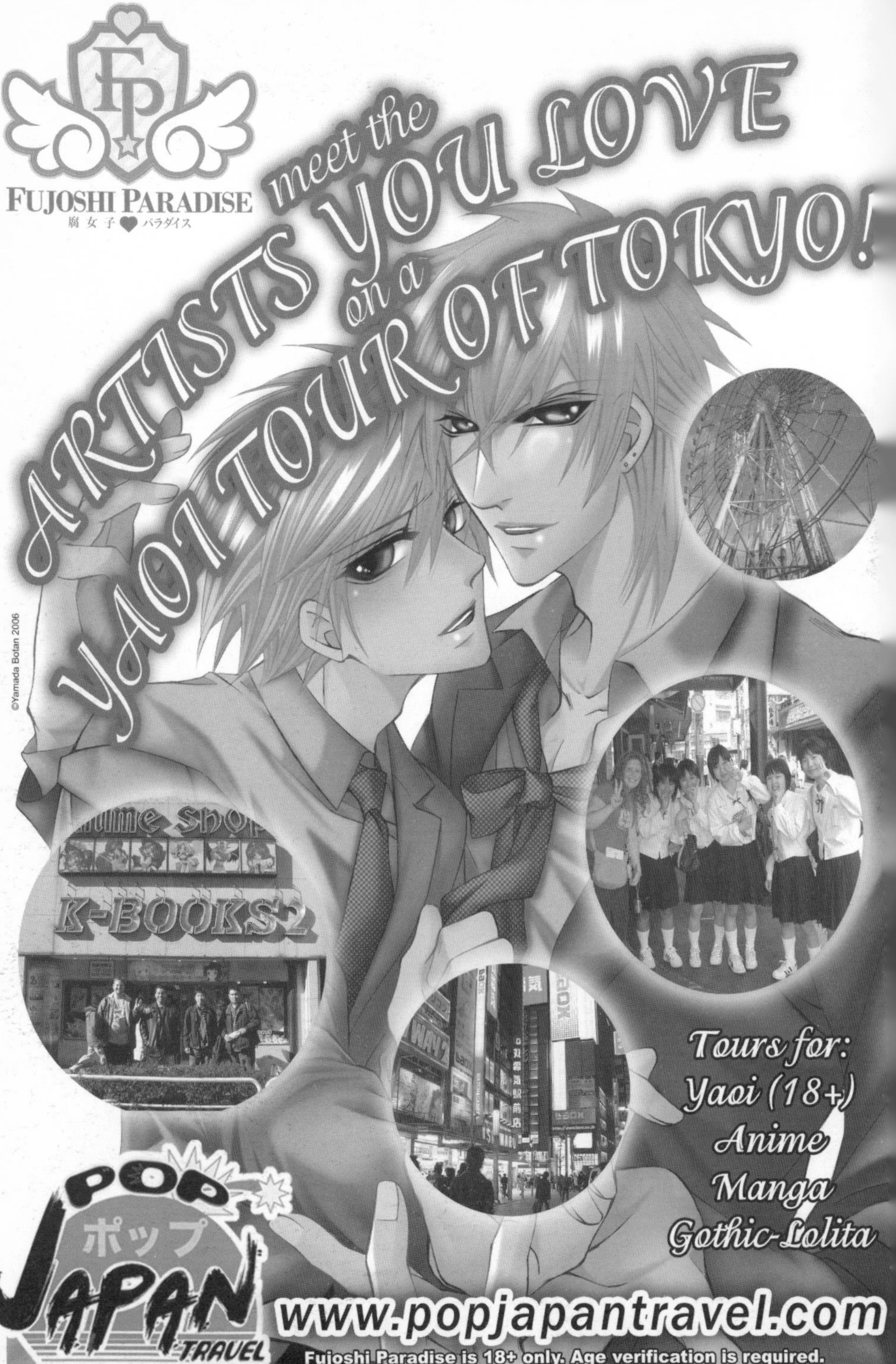
FP
FUJOSHI PARADISE
腐女子パラダイス
meet the
ARTISTS YOU LOVE
on a
YAOI TOUR OF TOKYO!
©Yamada Botan 2006
K-BOOKS 2
Tours for:
Yaoi (18+)
Anime
Manga
Gothic-Lolita
POP
ポップ
JAPAN
TRAVEL
www.popjapantravel.com
Fujoshi Paradise is 18+ only. Age verification is required.

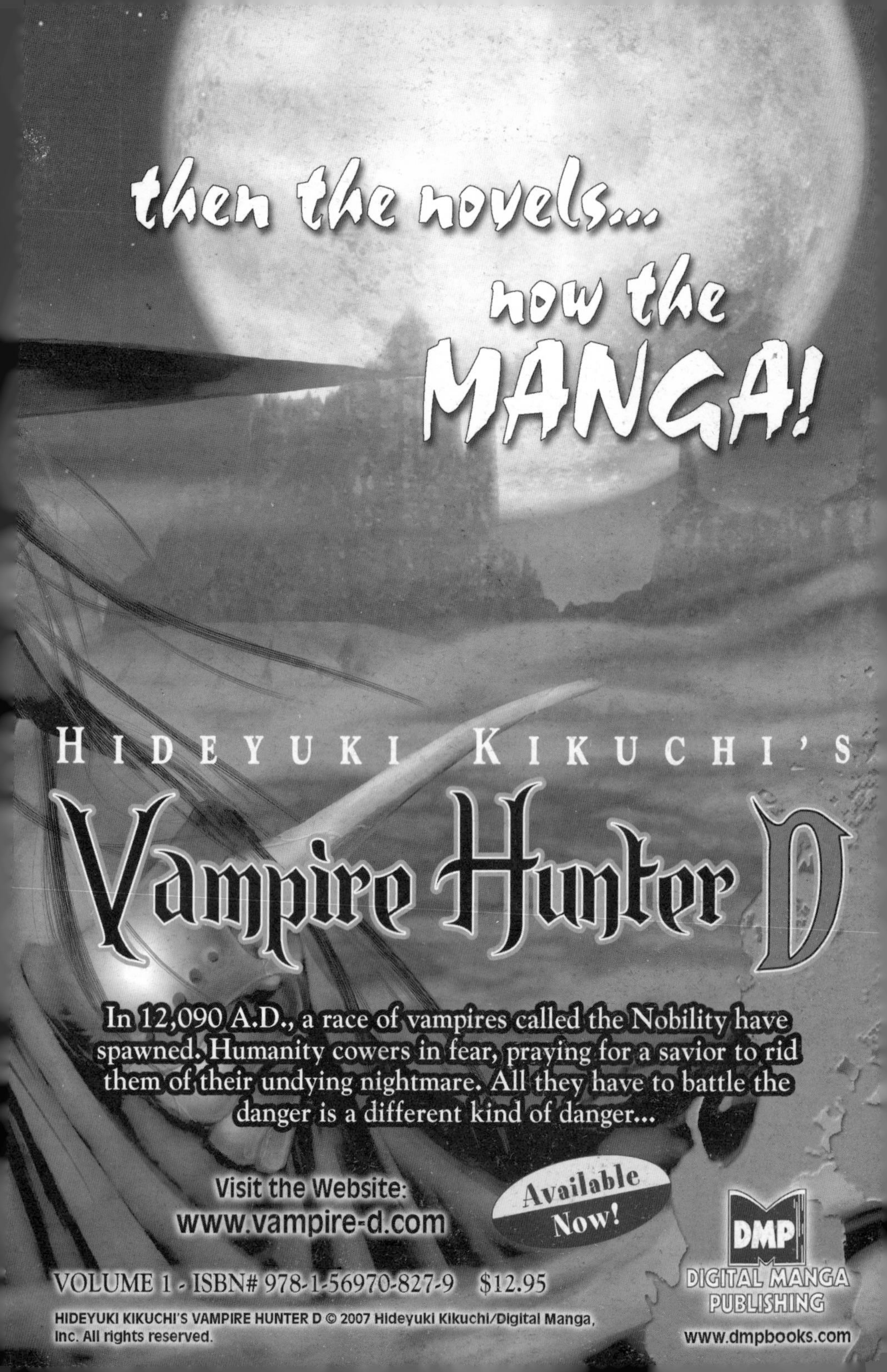
then the novels...
now the
MANGA!
HIDEYUKI KIKUCHI'S
Vampire Hunter D
In 12,090 A.D., a race of vampires called the Nobility have spawned. Humanity cowers in fear, praying for a savior to rid them of their undying nightmare. All they have to battle the danger is a different kind of danger...
Visit the Website:
www.vampire-d.com
Available Now!
DMP
DIGITAL MANGA PUBLISHING
VOLUME 1 - ISBN# 978-1-56970-827-9 $12.95
HIDEYUKI KIKUCHI'S VAMPIRE HUNTER D © 2007 Hideyuki Kikuchi/Digital Manga, Inc. All rights reserved.
www.dmpbooks.com

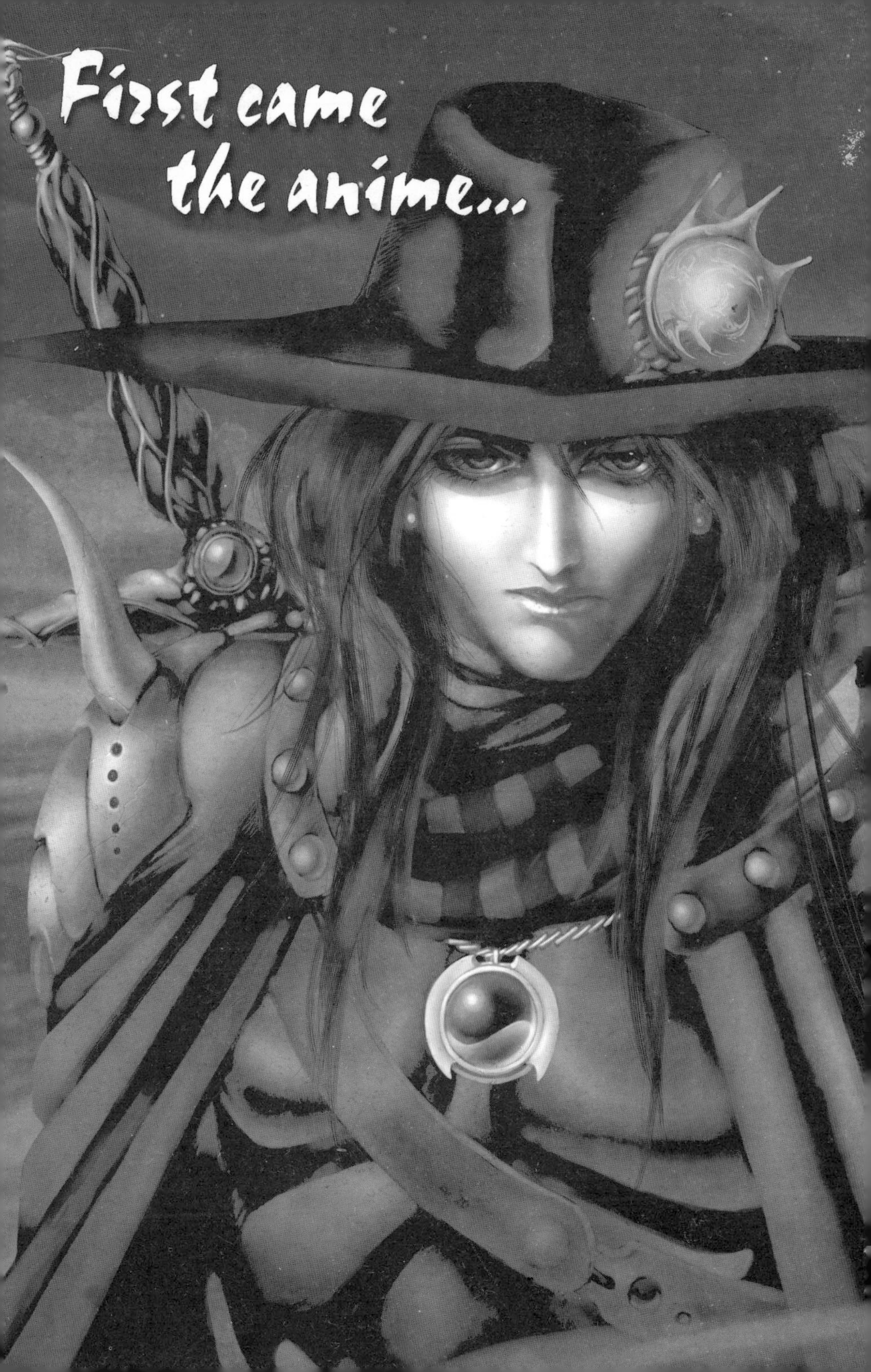
First came
the anime...

STOP

This is the back of the book!
Start from the other side.

NATIVE MANGA
readers read manga
from *right to left*.

If you run into our **Native Manga** logo on any of our books... you'll know that this manga is published in it's true original native Japanese right to left reading format, as it was intended. Turn to the other side of the book and start reading from right to left, top to bottom.

Follow the diagram to see how its done. **Surf's Up!**

NATIVE MANGA

READ RIGHT TO LEFT